LIVING U.S.-CHINA RELATIONS
From Cold War to Cold War

DAVID M. LAMPTON

*To Lea,
with all the best,
Mike*

ROWMAN & LITTLEFIELD
Lanham • Boulder • New York • London

Acquisitions Editor: Ashley Dodge
Assistant Acquisitions Editor: Laney Ackley
Sales and Marketing Inquiries: textbooks@rowman.com
Credits and acknowledgments for material borrowed from other sources, and reproduced with
permission, appear on the appropriate pages within the text.

Published by Rowman & Littlefield
An imprint of The Rowman & Littlefield Publishing Group, Inc.
4501 Forbes Boulevard, Suite 200, Lanham, Maryland 20706
www.rowman.com

86-90 Paul Street, London EC2A 4NE

Copyright © 2024 by The Rowman & Littlefield Publishing Group, Inc.

British Library Cataloguing in Publication Information Available

Library of Congress Cataloging-in-Publication Data
Names: Lampton, David M., author.
Title: Living U.S.-China relations : from Cold War to Cold War / David M. Lampton.
Description: Lanham : Rowman & Littlefield, [2024] | Includes bibliographical references and
   index.
Identifiers: LCCN 2023041563 (print) | LCCN 2023041564 (ebook) | ISBN 9781538187241
   (cloth) | ISBN 9781538187258 (paperback) | ISBN 9781538187265 (epub)
Subjects: LCSH: Lampton, David M. | Sinologists--United States--Biography. | Committee on
   Scholarly Communication with the People's Republic of China (U.S.)--Biography. | United
   States--Relations--China. | China--Relations--United States.
Classification: LCC DS734.9.L355 A3 2024 (print) | LCC DS734.9.L355 (ebook) | DDC
   303.48/251073092 [B]--dc23/eng/20231115
LC record available at https://lccn.loc.gov/2023041563
LC ebook record available at https://lccn.loc.gov/2023041564

For Susan

Contents

LIST OF FIGURES

PREFACE AND ACKNOWLEDGMENTS

The defining and unique characteristic of this volume is that it tells the story of U.S.-China ties as the relationship between two *societies*, not just two *states*, and it does so through my lived experience over the last nearly sixty years. This account and explanation have nuance and avoid black-and-white caricature—this account is empathetic.

In retrospect, it was almost inevitable that I would make China my life's work.

Born in 1946 following my father's return from military service in Europe during the Second World War, I grew up during the Cold War when the United States regarded both the Soviet Union and China as implacable enemies. America fought two wars in Asia during my youth—one in Korea and another in Vietnam. Both involved China.

My preoccupation with China began in my teenage years, in 1964. The Cold War was at its height. At Palo Alto Senior High School ("Paly High" as it was known to the students), I took a course on Far Eastern history that changed my life.

After graduating from Paly High in 1964, I spent my freshman college year at Willamette University in Salem, Oregon, then transferred for my sophomore year to Stanford University, majoring in political science with a focus on China, first as an undergraduate and then as a graduate student, receiving a PhD in 1974. The period of rapprochement between China and the United States began in earnest with President Nixon's visit to China in February 1972, though formal diplomatic relations between the People's Republic of China (PRC) and the United States were not established until January 1, 1979.

The period that followed was one of flourishing cultural, economic, diplomatic, and academic exchanges, lasting into the second decade of the new millennium—the period of constructive engagement. Most of my working career has been devoted to understanding and addressing issues related to China and U.S.-China ties as they unfolded in that era. Sino-American ties were more inter-societal happening than a well-thought-out strategy.

It was at Stanford, as an undergraduate, that I became a firefighter. The job not only gave me room and board but also provided sufficient money to get through college. Above all, being a firefighter gave me a different perspective on China.

The life of a firefighter is characterized by periods of quiet and solitude, punctuated by frenetic calls to fires, medical emergencies, and false alarms. One incident for me became a metaphor for U.S.-China relations—a child stuck his head between the bars of a metal balcony railing and could not get it back out. The more the child struggled to free himself, the more his increasingly swollen ears prevented his extraction—we used the "jaws of life" to pry him out.

Norman Maclean's classic 1972 book, *Young Men and Fire*, is about the Mann Gulch fire in Montana that started in August 1949. Fires can ignite for many reasons—negligence, arson, an accident, a lightning strike, or spontaneous combustion. Once started, they can be accelerated or retarded by a myriad of factors including the moisture content of the air, wind speed, direction and variability, and the nature of the underbrush below the forest canopy. In cities, additional considerations are important, such as gas and electricity lines in high-density areas and tall structures, which contain all sorts of hazardous conditions and combustible substances.

Maclean's story revolves around fifteen smoke jumpers who were inserted into a fire that initially looked fairly routine. Tragically, however, a concatenation of individually low-probability developments soon converged to create an inferno from which only three of the fifteen men escaped alive. Maclean's book is a parable about fate, nature, science, misjudgments, and fickle circumstances.

Working over the years to keep the U.S.-China relationship intact has required constant efforts by numerous people to stamp out the endless small fires of misunderstanding and misperception that could easily get out of hand. Over the decades, the colleagues and partners with whom I have worked in China, the United States, Russia, Southeast and Northeast Asia, and Europe have sought to keep the combustible underbrush of the relationship below a critical threshold and to deal with spot fires as they have ignited, often without warning. I have endeavored to put fires out from the perch of nongovernmental organizations, educational institutions, think tanks, and as a consultant to governmental, philanthropic, and corporate organizations at home and abroad. The task of suppressing fires sparked by the vicissitudes of international relations never ends.

In this, the third decade of the new millennium, developments in the U.S.-China relationship are converging in a fashion that is setting off alarm bells. At this moment, in 2023, the underbrush is plentiful, the winds unfavorable, and the atmosphere parched. Friction between America and China is increasing, unlike anything we have seen in a half century.

On February 4, 2022, Xi Jinping and Vladimir Putin declared that their partnership had "no limits," and about three weeks later Russia invaded Ukraine. China initially offered no condemnation, and over the months following the invasion, Beijing became increasingly aligned with Moscow. Washington continued shoring up its power in Asia to compete better with Beijing. China was using its mounting economic clout to make friends wherever they could be found, all the while pushing its defense perimeter outward. Solutions to the new conflicts and problems confronting world order are far from obvious and unlikely to come soon.

This volume explores many issues. How and why have China and America each changed, and how has the relationship changed? How can we increase cooperation, not only to avoid bloody conflict but also to realize the benefits that would surely accrue by jointly addressing practical and grave global issues?

Managing U.S.-China relations, even under the best of circumstances, is problematic. But this is not the story of Chinese villains in black hats and Americans in white ones, or vice versa. Rather, it is an accounting of two large, powerful, and above all proud peoples trying to maximize their welfare, power, security, and sizeable national egos. This book speaks to the importance of political leaders—how they use external foils to enhance their domestic leverage, and how domestic circumstances limit their choices. Finally, it underscores the importance of organizations and fields of study, institutions that are not easy to build and maintain.

In the more than half a century recounted in this book, I experienced events worthy of celebration, moments of humor, and times when I shook my head in disbelief at the absurdity, and sometimes the tragedy, of the moment. Ranking high on my scale of recent absurdities has been how America and China reacted to each other during the COVID-19 pandemic from 2020 to 2023.

Many individuals helped in this volume's research, editing, manuscript preparation, and physical production. From its inception, this project has had the research assistance of my granddaughter, Zoe Vittoria Balk. I also want to thank two individuals who thoroughly read earlier drafts of this work, enriched it through their insight, and, on occasion, saved me from myself: Dr. Anne F. Thurston has my undying gratitude. From the start of this project, through successive drafts, she forced me to say what I meant. She unfailingly encouraged me when I had doubts. Her ability to write graceful, clear prose is an inspiration. I also must thank her for being such a valued colleague in the Johns Hopkins School of Advanced International Studies (SAIS) China Studies Program over many years.

Since our graduate student days at Stanford, Terry Lautz has been a colleague and friend, and together we have lived through much of the history recorded here, geographically, professionally, and intellectually. In this current endeavor, Terry brought his historian's eye, knowledge, writing skills, and experience to the service of improving this effort.

Without the help of Ashley Dodge at Rowman & Littlefield, and Samuel S. Kim as Asia in World Politics Series Editor, this volume would not have been possible. Laney Ackley, also at Rowman & Littlefield, has my undying gratitude for her skillful copyediting and manuscript preparation. I also want to thank Rowman & Littlefield's editing, production, indexing, and marketing professionals and express my gratitude to the anonymous peer reviewers who made suggestions that I trust they see reflected in the following pages. Adam Lampton adeptly used his talent to prepare my photos for this volume.

This book's narrative skeleton is chronology, and the content is based on both documentary research and personal interactions and interviews in China, the United States, and elsewhere. I have protected sources when I thought it important to do so. In contrast to my previous books, this account is leaner on footnotes, though I have provided sufficient specificity within the text to signal the kind of information upon which I have relied. I draw extensively on my Chronological Files (correspondence) and my extensive meeting notes and interview files, as well as the yet more extensive files of the National Committee on United States–China Relations (NCUSCR), all deposited in the Rockefeller Archive Center (RAC) in Sleepy Hollow, New York.

In this, as in every venture I have undertaken since we were married fifty-five years ago, my wife, Susan, has encouraged and supported me, including commenting on repeated drafts of this manuscript. It is to her I have dedicated this volume. China has meant separations of various lengths for our family, and her support helped me get through them. China also has brought us together as Susan and I shared adventures, from our residence in Hong Kong to riding out a raging storm on the Yangtze River, and from hiring a taxi in Xinjiang and heading out the Karakorum Highway toward Pakistan to going by land through Thailand and Laos to Boten on the PRC border. My trip with my daughter Kate in 1990 was memorable for us, as described later. As for my son, Adam, we shared many adventures on a 1995 trip through the Gansu Corridor to Xinjiang and the Flaming (*Huoyan*) Mountains, where we had to decide whether or not to seek refuge from the 113-degree heat by descending into an underground cistern in the ancient *karez* irrigation system filled with Uighurs smoking their strong Turkish cigarettes by the cool water. We chose to descend into the cistern to avoid the heat and in so doing entered an entirely non-Chinese world.

Most of all, Susan and I share pride and joy in our children, grandchildren, and extended families.

CHAPTER ONE

The Chinese Kaleidoscope

(The Early Years)

Audience Question: Mr. President, your China trip will soon come to its end. Could you tell us what impresses you most during this visit, and what impressions you especially want to convey to American young people when you are back home?

The President: What impressed me most? I'm still sorting it out. [Laughter] It's a kaleidoscope.
        PRESIDENT RONALD REAGAN, FUDAN UNIVERSITY, CHINA, APRIL
30, 1984

RONALD REAGAN CAPTURED A FUNDAMENTAL TRUTH ABOUT CHINA. Anyone who has visited the country for more than a few days is struck by the constantly changing kaleidoscope of sights, sounds, and dynamism. Leave sprawling, modern cities and find villages of mud-walled houses that could have been constructed centuries earlier. Adjust the eyepiece of your kaleidoscope, go to China's west, and in many places horsepower still is power. Similarly, talk to urban intellectuals, and the future they envision is much closer to that of their Western interlocutors than when one speaks to rural folk holding traditional views of governance, indeed life. China's development has created vast reservoirs of new power, but turn the eyepiece ever so little, and one is more impressed with China's soft spots—weaknesses. China's leaders strut the world stage, even as they are unsure of their grip on power at home. China's party does not promote religion, but for much of the opening and reform period, the number of Christians grew by leaps and bounds.

The kaleidoscopic quality of China is anchored in its geographic scope, the number of touch points with a vast, diverse periphery, its multicultural character and geoeconomic diversity, its sheer mass, its deeply entrenched problems, and its often precarious stability. Because China's problems change and its leaders have considerable discretion, policies can wildly oscillate. With each policy change, China presents an altered face to the world. In the last nearly fifty years I have lived through Mao Zedong's pro-birth policies anchored in the idea that more people equals more power, Deng Xiaoping's draconian one-child policy, and Beijing's current push for couples to have two or more offspring.

China's mass, dynamism, and potential make it enormously consequential to the outside world, not least America. Working with this huge force as productively and effectively as conditions and underlying interests permit is critical. Coming out of World War II, events pushed America and China into ever-more costly confrontation and lost opportunities, to be followed by an even longer period of engagement from the 1970s until well into the new millennium. Now, once again, after a long period of relative cooperation, we again see the earlier pattern of conflict unfolding with alarming rapidity.

This book covers a full cycle of changes in ties between the United States and China, from estrangement (1950s and 1960s), to engagement (1970s–2010s), followed by the currently mounting strategic suspicion and friction that threaten to engulf us. Can we avoid another Mann Gulch inferno? The future is uncertain.

COMING OF AGE AND ENGAGEMENT

When I entered the China field in the late 1960s, mainland China was migrating into American thinking from the category of communist enemy to that of useful offset to the Soviet Union. In 1967, before he became president, Richard Nixon gingerly began to consider and promote a new, more flexible, forward-looking policy toward the PRC. By 1969, when he assumed the presidency, the Sino-Soviet conflict was reaching its peak, and Washington was becoming increasingly alarmed at Moscow's military buildup, not least its swollen missile and nuclear warhead stockpile. Having graduated from Stanford as an undergraduate in 1968, immediately doing a stint of active duty as a medic in the enlisted ranks of the U.S. Army Reserve in 1968–1969, I entered Stanford's Political Science PhD program in the summer of 1969, the year of serious Sino-Soviet military clashes along their long border. The Nixon administration even sought to deter Moscow from attacking China.

Following Nixon's and Mao's bold move toward rapprochement in the early 1970s, the four-plus decades that followed witnessed increasing interaction and openness between China and the United States.

With Mao Zedong's September 1976 death, the rise of Deng Xiaoping, and his promotion of the policy of opening and reform in 1978–1979, the Middle Kingdom began morphing in the popular American imagination into a reforming society achieving important gains for its people, as well as providing economic opportunity for the outside world, not least the United States. Americans were no longer dying on forsaken Asian battlefields after the conclusion of the Vietnam War in 1975. Joining with Beijing to address global issues gradually became more central to the rationale for engagement. Forging cooperation on these issues was never easy and progress grindingly slow.

The period of engagement was never a plan. It was not a strategy. Rather, it was a happening. At any given moment in engagement's long life span, there was an explanation for the then-current U.S.-China relationship, but each was more a fleeting rationale, an intellectual construct, than a long-term set of objectives, with carefully planned and implemented intermediate steps. Engagement was energized and defined by a cacophony of interests and explained publicly by a series of shifting rationales. As conditions and interests changed, so too did the rationales, the contours of the relationship, and the modes of engagement.

During these years, America and China segued from an elite-centric relationship (Nixon-Mao, Carter-Deng) to an increasingly society-to-society, globalized relationship.

3

When U.S.-China relations began to visibly worsen from 2010 on (already having taken a big hit in the Tiananmen bloodshed of June 4, 1989), Beijing increasingly became a competitor, then an adversary, and by 2022 an enemy in fact, if not words; echoes of the first Cold War. All along the way, each side has responded to the other by stoking the fire.

Coming of age on the Pacific Coast during the Vietnam War, I had a largely inchoate sense that both America and China could be doing far better dealing with each other. When the Vietnam War was over and China's suppression of the popular demonstrations in Tiananmen Square was still in the news, the lyrics of Billy Joel's "We Didn't Start the Fire" captured perfectly for me the jumble of events and personalities that had shaped me.

FAMILY INFLUENCES

My father, Jack W. Lampton, was born during World War I and lived through the Great Depression. He married my mother, Mary Jane, in May 1938; enlisted in the Army Air Force (Corps) in late 1942 during the Second World War; and became a member of the 439th Troop Carrier Group Headquarters, serving principally in Britain (Devonshire) and France (Chateaudun), where he took us in 1965 to meet the family he bonded with during the war. On D-Day and thereafter, the Troop Carrier Group supported air sorties and glider flights during the European invasion originally scheduled for June 5, 1944, but postponed until June 6, due to foul weather. One of my father's most treasured possessions was his copy of the June 5, 1944, letter from Supreme Allied Commander General Dwight D. Eisenhower saying: "We will accept nothing less than full Victory! Good luck! And let us all beseech the blessing of Almighty God upon this great and noble undertaking."

Mustered out of the service in the fall of 1945, my father returned home to the family business in southern California. He was an entrepreneur with a keen appreciation of risk, prudence, and deep morals. He believed in personal integrity, responsibility, duty, the power of compound interest, and that "the customer is always right." He also believed in luck. In his memoir, titled *The Luck of the Draw!*, he recounted how he missed his Army Air Corps transport flight back to France from London near the war's end. The plane he was scheduled to take crashed into the Cliffs of Dover, killing all aboard. Given his compulsive habit of being on time, my father saw missing this flight as a real stroke of luck. He called this "my third divine intervention."

My mother, Mary Jane, was of the Adams family—not the presidents, but rather the loyalists. She was a spiritualist and sacrificed her personal ambitions to sing opera professionally to raise her two boys (my younger brother Pat and me). When she was young, she was a featured TV performer in the early days of television. At the other end of her life, then in her mid-eighties, she created music and lyrics for a musical, "Stacy Jane," that premiered at a sold-out house in Ely, Nevada. One of her songs was titled, "What Road Shall I Take."

In Palo Alto and Los Altos, California, where we lived for most of my youth, our home was alive with my mom and her friends singing opera. Her spiritual journey consisted of testing the religious waters of everything from Catholicism to Christian Science, never fully comfortable with any single dogma or religious bureaucracy, but convinced that life had to be anchored in transcendent values and a loving God. She sang professionally for places of worship and took my brother and me along as she crossed all the denominational boundaries—she believed her boys should have spiritual grounding, even if anchored in no particular religious organization. Her beautiful mezzo-soprano voice still rings in my ears and heart. She sang Giacomo Puccini's aria in Gianni Schicchi, Act 1, "*O mio babbino caro*."

The personalities of our extended family also shaped me. Sunday dinners usually included members of three generations, the Chinese ideal of family life—grandparents, parents (aunts and uncles), and "the kids." I was the oldest of the cousins and usually got to eat with the "grown-ups." Arguing about history and politics over dinner was a verbal contact sport, and the voices talking over each other ran the spectrum from squishy left to hard right. Deciding whether to grab another piece of chicken or fight for your principles was part of the meal!

My maternal grandfather, an Adams, had been an enlisted man in the U.S. Army in World War I. A picture of him riding a horse through bombed-out European terrain in 1918 remains in our family album. Subsequently, in World War II, he was a Lt. Commander in the U.S. Navy at Bremerton Shipyard near Seattle training "Rosie the Riveters" who made America, what a December 1940 radio address by FDR called the "arsenal of democracy."

Most members of the family referred to my maternal grandfather as "Gramps" or "OD" (his initials), but some called him "the Commander" in deference to his military service. He was an expert in vocational education and state director of vocational education in Oregon before World War II. America needed to train welders and other trades to build the weapons of war, not least ships. With so many men fighting overseas, women came into the formal workforce in droves.

Sometime after World War II, Gramps became Assistant Superintendent of San Francisco Schools for Vocational Education. He believed that many people had an aptitude for making things with their hands and that teaching people technical skills was what they needed and desired. Learning a craft or trade was their ticket to a meaningful job of dignity, a pathway to the middle class. He believed that working with one's hands was every bit as noble and dignified as academic or white-collar pursuits, though he received his PhD from Stanford in the early 1950s at age sixty-three. One of his sons, my Uncle Bob, years later followed in Gramps's footsteps and helped found Linn-Benton Community College in Oregon's Willamette Valley, a school emphasizing vocational education, or occupational training. Uncle Bob had been in the Pacific in World War II as a "Seabee."

Another uncle, Ralph, fought in the Korean War. Ralph had been so traumatized by his U.S. Army wartime experience in Korea fighting Mao Zedong's "Red" Chinese that more than once at Sunday extended-family dinners, he gave me the latest U.S. Government Printing Office–published *Hearings and Investigations of the House Un-American Activities Committee*, enjoining me to "read this and don't ever get mixed up with any of these groups!" The "House Un-American Activities Committee" might be likened to Star Chamber proceedings, some of which aired on TV newsreels. Uncle Ralph was a foot soldier in the army of the California right. Ironically, much of my subsequent career involved interacting with countless members of the Chinese Communist Party. I never knew what Uncle Ralph thought about that. He was a man of few words and furrowed brows.

Later, no matter how much I objected to the war in Vietnam, going to Canada, or going to jail, never were options. Every living older male in my family served in the Army or Navy. "Draft dodging" would have been beyond the pale.

In 1968 I was in a dilemma like so many other young persons of that period. I opposed the ever-deepening involvement in Vietnam, not only for moral reasons but also because I did not want to perish in the misbegotten effort. The entire effort in Southeast Asia showed that we had learned nothing from the French defeat in the spring of 1954 at Dien Bien Phu. I had read Bernard Fall's 1966 masterpiece *Hell in a Very Small Place*.

But nothing was more important to Susan's and my Vietnam decision-making than my ongoing correspondence with Gramps. On September 19, 1968, a month before I went into the Army, in a letter to him, I laid bare my anguish: "Yet, I feel this portion of the earth [Asia] and the men who inhabit it represent a great potential for human reconciliation; reconciliation desperately needed if life as we know it, is to continue."

The month before, Gramps had written me on August 6, 1968, saying:

> While there are many ways of looking at the present situation, with good arguments in opposition to the undeclared war, nevertheless, it isn't any easier for those boys who find themselves in the armed services and have to do their part to face up to their duty either. Our family have all had, that is the men, some military experience. My brother Hal and I in the First World War, my younger brothers were too young. Your father, Jack, your uncles, Ralph and Bob, all had overseas duty and Roger served his required time here in this country. So most of us have stood up to be counted. . . . SO THE BEST THING TO DO IS TO PLAY BALL, MAKE A GOOD RECORD, AND GET IT OVER WITH [Emphasis in original]. . . . You must get an attitude of mind through this whole experience that will preserve your integrity, your identity, and bring you through by the events that transpire. . . . It takes

a great deal of wisdom to profit from another's experience—even that of your grandfather.

FAMILY AND CHINA

My family gave me values, a sense of well-being by belonging, and equipped me with life skills. Later in my professional years, China inevitably became part of family life to various extents. One vignette stands out with particular vividness in my mind, showing how intertwined family and profession can become.

Not long after the June 4, 1989, bloody violence in Beijing, with its carnage broadcast live on CNN, a tragedy that again powerfully injected human rights into China's relations with the West, I delivered remarks at the Diaoyutai State Guesthouse in China's capital. Once the imperial fishing hole, Diaoyutai had been expanded in 1958, one of the most excruciating years in Chinese communist history, into a retreat for high-ranking party officials and foreign dignitaries. The large compound on the western side of the capital was dotted with many lavish guesthouses, connected by waterways, lakes, and traditional arched bridges, all beautifully landscaped.

I had been invited by an arm of the Foreign Ministry to speak at a bilateral dialogue. My daughter, Kate, accompanied me on what was her first visit to China. In the very early hours of the day that I was to deliver my remarks at Diaoyutai, I took Kate to the open-air bird market, also on Beijing's west side. The local citizenry was waking up and hanging beautifully crafted bamboo and wooden cages with chirping birds on the sparse trees, and beginning to peddle a variety of artifacts, from cricket cages of all descriptions to the live crickets meant to inhabit them. The darkly clad citizens out at that early hour seemed more engaged in recreation than serious commerce.

I hoped that Kate would experience the Chinese culture of haggling, its energy, and the sheer fun of it. I also wanted her to understand that not every tough word in the course of negotiations was to be taken seriously. In such a bargaining culture, mock shock, and alternately insulting the buyer's and seller's seriousness and possessions, are all fair game—and to be expected. It was great improvisational theater. Better yet, these were

Figure 1.1.   Zhongnanhai, Beijing, September 7, 2019. Photo by David
M. Lampton.

lessons that could be more broadly applied to dealings with China, and perhaps others.

In those days any foreigner on the street attracted a crowd, but Kate, with her bright red hair (passed on by her strong-willed, English-stock maternal grandmother, Ora Mae), attracted inordinate attention and even hair-stroking by the crush surrounding her. She entered the bidding fray with me doing the translating and kibitzers all around chiming in and offering advice. They generally sided with Kate, trying to chisel the seller down. I can't even remember what she bought.

After Kate had completed her transaction and we were walking away and had an opportunity for a quiet time together, she turned toward me saying: "Dad, I see why you like the Chinese people!" In that moment, all the separations and lost family time due to my frequent trips to China, Taiwan, and Hong Kong took on a different meaning. My daughter understood me—and China—in a new and different way.

Kate was already on her way to the Beijing airport to return home, escorted by a Chinese military officer who would take her safely through departure formalities, by the time I was delivering my remarks at Diaoyutai. My talk cataloged the problems and global moral outrage that the Tiananmen bloodshed had created, thus making the stable and productive management of bilateral relations between the United States and the PRC more difficult—and important. Feelings in the room were raw. I thought a personal anecdote would break the ice. I recounted the scene earlier that morning with Kate at the bird market.

During the story about my daughter's bargaining and her proclamation to me about the Chinese people, I suddenly lost my composure. China and my family had collided in a jumble of emotions before the audience. Chinese and American leaders of considerable gravitas were present, Robert McNamara among them. It was not the kind of controlled, diplomatic moment I had intended. My remarks did break the ice, but not the way I had envisioned.

THE IMPORTANCE OF PLACE—CALIFORNIA

The California of my youth, in the 1950s and 1960s, was a bastion of the Chiang Kai-shek–oriented "Committee of One Million against the

Admission of Red China to the United Nations." California's senior U.S. Senator, William F. Knowland, was a powerful pro-Chiang ("Free China") voice in American foreign policy. He exerted influence from his various senatorial perches, having served as both Minority and Majority Leader for Senate Republicans. And he was a scion of *The Oakland Tribune* fortune when newspapers still made money. California churned politically with outsized personalities, and every one of them had an opinion about China.

California has a long tradition with China. Leland Stanford built much of his fortune on the backs of Chinese who pick-axed and blasted through the Sierra Mountains building the western portion of the Transcontinental Railroad.[1] In the town of Truckee, in the Sierra Mountains near where I spent part of many summers, the railroad Stanford helped build clung to the cliffs, running through long sheds to protect the tracks from constant landslides and snow avalanches. That railway and the fortunes it spawned made America a Pacific power—indeed an imperial power.

The railroad made robber barons such as Leland Stanford fabulously wealthy, enabling him and his wife, Jane, to found a great university that eventually built exceptionally strong science and engineering departments. After a rocky period following the university's 1885 founding, with the early death of Leland Stanford in 1893 and the probable 1905 murder of his wife, who was a driving, quixotic force in the school's early governance, from the 1930s on Leland Stanford Junior University came to fuel what eventually became Silicon Valley (so named in 1971).[2]

California was also the home of the "Asia Firsters," those who believed that the sun already had set over the Atlantic. Ironically, the most conservative political figures of the era were also those who had the greatest faith in the proposition that Asia was the future. The California perspective was simple. European feuds kept sucking America into wars. The future, many Californians believed, was with Asia's growing markets and energetic people. The communist takeover of China in 1949 naturally caused considerable consternation, but it also fostered a new political opportunity for enterprising politicians promising to make Asia free. Making Asia free meant making China free. And making China free would change the world's geopolitical map and give a decisive blow to the Soviet menace.

In 1952, California's junior senator, Richard Nixon, whose political trademark was uncompromising anti-communism, was catapulted onto Eisenhower's presidential ticket to solidify Ike's credentials with the right wing of the Republican Party. The former Supreme Commander of the Allied Expeditionary Force in Europe was viewed as a little too soft on the "reds" for their taste, viewing Eisenhower as an Atlanticist who had not yet seen the light that Asia was the future. With Richard Nixon as his running mate in the general election, Eisenhower gained credibility with the anti-communists.

The actor Ronald Reagan, who peddled "20 Mule Team Borax" detergent booster on television and hosted the TV series *Death Valley Days* in 1964–1965, was also coming to prominence as a stalwart anti-communist Californian. The TV series he hosted embodied the rough-hewn values of America's West together with anti-communism. Reagan was initially a Democrat, turning Republican in 1962.

During the presidential campaign of 1964, I was asked (for what reason I no longer remember) to escort Barry Goldwater, Republican Senator from Arizona running against Lyndon B. Johnson (LBJ) for president of the United States, to the dais at a hundred-dollar-a-plate fundraising dinner in San Jose, California, about twenty miles south of my home. I remember reading Goldwater's *The Conscience of a Conservative* in preparation for my brief brush with him. My initial impression of him was that of a straight shooter, a man of deeply embedded principles, and not as smooth as Ronald Reagan.

California and its political personalities have periodically inserted punctuation marks into my later life. In November 1991, I met Richard Nixon in his New Jersey office not far from his Saddle River residence long after his August 1974 forced resignation as president. The former president's aide, John Taylor, who helped arrange the meeting with a visiting Chinese group that I accompanied, suggested we meet Nixon early in the day—the former president's thinking was clearer in the mornings he advised. After the formalities of welcoming his Chinese guests and me, with an ever-present yellow pad in hand, the ex-president delivered a forty-five-minute tour de force exegesis on U.S.-China relations, past achievements, and the challenges doubtlessly lying ahead.

As we rose from our chairs to depart, I mentioned to the former president that when he ran for governor of California in 1962, he had landed by helicopter in our local baseball diamond, flashing his signature double "V" gesture. A smile passed across his face, though his 1962 gubernatorial loss to Pat Brown was nothing he probably wanted to recall.

Years later, former governor of California Pat Brown was on the Board of the National Committee on United States-China Relations (NCUSCR), which I then headed. Brown's son, Jerry, who later also became governor of California, hoped to involve China's firms in building a high-speed rail line between Los Angeles and San Francisco.

THE IMPORTANCE OF PEOPLE IN SHAPING EVENTS

Social science often downplays the decisive role of individuals, with all their idiosyncrasies, though in our personal lives, we understand that individuals, whether noble or craven, have an impact. In my 2001 book, *Same Bed, Different Dreams*, one chapter is titled "People Count." I pay particular attention to persons who left deep impressions on me or the larger environment, trying to understand and explain the context in which they acted.

Those who have left me with the deepest impressions are not necessarily those with whom I had the longest association or were of exalted social or bureaucratic status. An old man in Beijing, whom I literally ran into in an alleyway (*hutong*) in mid-October 1976 for fewer than five minutes, very early one overcast morning (an encounter recounted in chapter 4), left nearly as deep an imprint on me as interactions with members of the Chinese elite in their monumental meeting rooms and resplendent imperial playgrounds—generally served by elegant *qipao*-clad tea ladies who had discarded their unisex, drab-colored, baggy pants soon after the Cultural Revolution.

Of course, I also remember many leadership meetings, including one in January 1998 with Chinese President and General Secretary Jiang Zemin in his office in Building 202 of Zhongnanhai, the inner sanctum leadership compound in Beijing, where he discussed the nature of memory, observing to my colleagues and me that "young memory leaves a deeper trace in the mind," going on to say that events in his youth still shaped his views and actions.

Illustrative of the importance of people and events, Richard Nixon gingerly began to suggest a new, more open policy toward the PRC in the 1967–1969 period, as the Sino-Soviet conflict reached its zenith, and as Washington became increasingly alarmed at the Soviet military buildup. President Jimmy Carter and Chinese paramount leader Deng Xiaoping pushed the Sino-American interaction across an ever-greater expanse of human interaction. Had Carter not been a devout Christian with prior experience with China, normalization might have been delayed.

Leaders matter. They can open new vistas or lead us into destructive *cul-de-sacs*. This fact struck me afresh as Donald Trump came into office shortly before I retired from regular teaching at Johns Hopkins—SAIS in mid-2018. A new set of national leaders in both Beijing and Washington—Xi Jinping and Donald Trump—had come to power and were driving U.S.-China relations in a more conflictual direction. A growing number of Western pundits and strategists began consigning Beijing once more to adversary status. My professional life was coming full circle: conflict, engagement, growing conflict. From Cold War to Cold War. Leaders matter.

But, when all is said and done, it is to my father that I remain ever grateful, as much for what he did not do as for what he did. He had the wisdom and courage to encourage me in my chosen endeavor despite his initial misgivings. He led me gently.

Since all of my father's overseas experience had been in Europe, he was understandably startled when I informed him that I intended to go into China Studies in 1968:

"China?" he said, "China? Who's going to pay you to do that?"

Later in his autobiography, my father remembered that moment:

One day, Mike [my nickname] came home and announced to his mother and me that he was changing his major at Stanford to political science, specializing in Asian studies, specifically China. Both his mother and I looked at each other, rolled our eyes, but thank goodness maintained our silence. At that time China had not been recognized by President Nixon, and it appeared on the face of it to be a field of limited opportunity to the uninformed. . . . With the passing of time, it became evident that his timing was perfect, and that those counseling him at Stanford University were proved to be correct.

Having had no direct exposure to Asia, much less China, my father's worries were understandable—his life was shaped by Europe; that is where he took our family when we went abroad. In the 1950s and early 1960s, America was still transatlantic in its economic and cultural orientation, despite the Pacific, Korean, and Vietnam wars. It had been European wars in which my mother's father ("Gramps") and my father had fought. It was the Soviet Union that had so many Americans digging backyard bomb shelters during the Cold War.

Moreover, it was not easy raising a child in the 1960s. Social mores were rapidly changing; new careers were emerging; the mechanical age was giving way to the electronic revolution with its epicenter in Palo Alto and the Santa Clara Valley, as it also was the epicenter of the "sexual revolution." What Carl Djerassi working on his oral contraceptive pill at Syntex Corporation and Stanford did not do for the sexual revolution, the University of California at Berkeley did.

In the post–World War II period, America had been mired in two large-scale Pacific conflicts in which total victory was not the objective—Korea and Vietnam. In the first "police action," U.S.-U.N. forces had been fought to a costly standstill, and the second conflict's eventual denouement would be a chaotic race to the exit—defeat in Southeast Asia. All this unfolded in our front yard south of San Francisco. As my dad explained in his memoirs, he and my mother were worried:

> We were in the volatile "sixties" and it seemed as though we went from one "crusade" to another, and Mary Jane and I found ourselves defending our values, formed during the 1930s Depression years and before, on a daily basis. Thank goodness, neither boy [my younger brother Pat and me] went over the brink.

Despite his misgivings and the era's uncertainties, Dad sublimated his concerns and encouraged me to follow my heart and head.

NOTES

1. See Gordon H. Chang, *Ghosts of Old Gold Mountain: The Epic Story of the Chinese Who Built the Transcontinental Railroad* (Houghton Mifflin Harcourt, 2019).

2. Richard White, *Who Killed Jane Stanford? A Gilded Age Tale of Murder, Deceit, Spirits, and the Birth of a University* (W. W. Norton, 2022).

CHAPTER TWO

"It's *Miss* Turner—And I Like It That Way!"

(The 1960s)

NOT ONLY DID I NOT GO OVER THE BRINK, I DISCOVERED MY LIFELONG passion during this time, while still in my teens. Miss Turner's class on Far Eastern History at Palo Alto Senior High School was the turning point. She inclined me in a wholly unanticipated direction, widening the aperture through which I viewed the world and opening my eyes to a different reality.

My most important reason for taking Miss Turner's class was Miss Turner (Florence) herself. Self-confident, cosmopolitan, determined, and captivating, her first words on the opening day of class were, emphatically, "IT'S *MISS* TURNER—AND I LIKE IT THAT WAY!" When she wanted to make sure her pupils were paying attention, she would say, "Now pay attention, because I'm going to drop some jewels." She taught what I still believe was the only course on "Far Eastern History" in the State of California Public Schools in the first half of the 1960s. My hazy recollection is that students had to "apply" to take her advanced course; if we did not actually apply, we nevertheless felt privileged to be in her class.

Visiting Asia in the summers, she would stop in Hawaii to spend time at the magnificent new East-West Center in Honolulu that had been established by Congress in 1960. The center was developing into a crossroads between East and West—at least until long-range Boeing

747 aircraft made it possible to bypass Hawaii entirely going to and from Asia. From her visits to Asia, Miss Turner brought back her lived experiences, interspersing her anecdotes with lessons on Chinese dynasties, Commodore Matthew C. Perry and the opening of Japan to trade, Confucianism, Opium Wars, and compradors.

She taught us that there was much of significance that had happened throughout Asia's long history and a lot was occurring there that would affect us ever more profoundly in the future. This region, she taught, had a different, but equally valid, experience, quite distinctive from that of the West. Much of what was happening in Asia had to do with the nationalism of diverse peoples, striving to modernize and gain control of their destinies. She had a broader view than that the United States was simply confronting a centralized master plot of ideological subversion run from Beijing and Moscow, aimed at America's heart.

Miss Turner was the embodiment of globalization before it had a name. Globalization was occurring all around me in Palo Alto, Stanford, and the peninsula south of San Francisco. Hewlett and Packard were in their legendary garage fashioning what became a globally leading technology company with a close connection to the Stanford Industrial Park. The Alioto family that owned the Pacific "Bear" Lines (Pacific Far East Lines) was sending its ships out of San Francisco Bay to the Far East in growing numbers—my wife Susan's Uncle Jack worked for Pacific Bear Lines and adopted a quasi-Chinese lifestyle and collected books on China. His books now grace my collection.

Asia was prominently in the news during JFK's final year of life before his assassination, and thereafter during the 1964 presidential campaign, when I decided to take Miss Turner's class. One of the issues in the campaign between the incumbent Lyndon Baines Johnson (LBJ) and conservative U.S. Senator Barry Goldwater from Arizona was whether the United States should become more involved in Vietnam, with all the attendant risks of war with China. President Johnson argued that Goldwater and the Republicans would get us into a nuclear war. To drive the point home, the Johnson campaign's signature television spot in the closing moment of the campaign was a young girl in a field plucking daisy petals and counting them as her life was extinguished in a nuclear blast before the viewer's eyes. Indeed, the viewer was looking into her eyes. It was such a shocking ad that it only officially aired once, though it was replayed endlessly by others. The spot closed with LBJ intoning that "we must either love each other, or we must die." Johnson won the election resoundingly. In my youthful eyes, I would soon come to believe that LBJ had invoked peace to win the election, only to wage war in Southeast Asia once victorious.

There was yet another reason for my attraction to Miss Turner's course—I had had enough of European history. It seemed that my European and American history classes never got through World War II before the academic term ran out. I never quite learned why we periodically had to seek refuge under our school desks on our knees with our hands on the back of our necks in "duck-and-cover drills" to protect ourselves from our World War II "allies," the Soviets and the Chinese. Moscow had detonated a hydrogen bomb in 1961, and Beijing detonated an atomic device in October 1964. It was an insecure time. One high school friend's family built a bomb shelter in their backyard. I helped dig it, only to be pretty sure afterward that there would be no room in it for me if nuclear bombs started raining down. I wanted to learn how we had come to this point.

So profound was Miss Turner's effect on me that more than four decades later, I wrote her a letter. I thought she might like to know that one of her former pupils had so taken her teachings to heart that he had been president of the National Committee on U.S.-China Relations in New York City and subsequently a chaired professor at Johns Hopkins SAIS leading its China Studies Program. Around 2005–2006, I sent her a letter, care of the current Palo Alto High School principal.

Some weeks later, the letter was returned to me with a note saying that Miss Turner had passed away in January 2005. The principal offered condolences.

My motive in writing Miss Turner had been simple. Teachers had changed my life, none more than her, and I wanted to thank them all through her. Having been a professor myself, first at Ohio State University in the 1970s and 1980s and later at Johns Hopkins in the late 1990s into 2018, I knew how gratifying it is for teachers to be told that they had made a positive difference. Upon receiving the returned envelope, I vowed thereafter to be prompt and fulsome in acknowledging the difference others have made in my life.

In retrospect, the interest in Asia I developed while still in high school seems almost inevitable. I lived in California; California faces Asia. The influences Asia exerted on the state were evident all around me, even in the Chinese-style roofs of the Maryknoll Seminary that sat on grass-covered hills a few miles from my home south of San Francisco. The priests who lived there in semi-seclusion were retired missionaries who had served in China and other parts of Asia. They might have been isolated in their hillside redoubt but were glad to talk to those of us brave enough to make the trek into the foothills, as my wife-to-be, Susan, and I learned when we hiked to meet them one day.

In 1964, the year I graduated from high school, the Olympic Games were held in Asia (Tokyo) for the first time in history, not yet even twenty years after Japan's total defeat in the Pacific War, a war ending in two atomic blasts. Asia was on the move.

Just before going off to my first year of college in the fall of 1964, I worked at the United Airlines flight kitchen at San Francisco International Airport. Sometimes I rode to work with my dad's carpool. One morning I suggested to my somnolent seatmates in the carpool that United Airlines ought to start planning to fly to China—it had a quarter of the world's people, and they were smart and entrepreneurial. In my optimism, I ignored the fact that my first passport said on page 4: "THIS PASSPORT IS NOT VALID FOR TRAVEL TO OR IN COMMUNIST CONTROLLED PORTIONS OF CHINA, KOREA, VIET-NAM OR TO OR IN ALBANIA, CUBA."

I was also ignoring the fact that Mao Zedong was using anti-imperialist ideology as his clarion call to consolidate power at home and fuel brushfire communist insurgencies globally to weaken and divert Washington. While I was thinking about flying to China, President Kennedy had been, and President Johnson was, preoccupied with building counterinsurgency capabilities and stopping Beijing's salami-slicing aggression in Asia and elsewhere. The carpool went back to sleep after a few guffaws. My advice was about two decades premature. United Airlines bought Pan

Am's Pacific routes in 1986 and built the largest American presence in the China air market thereafter.

All in all, Miss Turner was singularly important in me taking what was, in the 1960s, the road less traveled. But, once I started down the path to Asia, I soon encountered others nudging me along this ever-more challenging trajectory.

MORE MOTIVATION

Professor Michel (yes, the spelling is correct) Oksenberg was my next source of inspiration. Mike was still working on his PhD degree in 1966 when he began teaching Stanford undergraduates, among whom I was one. He was on the leading edge of what was becoming a dynamic China field. Although most outsiders, my father included, could not imagine a future in studying China, beyond sheer intellectual interest or a possible national security career, in reality, demand for China knowledge was growing quickly.

The Ford Foundation and the U.S. government, in the form of the National Defense Education Act of 1958 (NDEA), were committing considerable resources to create both the human and physical infrastructure for what would become a vibrant China field, a field that was decimated during the McCarthy era when many China specialists had been accused of being sympathetic to communism and were pilloried and removed from posts. Now new attention to China and Area Studies was being justified by the need for national security.

STEM fields and the study of foreign languages and strategic nations and regions received emphasis, justified as necessary to enable the United States to catch up with the Soviet Union following Moscow's successful launch in 1957 of Sputnik, the first earth-orbiting satellite. For its part, the PRC was periodically raising alarm in the Taiwan Strait and supporting far-flung insurgencies. The CIA, the Foreign Broadcast Information Service, and the Joint Publications Research Service, along with the U.S. Consulate General in Hong Kong, translated and disseminated almost every broadcast and periodical from China they could lay hands on, pumping out so much paper that soon every serious China scholar's bookshelves and basement were full with the output.

My graduate education was entirely paid for by the Ford Foundation, NDEA, and the Fulbright-Hays Dissertation Research Abroad Program. The Fulbright Program administrators got creative and approved my research in Hong Kong where I could interview refugees from the PRC. Being the colonial power in Hong Kong, London had to approve of this arrangement. The US defense structure and the Ford Foundation began infusing the field with money to acquire primary language source materials and fund four-year graduate fellowships. In exchange for that support, the grantee had only to promise to study (in my case) the Chinese language and then do something of public benefit for several years following degree completion—teaching counted as public benefit. While this effort to build national capabilities served America well, the security dynamic of the period warrants a cautionary note.

In the United States, "national security" is a trump card in establishing national policy and budgetary priorities. Projects hooked to a plausible, pressing national security concern have a much better chance of receiving federal funding than those that are not. President Eisenhower was not exaggerating when in early 1961 he said:

> We annually spend on military security alone more than the net income of all United States corporations. Now this conjunction of an immense military establishment and a large arms industry is new in the American experience. The total influence—economic, political, even spiritual—is felt in every city, every Statehouse, every office of the Federal government. We recognize the imperative need for this development. Yet, we must not fail to comprehend its grave implications. Our toil, resources, and livelihood are all involved. So is the very structure of our society.

At the time, Mike Oksenberg had not yet finished his PhD degree but was ascending rapidly in his career because he was brilliant, the demand for talent was great, and the immediate supply of modern China skills was limited. A crash national effort was underway as several university centers became magnets for material investment and human resource development—Stanford, Columbia, Michigan, Harvard, and the University of California at Berkeley, with other important efforts underway at the University of Washington, Princeton, and Cornell, among others. In the mid-1970s and thereafter, Middlebury College's Department of Chinese Language and Literature became a gold standard in Chinese language training under the leadership of its founding chairman John Berninghausen. In the think-tank world, the RAND Corporation, Stanford Research Institute (SRI), and the Brookings Institution stood out. In 1968 Oksenberg left Stanford to teach at Columbia University, where his mentor, A. Doak Barnett, was located. In 1969 Barnett left Columbia for Washington, D.C., to work at Brookings, and later still at Johns Hopkins—SAIS. I eventually succeeded him there.

In the latter half of the 1960s, body bags were coming back to America in increasingly obscene numbers from Vietnam, the count peaking in 1968. China had a significant number of troops in Vietnam (principally in North Vietnam as advisors, engineers, and anti-aircraft personnel) contributing to the U.S. body count, with a few observers in South Vietnam as well. The Johnson administration did its best to obscure PRC involvement from the American public, fearing that the backlash would corner the administration, forcing it to either expand the war to China or precipitously withdraw without achieving what President Richard Nixon called "the decent interval" or "peace with honor." When America left and Saigon fell, no president wanted his fingerprints on an unseemly rush to the exits.

Even before becoming president in 1969, Richard Nixon had called for changes in China policy in a 1967 *Foreign Affairs* article. Nixon wanted to use improved relations with Beijing to divide Soviet troops between the European and Far Eastern theaters, weaken Moscow and Beijing's support for Hanoi's war against U.S. intervention, and to promote arms agreements with Moscow, enabling him to assume the posture of peacemaker for domestic electoral advantage. In the two or so years after his *Foreign Affairs* article appeared, the political and strategic stars gradually aligned in Beijing and Washington, making a breakthrough possible.

I was a junior in the spring of 1967 when I enrolled in Mike Oksenberg's class on "Chinese Foreign Policy." The course required writing an original research paper. I chose to write about the recent bloody

"September 30, 1965, Incident" and its aftermath in Indonesia. A very large but unknown number of ethnic Chinese across the archipelago had been slaughtered by some in the majority Muslim population and by elements of the Indonesian National Army, using the association of the Indonesian Communist Party (PKI) with Mao's China as a rationale. While not endorsing the slaughter, Washington was relieved that the "Chinese threat" in that strategic island chain had been extinguished. Most ethnic Chinese in Indonesia were not communists (indeed, many were highly successful capitalists), but the Cold War was not an era of careful distinctions. The intercommunal violence had more to do with religion, nationalism, and unequal distribution of wealth than political ideology.

As part of my research paper, I wanted to know why locals in Indonesia were killing Chinese, how and why Beijing responded as it did, and why America was fighting authoritarianism in Vietnam while turning a blind eye to it and ethnic slaughter in Indonesia. A CIA report on the Indonesian carnage I read at the time has stuck with me ever since—"The Medan River [in Sumatra] is choked with the bodies of dead Chinese."

This research paper taught me not to underestimate the power of hatred in Asia, whether derivative of ethnicity, nationalism, religion, or ideology. To a boy from California who had Jewish, Catholic, Mormon, Protestant, and Christian Science neighbors and friends, and a spiritually ecumenical mother, I had grown up without experiencing the types of societal divisions animating politics and life in much of the world.

One of my earliest experiences in Asia confirmed the conclusions I had drawn in the paper I had done in Oksenberg's class. In the summer of 1973, Susan and I went to Indonesia (Java, Bali, and Sumatra, traveling mostly by car). Susan had a contract to revise and update travel publications on Indonesia for Lane Publishing (*Sunset Magazines & Books*). She brought me along as her photographer. A colonel in the Indonesian military (everyone seemed to be a colonel) was assigned to guide/watch us.

We asked to see the site of the 1955 Conference held in Bandung, an iconic meeting for those who follow Chinese foreign policy. This was the conclave at which Premier Zhou Enlai launched Beijing's kinder and gentler foreign policy—the "Bandung Line." Zhou had had a close call on his trip, echoing my own father's good fortune in missing a plane. On his way to the Bandung Conference, Zhou missed (whether by design or accident, we do not know) his plane out of Hong Kong. That plane was bombed, crashing into the waters off Sarawak. All but three aboard died. Zhou arrived on another plane.

As Susan and I exited the Bandung Conference site, which looked like a run-down YMCA, our military escort literally exploded when I asked to visit Bandung's Chinatown: "I don't like Chinese, I hate Chinese, and I won't take you." Shortly after our visit in the summer of 1973, a minor traffic accident in Bandung snowballed into an anti-Chinese tsunami, destroying 1,500 ethnic Chinese businesses in the city.

Mike Oksenberg's course led directly to my decision to become a China specialist. Everyone who ever knew Mike experienced his infectious enthusiasm and idea-a-minute mind. One sunny day, I stopped by his office located on Stanford's beautiful quadrangle constructed of tan-colored early Eocene Arkosic Sandstone blocks. I sat down and blurted out that I was wondering what to do with my life.

Without skipping a beat, he said, "You ought to go into China Studies." To which I responded, also without skipping a beat, "OK!" In later years, Mike often told this story, in part to tease me about my thoughtful decision-making style and maybe in part as proof of his own persuasive capacities. We became lifelong friends and colleagues.

Despite Mike's move to Columbia University, after my year-long interlude in the U.S. Army Reserve on active duty (1968–1969), I chose to stay at Stanford for graduate school, instead of attending Yale or Columbia. Stanford had the balance I was looking for between political science as a discipline and China as a geographic concentration. Stanford's political science department was behavioral, data-based, without going over the quantitative deep end. At that moment in time, Stanford had an abundance of professors who shaped my study of China greatly and who were among the undisputed leaders in the field.

The faculty to whom I was drawn at Stanford, and who shaped my own study and research, all had written about China in innovative ways, some using social science frameworks, another utilizing Korean prisoner-of-war interviews, and still others using comparative case studies: John W. Lewis, Alexander George, Robert North, and Dennis J. Doolin (all in political science); G. William Skinner (anthropology); Lyman Van Slyke (history); and Dr. Paul Basch (international health at Stanford Medical School) had particularly strong impacts on me. So did Gabriel A. Almond, the era's pathbreaker on comparative development, political culture, and functionalism—concepts that shaped my thinking.

As busy as Professor Almond was, even when I was an undergraduate, he agreed to meet with me every Friday afternoon to talk about my undergraduate Honors Thesis on Henry David Thoreau, addressing the question of why Thoreau's ideas never became the basis for a mass movement. Nobody else in the Department of Political Science would so much as touch Thoreau, whose political philosophy was about as far away from emerging political science methodological trends as could be imagined. Our meetings started at 2:00 p.m. when, on Professor Almond's instructions, I would knock on his office door and gently wake him from his power nap. The principal conclusion of my honors thesis research was that Thoreau provided no basis for mass political action because he was an individualist. That was a pretty rudimentary conclusion—but I was able to read a lot of Thoreau!

Professor John Wilson Lewis became my PhD advisor and shaped my path forward—another motivator.

"THAT SOUNDS LIKE A WONDERFUL TOPIC"
Much could be said about graduate school life. The reality is that it is more a perseverance test than an intelligence test. Beyond the exhausting tasks of trying to learn the Chinese language adequately enough to conduct field and documentary research using original sources and learn a discipline adequately enough to know what has been done before you, lies the job of writing a dissertation.

The core challenges of a dissertation are defining a researchable question that other scholars will judge significant methodologically and substantively, adopting or creating an analytic framework to shed light on that topic, and then producing a publishable "original and significant contribution to knowledge." Simply put, the challenges are explaining: "What is the question?" "Why does it matter?" "What are you telling your chosen academic field that it does not already know?" And, "how do you know?" In forcing me to answer these questions, without creating a topical or intellectual straight-jacket, John Lewis left an indelible mark on me. Sometimes encouragement and freedom are the greatest gifts a mentor can bestow.

John Lewis was a dynamo. He emitted an almost electrical field, energizing all in his orbit. Early in my PhD training, John advised me to "NEVER use the passive voice!" I think he was instructing me on a general posture toward life, not simply grammar. His underlying advice was "act, do not be acted upon!" John provided energy and meaning to tasks larger than himself. He was constitutionally unable to be a spectator to a crisis. He believed that knowledge of a problem or injustice demands action.

John always had one or more global problems in his sights. His preoccupations, commitments, and contributions included a fact-based opposition to the war in Vietnam; moving toward and beyond normalization with China; fostering intelligent management of the Korean Peninsula, particularly as this related to North Korea; arms control; U.S. relations with the Soviet Union and later Russia; and Taiwan.

His work with George McTurnin Kahin, *The United States in Vietnam: An Analysis in Depth of the History of America's Involvement in Vietnam* (1967), informed and energized me, providing the basic facts about increasing U.S. entanglement in Southeast Asia. Aside from *The Pentagon Papers*, the Kahin-Lewis volume probably was the most significant intellectual contribution to the antiwar movement. It became the touchstone for many of us graduate students who went to churches and schools throughout Northern California spreading its knowledge and wisdom and, in the process, picking up valuable experience in lecturing, teaching large groups ("teach-ins"), trying to link academic findings to problems in the public square, and attaching importance to public education in a democracy.

There were two broad categories of antiwar graduate students during the Vietnam War. One kind, which included many of John's students, thought America had made a tragic blunder by stepping into the

Vietnam quagmire, a misstep that could only be rectified by knowledge, persuasion, public education, and democratic involvement. The other subset saw the war as a reflection of the predatory nature of the American system itself. In the view of this subset, fundamental systemic transformation was essential if anything was going to change. I considered myself clearly in the first camp—correct the error, but don't challenge the system's legitimacy.

Reflective of this split among students (and faculty) was the composition of the Committee of Concerned Asian Scholars (CCAS), founded in the late 1960s. I became a "member" in graduate school (with no discernible process by which one became one). In 1971 the group sent a much-publicized delegation to the PRC in which I have been said to have participated.[1] I did not go on that trip. After that group's return to the United States, CCAS initiated a selection process to dispatch a second group to China. I was so concerned about what I considered an ideological litmus test for inclusion in the group that I declined to enter the selection process. This was a fraught period. Everyone wanted to go to China, but seemingly endorsing Chinese foreign policy was more than I, and several other classmates (particularly ones with military service), could do.

In short, John gave us the twin gifts of information and purpose as we sought to extricate our nation from the tragic conflict in Indochina. He also showed us how essential it was to build organizations to effect enduring change. He helped establish and build the NCUSCR, which I later headed and which so many of my Stanford peers, such as Harry Harding and Douglas Murray, did so much to develop. And last but not least, John was chair of the Joint Committee on Contemporary China at the Social Science Research Council (SSRC) where he was instrumental in bringing China Studies into the social sciences—my long-time colleague at SAIS, Anne Thurston, was the China staff at SSRC in that era.

Toward the twilight of his career, John wrote another book, *Imagined Enemies*, in which he sought to warn America and China to avoid another descending spiral, this time involving Taiwan. At every step of the way, he sought to reduce the prospects for conflict, possibly nuclear, on the Korean Peninsula and across the Taiwan Strait.

For John, the central problem of political life was how to understand "the social limits of politically induced change." I believe he meant that humans are not simply cerebral and rationally calculating, but also social and visceral, driven by durable attachments to community, values, culture, perceptions, divergent interests, and institutions. With political behavior anchored in so many powerful motivations, imagining change in human affairs is easier than producing it.

GIVING STUDENTS WINGS

John had a small army of graduate students, and several were involved in a large study he had underway on Tangshan, a city in North China, devastated in 1976 by a gigantic earthquake, killing an enormous number of citizens; estimates run to more than six hundred thousand. The core of John's Tangshan research was to understand this locality by various individuals researching and writing numerous varied case studies, aggregating them, and hoping that as knowledge of this single area accumulated, scholars would gain insight into how China worked, from a variety of perspectives. This project could sustain many potential PhD dissertations.

As one of John's students, I only had one problem. I was not particularly interested in Tangshan.

For what seemed like months around the end of my second year of graduate school, I grappled with how I would tell Professor Lewis that I was not particularly interested in Tangshan. Without any real basis, I had assumed that he expected me to do something germane to his overall project. Instead, I wanted to do something with which I had some life experience—something in the field of medicine and public health, something germane to national politics and policy.

The Great Proletarian Cultural Revolution (1966–1976) was underway in China at the time, and health delivery innovation was one seemingly constructive development in the PRC amidst the mayhem. I thought this would be a good avenue to understand how the Chinese government, party, and citizenry interacted on life and death issues of universal, daily importance. My germinating topic got away from the era's preoccupation with the "Great Leader" (Mao) and ideology and focused on universal policy problems that cannot be wished away by sloganeering.

The need for skilled doctors and nurses, rational organization, and money were essential, not ideological cant.

Finally, I screwed up my courage, made an appointment to see John, and walked into his office. After telling him my news, he replied, "I think that sounds like a wonderful topic!"

Thereafter, John provided me with essential interview contacts to get my research underway, one of whom was a former Ministry of Public Health bureaucrat living in Falls Church, Virginia. He also recommended I talk to a female Chinese medical doctor he knew who had fled the mainland to Hong Kong. And finally, he contacted Professor Ezra Vogel at Harvard on my behalf, knowing that Ezra had conducted refugee interviews in Hong Kong related to medical care and public health in the PRC. Ezra graciously opened up all his files to me, a student he did not even know, sparking a career-long friendship and admiration on my part.

CONCLUSION

We all need inspiration, motivation. We all need a sense that our lives can be very different from those our parents and others have lived. Young persons need this, not as an act of rebellion, but rather to follow their correct instinct that the future will be different from the past and they must adapt to that future and help shape it. The métier of a teacher is to convey to others, in the most rounded fashion possible, what happened in the past and why it happened, knowing that we could be off the mark. Our task is to empower students to fashion a different, better future. I was blessed with more such teachers than anyone could rightfully expect. My mother and father overcame their doubts to liberate their son. Miss Turner was the first beacon in turbulent waters. Mike Oksenberg and John Lewis sent me sailing.

NOTE

1. Pete Millwood, *Improbable Diplomats: How Ping-Pong Players, Musicians, and Scientists Remade US-China Relations* (Cambridge University Press, 2023), 104.

CHAPTER THREE

To the Field

(The Early 1970s)

GRAMPS BELIEVED THAT WE LEARN NOT ONLY THROUGH OUR HEADS but also through our hands, by doing. I share his beliefs, which grounded my teaching and writing in direct, hands-on experience.

I revel in interaction with people, places, and institutions. My experiences on the ground have shaped the questions I have asked and the information sought. I delight in talking with people, visiting factories and work units, and getting out to the field, with my research taking me to such far-flung places as the jungles of Laos where I was researching the construction of a high-speed railroad, an effort fittingly captured in one of my favorite photographs, showing me and two colleagues, one Malaysian and the other Singaporean, slogging through the jungle with red, gummy soil caking our shoes. We were hiking to a tunnel-boring site being constructed as part of the Chinese-built high-speed rail line in Laos. *Rivers of Iron: Railroads and Chinese Power in Southeast Asia* was the result of this five-year, nine-country project substantially conducted in the field.

Much of my research has focused on topics involving issues arising from friction along the boundaries of human communities and administrative organizations. I believe that understanding is achieved by talking to participants in boundary-line friction.

In the early 1970s, when I set out to do my dissertation with John Lewis's contacts and encouragement as initial boosts, what today I can

Figure 3.1.   Research Team at tunnel-boring site in Northern Laos, June 2017.
(Left to right: Cheng-Chwee Kuik; Selina Ho; author). Photo by David M. Lampton.

describe as my research approach was a scarcely articulated impulse. In 1972–1973, my immediate tasks were to develop my dissertation topic and the strategy to tackle it and get into the field with the necessary linguistic and methodological tools.

By my third year of graduate school support, the clock was ticking and I still had to refine my topic, develop my analytic framework, finance the undertaking, go to Asia for research, write up my findings, and defend the dissertation before the money ran dry. I had no time to take the better path followed by several of my fellow graduate students at Stanford—going to Taiwan for a year to burnish my Chinese language. Consequently, my Chinese language is only utilitarian, which I still regret.

WHERE DID MY IDEAS COME FROM?

The Big Idea: For Sir Isaac Newton, the "big idea" came under an apple tree. Mine came under an oak tree outside Encina Hall on the Stanford campus in late 1971.

I was waiting for Susan to meet me at the end of the day, turning over in my mind potential dissertation topics and approaches, asking myself, "What do I actually know something about?" "What are the Chinese themselves talking about as important issues in their own country?" "What topic is intrinsically comparative?" "What is a problem in China that also is of universal concern, and how has the PRC adopted different, or similar, solutions to this challenge?" "Can we discern patterns common in human society that account for the similarities and differences we observe in China?"

In the recesses of my mind was the instinct that something was missing in much research being conducted about the PRC. Then analysts were preoccupied with the machinations of one elderly, deeply flawed, perhaps demented, and awesomely powerful leader, Mao Zedong, and the sycophants, hangers-on, and factions within and outside his orbit. This was a period rather similar to today's preoccupations with Xi Jinping and his acolytes.

Instead, I wanted to focus on a universal issue connected to meeting human needs, whether it be medical care, water management, transportation, civil nuclear power, or education, all subjects that I eventually tackled over the next fifty years. I wanted to look at issues that most people in China, most of the time, were concerned about.

I knew that elite politics and leaders were unquestionably important and that the stability of the political system was enormously consequential. Many times throughout my career, I have focused on these. But I have always come back to the perspective that the daily grind of politics concerning recurrent, universal issues was a vantage point holding the prospect for understanding politics as it was often practiced in China, the unpredictable and precocious riptides of mass political campaigns notwithstanding.

I considered that much analysis of elite politics being done by Western scholars suffered from a disability. That disability was that no one who knew directly about elite politics in Beijing or in provincial capitals throughout China would, at that time, speak with the likes of me, and anyone talking to me likely knew little about such sensitive issues. In the late 1970s and throughout the 1980s and 1990s, when it became possible to talk to an increasing range of leaders (and people who knew them) at all levels in China, I would seize the opportunity to do so. Two of my books, *Paths to Power* (1986) and *Following the Leader* (2014), are explicitly about leaders and leadership. But in the early 1970s, direct exposure to leaders, or even people who plausibly knew them and would talk, was exceedingly rare. I initially focused on universal issues about which many people had personal knowledge.

As I thought about what specific dissertation topic I might pursue, my previous idiosyncratic, unplanned, unconnected life experiences collided to produce a gestalt. These experiences require a detour in the narrative.

The Fire Department

In the second half of my undergraduate career, I had been a student firefighter, an on-campus job with a colorful history dating back to 1883 and Leland Stanford's determination to protect his riding stables and mansion. I lived in the old firehouse (built in 1904) at the center of the Stanford campus on Teresa Street—a wooden clapboard structure with a hose drying tower on top, a utility barn and training space behind, and

Figure 3.2.   Stanford University Fire Department, home to student firefighters, built 1904, at heart of campus. Photo by David M. Lampton.

the emergency radio we shared with the police department next door. At that time, about twenty-two of the fire department's workforce consisted of professionals who were paid a regular salary and generally had military experience. They were the "paid men." Then there were about fourteen students who got sleeping quarters, laundry service, monthly stipends, and meals for a dollar a day. Predictably, the views of the paid men on the Vietnam War clashed with many of us students who, in our leisure time, were to be found on the sun deck listening to the music of Bob Dylan or studying away in our "study shacks" out back. There was constant political sparring between the paid men and the students, mostly, but not always, good-natured.

The paid men drove the fire trucks, manned the pumps, and performed most of the technical tasks while the student firefighters rode on running boards, provided the manual labor, helped maintain equipment, were trained, laid hoses from hydrants, helped administer first aid, climbed ladders, and entered buildings during incidents, some of which were significant and some of which were nothing more than burnt toast. The students worked "24 hours on, and 24 off." Our bunks were on the second floor, with the trucks nestled below, connected by a brass pole through a hole in the floor. One late night, the alarm went off, lights flashed on, and I awoke bleary-eyed, pulled up my fire pants, ran to the floor hole, and failed to grasp the pole. I reached the ground in record time. Fortunately, there was a protective spongy surface at the bottom to protect against injury.

There was also a university-wide alarm system to alert us if we needed to leave class to respond to a call. I was never actually pulled out of class. Over half of all blazes occur between 10:00 p.m. and 6:00 a.m., the hours when students, staff, and visitors are generally scarce. Student firefighters received compensation during the academic year and also had a well-paid summer job if they wanted one. Indeed, with every other day off in the summer, I could hold down another job to earn more money. This is how I earned enough to supplement my family's great help in paying Stanford tuition, admittedly much lower in those days. As the July/August edition of *Stanford Magazine* stated in a 2002 article, "In those days—before major liability concerns and government regulations—recruitment was casual and almost entirely by word of mouth. If a young man had a friend working at the firehouse and could present a manly bicep, he got the nod." My best friend from high school, Steve Wood, also was a student firefighter. We are lifelong friends to this day.

I learned a great deal in the fire department, including how teams work, how public institutions operate, how groups (indeed myself) function under stress, and how to deal with lots of different people. Coping with emergencies breeds a combination of confidence and sometimes resignation or feelings of inadequacy. As well, it was exciting.

There was an implicit hierarchy for the student firefighter, measured by the truck to which each of us was assigned. The rookie truck, most impressive to the outsider, was the aerial truck. In our case it was a Seagrave ladder truck built in Columbus, Ohio, where I later taught at The Ohio State University. The Seagrave had an eighty-five-foot aluminum extension ladder that swayed when you were at the top. Training for rookies included repeatedly climbing the ladder, gradually overcoming the queasiness created by the height and swaying. The most junior student firefighter was assigned to that vehicle for the simple reason that it was the least used and "all" one had to do was climb to the top, dragging a hose over his shoulder up the rungs, hoping that the pump engineer below did not prematurely "charge the line" before the rookie got anchored firmly at the top, thereby taking him on a wild ride on a gyrating hose to the ground eighty-five feet below. And, of course, if you got to the top, you might end up having to carry someone down. None of that happened to me.

As a firefighter's seniority grew, he moved to a secondary pumper truck, then the Rescue Truck, or the lead engine that responded to every emergency call. Not all trucks went on all calls. The student's goal was to be assigned to a truck that was first on the scene, went to all incidents, and allowed him to be the first one into the building in which there was a presumed emergency. Many calls were false alarms, some accidental, others misguided pranks, and still others malicious.

Covering over eight thousand acres, Stanford had its own fire department (two stations), having all manner of incidents, from grass fires to chemical, radiological, and electrical emergencies, incidents in both low- and high-rise buildings, and arson cases. Twice during the Vietnam War when I was in the department (March and May 1968), arson fires burned down the on-campus Naval Reserve Officer Training Corps building that was located in an isolated eucalyptus grove. Of course, there were also student-related incidents (including suicide, drug overdoses, as well as bicycle, auto, and motorcycle accidents). Stanford thus confronted a big city's range of challenges with a small-town fire department. If things got out of hand, we had "mutual aid pacts" with surrounding jurisdictions upon which we could rely.

I remember the night Robert Kennedy was shot, June 5, 1968, 12:15 a.m., dying hours later. The very loud incident alarm in the station had just gone off, the lights automatically flashed on, and we all hustled out of our bunks, pulled on our black rubber boots and yellow overalls with black suspenders, slid down the brass pole from the second floor to the truck bay below, and piled onto our assigned vehicles. I jumped on the rear running board of the lead engine as someone yelled that Senator Robert Kennedy, then campaigning for president, had just been shot in Los Angeles. It was disorienting riding to the campus incident on the rear running board going through the darkness "code three" (lights and siren, which permitted violation of ordinary traffic regulations), feeling that life was at the margins of control. I grasped the grab bar especially tight that night.

It was also at the firehouse, particularly after getting assigned to the rescue truck, that I had my first encounter with the world of medicine beyond my own family doctor. The basic task in the paramedic's world in an event is to quickly assess the overall situation, prioritize casualties by tending to those for whom your attention can make a critical difference, stabilize patients, and get them quickly up the referral chain to ever-more capable hands. The definition of success was keeping the patients alive long enough to get them to people who could provide that next level of care and holding off attention for those who could wait or were beyond hope.

The overall thought I had as I waited for Susan in front of Encina Hall that evening in late 1971 was that China and its medical/public health system were in a position in which its leaders had to try to deliver emergency care, curative care, and public health services in a circumstance of insufficient resources and overwhelming needs. The PRC was a mass casualty event.

One could readily understand why Mao Zedong called for emphasizing prevention and public health, rather than high-cost, high-investment Western-style curative institutions. During the ongoing Cultural Revolution, Mao was promoting "barefoot doctors," who were poorly trained paramedics, with far less equipment and support than paramedics in the United States enjoyed and I had at the fire department. How did the Chinese make decisions, cope with demand, expand capacity, and assure quality and safety? To what effect? How did they pay for health care? Who got it? Who and what organizations performed the food and drug assurance function? While much of the contemporary China studies field was preoccupied with ideological struggles and mass disorder, important concerns, I was more interested in recurrent issues affecting the Chinese people as a whole.

In contrast to elite politics, everyone in China had personal experience with the public health and medical system. Everyone was a potential informant. And the issue was intrinsically important and universal, with a rich comparative literature. On top of that, I knew something about the subject.

U.S. Army Medic

Another set of formative experiences that percolated in my mind that day on the Stanford street corner in the early 1970s was my active-duty time in the U.S. Army Reserve. Immediately following graduation from Stanford as an undergraduate in June 1968, I enlisted in the U.S. Army Reserve with my draft board nipping at my heels. The prospect of being drafted and fighting in Vietnam was imminent.

For that year's college graduates, the draft was very real—the lottery system of 1969 came along after I had to make a decision. Had I been in the lottery the following year, my number would have been 112, which probably would have gotten me drafted anyway. I was destined to be in the Army, as had been Gramps, my father, and two uncles.

The war just seemed so pointless, unnecessary, and counterproductive. China, Laos, and Cambodia constituted support areas for the Viet Cong and the North Vietnamese Army (NVA). These areas proximate to the Democratic Republic of Vietnam (North Vietnam, or the DRV), and bordering South Vietnam, were used to outflank American forces and their South Vietnamese allies and constituted amoeba-like bases from which Hanoi could provision its troops.

DRV forces and those of the Viet Cong in South Vietnam were sustained by the unshakeable belief that the Americans, like the French and the Japanese before them, eventually would become exhausted and go home. This is what happened with the eventual, rapid collapse of Saigon in April 1975. Washington witnessed a very similar process unfold in Afghanistan in 2021, with provincial capitals falling like dominoes. Nonetheless, given the military service tradition in our families, not serving somehow was not an option.

Susan and I looked for a way out of the "go to jail, go to Canada, or go to Vietnam dilemma." Miraculously, the opportunity presented itself in the form of openings in a U.S. Army Reserve unit at the San Francisco Presidio—Sixth Army's 6253rd U.S. Army Hospital unit.

The unit had one thousand hospital beds and all associated equipment stored in a warehouse somewhere waiting for something akin to general war. The reserve unit itself was composed of all the personnel necessary to run that hospital if the equipment ever was taken out of crates to see action. The unit was subject to rapid mobilization. Hospital personnel were trained on active duty (in my case for nearly a year), and then obligated to attend monthly reserve meetings that often occurred in military hospitals or Veterans Administration facilities around the country. Each summer the reservist spent two weeks at "summer camp." The duration of such a commitment was six years, unless extended. At sign-up I knew I would be trained as a medic, eventually becoming an x-ray technician. My feeling was that if I couldn't stop the carnage in Vietnam, I could at least patch up its American victims. In retrospect, the experience was very good for me and compatible with my beliefs and obligations.

I remained in the U.S. Army Reserve for longer than I initially would have imagined, starting in the enlisted ranks in 1968 in the Medical

Corps as a specialist, and later being promoted to be an officer in 1980 in a Military Intelligence Detachment in Columbus, Ohio (the 442nd MI, Det.). I was honorably discharged in June 1986.

Irony abounds in the U.S. Army. I was promoted to be an officer because I spoke Chinese, but the military intelligence detachment to which I was assigned only worked on the Middle East, going to the Pentagon in the summers. At that time, China in the Middle East was the furthest thing from anyone's mind. However, this experience exposed me to the Pentagon and military intelligence practices. In 1986, I decided to terminate my reserve service, feeling that my expanding work in public policy and exchange with the PRC could be adversely affected by the armed services' intelligence affiliation.

Nevertheless, the 1968–1969 period, during which I was on active duty for basic training and medical specialization, was key to my development and informed my choice of dissertation topic.

In October 1968, I was ordered to Fort Polk, in a Louisiana swamp, for basic combat training. Ft. Polk was home to "Tiger Land" and countless snakes. After completing basic training, I was assigned to the Army Medical Field Service School (MFSS) at Fort Sam Houston in San Antonio, Texas, for medic and x-ray technician training. Normally, trainees were required to sleep on base without their spouses, but my commanding officer agreed to permit Susan and me to live together off-post. We had been married a few months earlier by Stanford's antiwar reverend, Robert McAfee Brown, in Stanford's Memorial Church. That officer who let us be together got my best work from that day forward. Susan got a job in a commercial art studio.

Upon graduation from MFSS, I had several months of on-the-job training at the burn ward of the Brooke General Hospital, also at Fort Sam. The burn ward was developing world-class treatments for severely burned patients which, tragically, the Vietnam War produced in profusion.

My experience in the burn ward shaped how I saw the purpose of my career, and upon reflection it inclined me to make sure that in my professional life I would do my best to help avoid another misbegotten and ill-advised war involving China, directly or indirectly. This experience also fed into my dissertation thinking.

Three incidents stick in my mind to this day. The first occurred literally on my very first shift at the burn ward after having gone through x-ray school. During training the student only took mock x-rays on manikins, obviously not wanting to over-expose every "trainee" with multiple doses of radiation over the sustained training period. I was particularly careful because as an infant I had been exposed to large doses of radiation to treat an enlarged thymus. Doctors subsequently cautioned me to minimize future radiation exposure.

Coming out of MFSS, I had a lot of theory and formulae for x-ray exposure settings rattling around in my head, but I had not yet actually "imaged" a *live* patient. Considerately, for my first night of actual hospital duty, my medical superior put me on the midnight to morning shift, thinking, perhaps, that nothing much would happen—one x-ray technician was working in the morgue and the other, me, up in the burn ward and surgical floor. However, something did happen that first night, and I had no help.

Several badly burned troops from Vietnam were ferried over by helicopter from nearby Lackland Air Force Base to Fort Sam/Brooke General Hospital. The arriving wounded had been stabilized in Japan and flown to the United States on large hospital air transports. These casualties would not even have been sent to Brooke had they not sustained massive burns. The receiving doctor told me: "Give them all full body x-rays!" That was a substantial number of images for each person, multiplied by several casualties. They were the first live patients I ever had to handle and I was not sure that my theoretical exposure formulae would actually work. People are different; weights and body densities vary. Thus, taking x-rays is something of an art. Mercifully, the first attempt at all the x-rays worked. When it was over, I nearly collapsed with shock, relief, and exhaustion.

After recovering somewhat, I walked through the waiting room to find a fairly senior officer seated there. He demanded to know "what was taking so long for him to be seen?" I, a lowly enlisted specialist, exploded, saying something like, "If it weren't for you and other army leaders, these troops would not have been here." What I said was unfair. In retrospect, I would even say it was cruel, but my outburst captured the moment. I imagine I could have been court-martialed but never heard further about the incident.

In another case, a young man who had been burned severely had had three limbs either partially or fully amputated. I did not know what to say to him, but I will never forget what he said to me: "What bothers me most, beyond that I cannot kill myself, is that I will never be able to kill the people who did this to me." It was from him that I first learned that the lessons of war do not always teach peace.

Many years later, in June 1997, Susan accompanied me to San Antonio where I had a speaking engagement, for FedEx as I recall. One free evening, I suggested we drive up to Brooke General Hospital to see what had changed. The old general hospital was situated on a mesa, and during the Vietnam War when I was there, it was lit up around the clock, a hive of activity. Now, coming up over the rise, the building suddenly jutted upward into the dusky prairie sky. The hospital was almost completely dark, except for exit stairwell lights. I blurted out to Susan—"See, this is what peace with China means. It means you can shut down entire hospitals."

My experience as a stateside medic during the war in Vietnam taught me never to forget that mistakes among nations, not least China and the United States, have consequences. I have never had much patience for armchair warriors.

In terms of the dissertation shaping up in my mind, I learned about how hospitals run and the dilemmas created by having massive surges in demand for medical and public health services and being under-resourced to meet them. This is the defining characteristic of medical and public health service delivery in China, certainly in the 1970s.

My Dissertation Takes Flight

Not long after the evening when Susan picked me up, I walked over to the Stanford Medical School and Hospital, wandered its halls, and stumbled across a sign in the hallway saying "International Health." I walked in and found Dr. Paul F. Basch, whom I had never met before, and who worked on the parasitic disease schistosomiasis, then prevalent in central China. After explaining my germinating topic, he not only encouraged me to pursue it, but agreed to be on my dissertation committee, and thereafter became a good friend. Sometime later he visited China, where he had a severe coronary event and was saved by some fine physicians in the lower reaches of the Yangtze River Valley, in Wuxi.[1] Subsequently, I had an article on anti-schistosomiasis work in China come out in *The American Journal of Tropical Medicine and Hygiene.*

These ruminations under that oak tree on the Stanford campus triggered the idea of undertaking field research on the politics of medicine and public health in China in the communist era. I had the comparative advantage of some experience. The topic lent itself to an interview strategy. Hong Kong provided access to large numbers of interviewees (refugees fleeing the PRC in the Cultural Revolution). Moreover, there was an ideal research base from which I could work. In 1963–1964 Harvard Professor Jerry Cohen and others helped secure a location in Kowloon, Hong Kong, to which scholars from around the world could come to do all manner of research on contemporary China. The Universities Service Centre (USC) was located at 155 Argyle Street, almost directly beneath the legendary flight path for harrowing landings at nearby Kai Tak Airport. Over the years, the Ford, Carnegie, and Mellon philanthropies were important funders of USC.

At USC a young and growing contemporary China studies field came together in its library, offices, and, above all, its lunchroom. USC also had a working copy machine that served to increase research efficiency. Among those of the era who did path-breaking work, there were Mike Oksenberg, Bernard Frolic, Kenneth Lieberthal, Steve Goldstein, Susan Shirk, Stan Rosen, Parris Chang, Richard Madsen, Bill Parish, Martin K. Whyte, Lynn T. White, III, Deborah Davis, Andrew Walder, Jean Oi, Suzanne Pepper, John Dolfin, Stanley Lubman, Charlotte Ikels, Lucian Bianco, Seiichiro Takagi, Nicholas Lardy, Anita Chan, Stephen Fitzgerald, Dick Solomon, Rod MacFarquhar, Vic Falkenheim, and Ezra Vogel. We became lifetime colleagues, in many cases friends. That congregation of scholars, overlapping in that small place, helped forge a field that cohered for decades.

In sum, during that afternoon waiting for Susan, my dissertation plan took form, consisting of the following elements: study PRC medical and public health policy; interview Chinese refugees in Hong Kong using them as a principal source; read local PRC newspapers and professional medical documents from China held in various Hong Kong archives; use the available resources of the U.S. Consulate in Hong Kong; and adopt a comparative perspective. The USC would be my base and community. It was here, too, that I met "Lao Yang" (Yeung Sai-cheung), who became my research assistant in a subsequent project some years later.

The Fulbright Program accepted my proposal and agreed to provide financial support and sponsor my project with the British authorities. In the summer of 1972, Susan and I flew to Hong Kong, our first journey to Asia.

Before our departure, we had the choice of buying a house near Stanford or using our scant resources to buy Pan Am around-the-world air tickets so we could see some of Asia and Europe on our way back home after the anticipated year in Hong Kong. We chose the air tickets, did not buy the house, and consequently missed all the subsequent phenomenal growth in property values in Silicon Valley. We still feel we made the right choice.

Living in Hong Kong
The Setting

We arrived in a sweltering, humid, summertime Hong Kong, about midday in mid-1972. As the pressurized door of our Cathay Pacific airliner opened, and as we processed the beautiful scene of Hong Kong harbor from atop the aircraft stairs, the pungent scent of the city engulfed us; the detritus of then about four million persons sloshed in the harbor, where it decomposed into a fragrant soup. On many of the hillsides within view of the aircraft door were precariously built structures, interspersed with shanties, clinging to the steep grades. Directly across the harbor from Kai Tak Airport on Victoria Island was a fresh scar on the iconic mountain's face where a June 18, 1972, landslide, caused by the 25.2 inches of rain in the preceding seventy-two hours, killed sixty-seven persons. Later that same day, a separate landslide killed seventy-one squatters in another part of the colony. Susan and I looked at each other as we deplaned, wondering what awaited us.

Hong Kong always has been a difficult city along many dimensions, and certainly 1972–1973 was no exception. However, Hong Kong also could be very comfortable for expatriates and the many locals living in relative or absolute opulence. The city also provided a path for upward mobility for destitute PRC refugees. I felt that while many people there might be poor, they were not impoverished of mind or spirit. They were pursuing that era's "Chinese dream."

Susan and I soon found an apartment on *Yuet Wah Gai* (Yuet Wah Street) in the industrial, largely ethnic Chinese, district of Kwun Tong in Kowloon—though not without an initial stumble. In the opening hours of our apartment search, we unknowingly wandered into what proved to be a bordello in "Chungking Mansions" at 36–44 Nathan Road in Tsim Sha Tsui, where rooms were available by the hour, day, and week. "By the hour" should have been the tip-off. After an awkward encounter with the "landlady," we moved on with our search. A rental posting on the USC bulletin board led us to the Yuet Wah Gai apartment that we quickly rented.

Our new home was a fairly distant 1-A bus ride from the USC office. Our landlords were Mr. and Mrs. Hung, a family in the textile industry who had packed up and departed Shanghai around the time of the communist takeover. The Hungs lived in a flat adjoining our own, with a small door linking our quarters to their kitchen. Their daughter, Debbie, acted as interpreter, effortlessly gliding among English, Mandarin, Cantonese, and Shanghainese Chinese dialects, with Mr. Hung speaking Shanghainese; Mrs. Hung Cantonese, Shanghainese, and Mandarin; me speaking Mandarin and English; and Susan speaking English. The Hungs had already resuscitated their economic fortunes. Their resilience, and adaptability, was the first lesson I learned in Hong Kong.

Living on the eleventh floor of the "Good View" apartment building (*Hao Jing Lou*), we indeed had a good view of Hong Kong life below. Kwun Tong was a magnet for refugees fleeing China, congregating there as they sought to rebuild their lives. In 1949 and 1950 in particular, the profitable textile industry substantially evacuated Shanghai, leaving *en masse* for Hong Kong seeking security from PRC expropriations and persecutions and skirting growing Western embargo-related barriers affecting Shanghai exports.

Our apartment window looked out over what the British colonial authorities euphemistically called "housing estates," huge residential blocks constructed of crudely poured concrete. The number of square meters allotted per capita was so limited that family members sometimes had to sleep in shifts and/or in bunk beds, as their breadwinners worked shifts around the clock in nearby factories. The lights never seemed to go dark; the clack of mahjong tiles never ceased. It is worth noting, however, particularly by devotees of the free market, that the Hong Kong colonial administration made Herculean efforts to provide public housing for the ever-growing number of refugees, a point I made to Milton Friedman years later as he talked about the virtues of the unfettered free market in the colony.

As in all things, deprivation in Hong Kong was relative. In between our modern apartment building and the "housing estates," a couple of hundred meters away, there was a large cardboard, sheet metal, and wooden squatter encampment. One day a fire started and ripped through the squalor below. When the fire department arrived, the firefighters refused to turn the water on until an acceptable price was negotiated with the victims, who were anxiously watching as every few seconds more of them lost their scant possessions and residences. Such corruption shocked me, not least because that would have been the last thing to occur to me as a firefighter back home.

Everything in Hong Kong was competitive. The Christian missionaries competed for souls. There were few Caucasians in Kwun Tong, and those few seemed to be missionaries of various sects and denominations, including some from the fire and brimstone school of religious outreach. The missionaries assumed that Susan and I were there also to enlist converts, and they avoided us, mistakenly seeing us as competitors in doing the Lord's work.

In 1972, immediately following one particularly strong typhoon in an active season of big winds, one missionary knocked on our door imploring us to "come to the Lord." Given that the recent typhoon had

Figure 3.3.   Hong Kong housing estates and shanty town fire in foreground, Kwun Tong, fall 1972. Photo by David M. Lampton.

howled powerfully through our cement flat (in which we kept open some windows so the pressure would not build up and blow out the glass), and given that potted plants had rained down from the balconies high above onto the streets below, I could see how proselytizers might make converts.

Also out our front window, we learned about rough justice and the absence of rule of law. From our high apartment window one morning, we watched as a taxi brushed against a pedestrian—a laborer crossing at a street corner below. Pedestrians and drivers were natural enemies, not only in Hong Kong but in much of the developing world. Drivers felt empowered, high status. Pedestrians, not least manual laborers, resented having neither a car, power, nor respect. A flash mob formed, and one worker grabbed a two-by-four piece of construction lumber and bludgeoned the taxi driver to within an inch of his life. The mob's fury subsided once the driver was down and bleeding—the equilibrium had been restored. No Royal Hong Kong Police (RHKP) intervened.

The RHKP seemed not overly concerned about Chinese-on-Chinese crime and violence. This gave the Triads room to operate, the Triads having their origin in the seventeenth century in China. Ruthless and organized geographically and ethnically, these gangs span the Hong Kong and PRC borders, gaining revenues from extortion and blackmail to prostitution and drugs, gradually expanding internationally far beyond Hong Kong. They physically controlled the Kowloon Walled City when we were in Hong Kong, with thirty thousand persons living within the walls of their domain into which the RHKP dared not venture.

Corruption was so rampant and open that in February 1974, the British Colonial Administration created the Independent Commission against Corruption (ICAC). Susan and I enlisted on weekends to help Elsie Tu Elliott, an English-born missionary turned social and political activist, write letters to various colonial offices trying to resolve injustices affecting indigent or illiterate residents.

Hong Kong as a Research Site

Hong Kong was an ideal base for my research. Taiwan was a theoretical alternative site in 1972–1973; but for me, Taiwan was not the best perch. Most of the mainlanders living there had fled China for the island of Taiwan (Formosa) in 1946–1949: an estimated 2.201 million strong. Most of them never had actually lived under effective nationwide communist rule. After 1949, direct cross-strait communication quickly became exceedingly limited, with propaganda balloons, artillery shells, blaring loudspeakers near Jinmen Island, and broadcasts comprising the major forms of cross-strait communication.

For me, wishing to understand how the post–1949 Chinese medical and public health system worked, how decisions were made, and how the system and citizenry interacted, Hong Kong was a far better vantage point, brimming with recent refugees (an estimated twelve thousand coming in 1972 alone), each of whom had their own story to tell from their personal experience. The refugees came in successive waves, the most recent of which was a result of the Cultural Revolution (about eleven thousand in 1967 and fourteen thousand in 1968). The biggest prior refugee waves under communist rule had been during the post–Great Leap Forward famine that engulfed the PRC; more than twenty-five thousand came to Hong Kong in 1961, almost seventy thousand in 1962. It was not unusual for corpses to wash into Hong Kong harbor, the corporeal remains of those intercepted by PRC gunboats or overpowered by treacherous currents.

The number of bodies washing into Hong Kong Harbor was a morbid, macabre indicator of the degree of violence and deprivation up the Pearl River in Guangdong Province. A common escape route was to enter the waters of the Dapeng Peninsula or Shenzhen Bay in the PRC and swim several kilometers into Hong Kong's Deep Bay. Hong Kong's total population grew from around 840,000 in 1931, to 3.1 million in 1961, to 4.1 million in 1972. (In 2022, the city's population was more than 7.6 million souls.)

One of my first required stops after arrival in Hong Kong was to present myself to the British immigration authorities, whereupon a gray-haired British civil servant admonished me: "Young man, we are watching you. There is trouble in China [the Cultural Revolution]. We don't want it spilling over to here. If you cause trouble with the Chinese, your visa will not be renewed." His underlying point was that the Hong Kong administration, and indeed the refugees with whom I would be speaking, were in a precarious position, balancing the concerns about the PRC, the local provincial government across the border, London, and the local PRC shadow administration run out of the New China News Agency.

So What Did I Find In My Research?

China Studies was a field rich in diverse traditions and research perspectives. Sociologists and anthropologists; social psychologists; traditional sinologists focusing on philosophy, literature, linguistics, and history; and of course political scientists and economists all found interaction with one another comfortable and fruitful. Despite the arguments in America about the appropriate relationship between academics and their governments and intelligence agencies, many scholars, myself included, felt comfortable sharing perspectives with government analysts who also were in the colony trying to understand what was occurring in the PRC a few miles away. It was exhilarating to be in a community in which academics, intelligence agents, diplomats, businesspersons, military officers, refugees, and missionaries all were a multinational human jumble united in a common quest to understand the behemoth across the border and convey that reality to the world.

The colony also was full of Communist Chinese front agencies and unions, effectively running a shadow government parallel to the British imperial administration.

In Hong Kong, U.S. Consulate personnel and many of us expatriate scholars interacted socially (American football at the Diocesan Boys' School in Mong Kok on Kadoorie Hill) and professionally, with academics given access to the U.S. government's "appearance file" that tracked the movements of Chinese leaders, an indispensable source in that era before computers. We assumed that if on any given day China's senior leaders all simultaneously went dark in public or unmentioned in the press, an important meeting might be occurring inside the PRC, foretelling a possible major policy announcement. If a leader stayed "missing," that could be indicative of a personnel change or elite struggle. Following each PRC senior leader daily provided a sense of what an individual's functional or geographic areas of responsibility might be.

Most foreign scholars I knew felt obliged to be open and transparent about their interactions with governments. The relationship was generally open, cordial, and mutually productive.

Often academic fields orient themselves around a broad dominant question. With that overarching question in mind, individual scholars then define their own sub-questions germane to the larger preoccupation and then bore in. In the second half of the 1960s and into the 1970s, a dominant question in the field concerned the violence and mayhem of the Cultural Revolution. Were the Cultural Revolution's origins to be found in factional fights among loyalty groups? If so, from what attachments did these loyalties spring? Was Mao a revolutionary whose individual resentments (against his father specifically, and authority figures generally) boiled over into his public behavior? Was the Chinese Communist Party (CCP) apparatus fighting the People's Liberation Army (PLA) for control? Was Chinese political culture given to cycles of political quiescence followed by the explosive release of accumulated mass resentments stemming from the very nature of Chinese family and public life? What role did ideology and organization play? And finally, a question of particular interest to me—did China have interest groups? If so, what united and divided them, and did such groups have means to coordinate actions?

Many avenues of inquiry had a common antecedent assumption—that the origins of Chinese political behavior resided in China's uniqueness, its ideology, its distinctive leadership and political culture. My guess at that time was, and remains, that much political and societal conflict in China reflects more general phenomena, such as bureaucratic and interest group politics, the need to develop budgets (allocate scarce resources), incrementalism, and the need to regulate sectors that resist supervision. Above all, in complex organizations, there is a gap between central intention and local execution—policy implementation is problematic, per se. "Principal-agent" problems are universal. And finally, the leader must always decide what mix of coercive, remunerative, and normative power to exert in each circumstance, knowing that ambitions can easily outrun resources. Power must be rationed.

Another thought I had concerning the then-prevailing approaches was that analysts often looked at policy rhetoric, rather than actual policy outcomes. China generally produced a healthier population at a lower income level than any other large developing nation, even discounting unreliable statistics and exaggerated claims coming out of the PRC. Why? How was this accomplished?

My first refugee interview was conducted in Falls Church, Virginia, not in Hong Kong—with a former Ministry of Public Health employee who had found her way to the United States and whom John Lewis had introduced to me. As I started to pose my first question to her, she, in effect, said, "Wait—let's look at the organization chart and see how things are organized." She was advising me that the researcher must understand the functional and territorial bureaucratic boxes in a policy process and how they are interlinked. Not all boxes are involved in all issues. Not all boxes are equally important in different spheres or contexts. In addition, staffing and how various actors perceive their own situation is critical. The analyst must understand the constraints imposed by formal rules and the informal pathways people find to skirt them.

Not all my research on China proceeded sequentially, neatly, and effortlessly. When I arrived in Hong Kong, I was almost immediately invited to present my work to the University of Hong Kong's (HKU) Centre of Asian Studies as a "working paper"; the audience was composed of professors, graduate students, and some of my colleagues from USC. This occasion (January 13, 1973) was my maiden presentation before such an august group. The dark, wood-paneled room oozed seriousness.

My fundamental question was, "What accounts for the observed changes in PRC public health and medical policy over time?" Fluctuations in policy had been dramatic in the 1949–1972 period. At that time, the generally accepted approach to addressing such a question was to assess Mao Zedong's preferences, the reigning ideology, and the instrumentalities that the CCP had to enforce edicts. Prevailing thinking emphasized the importance of factional (personal) alignments. In contrast, I argued that interest groups and bureaucratic politics were a major part of the explanation and that varied interests existed within and among rural constituencies, urban groups, medical professionals, and manufacturing organizations such as the pharmaceutical industry. Policy was not simply ideologically driven, or personalistic, but also represented the ongoing struggle among interests. One fruitful starting point for analysis, I argued, was that ideological struggle often was a cover for contending embedded interests. Mao's desires were only part of the equation.

After making my initial remarks in the academic hall, remarks heavy on theory and light on specifics, a hand shot up. It belonged to one of HKU's Political Science professors, Peter Harris, as I recall. He asserted that my proposed research question and methodology were deficient (I remember the word "garbage" but am unsure he actually said that), and he went on to criticize some of the theoretical underpinnings I had used, not least the work of Stanford anthropologist G. William Skinner, who argued there were policy (compliance) cycles in China. Other commentators that day were kinder, but Professor Harris had a point by warning against building intellectual castles in the air. Still reeling from the blast, I boarded a bus to the Star Ferry pier in Central Hong Kong where even the usual delight of the boat ride to Kowloon did not lighten my mood.

Upon my return to the sanctuary of our flat, and further reflection, I realized that Professor Harris did me a favor, though his bedside manner left a lot to be desired. He pushed me in the direction of my natural inclination of not letting the intellectual superstructure overwhelm the substantive foundation. I vowed that my future research would be heavier on facts, learning another lesson from this incident too. While scholars should be receptive to guidance and take critiques seriously, we should not let others cause us to prematurely abandon what might turn out to be a productive avenue. The line between persevering and being obstinate is fine.

As my dissertation took shape, I came to several conclusions:

1. In understanding the way systems behave, prior institutional structures and organizational cultures differ, they persist, and they are important.

2. Budgets matter. People fight over money. I often have been surprised by how few analysts talk in-depth about budgetary conflict.

3. Medical care and public health inequalities are enormous generators of political conflict, everywhere.

4. Interest group politics and coalition building is central. Mao literally started the Cultural Revolution by mobilizing his revolutionary rebel constituency with denunciations and derision of what he branded the "Ministry of *Urban* Health" in June 1965, highlighting the divergence between the services urban elites received and those available to the still largely rural population. Mao said,

> Tell the Ministry of Public Health that it only works for fifteen percent of the total population of the country and that this fifteen percent is mainly composed of gentlemen, while the broad masses of the peasants do not get any medical treatment.[2]

5. Bureaucracies are staffed by professionals. Professions have ethical codes, values, and corporate interests, even in communist, authoritarian systems.

6. With respect to policy implementation, in China's bureaucratic system with many horizontal administrative levels extending from Center to village, and numerous vertical functional stovepipes, as policy passes down through successive layers, at each level and within each stovepipe, policy is deflected in the direction of the implementer's interests. The cumulative distortion can be enormous.

I learned a great deal about China's pharmaceutical industry. One interviewee briefly mentioned that domestically manufactured pharmaceutical products generally were considered less safe and effective by patients than foreign-made alternatives. Several interviewees referred to "twitching" and other side effects from domestically made antibiotics. Patients therefore preferred foreign drugs, except in the few cases of Chinese traditional remedies widely thought to be more effective than Western medicines. In light of the high demand and scarce availability of foreign-manufactured drugs (and the trade embargo), and the perceived risk in using domestic alternatives, corruption in the doctor-patient prescription process was endemic. The medicine supply system was shot through with corruption and regulatory negligence. These problems have not been resolved. Decades later in an instance of gallows humor, one Chinese informant recounted to me that a female student was depressed upon a breakup with a boyfriend, and she couldn't get prescription sleeping pills to kill herself, so she ordered sleeping pills from China on the internet, but because the pills were fake, they did not kill her. "So bad things can turn into good things."[3]

With respect to the safety and quality of domestic drugs, the question arose as to where the PRC's Food and Drug regulator was and why it functioned poorly or not at all. The answer was simple in outline. Most medicines in China were subject to provincial regulation, meaning that there were no uniform national rules. Even if some rules nominally were national, implementation, oversight, and enforcement were provincial matters. Various provinces had divergent capabilities, not to mention predispositions. We have seen a somewhat analogous situation in America during COVID-19, where the Centers for Disease Control and Prevention (CDC) had "guidelines" but some U.S. governors entirely disregarded them and in other instances openly opposed Washington's regulations, much less mandates.

In China enforcement was weak, in part, because the drug producers were state-owned enterprises (SOEs) that could resist oversight by other players at their administrative rank. With no hard budget constraints on SOEs, monetary fines would be a meaningless sanction against the firms—they would just turn over less profit to government at various levels. Beyond that, much medicine was "traditional Chinese medicine" (*Zhong yi*). People had used herbs, medicinal concoctions, and acupuncture for thousands of years, and generally speaking those remedies were exempt from regulation. Chinese politics functions in many areas in perfectly predictable ways if one understands the contexts, constraints, and institutions.

Armed with these insights, I returned to the United States to submit my dissertation and find a position that would offer me the opportunity to publish my dissertation and other spin-offs to establish a research record that would be competitive in the job market. Luckily, I was able to spend a postdoctoral year (1973–1974) in Ann Arbor, at the University of Michigan's Center for Chinese Studies ("Corner House") with the support of the Josiah Macy, Jr. Foundation, whose president, John Z. Bowers, was very interested in Western medicine in China, importantly including the medical activities of the Rockefeller Foundation, Yale-China Association, and Johns Hopkins University. Mary Brown Bullock has written the definitive study of much of this philanthropic involvement in her wonderful book: *The Oil Prince's Legacy: Rockefeller Philanthropy in China*.

At Michigan I had an office across the hall from former U.S. government official Professor Allen S. Whiting. With the center's generous support and great colleagues including Whiting, Mike Oksenberg, Robert Dernberger, Albert Feuerwerker, Alexander Eckstein, Myron Wegman in the School of Public Health, and many others, I refined my dissertation into a book titled *The Politics of Medicine in China: The Policy Process, 1949–1977*, and wrote several articles and a monograph.

Our daughter, Kate, was born in Ann Arbor at Women's Hospital in the spring of 1974, and I started teaching at The Ohio State University (OSU) in Columbus that fall. Our son, Adam, was born in 1977 in Columbus. Kate was our Wolverine and Adam our Buckeye. Our family thus covers both bases in the Michigan–Ohio football rivalry.

NOTES

1. Mary Brown Bullock, *China on My Mind* (Xlibris, 2023), 85–86.

2. David M. Lampton, *The Politics of Medicine in China: The Policy Process, 1949–1977* (Westview Press, 1977), 185.

3. David M. Lampton, "Interview," September 17, 2012, 5–6. Hereafter in notes and text, "RAC" refers to documents located in the Rockefeller Archive Center, Sleepy Hollow, New York.

The Old Man and the Dirt

(Post-Mao China)

OHIO: GATEWAY TO THE PRC AND TAIWAN

Nineteen seventy-four Ohio was a quintessentially American place. Big farm interests and large industrial cities. Cleveland, Dayton, and Akron were already beginning to fray economically, heading toward what by the late 1970s and into the 1980s would be referred to as the "Rust Belt" era. Public opinion and consumer polling firms considered Columbus, Ohio, more like America than any other place in the country. Its airfield consisted of one small terminal; you could arrive there five minutes before departure and make your plane. As one exited the airport grounds to go downtown, a cheery sign welcomed you to "The All-American City."

Thus, when Ohio became a pacesetter in constructing relations with China in the late 1970s and the early 1980s, it was clear that something fundamental was happening, not just in the Midwest, but throughout the entire nation. Better relations with China were not foisted on an unwilling heartland by coastal elites. Rather, there was a seemingly odd fit between local politicians in Ohio and the hard-bitten revolutionaries running China. They found common ground in their respective struggles for economic development.

My arrival at OSU in the fall of 1974 to assume a tenure track assistant professor position in the Political Science Department was quite fortuitous: fortuitous that I got the job, fortuitous that there were relatively few other academics in the state focused on policy-relevant contemporary China issues just as demand for that knowledge was surging, and fortuitous that a political science department striving to be a top department nationally by the cannons of an increasingly quantitative discipline made room for an area specialist like me. Ohio State let me spread my wings and gave me many chances for exposure to media, state officials, and the state legislature, as well as to become involved in public outreach.

Had I been in the relatively more crowded professional communities of the East or West initially, many of these opportunities may not have come my way. Also, being a land grant university, OSU had a large agricultural extension mission. Many students came from farms and rural areas. They taught me a lot, not least that farmers in this age of global markets are cosmopolitan; developments anywhere could affect commodity prices.

One of my first big public lectures for OSU was in Urbana-Champaign, Illinois, in a tent full of farmers in overalls. Incongruously dressed in a dark pin-striped suit and a tie, I was speaking to the Land of Lincoln Soybean Association. As the moderator introduced me to the audience, he turned to me saying (so all could hear through the open microphone), "Sonny, you are looking at more millionaires than you will ever see again in one place." Soybeans had just hit $10–$11 per bushel. Indeed, soybeans became one of the major U.S. exports to China over time, right along with Boeing aircraft.

In localities such as Ohio, Iowa, and Illinois, cosmopolitanism and parochialism coexist. It is a great advantage to appreciate the complexity of one's own nation before trying to untangle the complexities of another. Professor Ezra Vogel of Harvard and I periodically talked about Ohio, where he grew up in Delaware, a city just north of Columbus on Route 23 going to Michigan. That experience affected both of us profoundly. One of my PhD students at Ohio State, Paul Schroeder, became the representative for the State of Ohio in China (posted in Wuhan). Later, Paul took a position at Case Western Reserve University in Cleveland in Political Science; Ezra, his spouse Professor Charlotte Ikels (a professor at Case Western), and I took great interest in Paul throughout his career.

He played an important role in developing the Ohio-Hubei Province partnership described later in this chapter.

At Ohio State, I had large lecture classes in Introduction to Comparative Politics and China-related courses on domestic and foreign policy. I enjoyed teaching, and in 1979–1980 and 1981, I won teaching awards for arts and sciences, something of which I am proud. Given the large classes and the heterogeneous nature of the student body, keeping student attention and reaching everyone was a challenge. In a moment of gallows humor, I half-joked with my department colleagues by noting that some previous winners of the teaching award had been denied tenure and that I hoped there was no cause-and-effect relationship between winning teaching recognition and not getting tenure.

Like many junior social science professors striving for tenure in a very disciplinary, theoretically oriented department, there was a constant tug-of-war in my mind between trying to achieve precision with respect to what I often felt were small-bore disciplinary questions for which the researcher could get numbers and generate coefficients of correlation, and exploring significant, less quantifiable questions that were less valued in the disciplines but germane to the outside world.

Getting a methodologically rigorous piece on the roots of interprovincial inequality in education and health services in China into the *American Political Science Review* (1979) gave my tenure quest an enormous lift where it counted—in my department. I am not sure how many scholars in the China field ever read that article; it was full of numbers and coefficients of correlation. Its principal finding was that how well provinces did in providing their people with medical and education services strongly correlated with the magnitude of investments that the central government made in various jurisdictions. Not all localities were treated the same. The more investment, the better the outcomes. Government decisions and priorities matter. A core political question was why different localities received more or less. Part of the answer was that some areas simply had more sway in Beijing than others did.

REACHING BEYOND THE UNIVERSITY

I have always felt a debt of gratitude to OSU. One reason was that the university supported me in the many outside experiences I asked for. I especially appreciated the university's (ninth) president, Harold Enarson. Enarson was interested in China, perhaps because he had been part of the first delegation of American university presidents to visit China, sponsored by NCUSCR in 1974, the year I came to OSU. Harold viewed China as an important area of opportunity for the university, the State of Ohio, and our nation. I worked with him to encourage the Economics Department to hire an economist of China, even though the department didn't really want one.

Although I chafed at the methodological orthodoxy in the Political Science Department, my colleagues (not least Chairman Randall Ripley, or "Rip") encouraged my desire for external policy-oriented links. I seized opportunities for outside experiences that shaped my understanding of Chinese politics, foreign policy, and how America itself works. Colleagues supported my endeavors concerning public policy, nongovernmental organizations, and public outreach. I trace my varied work with Ohio's government; the National Academy of Sciences (NAS); the Central Intelligence Agency (CIA); the Department of Health, Education, and Welfare (HEW); NCUSCR; the Asia Society; and the Kettering Foundation in Dayton to those early years at OSU from 1974 until I permanently left for New York in 1987.

The National Academy of Sciences

The first opportunity I had to travel to the PRC was in the fall of 1976. The Committee on Scholarly Communication with the People's Republic of China (CSCPRC), which later became the Committee on Scholarly Communication with China (CSCC), housed with the NAS in Washington, D.C., was planning to send a Steroid Chemistry and Biochemistry Delegation to China. Even before Richard Nixon's February 1972 trip to the PRC, there was considerable competition among China specialists to get to the mainland.[1] How could one speak authoritatively about a place one never had been—especially when others now were going?

Initially, the Steroid Group was to be led by the developer of the active hormone ingredient in the birth control pill, Stanford Professor Carl Djerassi. The Chinese were very interested in this technology, looking toward the day when they would jettison Mao's pro-natal policies in an attempt to boost per capita income growth by limiting population increase. Beyond promoting hard science exchanges and eventually collaborative research, the CSCPRC also had a policy of piggy-backing humanists and social scientists on hard science delegations to China.

This practice strengthened the social sciences and humanities in the PRC, areas of inquiry that had been savaged during preceding decades. This practice also strengthened China Studies in America by including a China scholar in each hard science delegation. Basically, the PRC was interested in hard science and technology; America was also interested in the social sciences and humanities. One hand washed the other in negotiations with Beijing. The implicit arrangement was you, China, accept sinologists, and we will provide access to the hard scientists you want.

CSCPRC (and NCUSCR, which followed the same practice) also wanted to include China specialists in delegations to have someone along to provide country-relevant historical and contemporary background, language capacity, and perspective for the U.S. scientists. Because I had written on health policy and had some knowledge of the PRC's pharmaceutical industry, CSCPRC selected me to accompany the group, originally scheduled to leave for China in September 1976.

Immediately before our scheduled departure, Chairman Mao Zedong died on September 9, 1976. The PRC shut its borders to entry by foreigners for thirty days of mourning and (as we would soon learn) to manage the precarious succession. Shortly after that postponement was announced, however, Beijing informed the NAS in Washington that our group was authorized to land in China on October 10, 1976. As Professor Djerassi was unable to come on the rescheduled dates, Professor Josef Fried of the University of Chicago became the group's delegation leader (*tuanzhang*).

That Beijing so quickly rescheduled our group was an early indication that Mao's death would accelerate China's opening to the United States and the world. The prompt invitation re-issue signaled that S&T would be a leading edge of the PRC's development efforts and that America would be important to that goal.

The Cultural Revolution, and the disorder that had preceded it since 1949, had severely damaged science and learning in China. One discussion among our group members before heading for the PRC concerned what each group member expected to learn from Chinese science in their own specialization. It was clear what China had to learn from us. After some back and forth, the delegation members generally concluded that they would learn a lot about China, but not much in their specialty beyond ascertaining where the PRC was relative to the field's frontiers. Nevertheless, all the delegation members agreed that the benefits of opening, the potential for future collaboration, and assisting China to move beyond the Cultural Revolution were reasons enough for openness and participation. Everyone was thrilled by the prospect of going to a place that had been beyond reach for so long.

In the run-up to our trip, another issue arose that shaped every subsequent negotiation I ever had with PRC institutions on this and related subjects. When CSCPRC sent Beijing the initial name list of our delegation members, the list was accepted, *except* that I had been struck from it. I was so junior that I did not take it personally but understood this action to reflect the PRC's distrust of social science and China specialists. The other delegation members all were globally known natural scientists. No one would ask why they were on the delegation. But me? CSCPRC, as an institution, and the delegation as a whole, agreed that if everyone on the original name list did not go, *no one* would go. When CSCPRC informed the Chinese of that decision, the list was quickly approved as originally submitted.

The basic principle under which we Americans operated was that the sending side would determine the composition of its own delegation and the receiving side would not interfere. Of course, the same applied to the composition of Chinese delegations sent to the United States by Beijing. Imagine what failure to observe this principle would mean. Each side would be free to exclude people who did not conform to whatever some bureaucrat's preferences of the moment may have been on either side. It would undermine the integrity of our own delegation in the eyes of fellow Americans if we permitted the PRC to pick off individual delegation members, and vice versa.

There were various unsuccessful exclusionary incidents of various types over the years. For instance, the Chinese attempted to exclude Dru Gladney, a leading specialist on Western China (including Xinjiang), from serving as a scholar escort for a Members of Congress Delegation to Western China with which I was involved. Chinese delegations visiting the United States tried to exclude particular Americans, such as Anne Thurston, from joining ceremonial events. And they once tried to exclude journalists from Falun Gong's *Epoch Times* from attending a public event with a Chinese official at SAIS.

To be fair, after the June 4, 1989, violence in Beijing, Premier Li Peng was radioactive in the United States, and there were awkward discussions among visiting Americans about whether they would meet with him, much less permit a picture. My approach has been that China gets to pick its leaders and we try to deal with them. We deal with China as we find it, not as we desire it. Conversely, China has to deal with America as it is, not as Beijing may wish it to be.

Beyond my appreciation for the Steroid Delegation's show of solidarity, this also was an inviolable and unwavering policy of the NCUSCR from its earliest days of exchange. Later, this was the principle that the Aspen Institute Congressional Program applied as well. This was essential, for failing to do so would call into question mutual benefit, equality, academic freedom, and, quite simply, justice.

The other lesson I learned from this incident concerned negotiation. When you have a reasonable principle, and are steadfast in its defense, often as not the Chinese will find a way to accommodate. And, when they don't accommodate, you stick to your guns. No bluffing. Another principle we observed concerning the Chinese interlocutors with whom we worked and negotiated over the years was that we would not trumpet the fact that they had been flexible when they accepted our steadfast proposal. We were more interested in preserving and improving the operational environment than ballyhooing PRC retreats to receive transient domestic praise.

Our Steroid Chemistry Group, arriving in Beijing on the night of October 10, 1976, aboard Iran Air, flight 801 from Tokyo, was the first U.S. delegation to arrive in post-Mao China. (Former U.S. Defense Secretary James Schlesinger had been in China on a private trip when the chairman passed away.) A young PLA-uniformed woman, sporting a red-star cap and wearing baggy pants, boarded the aircraft parked on the darkened tarmac and abruptly told us to remain seated as she sprayed us with what we presumed was insecticide. (DDT was banned in the United States in 1972, though I do not know the substance used that evening.) After deplaning, we walked into a small terminal, more like a house, and saw a chalkboard announcing in handwritten characters flights arriving that day from abroad—there were about two, a minuscule number for the capital of a country then with a quarter of the world's people.

Because our delegation wrote an exhaustive CSCPRC report on the trip and our findings, *Oral Contraceptives and Steroid Chemistry in the People's Republic of China* (1977), here I will focus on several experiences that had an enduring impact on my thinking about China.

Incident One: The Old Man and the Dirt
After arriving at Capital Airport, we were driven down a darkened two-lane road clogged with donkey and horse carts to the then newest wing of the Beijing Hotel. There was virtually no one in the huge lobby. Instead, we were greeted by a sign in Chinese characters proclaiming, "We Have Friends All Over the World." I spent a restless night in the Spartan hotel room, with the cadence of double-timing troop boots reverberating outside my window on *Chang An Jie*, the Avenue of Eternal Peace. I was eager to get outside the hotel to see Beijing awaken with the sunrise, to have a couple of hours free of (visible) supervision before breakfast.

In these early days, each visiting group ate separately from others, screened off from Chinese or other foreigners. Diners were offered a choice of Western or Chinese breakfast—and mixing and matching elements of the two genres was *not* permitted—no coffee with Chinese breakfast and no tea with Western breakfast!

I decided to adopt the practice of early each morning heading in a different direction for an hour, knowing it would take an hour to return to the hotel. Six days in Beijing would allow me to hit all four directions, and then some, without covering the same ground twice. Maps were unavailable in that secretive-minded, insecure era. China was under threat from the Soviet Union, its leaders remained uncertain about the United States, and generally the regime treated all locational, numerical, organizational, and biographic information as classified.

On about the third or fourth day in Beijing, at 5:30 a.m., I headed out the Beijing Hotel's front door clad in my newly acquired PLA olive drab overcoat with a brown fur-like collar and Beijing winter hat—marmot. Passing through the city's Front Gate (*Qian Men*), I walked south, eventually turning left into the then extensive alleyways (*hutong*). The tiles on the ancient roofs were covered with fine dust providing soil for grass to spout and grow. I had noted on my previous morning walks that people would see me coming and head to the other side of the street, or duck back into their homes. That morning I was determined to blend in wearing my Chinese garments, hoping to be sufficiently inconspicuous to get close enough and talk to someone, anyone, in my hard-won Chinese.

Rounding a corner, I almost literally bumped into an old man, still in his pajamas, standing at an outside water tap on the corner of a gray brick residence brushing his teeth. Our eyes met, and he had nowhere to easily retreat. A wave of alarm washed across his face. Being a morning person, I cheerily said, "Good morning (*zao*). How are you? I am an American" (*ni hao, wo shi Meiguoren*). Now he seemed truly alarmed, first that I spoke Chinese and second that I was an American. Trying to reassure him, I asked him what I thought would be an innocuous question, presuming that the Public Security Bureau would be interrogating the anxious man once I departed. All around us were mounds of dirt in the street piled against the walls of surrounding structures. I thought dirt was a safe topic.

The preceding July 28, there had been a cataclysmic earthquake with its epicenter in Tangshan, southeast of Beijing, in neighboring Hebei Province (killing more than two hundred thousand, perhaps many more, with some estimates reaching six hundred fifty thousand). The quake dramatically affected the capital, creating mounds of earthen and other debris in the streets, and many residents still lived in structures cobbled together in the earthquake's wake. But Beijing also was engaged in a tunnel-building effort (bomb shelters) to protect citizens from attack by the Soviet Union, principally. It was this latter fact that made my question so inadvertently sensitive. "What is all the dirt for?" I innocently asked. The old man looked at the dirt, looked at me, looked again at the dirt, and then again at me, saying, "What dirt?!"[2]

This response has stuck with me ever since, for two reasons, beyond admiring his quick, clever mind. To start, one is never quite sure what the entire context for one's interaction with individuals or organizations is in China. Trying to be reassuring can be problematic when you don't know what your interlocutor actually is worried about. And second, when Chinese do not wish to deal with an issue, they may simply deny its existence.

Incident Two: Hua Guofeng and Succession Politics

When our delegation arrived in Beijing from Tokyo, Hua Guofeng had at least nominally been appointed to Mao Zedong's formal positions, the decisions having been made in secret. The PLA had been central to the outcome, but the Chinese populace did not know this until Hua appeared in a PLA uniform on national television on October 21, by which time our delegation was in Guangzhou. Hence, a quarter of the world's people had been uncertain about who their national leader was for about six weeks (September 9 to October 21). Though we knew nothing of this at the time, in the hours after Mao's death, there was debate as to whether to cremate his remains (as per the Chairman's wishes) or preserve him. They decided to embalm him, but they had only primitive means by which to do so.

When Hua's appointment was formally announced, he was by no means a household name. One cadre who greeted us in Shanghai after the announcement about Hua got into my car and purposefully asked, "Who is Jimmy Carter?" a previously little-known Southern governor from Georgia then having success in his run for the U.S. presidency. I laughed and said, "We know as much about Jimmy Carter as you know about Hua Guofeng." My Chinese interlocutor laughed nervously. As

Figure 4.1.   Beijing *hutong*, October 1976. Photo by David M. Lampton.

for Jimmy Carter, about two weeks later, he was elected U.S. president, having defeated President Gerald Ford. To say 1976 was the year of dark horses is an understatement.

In Beijing, residents seemed to be holding their breaths, waiting to see who their next paramount leader would be; what individuals, leadership factions, and organizations would dominate the new constellation of power; and whether political order would be maintained. On my first night in China's capital, I noted calligraphy on the vermillion walls of the Forbidden City proclaiming, "Love the People's Liberation Army," ominously implying that some citizens did not.

After six days in Beijing, those in charge of our itinerary still seemed unsure about what to do with us. On October 16, 1976, we were informed that we were leaving on CAAC flight 139 to Guilin, Guangxi Zhuang Autonomous Region, bordering Vietnam. The declared purpose of our visit was sightseeing, but I have always suspected that our delegation's security was a principal concern. Guilin was almost as far as you could get from Beijing, so far off the beaten path that the mass campaign billboards with slogans were faded, one or two iterations behind the reigning slogans in the capital. So rare were foreigners at this time that our young female local guide who led us through a rural cavern misidentified us as a group of Japanese.

This experience was a graphic illustration that China, then and now, has no constitutionally binding, norm-bounded, succession process. A peaceful and predictable transition of power between national leaders is basic to an institutionalized, stable system, something that Americans had to re-learn in the wake of the January 6, 2021, insurrection against the U.S. Congress and Constitution following the 2020 presidential election. Only a thin membrane of norms maintains the separation between order and chaos.

In China succession meant power struggle. Unless it spilled out into the streets, the average citizen was in the dark, even though the identity of the leader was crucial in this centralized system not governed by law. In this Mao to Hua Guofeng succession, China lucked into a manageable transition with Hua performing as the bridge until Deng Xiaoping could (re)assert his authority.

Deng created conditions that enhanced the odds of a smooth transition from himself to Jiang Zemin, and even thereafter for the transition from Jiang to Hu Jintao. Deng set retirement ages and introduced the rule of limiting PRC presidents to two five-year terms and established the norm that the leader of the party could not serve a new term beyond sixty-eight years of age. Decades later, in March 2018, Xi Jinping engineered an amendment to the state constitution allowing for a third term as president, thereby implying that the party's age norm was no longer applicable, facts subsequently confirmed at the 2022 Twentieth Party Congress and the Fourteenth National People's Congress the following March. Xi thus has the prospect of holding power for life, increasing the odds of instability when he departs.

At the moment of the official announcement of the succession from Mao to Hua Guofeng, our delegation was in the Lou Gang People's Commune outside Guangzhou. It was the morning of October 21, 1976, having departed Guilin for Guangzhou on the afternoon of October 19. We were ushered into Luo Gang's austere recreation hall along with commune members who had been summoned to watch an important live broadcast from Beijing without, as far as I could tell, prior explanation. The audience was expectant. The rec room had an old black-and-white tube TV with images barely distinct. I saw the fuzzy picture as a metaphor for the lack of transparency in Chinese politics.

Suddenly Hua Guofeng appeared on the screen in the center of the Tiananmen Gate leadership lineup. He was clad in a military uniform. There was an audible inhalation from the audience, followed by chatter. It appeared that some people didn't recognize Hua, and others were surprised that he wore a PLA uniform, given that the military had not been Hua's prior persona.

Some six weeks had passed before the new regime was able to orchestrate this event, a moment preceded by inner-party struggle, the development of a new propaganda line, and the notification of all the party branches down the hierarchy so they all were on the same page. The PLA's backing for all this was key. If one had to put a name on what transpired, "military coup" would be imperfect but adequate.

Figure 4.2. Photo taken at Luo Gang People's Commune near Guangzhou, October 1976. First televised image of Hua Guofeng as China's first nominal post-Mao leader. Photo by David M. Lampton.

Later that day, we departed Guangzhou on the 4:00 p.m. CAAC flight to Shanghai, arriving two hours later. Our departure from Guangzhou signaled that the authorities felt Shanghai was presentable and safe.

Incident Three: The Night the Lights Went on in Shanghai, October 21, 1976

Having landed in Shanghai at 6:00 p.m., driving into the city was like I have always imagined Paris to have looked and felt when liberated from the Nazis by Allied troops on August 25, 1944. Neon lights that had not shone for a long time were again ablaze. Drums and gongs sold out at the Shanghai Number One Department Store. The next day, I joined the throngs and with their help deciphered the meaning of big character posters pasted on the facades of treaty port-era buildings along the Bund. Military troop trucks hauled naval personnel from the East China Fleet back and forth to demonstrate the PLA's presence.

Shanghai was celebrating not only the fall of the "The Big Gang of Four" in Beijing (Jiang Qing, Yao Wenyuan, Zhang Qunqiao, and Wang Hongwen) but also Shanghai's "Little Gang of Four" led by Ma Tianshui, Wang Xiuzhen, Xu Jingxian, and Ma Zhenlong. The two "gangs" were Mao Zedong's core acolytes. The acolytes were mortally threatened by the impending reversal of the verdict on the entire Cultural Revolution and the return to power of the Cultural Revolution's victims, not least of whom was Deng Xiaoping. In China political losers do not go off and write their memoirs and live comfortably thereafter.

That first night, as we drove through the streets clogged with early evening revelers pasting up big character posters as high on the walls as stepladders, or the boost of a friend, would permit, I was struck by the exuberance of people packed into the streets cheek by jowl. The sentiments expressed on the posters were graphic: revenge, hate, and violence were all pictorially directed at the now-fallen leftists, the most reviled of whom was Mao Zedong's (fourth) wife, Jiang Qing. The hand-drawn and painted cartoon-like figures portrayed various ghoulish scenes such as the righteously indignant Chinese masses boiling the Gang of Four in oil, portraying them as vile serpents, being bayonetted, and the gang literally being squeezed to death in the clenched fist of the irate Chinese masses. A major theme was the hypocrisy of these leftists who enforced an almost Taliban-like asceticism on the Chinese people for a decade, while behind high walls in their villas, they ate, drank, gambled, watched Western movies, debauched, and wore beautiful Western attire. Monumental hypocrisy. My photos were published in a four-page spread in the *Columbus Dispatch Magazine*, December 12, 1976, under the title, "Eight Days in Shanghai."

The morning after we arrived in Shanghai, I arose early and peered through my upper-floor window in the North Building of the Jin Jiang Hotel overlooking the old French Club where Mao occasionally swam in its luxurious pool. On the street below, I saw white characters painted on the macadam which said: *"Da Dao Siren Bang"* [Strike down the Gang of Four]. I asked the service person on my floor of the hotel, "Who is the Gang of Four?" to which he responded, *"Wo bu qing chu."* ["I am unclear."] At this moment, no one with whom we dealt had certainty

Figure 4.3. Anti-Gang of Four demonstrations, Shanghai, October 1976. Photo by David M. Lampton.

about what was happening in either the local or national leadership. No one had a clear idea of what was ideologically acceptable behavior and no idea what they could safely tell foreigners. The prudent path forward for PRC citizens was to do and say as little as possible, and only do that if authoritatively instructed.

A striking example of this process was our schedule for the evening of October 26. The itinerary we were initially handed indicated that we would see a film version of the ballet *White Haired Girl,* a Cultural Revolution–era approved "opera" closely associated with Jiang Qing, Mao's widow. Our handlers were in a dilemma because the situation had changed since the itinerary had been set. If our minders did not show us the film as scheduled, and the Gang of Four somehow staged a comeback, then our hosts would have made a grave political error and displayed anti-Mao tendencies. Conversely, if they showed the film to us and the Gang of Four was permanently overthrown and more reform-oriented forces prevailed, they then would appear to have been holdouts for Gang of Four ideology. Our hosts' solution? They loaded an ancient motion picture projector with the film, started it, and locked us in an otherwise empty hotel auditorium, with the clickety-clack of the film going through the projector sprockets. They remained outside and permitted no Chinese to view the production. They had done what they were told by showing us the film while minimizing their risk by not viewing it themselves or contaminating fellow citizens with now heretical thoughts.

Incident Four: The Shanghai Fire Department

One of the things I learned in Shanghai was the difference between Chinese and American firefighters. I was on an early morning walk through the old French Quarter as the city awoke. In the middle of a block, I came across a fire station with firefighters outside milling about, getting ready for the day ahead. The scene looked to me like what you might expect to see at any fire station anywhere in the world. I thought to myself, "This is perfect. Having been 'one of them' not so long ago, knowing that firefighters generally are gregarious, I could go up, explain myself, establish a kinship of sorts, take a tour, and deal with people on a different level than that of foreign scholar visiting amidst all of the uncertainty in the wake of Mao Zedong's death." I walked up to the nearest firefighter and explained myself. With an expression of surprise and anxiety, the firefighter told me to go away.

Upon getting back to the embrace of my "*peitong*," our watchers at the hotel, I learned that fire departments in the PRC were part of the public security apparatus. I had assumed openness would be forthcoming, but, instead, found that I had walked right into the domestic security system. I concluded then and there that as a researcher, I had to fight the polar opposite impulses to either think that things in China are really like, or completely dissimilar to, conditions at home. Reality is complicated.

WHAT WE LEARNED

As to the findings of the visit, there was more serious research and pharmaceutical manufacturing work in Shanghai than in Guangzhou, much less Guilin. Shanghai was more active than Beijing. Our overwhelming impression was how far behind China was in both research and pharmaceutical manufacturing. In terms of plant safety, a factory tour was perilous for those without good eyesight and balance, given the disrepair of facilities—elevated gangways with no (or creaky) railings and poor lighting being examples. The workers' paradise paid little attention to workers.

The Chinese were anxious to introduce our delegation to work that could be regarded as cutting-edge—their candidate for us was a new substance called "Anordrin," about which we learned little.

Our delegation did, however, learn about decision-making in drug development, testing, safety, distribution, and pricing. There was a veneer of central control, but, as mentioned earlier, in reality much actual regulation and oversight was delegated to provinces having little capacity, will, or knowledge to exercise effective regulatory oversight of drug development, testing, safety, and quality. Whether nationally or locally, assuring safety and efficacy before mass administration of pharmaceuticals was not a high priority.

Even today, with the development of a COVID-19 vaccine in China, for example, one sees similar problems of rushing things to mass distribution to meet whatever the priority of the moment may be. The reliability and efficacy of Chinese-made pharmaceutical products remain variable, and often deficient. We saw many of today's shortcomings forty-five years ago.[3]

I hasten to add that Western pharmaceutical makers with production in China today adhere to their global quality assurance standards. It is troubling (in the context of the COVID-19 pandemic) that China has had the foreign exchange to purchase more effective Western vaccines and antivirals, or licenses to manufacture them (rights offered under generous terms), but Xi Jinping was unprepared to acknowledge the quality differences that such purchases would signify, even as the outbreak became severe, inflicting enormous economic and human costs on the PRC and, even more disturbing, preventing Chinese from receiving higher quality pharmaceuticals. Pride and the protection of a domestic industry trumped prioritizing citizen health. Massive population lockdowns under the "Zero COVID" policy were the highly disruptive path taken. Subsequently, when the policy was summarily abandoned in January 2023, there was inadequate preparation and stockpiling of essentials, many elderly distrusted what vaccinations were available, and the death rate among the elderly spiked dramatically. Of course, the U.S. response on the front end of the global pandemic was deficient and contributed to a million deaths in America.

The Central Intelligence Agency and Post-Mao Leaders

The post–Mao succession process, the first part of which our Steroid Chemistry Delegation witnessed in late 1976, rapidly began elevating people from relative obscurity to the Politburo and vice premierships.

Foreign intelligence agencies and academic analysts of PRC elite politics had large blind spots about simple biographic facts concerning emerging leaders, much less how they positioned themselves to rise and the implications of their presence for future policy. Scholars and intelligence personnel had a few helpful standard biographic dictionaries, and the U.S. Consulate in Hong Kong did its best to follow Chinese leaders and make data available. Nonetheless, we were flying nearly blind with respect to the new leadership, its activities, character, and internal processes. In many cases, we did not know basic details such as: What is the person's real name (many had civil war–era *noms de guerre*)? Were they married, did they have children, and if so, who were they? Where did they go to school (if anywhere), and in which skills were they proficient? Did they have prior foreign connections or exposure to other cultures? What were their factional affiliations, and who were their patrons? What was their work experience, and how had they performed? Where had they grown up? What were their policy predispositions? Why, and through what sequence of positions, did they rise? And what political strategies did they employ, and how would their past shape their future behavior? In short, we had little information important to understanding China's political elite, either individually or collectively.

The few sources we had were of varied accuracy, often from Hong Kong media or Taipei intelligence services. Within the ROC government in Taipei, the Ministry of Justice's Bureau of Investigation, and the Ministry of National Defense's Intelligence Bureau were important sources, along with the Institute of International Relations (IIR), affiliated with National Chengchi University, historically a cadre training school for the *Guomindang* (the Nationalist Party or the KMT) founded in Nanjing in 1927 and reconstituted on Taiwan in 1954.

Concerning Taiwan, knowledge about the PRC possessed by those on the island quickly became stale post-1949. In Hong Kong, information came from refugees, rumors, and printed materials finding their way out of the mainland into the Colony. If one paid interviewees in Hong Kong or Taiwan, the interviewee had the incentive to talk even if what they said was fiction. I never have paid for an interview.

The most basic problem of all, however, was that the communists had for decades before 1949 been an underground, secret organization, particularly in the "White Areas" (locales controlled by forces hostile to the "Reds," especially the KMT and the Japanese). Consequently, what we knew about the communist leadership before the 1949 takeover was fragmentary and uncertain. What had happened before the "Liberation" was obscured in a fog of combat, a tissue of lies and misdirection, and intrigue. The CCP's operational code was that any scrap of information of interest to the enemy was to be concealed.

After 1949 and the implementation of Washington's containment and nonrecognition policies, Americans had very few opportunities to meet anyone of political consequence in the PRC for twenty-plus years, except in the context of highly structured, sporadic diplomatic encounters in Geneva and Warsaw. By the time Mao died in 1976, ROC information was out of date at best, and unreliable at worst. Information from Hong Kong was sketchy. Only with the Kissinger-Nixon initiatives of 1971 and thereafter did Washington gradually obtain more firsthand knowledge of Beijing's leading figures.

In early 1978, the Carter administration, in the persons of Michel Oksenberg at the National Security Council (NSC) and Charles Neuhauser at the CIA, inquired as to whether I would undertake research and write a set of six focused, comparative biographies of new senior PRC leaders. I could select six individuals whom I considered significant in the emerging Chinese elite. I would be free to undertake a global search for information, and I would have access to unspecified classified material possessed by the U.S. government. The contract would run from

1978 into 1980, and I would have my own budget, which my accountant and I would administer. My duties at Ohio State would continue. Little did I know then that, within the year, Beijing and Washington would establish formal diplomatic relations and U.S. officials might be interacting with my research subjects.

This was a great opportunity. I would examine public and government archives in several world areas (particularly Taiwan). My research would address a topic of widespread interest to both academe and a White House determined to engage Chinese leaders across many functional bureaucracies and geographic areas. This project would permit me to say something about leadership questions important to political science, one of which was, "Who gets ahead and why?" Now I could directly explore the dynamics of elite politics that I had previously deemphasized.

In terms of my own long-term development, this provided an opportunity to see firsthand how "Greater China" (Taiwan, Hong Kong, and the PRC) interacted and to understand each locality as a research site, each with strengths and drawbacks.

The offer also triggered concerns. In the 1960s and 1970s, the relationship between academics (and journalists) and intelligence agencies had become problematic. Many earlier connections between intelligence agencies and scholars and journalists had been hidden from public view, and consumers of the data and analysis had no idea whose interests were being served by the information acquired and released. Government money could distort the research agenda. Universities are built on the proposition that research should be open to the public and other scholars so that competing hypotheses, assertions, and data could be evaluated and compared. With classified research, or research that drew on classified materials, this became difficult or impossible. How could one know whether unseen funding was shaping conclusions for nefarious purposes?

As an organization, the CIA and the entire military-industrial complex had been brought into moral question in the minds of many during the Vietnam War and associated scandals such as Watergate. This is one reason the CIA at this time tried to have at least some outreach to the civilian world under its new director, Admiral Stansfield Turner, and President Jimmy Carter.

The initial CIA contract offer did not include provisions that I could openly publish the results, in part because I would have by then seen internal government sources. This was a gigantic problem for an academic like me because the world of a junior professor is "publish or perish." I could ill-afford to spend two-plus years on a project that might never see the light of day in academe and beyond. I was determined that this project would result in a book published by a highly credible academic house, which in this case was the University of Michigan's Center for Chinese Studies. I was committed to publicly acknowledging in black-and-white the source of the project's funding—the CIA.

Mike Oksenberg was a scholar who saw my dilemmas and was willing to help from his Old Executive Office Building vantage point. Charlie Neuhauser at CIA was a first-rate analyst who went to work on my behalf to get a contract meeting my needs and agency strictures. Neuhauser, who had been John Updike's roommate at Harvard, had a reputation as a curmudgeon—I enjoyed working with him.

The arrangement the CIA and I had deserves some elaboration since it is one approach to handling the problems arising at the intersection of the academic and intelligence worlds. We agreed that the first, and most extensive, phase of my research would be a potentially global, all open sources, search for materials and information that eventually took me to Taiwan (two months in the summer of 1978), Hong Kong, and public archives in the United States.

The second step would be for me to write my book entirely using open sources obtained to that point—I had to put my sources in footnotes. No classified materials; indeed, I had not yet seen any. Upon completion of that manuscript based entirely on nonclassified, public sources, two copies would be put into two separate sealed manila envelopes, with one copy retained by me and the other for the agency. There would be no CIA (government) review of my manuscript copy or restrictions on its publication. The sealed envelopes would be the evidence of what my open-source research had revealed before I had even looked at any classified information.

The third step would be for me to then go to the CIA in Langley, Virginia, to examine whatever resources the agency chose to make available to me (I never knew what I didn't see), and I would annotate by hand the CIA copy of my public book in the confines of the building based on classified and internal materials, leaving that sole annotated copy in the agency's possession. I did not, and do not, possess a copy of that manuscript.

Even this arrangement had a danger—what if I discovered a vast data trove inside the government that I could not convey externally and that changed the interpretation of the data I had collected in the open search? That was a risk I assumed. In fact, there was virtually *no* significant data (or almost none at all) acquired internally that I had not already found externally in open sources. It also may be, and I do not know, that the agency simply chose not to provide much. The final book (my copy) was published in 1986 and was reissued in a second edition in 1989.

As to the six subjects of my research, I selected relatively little-known individuals who had risen to the positions of Politburo Member and/ or Vice Premier as of March 1978: Ji Dengkui, Peng Chong, Gu Mu, Yu Qiuli, Xu Shiyou, and Chen Xilian. Two of the six rose through the central State-Party bureaucracy, two through the military, and two from subnational territorial units (provinces or localities)—these were the three basic launching pads for elite careers in the PRC.

In the course of the project (1978–1980), I was unable to interview any of the six subjects, though I did travel to the Luoyang Mining Equipment Factory (November 1980) where Ji Dengkui had worked, and I talked with a person who knew him as that factory was being built in the mid-1950s under the First Five-Year Plan. It was one of the 156 key industrial projects built with the USSR's help.

After completion of the book, and its nonpublic (*neibu*) translation into Chinese by the PRC (without my knowledge or approval), an intermediary arranged for me and National Committee Vice President Jan Berris to interview Gu Mu (on March 31, 1993) in Villa Number 15 (enormous at 53,819.6 square feet) of the Diaoyutai State Guest House in Beijing. As I greeted Gu, I said, "Though this is the first time we have actually met, I feel that we are old friends from my research about your life."[4] That broke the ice. He had an infectious smile. Well after publication of the book, an offspring of one of the other subjects, by then residing in the United States, contacted me after reading the volume and having heard me speak. The tenor of that person's evaluation was to express appreciation that I had truthfully told their father's story.

I concluded several things from this experience: The first was that it is a mistake to view China's leaders as faceless, homogenized party apparatchiks. They each had distinct life experiences that shaped their behavior and distinct personalities with differentiated priorities. Who wins contests for power matters, as we have seen in the Mao to Deng transition and as we more recently have witnessed in the shift from Jiang Zemin through Hu Jintao, to Xi Jinping.

The six leaders I studied had different skills. Some were good in small groups; others were adept at mass mobilization. Some were pragmatists and others ideologues. Some were grateful to Mao for his support, while others rose without his obvious patronage. The book was titled

Figure 4.4.   Former Vice-Premier Gu Mu meets Author and Jan Berris [not in photo] in Diaoyutai State Guesthouse, Beijing, March 31, 1993. Photo by David M. Lampton.

to underscore the diversity of those who have led, and who will lead, China: *Paths to Power: Elite Mobility in Contemporary China*.

One lasting impression stemming from this project relates to my research in the ROC in the late 1970s. Martial law was still in effect in Taiwan (ending in July 1987), and the U.S. government worked with the Defense, Justice, and Foreign ministries in Taipei to gain access for me and Lao Yang, my veteran research assistant, to archives containing biographic materials concerning the Chinese Communist "bandits." Lao Yang had been a cadre in the PRC but was able to get to Hong Kong, thereafter working with Western researchers. The pre-1949 materials held in the Taiwan archives were particularly important because they covered the era when Chiang Kai-shek's forces were on the mainland trying to find out all they could about their shadowy adversary. However, these materials turned out to be full of contradictions, inaccuracies, and speculation.

The post-1949 materials were even less reliable. Frankly, when we compared data gathered from publicly available PRC Chinese-language materials such as local newspapers, much of the Taiwan data and analysis did not appear either exhaustive, accurate, or insightful. I came away questioning the quality of the information Taipei was acting upon and sharing with Washington. Of course, Lao Yang and I had no idea what we were *not* shown in Taipei, just as was true in Washington.

Nevertheless, some of the most significant materials on Communist China in this era were obtained by the ROC and became publicly available in the West. *The Work Bulletin of the PLA* (Gongzuo Tongxun) and records of a coastal commune (*Rural People's Communes in Lien-Chiang*) were to become critical to our understanding of rural life and how people's communes worked. The PLA papers opened our eyes to the military's problems in the years of deprivation and mass starvation following the Great Leap Forward and provided insight into lines of communication and authority within the PRC's military.

Another lasting impression from our Taiwan research was a sense that we were deeply distrusted by our KMT hosts. Before our trip, I had naively assumed that door-opening by the CIA would facilitate our work. I soon discovered, however, that opening doors does not mean cooperation when you are in the room. We were quite limited in the quantity of materials we could request; the card catalog gave us little idea of each document's content. Often as not, the librarian, who was the only person authorized to enter the stacks, would return empty-handed after we had submitted a request the previous day. Some days the only person authorized to enter the stacks was out "sick." The basic rule was one request per day.

In short, in 1978 the KMT apparatus was not all that different from the CCP's. As our research in Taiwan ended, I asked Lao Yang, "*Lao Yang, Guomindang ye Gongchandang you shemma butong?*" ["*Lao Yang*, what is the difference between the Guomindang and the Communist Party?"] His reply: "*Meiyou shemma butong.*" ["There is no difference."] This captures the spirit of our experience. Both the CCP and the KMT of that era were Leninist organizations, and information control was the coin of their respective realms.

Stepping back, however, the distrust the KMT felt for us and the United States, its then-treaty ally, is understandable. To begin with, my research assistant had previously been a Chinese Communist cadre. I can only imagine what Taiwan security-minded authorities must have thought about him rummaging through their archives, given his personal history.

There were probably several further considerations. To start, Chiang Kai-shek (who died in 1975), and for that matter, his son Chiang Ching-kuo, who succeeded him, didn't trust Washington. Dependent clients always live in fear of abandonment by their inconstant patrons, as the United States had done in 1949 when it was clear that Washington's patience with the KMT had been exhausted, as city after city on the mainland fell to the communists and U.S. advice was ignored. Clients constantly fear handing their patrons information revealing weakness, incompetence, or corruption, knowing that might erode patron support.

Moreover, although I had secured from the CIA explicit rights to publish my findings, there was no reason to think Taipei would be enthusiastic about this, even if the CIA was in a moment of openness. It was only with the democratization of Taiwan in the 1980s and thereafter that Washington ideologically recommitted to the island. When I was there in the summer of 1978, it was a transactional relationship between Washington and Taipei. Washington got a platform to observe the PRC, and Taipei got protection. That did not mean the ROC liked dependence or suddenly became transparent.

By the time I was in Taipei with Lao Yang, even this transactional relationship was cracking. Henry Kissinger's secret trip of 1971, and Nixon's China journey early the following year (during which Nixon signed the Shanghai Communique), were signals to Taipei that future reliance on Washington was a dubious proposition. ROC leaders and citizens alike could only have been alarmed by what the Shanghai Communique's third paragraph said: "During the visit, extensive, earnest, and frank discussions were held between President Nixon and Premier Chou En-lai [Zhou Enlai] on the normalization of relations between the United States of America and the People's Republic of China, as well as on other matters of interest to both sides."

The Nixon-Kissinger approach was to keep discussions with Beijing and imminent policy changes hidden from the U.S. Congress and the State Department, viewing them as sympathetic to Taipei and prone to throw up roadblocks. For the same reasons, the Carter-Deng normalization agreement of December 1978 followed the secretive path Nixon had trod. If I had been our KMT hosts in the summer of 1978, I too might have had limited ardor to assist my research.

On the day before Lao Yang's and my departure from Taiwan to return home after about two months on the island, IIR Director Tsai Wei-ping invited me to come see him to say goodbye. I genuinely wanted to thank him for his institute's many courtesies.

Beyond courtesy, however, Ambassador Tsai had on his mind rumors then circulating that President Carter was contemplating shifting formal diplomatic relations from Taipei to Beijing. I, like everyone outside a very small circle in Washington, had no knowledge that the administration would move quickly. I offered Ambassador Tsai my analysis, and that of about everyone else I knew, that President Carter would not jeopardize his reelection chances in a presumed 1980 reelection bid by seeming to precipitously cut loose friends of long-standing, leaving the island to the tender mercies of the communists. I told Ambassador Tsai that I thought

President Carter did want to normalize with Beijing, but he would wait until a possible second term.

A couple of months after that conversation with Ambassador Tsai, on December 15, 1978, the Carter administration announced the change in formal diplomatic relations, almost two years before the 1980 election in which Carter unsuccessfully ran for a second term. Taipei was given an extremely short heads-up on the de-recognition announcement for fear of the news reaching Congress before the fait accompli.

I always have felt uneasy about that farewell conversation with Ambassador Tsai. I had provided him my analysis—which had proven wrong. Subsequently, when I flew home from a domestic trip the evening of December 15, 1978, and Susan picked me up at Columbus Airport and told me that Washington and Beijing had normalized relations, I thought there must be some mistake. I had not heard the news. But, in fact, Susan was absolutely right. This was a stark reminder that political leaders can do the unexpected, sometimes to large effect.

What I learned from my ongoing interactions with Taiwan is that American foreign policy is unpredictable and that those who rely on our help are right to be wary of Washington's open-ended promises that may be inconvenient to deliver on in an uncertain future.

Ironically, as I write these words on August 18, 2021, U.S. forces, American and foreign citizens, and nationals of Afghanistan are fleeing the Taliban, hurriedly lifting off from Kabul Airport in a mass rush for the exits, leaving thousands of Afghan citizens who had helped Washington over the years stranded, fending for themselves. At least one desperate fleeing citizen was crushed in an airplane wheel well, reminiscent of the scene in Saigon more than forty-five years earlier. I still think of the young women of Afghanistan I met on a 2014 trip to Kabul so proud of the schooling that they again will be denied.

So, I began my career seeing news photos of helicopters lifting off from Saigon only to reach the twilight of my career seeing the same pictures, this time in Kabul. In reaction to the precipitous Afghanistan withdrawal, President Tsai Ing-wen of Taiwan said in mid-August 2021: "Taiwan's only option is to make ourselves stronger, more united and more resolute in our determination to protect ourselves. . . . It's not an option for us to do nothing . . . and just to rely on other people's protection."[5] Beijing declared that U.S. "abandonment" of Afghanistan was an "omen of Taiwan's future fate."[6]

Taiwan under the Nationalist Party was leery of Washington, as has been its Democratic Progressive Party (DPP) competitor in more recent times.

My conclusion from all this? Democracies articulate lofty principles and make explicit or implied commitments, the fulfillment of which depends on popular will and capacity to sustain once the costs begin to mount. It is easier to get committed than to extract oneself, like that little boy at Stanford with his head wedged between the balcony railings during my firehouse days.

NOTES

1. From the 1972 visit of the Chinese Ping-Pong Team until normalization of relations in 1979, CSCPRC and NCUSCR were the two principal organizations sending American delegations to China and welcoming Chinese groups to America.

2. Carrying the tunnel digging campaign forward, in a November 23, 1980, letter home from Zhengzhou, I recounted that: "We went into a long (13 km) air raid shelter deep underground where they had 'The Sound of Music' and 'Red River Valley' piped in. Bazaar!"

3. David M. Lampton, "Administration of the Pharmaceutical, Research, Public Health, and Population Bureaucracies," *The China Quarterly*, 74 (June 1978): 385–400.

4. David M. Lampton, Interview with Gu Mu, 2 (RAC).

5. "Tsai Says Taiwan Needs to Be Stronger," *Taipei Times*, August 19, 2021, https://www.taipeitimes.com/News/front/archives/2021/08/19/2003762844.

6. Editorial, "Afghan Abandonment a Lesson for Taiwan's DPP," *Global Times*, August 16, 2021.

Normalization

(Into the 1980s)

THE TELEPHONE IN THE KITCHEN OF OUR SMALL WHITE CLAPBOARD house in Columbus, Ohio, played its minuscule role in the process of normalization. On November 24, 1978, Mike Oksenberg and his son David drove from Ann Arbor to Columbus to be our overnight guests for the Ohio State–Michigan football game the following day. We had a tradition of alternating as hosts depending on where the game was being played. That year OSU lost fourteen to three.

Sometime during Mike's stay, National Security Advisor Zbigniew Brzezinski ("Zbig") had a call placed to our home. He wanted to speak with Mike. It was freezing outside, but Mike asked all of us, including the kids, to stand outside on our front porch, where we shivered out of earshot. Mike tantalizingly told us that he would someday tell us what had just happened. Later I learned that it was during that phone conversation that they had finalized the decision to invite Deng Xiaoping to visit the United States soon after normalization. Deng's code name during the call was "the little one."

President Jimmy Carter and China's new (but interim) leader, Hua Guofeng, announced the establishment of formal diplomatic relations on December 15, 1978, to take effect on January 1, 1979. With normalization in effect, newly restored de facto leader Deng Xiaoping made his first, and only, visit to the United States in January and February, an earlier visit to the United Nations not being officially considered "to the

United States." From the start, the Carter White House sought to institutionalize the bilateral relationship so that ties became stronger than simply a relationship between Jimmy Carter and Deng Xiaoping. Central to this effort was their signing of "The Agreement on Cooperation in Science and Technology" on January 31, 1979.

Cabinet-level exchanges were encouraged, and among the first such visits were officials in foreign affairs, national security, science and technology, and the departments of Treasury, Agriculture, and Commerce. Zbigniew Brzezinski, and the president's science advisor, Frank Press, coordinated the many implementing departments and agencies, such as the Department of Health, Education, and Welfare (HEW) and the Environmental Protection Agency, among many others. From the start there was a systematic effort to institutionalize ties. Parenthetically, fast-forwarding almost forty-five years as this volume goes to press, there is a severe internal debate occurring in Washington about the S&T Agreement and whether to renew, modify, or let this foundational piece of the U.S.-China architecture expire.

In any event, in parallel with this national-level effort in the late 1970s and 1980s, in the states and in the private sector (foundations, universities, and companies), a process of spontaneous combustion ignited having its own momentum and logic. Through luck and circumstance, I could view this process from several vantage points: national, state/local, and private sector.

My central conclusion from this experience was that the growth and institutionalization of the new relationship with China were not foisted on an unwilling bureaucracy, states, localities, or private sector by an overzealous and naïve White House. Nor had the people or officials been sold a bill of goods by hopeful, mistaken, or self-interested academics. Instead, once normalization switched on the green light, nearly all bureaucrats, local politicians, private sector leaders, and academics perceived opportunities for gains important to themselves, their businesses, their communities, their organizations, and, in many cases, their values. Not only are businesspeople entrepreneurs, but so are central government agency leaders, local politicians, and private sector organization heads from foundations to universities and nongovernmental organizations

(NGOs). Many religious organizations and figures, such as Father The-odore Hesburgh at Notre Dame, saw engagement as a moral imperative for reconciliation and peace. China was the macro story then, and nearly everyone wanted to be part of it. In this endeavor, most people not only saw opportunity, they also saw *virtue*—we were building what Richard Nixon had called "the structure for peace." "Doing well by doing good!" was the prevailing ethos. More than three decades passed before this fundamentally changed.

ONE THING LEADS TO ANOTHER

After returning from the CSCPRC Steroid Chemistry Delegation's trip to China, I had buried myself in teaching, publishing my book on *The Politics of Medicine in China* (1977), and writing assorted articles on health care for *The China Quarterly* (1978), *American Journal of Tropical Medicine and Hygiene* (1978), and *World Development* (1978). In December 1972, I wrote a piece for HEW's widely distributed *Health Services Reports* on developments in medicine, health care, and public health in China over the preceding two decades.

Although these pieces aimed at health and development profession-als probably did not convince many of my Political Science Department colleagues at Ohio State that I was really one of them, when the Carter administration, most particularly HEW, was searching for advice on how to structure two agreements to be signed in Beijing (one for health and one for education) and to help prepare for HEW Secretary Joseph A. Califano Jr.'s trip to China in June 1979, they called me.

I MEET JOSEPH CALIFANO AND HE MEETS CHINA

Under the "Agreement on Cooperation in Science and Technology," a large number of fields for cooperation were enumerated, including health, energy, space, environment, education and scholarly exchange, earth sciences, engineering, science and technology, biological sciences, and other areas as might be agreed upon later.

In many fields, the U.S. scientific community saw substantial opportu-nities—knowledge for the world, as the Johns Hopkins University tagline put it. China was a geologically active piece of real estate—geophysicists were interested, not least in the Himalayas. China had rather immobile communities and regionally specific diseases (e.g., certain cancers), a circumstance providing the opportunity to determine if regionally distinct environmental or other factors correlated with regionally specific cancers, as well as the opportunity to understand why China and the United States had different rates of specific cancers. Of course, the humanities and social sciences (not least China Studies) also saw opportunities for field, interview, and archival research. Ties between the two countries were in many respects a two-way street.

That so many areas for cooperation were identified in the bilateral agreement also meant that a large number of government agencies had to be coordinated and jurisdictional disputes resolved. For instance, some aspects of possible biological science and genetic cooperation (recombinant DNA) became a subject of interagency friction. In some situations, there were national security considerations. Cooperation in space has always been a problem with Washington's concerns severe in this area.

Budget issues intruded as well. While departments were encouraged to establish links with PRC counterparts, generally speaking, no additional funds came with that encouragement. This pitted new China activities against other, ongoing agency missions. Consequently, how durable and active various programs with the PRC proved to be was a function of agency-head commitment and the perceived benefits. These calculations changed across administrations and agency heads.

Even before normalization, during Frank Press's July 1978 trip to China, President Carter had approved what soon would become almost unlimited access to American universities by Chinese students and scholars, so long as the U.S. taxpayer did not foot the bill. This was a far different approach to managing educational exchanges than existed with respect to the Soviet Union, where the principle of one equivalent scholar/researcher from the USSR for one equivalent American scholar/ researcher reigned. Before long, more Chinese students and scholars annually were studying in the United States than the cumulative total Moscow had sent to America in the USSR's entire existence.

This open access for Chinese students was a strategically consequential decision. By 2020, 370,000-plus Chinese tertiary-level students were in American institutions of higher learning. No one in 1978 had imagined these kinds of numbers. Nor had anyone imagined that Chinese students would become an important source of tuition and skilled members of university research and teaching teams.[1] America's role in training Chinese became yet still more extensive with the growing flow of "visiting scholars" and trainees receiving vocational education as part of commercial contracts with U.S. firms.

Beyond the huge numbers of tertiary-level students flowing from these initial decisions, collaborative research, university-to-university partnerships, and institution building in China took off. Somewhat later, American companies established research facilities in the PRC. Chinese primary and secondary students enrolled in American K–12 education.

Because each area of S&T cooperation had its own galaxy of federal entities and private sector stakeholders, overall coordination (to the degree there was any) was provided by the White House Office of Science and Technology Policy headed by the geophysicist Frank Press, the president's science advisor. On national security issues, the NSC was key.

Frank Press was a renowned scientist who (with Raymond Siever) wrote the classic textbook on plate tectonics—*Earth*. After his service in the Carter administration, Dr. Press became president of the NAS where I was proud to work with him when I was at the CSCPRC, on leave from Ohio State from 1983 to 1985.

In the U.S. system at that time, the health, education, and welfare functions of the federal government were under the purview of a single cabinet-level agency (HEW). In China the medical and educational functions were divided between two separate ministries, the Ministry of Public Health and the Ministry of Education. In reality, in both countries, these functions were dispersed widely among many different agencies, levels, and sectors of the two governments and societies. In the United States, most education activity is under dispersed local control, for example. This meant that as HEW moved ahead with the PRC, it had to deal with two Chinese ministries and myriad actors at home.

HEW and its Chinese counterparts initially moved faster on the health side than the educational side, and they soon signed a Health Agreement and an Accord in Education as described next. As a whole, however, the expansion of educational ties in the months and years ahead moved faster than Washington could follow, much less control.

I was in my Derby Hall office (with its plastic windows, a relic of anti–Vietnam War protests of the early 1970s) on the Ohio State Oval in the spring of 1979 when I received a call from HEW's Office of International Affairs. As PRC ministries have "Foreign Affairs Offices" (*Waiban*), U.S. cabinet departments also have organizations managing international agreements and events, receiving foreign dignitaries, and arranging the Secretary's travel schedule, including security.

At this time at HEW, Peter Bell was the deputy undersecretary for International Affairs, and David E. Hohman was deputy director of the Office of International Affairs. The voice at the other end of the line from HEW's Office of International Affairs stated that Secretary Joseph A. Califano Jr., and his Deputy Undersecretary Peter Bell, would like briefings on health care, education, and related issues concerning China and advice on a pending trip to the PRC that the secretary would be taking from June 21 to June 30, 1979.[2] Could I be in Washington on April 4 to see Bell and his associates and meet subsequently with Secretary Califano on April 30, 1979, at 3:00 p.m. in his office at the Hubert Humphrey Building on the National Mall? My answer was "Yes and yes."

At the first briefing, I told Bell and his associates that the agenda of such a trip would necessarily be extensive. Concerning the medical and public health dimensions, they would need to address health care delivery (both urban and rural), birth control, parasitic diseases, environmental issues, food and drug regulatory concerns, medical research and education, traditional Chinese medicine, and mental health. Another part of the trip agenda would include visiting and building cooperative relationships with institutions and prominent figures in the educational realm. Issues pertaining to HEW's responsibilities for international health in the region were also an important topic, with refugees and their health status of particular concern. Then, having defined our priority interests and needs, we had to specify exactly who they needed to see in China. Of course, the Chinese had their ideas on all these subjects.

Health care and education had been savaged during Mao Zedong's Cultural Revolution. Putting it in terms that would be meaningful to those with whom I was talking, I said that annual per capita health expenditures by the Chinese government then were between U.S. 81 cents and $1.05, and that was probably an overestimation.

The April 4 briefing with Bell and his colleagues went well. On April 30, I was alone in the Secretary's office, with windows overlooking the Mall and the Capitol, waiting for him. It was the Secretary's habit to jog on the Mall when he could, and he was, as I recall, wearing lime green jogging shorts when he walked in with me already there. He welcomed me but, quickly getting to the point, told me that his staff had become aware of my work, that they needed some advice in thinking about the U.S.-China agreements and preparing for the trip. They wanted someone who had China experience to accompany his delegation.

Califano, as HEW secretary, would be the ninth cabinet-level official to visit the PRC. The delegation would be a *Who's Who* of the U.S. government medical world, including Dr. Julius Richmond, Surgeon General; Tom Malone, Deputy Director of the National Institutes of Health (NIH); David A. Hamburg, a renowned psychiatrist and President of the Institute of Medicine; and former Congressman and former Chairman of the House Subcommittee on Health, Paul Rogers. In addition, a twelve-person press contingent would accompany the delegation, including journalists from the *New York Times*, *Newsweek*, *Washington Post*, AP, ABC-TV, UPI, and NBC-TV. The Secretary told me that it was his habit to make sure he was compatible with people who worked and traveled with him. I told him I would be honored to contribute in any way possible. I guess that our meeting was sufficient to reassure him about me, as I was asked to join the group.

The logistical efforts required for such a delegation were considerable. The group's very thick blue briefing books were full of warnings: do not drink the tap water—only the hot water from the thermos bottle put outside the room door in hotels or guesthouses; bring all essential medicines, including an extra pair of eyeglasses; do not bring credit cards because they are not used in China; bring instant coffee; take strict care to protect your private information from outside scrutiny; bring wind-up alarm clocks because Chinese electrical systems carry different voltage than U.S. systems; do not take photos of sensitive facilities or pictures from airplanes; heed warnings about the arduous character of placing phone calls, particularly internationally; and, there was a long section highlighting the exotic nature of Chinese cuisine, ending with the assurance that "but, it is all interesting and much of it delicious." When visiting a local restaurant, we were forewarned that we "should be prepared for certain pitfalls: Chinese patrons may be abruptly moved so that foreign guests can have a table."

By June, Secretary Califano's schedule had become so packed that our itinerary had become completely contorted. First (June 18, 1979), our entire delegation flew from Andrews Air Force Base outside Washington to Stockholm, Sweden, via Keflavick Naval Air Station in Iceland (for fuel), for Califano to deliver a speech to the "Fourth World Conference on Smoking and Health" on June 19 at 1:30 p.m. After his speech, at 6:00 that evening, we reversed the flight direction (transiting over the Soviet Union was not possible until 1990), now flying west, once again stopping at Keflavick, then on to Alaska's Elmendorf Air Force Base in Anchorage, to refuel, setting down again in Tokyo, and landing finally in Beijing, June 21, 1979, at 4:55 p.m.

Among those who greeted the delegation at the Beijing Airport were U.S. Ambassador Leonard Woodcock (former president of the United Auto Workers), Chinese Minister of Public Health Qian Xinzhong, PRC Ambassador to the United States Chai Zemin, and U.S. Embassy Deputy Chief of Mission J. Stapleton Roy, later himself ambassador to the PRC.

Some context for the trip is necessary. First, Secretary Califano was promoting a domestic and global effort to curtail smoking and was being attacked relentlessly at home by such organizations as the Tobacco Institute (an industry lobbying association). Always a cheap luxury in the China of that era, smoking was pervasive, and the Cultural Revolution compounded the need for stress reduction. Moreover, the PRC Ministry of Finance received huge revenues from tobacco sales. That Mao had smoked, Deng smoked, and our host State Science and Technology Commission head Fang Yi smoked (though not in Califano's presence) did not help advance the anti-smoking cause in the PRC.

The accompanying American press was interested in the awkward byplay between the nonsmoking Americans and the chain-smoking Chinese trying to control their nicotine urges. Chinese meeting participants at intervals would discreetly leave the room, take a drag in the hallway, and reappear looking visibly relieved.

For Califano, China was an almost perfect screen on which to project his global anti-smoking crusade. In American interest group politics, China almost always becomes the biggest example of whatever the issue at hand might be. China is an endless resource for domestic politics, just waiting to be used.

Another issue leading to some friction was China's backing of the murderous Pol Pot regime and its remnants in Cambodia. Beijing had supported Pol Pot because Phnom Penh under him was fighting the Vietnamese, and Vietnam was a Chinese enemy with which the PRC had waged a short, high-intensity, high-casualty war along the Sino-Vietnamese border earlier in 1979. The issue came up during a meeting from 6:00 to 6:45 p.m. on June 23, in the Great Hall of the People with Vice Premier and Alternate Politburo Member Chen Muhua, a physically imposing female in front of whom her male subordinates figuratively genuflected.

Secretary Califano strongly implored Vice Premier Chen to cease support for the remaining murderous thugs in Cambodia and expressed his hope that the PRC would provide more assistance to refugees being pushed out of Vietnam. In her response, I understood Vice Premier Chen to say, "If Cambodians must bleed for Chinese interests, so be it!" Vietnam had invaded Cambodia in 1978, ending the Pol Pot regime in January 1979, a bloodthirsty gang that had killed around two million of its own citizens. Because Vietnam was Beijing's enemy, and Pol Pot's Cambodia a nominal PRC ally, Beijing would support any Cambodian political or military forces opposed to Hanoi, a chilling example of "the enemy of my enemy is my friend" logic.

Secretary Califano also pushed Beijing to take more of the ethnic Chinese refugees that were being driven from Vietnam—hoping that Beijing could be persuaded to construct refugee resettlement or processing centers in the PRC.[3] Many refugees, a large number of whom were boat people of Chinese extraction, were in overcrowded detention camps in Hong Kong. In August 1979, there were 66,038 refugees in twelve Hong Kong camps with most of the detention facilities in Kowloon. Sometime later, I visited one such Hong Kong refugee camp where people were stacked five or so high in bunk beds.

A day after our meeting with Vice Premier Chen, we met with Vice Premier Li Xiannian, also in the Great Hall of the People. Our meetings with the two vice premiers brought home just how constrained and threatened Chinese leaders felt at the time and how low refugees and the governance of neighboring countries ranked on their priority list. Vice Premier Li Xiannian ended our meeting on June 24 by underscoring China's economic and stability challenges and saying something like, "I cannot guarantee results, but I'll guarantee no starvation."[4]

Despite the humanitarian fiascos arising from the refugee crisis, many countries in Southeast Asia and elsewhere frankly were not of much help either. Vice Premier Chen was noncommittal about accepting more refugees, arguing that China already had taken large numbers (230,000) of such persons, and this was taxing PRC capabilities. My notes record her as saying: "There are 230,000 refugees to China, and great difficulties have resulted." My assessment: "She was worked up." Secretary Califano responded to both the situations in Vietnam and Cambodia by saying that "there is extraordinary brutality, and every pressure [should be] brought to bear to halt these acts."[5] In the meeting with Vice Premier Li Xiannian the next day, Califano told him: "We are appalled and disgusted at the North Vietnamese pushing of 6,000–7,000 refugees to the United States per month. The burden needs to be spread around."[6]

Some might ask how it was the HEW Secretary felt empowered to address sensitive high foreign policy and security issues in Beijing. The principal reason was that he was the administration's point person for responding to the refugee crisis, an issue to which many foreign policy topics were linked. Moreover, earlier in his career, the Secretary had dealt with defense and foreign policy. Joe Califano was no shrinking violet.

The Chinese leadership was steadfastly devoted to its overriding goal—modernization. Chairman Mao left China with an annual per capita GDP of less than $200, not much more than Cambodia after Pol

Pot. From Beijing's perspective, Hanoi was pushing out ethnic Chinese, and were the PRC to take them, it would, in effect, be facilitating Hanoi's ethnic cleansing. For its part, Hanoi was scapegoating ethnic Chinese in Vietnam to deflect criticism of the economic privation in the now unified country after the American war ended.

The uncomfortable meeting between Secretary Califano and Vice Premier Chen Muhua was made more so because she was the most powerful woman in the Chinese Government and Party, a key player in the family planning, economic, foreign aid, and international trade areas. Importantly, she was Minister of Foreign Economic Relations and Trade. In our discussions on health care, she talked laudably about the utility of Chinese traditional medicine and acupuncture, a topic that figures in this story. My meeting notes recorded my reaction: "She doesn't seem too knowledgeable" about the health care portfolio.

Secretary Califano was concerned about what was shaping up as the increasingly stringent one-child-per-family birth control policy in the PRC, a campaign that started the previous year in Anhui Province. Though knowledge of this evolving campaign was limited at that time, and the policy itself ever-changing, Secretary Califano was offended as a person, a liberal, and as a Catholic. We came armed with a lot of questions. Knowing that Beijing now, in 2023, encourages couples to have three children is enough to cause whiplash.

One other phenomenon taking place in the PRC during our visit created a sense among us that China might have the potential for fundamental political changes, though the movement giving rise to the optimism—Democracy Wall—was getting shut down as we were there.

In December 1978, a twenty-eight-year-old electrician named Wei Jingsheng challenged Deng Xiaoping directly and publicly by declaring that Deng's Four Modernizations required a "Fifth Modernization"—Democracy. Wei's "big character poster" sparked a popular movement epitomized by the appearance of what came to be called Democracy Wall, literally a brick wall in central Beijing where citizens posted criticisms of the Communist Party's ruling elite and aspirations for a more democratic future.

Democracy Wall had reached its zenith before we arrived in Beijing. Though no longer at its high tide, localized popular democracy promotion activities in the capital were ongoing during our visit. At every available opportunity, I would head down to the brick "Wall" at Xidan in Beijing's Western District to see what new posters were being put up and grab copies of blue mimeographed broadsheets on onion skin paper with names like *Qiu Shi Bao* (Seeking Truth). I am sure that our hosts were discomfited by our group's exposure to Democracy Wall, but it was not a formal item of discussion.

Califano had come to China with a full plate: health and education cooperation, anti-smoking, refugee policy, birth control, and more. The "Protocol for Cooperation in the Science and Technology of Medicine and Public Health" was signed on June 22, 1979, in the Great Hall of the People, followed by a banquet hosted by Minister of Public Health Qian Xinzhong. The next day, the "Memorandum of Understanding on Educational Exchange" was signed, with the details to be fleshed out in subsequent discussions.

Figure 5.1. Democracy Wall, June 1979, during HEW Secretary Joseph Califano's trip to the PRC. Photo by David M. Lampton.

In his June 22, 1979, banquet speech celebrating the signing of the Health Agreement, Secretary Califano explained that while he was the ninth cabinet-level official to visit the PRC in the Carter administration, this trip was moving the bilateral relationship to an entirely new level, with the Secretary saying, "This visit and this evening symbolizes not that we are dealing with ninth-ranking and less important relationships but that we are penetrating to the most fundamental of all problems: those that deal with the mind and the body." While this was a welcome step to many Chinese and all the Americans, it was precisely the dealing with the "mind" that still continued to worry many in the PRC's education and propaganda systems, bureaucracies still riddled with Cultural Revolution ideological holdovers.

The policy issues that the two sides were addressing in China had serious domestic and/or international political ramifications for both countries, as well as moral content. Accordingly, the press presence on the trip was considerable. But as the trip proceeded, a certain disconnect developed between the seriousness of our mission and how the mission was being portrayed in U.S. mass media.

Our delegation was not the only American group in China at that moment. Bob Hope was in Beijing independently for his "Bob Hope on the Road to China" television special with Big Bird and Mikhail Baryshnikov. Though Bob Hope was in Beijing independently, Califano and our group met with him and his wife, Dolores. David Hohman and I picked up the couple to bring them to the guest house (No. 14) near Beijing's Front Gate where we were staying—the old Belgian Embassy compound in the pre-1949 Legation Quarter.

One of the journalists in the Califano entourage was the satirical columnist Art Buchwald, who was turning out real-time columns that created discussion and raised eyebrows back home. The Bob Hope–Art Buchwald combination reached back home in one of Buchwald's columns in the *Washington Post* (July 30) in which he wrote: "Bob Hope is doing a three-hour special in China to be aired this fall.... Large crowds gather to watch. At first it was believed they knew who he was. But much to Hope's chagrin, he has discovered that all the Chinese people want to do is stare at his television equipment."

Buchwald's drip, drip, drip of satirical columns mystified the Chinese and disconcerted President Carter. One of Buchwald's offerings was devoted to the question of why the pandas China had given President Nixon—Hsing-Hsing, the male, and Ling-Ling, the female—weren't reproducing in the National Zoo in Washington. Buchwald interviewed China's foremost panda breeding expert at the Beijing Zoo, asking her why Hsing-Hsing wasn't more amorous, like another male panda at the Shanghai Zoo named Du-Du. The question of the day, Buchwald intoned, was "Why Du-Du does and Hsing-Hsing doesn't."

Another strain beneath the surface was bureaucratic politics at home involving President Carter and the Secretary. Califano was in a struggle to keep the "E" (Education) in his department name, HEW. During the trip, Joe explained to me why he thought it important to fight against what proved to be President Carter's unwavering commitment

Figure 5.2.   Art Buchwald and Author, Forbidden City, HEW Secretary Califano's trip, June 1979. Photo by David M. Lampton.

to establish a freestanding Department of Education (DOE) as occurred on October 17, 1979, leaving the remainder of HEW to be renamed the Department of Health and Human Services (HHS). Secretary Califano felt that the federal government's (limited) education function was best protected and expanded when it was part of a huge institution like HEW, with rivers of money flowing through it (e.g., Social Security checks until 1995), rather than creating a free-standing Department of Education that would be a bureaucratic guppy in a shark tank.

I think that Califano may have hoped that signing the education agreement with Beijing might bolster his position in that larger domestic argument, beyond his own commitment to ties with China. Whatever his reasons, Califano was committed to signing an education agreement that would lock in as many concrete details as possible with the Ministry of Education. But as the time to sign the agreement drew near, Joe still had not received final authorization (or budget approval) from Washington. Moreover, the Chinese were having their own internal tussles.

On June 21, we received a State Department cable saying, "It is clear that jurisdictional and funding problems on Chinese side will preclude formal agreement. Nevertheless, we are hopeful that joint communique are [sic. or] similar document outlining some of the cooperative activities in proposed [Education] Annex can be issued." On June 23, 1979, Califano and Minister of Education Jiang Nanxiang signed the "Memorandum of Understanding on Educational Exchange Programs between the United States and the People's Republic of China."

Califano was a tough politician of the LBJ tradition. He had been President Lyndon Johnson's special assistant for Domestic Policy from 1965 to 1969. He also had served in the upper reaches of the Department of Defense under Robert McNamara. He knew about domestic and foreign policy and big-league bureaucratic politics. When he organized this trip to China, he was mindful of domestic impacts and wanted maximum coverage by the press.

This created a schizophrenic circumstance. Concerning substance in China, the trip was very successful, resulting in the long-term institutionalization of health and education links between the two governments and their citizens. On the other hand, some of the extra-curricular activities

Figure 5.3. Minister of Public Health Qian Xinzhong and HEW Secretary Califano shake hands at negotiations for bilateral health agreement, June 1979. Orange soda (*qi shui*) was the drink of choice. Photo by David M. Lampton.

on the trip created controversy or diversionary interest. All this, plus President Carter's natural desire to go into the upcoming reelection campaign (1980) with his strongest possible team, not to mention the personal friction between Califano and President Carter's most senior aides, cascaded to produce the Secretary's dismissal on July 19, 1979, shortly after his return from the PRC. The day he left the administration, I received a note from him thanking me for my help on the journey. Incidentally, Treasury Secretary Michael Blumenthal, who had been NCUSCR's chairman, was fired later that same day in a politically bloody cabinet reshuffle.

In the wake of Secretary Califano's dismissal, Congressman Charlie Wilson of California (of the movie *Charlie Wilson's War* fame) commented: "They're cutting down the biggest trees and keeping the monkeys." Ralph Nader described the situation as "like firing Mickey Mantle because he couldn't get along with the bat boy." The former editorial page editor for the *Washington Post*, Philip Geyelin, concluded that "the People's Republic of China is not yet ready for Joe Califano and Art Buchwald."

The substantive results and details of the trip were enumerated in the official report, "Cooperation in Health: Report of Secretary Califano's Visit to the People's Republic of China 1979" (available online). Here I want to focus on a few aspects of the trip not covered in that document that shaped my future thinking.

First, Califano's two counterpart Chinese ministers, Qian Xinzhong at the Ministry of Public Health (*Weishengbu*) and Jiang Nanxiang at the Ministry of Education (*Jiaoyubu*), both had been early and prominent victims of the Cultural Revolution. Their two ministries had been among the earliest and most savagely attacked, with Mao denouncing the health bureaucracy as the ministry of "urban overlords," among other things. I inadvertently came to understand something of Minister Qian's ordeal when we were at a swimming pool and I saw the scars of the flaying to which he had been subjected by his Cultural Revolution tormenters. This trip by Secretary Califano was in a sense a personal and institutional vindication for both Jiang and Qian. The trip was a demonstration that, as post-Mao China emerged from the grip of Cultural Revolution Luddites, science and knowledge would figure prominently. The visit also was tangible evidence that China had real friends, not just the empty propaganda slogans I had seen in the Beijing Hotel's lonely lobby on my first trip to China in 1976.

A second impression that stays with me has to do with what it means to say a country is not a "rights" culture but rather a "duty" culture. China had precious little advanced science and technology at the end of the

Cultural Revolution, yet our hosts felt compelled to show China to good advantage, a country full of innovative, intelligent people—which it is. At this moment, our hosts were promoting what was being sold as a great advance in surgery: surgery under acupuncture anesthesia. Our delegation witnessed, live, in operating rooms themselves, a cerebral surgery and a subtotal gastrectomy. In the latter case, on the morning of June 25, our delegation was ushered into an operating room of the Kunming Medical College and Hospital of Traditional Medicine. However, the patient, who was "under" acupuncture anesthesia (seemingly wide awake), went into distress on the operating table, and we were hurriedly ushered out.[7]

Those patients put on display for foreigners, whether coerced or complying out of a sense of duty, seemingly had no choice and dutifully smiled as the procedure proceeded with all the onlookers. That a foreign delegation should be in an operating room where sterility should have been a prime concern, with no patient confidentiality, seriously violates medical best practices. But I heard no protests from our delegation, and our hosts did not give it a thought. In retrospect, I feel that I should have said something. Patient "rights" paled before the Chinese patient's "duty" to help project the China of the regime's dreams. Art Buchwald, to his credit, wrote a satirical piece in his syndicated column, "Getting Inside the Chinese Mind: The Direct Route." The piece noted that one would have to "be kidding" to think that the patient had been able to solicit a second opinion before undergoing this spectacle.

In these early post-normalization days, domestic politics drove much American behavior, but I greatly credit President Carter, Frank Press, and Zbigniew Brzezinski and his staff at the NSC, not least Mike Oksenberg, for building a network of interagency connections knitting the Chinese and American bureaucracies together, to stabilize things when the relationship hit inevitable rough patches and leaders came and went. The vision held well into the 2000s. But nothing lasts forever.

Looking back, some interagency agreements of that era proved more active and productive than others. An objective analysis would say that the health and education relationships remained very active and productive for both nations. To the degree which some interagency agreements fell by the wayside, while others remained active and adapted, owes to the vagaries of budgets, elections, variations in agency-head interest, and changes in technology, as well as the overall volatile character of U.S.-China ties. Space was one area initially identified for cooperation but which, over time, particularly in the United States, became progressively more impossible, especially after the 1999 publication of the "Cox Report" alleging widespread and protracted PRC theft of missile and warhead designs. I felt, and continue to feel, that not undertaking selective space cooperation was a lost opportunity.

Mental health cooperation was a sensitive area too. In a visit to a mental health facility during the Califano trip, the onsite medical personnel told our delegation that there was no schizophrenia in China, to which Dr. Hamburg, a leading psychiatrist on our delegation, replied: "If that is true, I will eat my hat!" One reason for this PRC assertion was that the Chinese line on mental health was that only diseased (capitalist)

Figure 5.4. (Left to right) Author; Yang Liwei (China's first person launched into space in the PRC program); and Phillip C. Saunders, Beijing, Space City, August 2007. Photo by David M. Lampton.

societies produce psychiatric disorders. Acknowledging mental disease would have been to acknowledge underlying societal problems.

There was one final aspect of the Califano trip that calls for attention; it concerns the CIA. The agency wanted to send an unacknowledged agent along on the trip. Califano refused to permit this unless the individual was explicitly identified and "okayed by the Peking regime." This "mind-blowing idea" was agreed to by the CIA. International affairs correspondent, Daniel Schorr, concluded his July 25 *Washington Post* report on all this saying, "John le Carre would have savored the moment when the Chinese Minister of Health Qian Xinzhong raised his glass to Phillips [the agent] at a farewell dinner and expressed hope that he had learned what he wanted to find out."

Thus far "normalization" has been implicitly discussed as a Washington phenomenon. But America has a federalist system. There are many points of initiative, what President George Herbert Walker Bush called "a thousand points of light." When Washington and Beijing cracked the doors open for two-way traffic American states and cities (and Chinese provinces and municipalities) individually seized opportunities as they saw them and were able. Creating relations (commercial, cultural, and educational) had a dynamic that was not entirely dependent on Washington or Beijing.

State, provincial, and municipal leaders in both countries saw gains to be made in moving toward each other. As it happened, I then was in Ohio and had a front-row seat to this process. While a Democratic Party administration in Washington enthusiastically promoted the U.S. relationship with China at the national level, an old-time Republican politician in Ohio was doing the same in his state. His name was James A. Rhodes.

NOTES

1. David M. Lampton, with Joyce A. Madancy and Kristen M. Williams, *A Relationship Restored: Trends in U.S.-China Educational Exchanges, 1978–1984* (National Academy Press, 1986).

2. American Embassy, Tokyo, Telegram, June 21, 1979, Unclassified, Beijing #3916, "HEW Visit-Schedule."

3. This refugee processing center idea was also a major theme of our meeting with Vice Premier Li Xiannian. "Meeting, Joseph Califano and Vice Premier Li Xiannian," June 24, 1979, 6:00 p.m., Great Hall of the People, Beijing, 5. (RAC).

4. "Meeting, Joseph Califano and Vice Premier Li Xiannian," 5–6. (RAC).

5. "Meeting with Vice Premier Chen Muhua," June 23, 1979, Beijing. (RAC).

6. "Meeting, Joseph Califano and Vice Premier Li Xiannian," June 24, 1979, 6:00 p.m., Great Hall of the People, Beijing, 5. (RAC).

7. Secretary Califano's "Schedule," June 21–June 30, 1979.

CHAPTER SIX

Ohio: The Heart of It All

(The Rust Belt Era)

JAMES A. RHODES, KNOWN TO MOST AS "BIG JIM," WAS OHIO'S MOST successful electoral politician of the modern era, serving as the state's sixty-first and sixty-third governor. A staunch Republican, he served two consecutive terms as governor from 1963 to 1971, sat out one term, and ran again, serving two more terms, from 1975 to 1983. He was physically imposing and jowly and adamantly believed that there were only three words in a successful politician's vocabulary: "jobs, jobs, and jobs."

For Jim Rhodes, "jobs" was the job. He was absolutely pragmatic in how he addressed that challenge, believing that foreign trade (exports) and foreign direct investment in Ohio were important job creators. Big Jim made international news when he persuaded Japan's Honda Motor Company to build an auto assembly plant in Marysville, Ohio, beating out other states to win the prize. When the assembly plant opened in 1982, it employed about 4,200 people and represented an investment of $4 billion. Big Jim's approach was different than some members of Congress, who five years later smashed a Toshiba "boom box" to smithereens on the steps of the U.S. Capitol.

In 1979, shortly after the normalization announcement in Washington and Beijing, Governor Rhodes set his gaze on China. Deng Xiaoping launched the reform and opening era at the December 1978 Third Plenary Session of the 11th Central Committee. By early the next year, modernization, openness, and de-radicalization were the PRC's goals, and America could play a big role.

For Governor Rhodes, China appeared to be a potential market for Ohio's machinery exports from firms like the Timken Company (bearings and power transmission) and Parker Hannifin (motion and control systems). Later he began to see opportunities for Chinese investment in Ohio. The more serious Ohio's rust belt problems became, the more energized Big Jim became to do business with China. Ideology did not matter. In a subsequent meeting with Vice Premier Yu Qiuli, Big Jim pulled out his wallet saying, in effect, that China and America spoke the same language—money.

Accordingly, state trade development officials began preparations for the governor to lead a State of Ohio Trade Mission to China in July 1979, one month following Secretary Califano's trip described earlier. In preparation for his trip, the governor's office asked me to come over to the Statehouse, just down High Street from OSU, to brief Big Jim and his cabinet on May 16, 1979. Seated at one end of the very long cabinet table, with the governor at the other end, he introduced me and asked me to tell them what they needed to know, what to expect in China.

Being an academic, and a young one at that, I started in the forty-five-minute lecture mode, explaining that his delegation was visiting the PRC at a notable juncture and that Deng Xiaoping represented a great departure from Mao. "The central problem China faced," I said, was "how to loosen up the system to get productivity, without generating uncontrollable demands and leadership division." Shortly after beginning my disquisition, the governor raised his hands in a referee timeout signal and said, "Dr. Lampton, I really just have one question here—do I have to eat Chinese food? Can I bring peanut butter in my baggage?" I learned several lessons from Governor Rhodes, one of which was—know your audience.

From such a seemingly inauspicious start, one might have predicted things would not go well for the governor in China, an old-time Republican engaging hard-bitten communists. On the contrary, the trip was a resounding success, with Governor Rhodes meeting grizzled Politburo Member, State Planning Commission Chair, Vice Premier, and a wounded war veteran Yu Qiuli (who had lost an arm in the "War against Japanese Aggression"). Upon reflection, it is not so surprising that Rhodes and China's immediate post–Cultural Revolution leaders got along well—these interlocutors were from the heartlands of their respective continental countries seeing themselves as having had to do battle with coastal elites and shoulder the burden of agricultural areas in the throes of industrialization. They were rough-hewn and plain-spoken.

Several things developed from the governor's China trip (on which I did not go), including Chinese exhibitions at the Ohio State Fair for years running, the sister state-province relationship between the State of Ohio and Hubei Province that benefited corporations in the state, and a very successful exchange between Ohio State University and Wuhan University (*Wuda*). This academic linkage soon provided field research opportunities for professors, including me, and PhD students.

The decision to couple Ohio with Hubei had been made on the basis that both Ohio and Hubei Province were located in their respective heartlands, both were big industrial areas, and both had very large agricultural sectors. They both were transportation hubs. There was a symmetry to the pairing.

One might have thought that the encounter between American and Chinese parochialism would have ended unproductively. But it was precisely the shared parochialism that bonded Governor Rhodes and his old revolutionary Chinese counterparts, Chen Pixian in Hubei and Yu Qiuli in Beijing. Chen Pixian was governor of Hubei Province and concurrently the province's Party Secretary. In 1982 he became the Secretary of the Party's powerful Central Legislative and Political Affairs Committee (*Zhengfa Xitong*).

Neither side treated the other with evasion or even much subtlety. They each stated clearly what they wanted. They all were economically motivated, with no ideological agenda. Dr. Paul Schroeder (a former PhD student of mine, later representative for Ohio in Hubei, and later still a professor at Case Western) recounts that during Governor Rhodes's dinner with Yu Qiuli in Beijing, the two men were simpatico, with Ohio's governor noting with surprise that tourists could climb the Great Wall for free—"You should charge money for that," Big Jim helpfully advised. Within a year, tickets were required to visit the Great Wall.[1] The following snippet of conversation captures the flavor of the trip and relationships:

> [Rhodes] plunked himself down in a chair and forged ahead with only "Hello, glad to be here" preliminaries. "First," Rhodes said, "We want to build an office building in Beijing." So far so good. "Second," he continued, without waiting for the translator, "We are proposing to build a tourist accommodation center at the Beijing airport. We believe tourism is your number one asset and it should be developed. The Center would include hotels and an amusement park and would be solely for foreigners so you can control them."[2]

DEVELOPING THE EDUCATIONAL DIMENSION OF NORMALIZATION AT THE STATE-PROVINCE LEVEL: OHIO STATE, WUHAN UNIVERSITY, AND THE YANGTZE (YANGZI) BASIN

After the governor's trip, building out the commercial relationship fell to the state's trade and development authorities and private enterprises across Ohio. But establishing academic relationships required the attention and commitment of the state's educational institutions to define with whom and how to work in China. Given OSU's location in the state capital and its relatively plentiful resources for dealing with contemporary China across disciplines, the lead role fell to Ohio State. This involved identifying key academic opportunities and enlisting committed colleagues at OSU, elsewhere in the state, and in China. Who in Hubei wanted to work with us? Finally, we had to strike a balance between student exchange and faculty and graduate student research. Beneath it all lurked the issue of how access to libraries, archives, and field research opportunities within Hubei Province would be handled. How would academic freedom fare? What did academic freedom even mean in the PRC emerging from the Cultural Revolution? How would Chinese students coming to Ohio be funded? What would be their needs, and could we address them effectively?

Wuda (Wuhan University) was the flagship university in Hubei Province. With a history dating back to 1913, it was a key institution under the direct supervision of the Ministry of Education in Beijing. It was OSU's natural partner, and we were quickly paired.

To translate the amorphous vision of state-level academic exchange into tangible, workable, and mutually beneficial activities, those on the OSU campus with the most interest drove the process—broadly speaking, this was the China Studies and Asian Studies faculty dispersed among the disciplinary departments. The interdisciplinary East Asian Studies Program was small and often headed by someone with a China interest. Initially, the key disciplinary departments were Political Science, History, Sociology, Anthropology, and Chinese Language and Literature. Each of these units had at least one champion. History Professor Samuel Chu played a key role, as did Languages and Literature Professor and chairman Timothy Light.

Over time other units of the university, such as the medical and agricultural schools, pursued their own avenues, whether under the umbrella agreement or entirely separately. I did what I could to assist the medical school during one trip I made to Wuhan, where I stayed alone in Mao's villa on East Lake, with PLA guards and wildlife as my only company. It was eerie. I could not help noting that the gorgeous physical setting that had served as a retreat for the then ruler of a quarter of humanity had poor lighting and no discernible heating.

For the OSU departments and programs involved, the core interest was gaining access to China for field or archival research rather than sending undergraduate students to the PRC for a classroom experience. Not many OSU undergraduate students at that time would have been interested, and there were not enough language-qualified students to sustain such a program if courses were taught in Chinese. For its part, *Wuda* was nowhere near ready to accept American undergraduate students into an English-only curriculum that its own faculty might have taught. And, at this early date, no one suggested sending Ohio State professors to China to teach American students at Wuhan University. Parenthetically, the Yale-China Association did have a few recent Yale graduates teaching English to Wuda students.

From the beginning, Wuhan University wanted to send students and scholars to us, and we wanted to send faculty and graduate students to

China for field and archival research. The OSU priority was not easily accommodated in early 1980s China because social sciences in the PRC were weak and still under something of a political cloud coming out of the Cultural Revolution. This baseline sensitivity had been compounded by the controversy caused by a Stanford anthropology graduate student (Steven W. Mosher) doing field research in China. Mosher had engaged in activities that made him untouchable there and caused Stanford to eject him from its PhD program. At this moment, the thought of foreign field researchers mucking around in villages and factories was viewed as intrusive and risky in terms of both politics and considerations of physical well-being (health). Hubei Province of the early 1980s was low on meat, high on cabbage, and low on doctors.

What we really needed in 1981–1982 was an initial, successful case of what was wanted so that we had a proven, viable template for the future. We hoped that OSU could have an initial success that would reassure the Chinese, meet the highest standards of academic freedom, and serve as an example to faculty and others of what was possible in China, in its heartland, off the beaten track. We went from the specific to the general, *not* general principles to be followed by a concrete program. In China things often work better if something new is designated an "experiment," tested, then popularized, leaving room for adjustment.

Given my interests in field research and interviewing, with my substantive focus being the provision of public goods, infrastructure, and water conservancy (flood control and hydropower), Wuhan was a natural place to go. My interest in water issues was sparked by Philip Selznick's *TVA and the Grassroots: A Study of Politics and Organization* and by Michel Oksenberg's dissertation, *Policy Formulation in Communist China: The Case of the Mass Irrigation Campaign, 1957–58.* I proposed that I go to Wuhan University under the OSU-Wuda signboard to examine the management and planning of the Yangtze River Valley.

The Yangtze River Valley drains about one-third of China. Any attempts to manage it holistically require up to nine province-level geographical jurisdictions to deal with each other, in addition to several ministry-level functional organizations in Beijing. My topic addressed core issues of Chinese politics without ever having to use the word "politics." Water conservancy could be treated as a "technical issue," not a political issue. The word *xie tiao* (coordination) is one of the most useful words in this context. Rather than talk about political conflict, as Americans are wont to do, Chinese generally speak of coordinating different units, leaving initially unspoken why they need to be coordinated.

Wuhan was home to the Yangtze River Valley Planning Authority (*Chang Jiang Liu Yu Gui Hua Ban Gong Shi*, or *Chang Ban*). That organization resembles the Tennessee Valley Authority (TVA). Wuhan, earlier an inland treaty port opened in 1858, is strategically located and the hub of water planning and research in central China. The Wuhan Hydrological Institute was adjacent to the *Wuda* campus. In Hubei Province beyond Wuhan, several large water projects recently had been completed, were underway, or were on the drawing boards, not least the Danjiangkou project up the Han River, the Gezhouba re-regulating dam at Yichang on the Yangtze, and the mammoth Three Gorges Dam for the more distant future upstream from Gezhouba. There also were numerous flood diversion, irrigation, and hydroelectric projects in Hubei to be considered. Hundreds of small earthen, often unsafe, dams dotted the landscape, some with small electrical generating capacity to provide badly needed power.

I planned to have six months of residence and visit projects and organizations throughout Hubei, reaching all four corners of the province. I would interview, use Wuhan University's library resources, gain access to the Yangtze River Valley Planning Authority and other water-related institutions, and write a series of articles on water policy in China. To finance the effort, I would use some Ohio State funds and apply for a grant from CSCPRC, housed in the National Academy of Sciences. To gain access to the field, I would use the combined connections of the Ohio-Hubei relationship and simultaneously obtain central sponsorship and necessary introductions through CSCPRC's National Program if I were selected.

A key consideration in the grant application evaluation process was whether or not the project was *feasible*. With a project having so much field research and requiring the support of two ministries (Water Conservancy, *Shuilibu/Shuidianbu*, and the Ministry of Education, *Jiaoyubu*),

Figure 6.1.   Author and engineer Liu at the Yangtze River Valley Planning Authority, Hankou, Wuhan, Hubei, late 1982. Photo by David M. Lampton.

my project would not be easily engineered bureaucratically. Ministries in China generally find interagency cooperation laborious. My proposal also required someone on the Chinese side to establish liaison with the multitude of localities and organizations where I would go for field observation, both in Hubei and in Beijing, explaining my purposes to each. I had the baseline challenge of explaining why a political scientist was interested in a "technical issue" such as water conservancy.

I had a lot of luck, testimony to the role of idiosyncratic convergence in life. Two events, each independent of the other, and each of very low probability, converged to make my project feasible, though I only gradually learned how this had come about.

A chance encounter established a personal relationship that created sufficient trust that Wuhan University would agree to host me for my research project and to bear the burdens and risks my presence would entail. The idiosyncratic event occurred in September 1979. I had been invited to a medical symposium in New Haven, Connecticut, convened by the Yale-China Association (on whose Board of Trustees I later served) where I presented the paper "Changing Health Policy in the Post-Mao Era," subsequently published in *Yale Journal of Biology and Medicine*. A vice president of Wuhan University who had received a PhD in biology from Yale in 1935, Dr. Gao Shangyin (Kao Shang-yin) also attended that symposium and was in New Haven for a week. Having overlapping interests, we became cordial.

Subsequently, I connected that earlier meeting with Dr. Gao to the needs of my water conservancy proposal and the developing overall OSU-*Wuda* relationship. Entirely fortuitously, Dr. Gao played a critical role, personally overseeing building ties with Ohio State, writing me in December 1981, and updating me on the status of three OSU scholars' plans for arrival and work in Wuhan. I realized Dr. Gao might be the perfect partner to facilitate my project. I eventually visited Wuhan, with Dr. Gao and his wife inviting me to their university residence for dinner. An invitation to dinner at a Chinese family's home was quite unusual in those days, and I consider it an honor to this day. Thereafter, Dr. Gao became a champion for our Ohio State–Wuda university-to-university cooperation and for my personal field research on the Yangtze River Valley.

The second hurdle to be cleared, with almost infinitesimal odds of occurring, was that two ministries in Beijing needed to approve my project—the Ministry of Education (responsible for educational exchanges under the National Program and the central oversight authority for Wuhan University) and the Ministry of Water Conservancy (responsible for most of the functional units to which I would need access during my field research). To the surprise of everyone, including the CSCPRC, the two ministries both signed off on my project. Only later did I learn how this happened.

Sometime later I was in a meeting at which a Vice Minister of Education, Huang Xinbai, was present. After we had been chatting for a while, he said something like, "Ah, Lampton, I know something that may be of interest to you." He then explained that his wife, Qian Zhengying (herself the daughter of a famous Cornell-trained hydrologist and one of China's first female engineers), was the minister of water conservancy, that my research project had come to their respective attentions through their ministries, and I understood him to say that they had resolved bureaucratic issues through what I jokingly called "pillow talk." Sometimes complicated things get resolved simply.

Through these convergences, bureaucratic approvals, and funding, on-the-ground access materialized, principally in Hubei, but also in Beijing at the Ministry of Water Conservancy. It was definitely luck, facilitated by the fact that at this moment all the involved Chinese and Americans wanted something positive to happen—in Beijing, in Hubei, in Washington, D.C., and in Columbus, Ohio. At a multitude of points, almost anyone could have thrown a spanner into my plans.

Consequently, in the second half of 1982, I lived at Wuhan University in the "Foreign Experts Building" (*Zhuanjia Lou*) on *Luojiashan* overlooking East Lake. For part of that period, I roomed with Barry Naughton, a valued professional colleague and friend ever since. Our window looked out over the lake where one could see the villa and swimming hole that Mao used during periodic visits to Hubei. Mao often took secret trips around China, providing scant notice to local officials where he was headed. Every province had an opulent place for him to stay, however infrequent his visits may have been.

The hardest part of my Hubei research stay was the family separation. My daughter, Kate, was eight, and my son, Adam, five. We had considered temporarily relocating the entire family to central China but were justifiably uncertain about medical conditions there and anxious about continuity in the children's education. We made the correct decision for our family, but leaving Susan, Kate, and Adam for six months was hard, with only miserable telephone connectivity and air mail that took a long time each way. In retrospect, had Susan, Kate, and Adam gone, they would have seen a China that has now generally vanished. The Wuhan of 1982 was a place where the daily nutritional deficits caused hair and weight loss and rodents often outnumbered residents. I learned to lure sizeable rats away from my bedroom with bean cakes strategically placed in an adjoining room. Foreigners were a genuine rarity off campus.

Walking the alleyways of Hankou, throngs of laughing, sometimes rambunctious children would often follow the outsider—out of lively curiosity rather than hostility. If I encountered a medical emergency, I felt that, if possible, it would be prudent to get to Japan or Hong Kong, not a speedy process then.

Wuhan is a three-part city (Wuchang, Hanyang, and Hankou), connected in the early 1980s principally by ferries, though there was the traffic-choked Wuhan Yangtze River Bridge, an engineering feat (completed in 1957) of which the Chinese were justly proud. The city is flood-prone with enormous dikes protecting its 4.1 million population. At that time, the Wuhan Bridge was the only span across the entire mighty river.

Field research took me from the southern border of Hubei (near Hunan Province) to Hubei's northern boundary with Henan Province on the Danjiangkou Reservoir. I walked through the internal tunnels of the Danjiangkou Dam below the waterline (eerily leaking gurgling water as one passed through the dim passageways lit by dangling bare incandescent light bulbs, infrequently spaced). I also visited the construction site of the Gezhouba re-regulating dam (started on Mao's birthday in December 1970) on the main channel of the Yangtze. That project was downstream from the future site of the Three Gorges Dam that began construction in December 1994. I address my research findings in chapter 13.

Being separated from my family for such a long stretch was difficult. Beyond rats and mosquitoes, I had an unwelcome companion—a certain degree of anxiety above anything I had experienced before.

Dissertation students and book authors frequently have recurrent worries that something will happen to their notes or manuscript, particularly as they near the end of their labors. Years before, in June 1972, I had that experience at Stanford. My office on the Quadrangle was about a mile from our home on the edge of campus. I was getting ready to head for Hong Kong for fieldwork and had all my notes and work in my campus office. One night at about dusk, I stepped outside our home on Bowdoin Street in "College Terrace," and the sky was orange in the direction of my office—I immediately assumed my work was going up in smoke. This was before the era when in seconds one could make an electronic backup of one's work on a flash drive—this was still the carbon paper era. I ran to campus to discover that indeed there was a huge fire, but it had ignited in another nearby building—Encina Hall. Nearly five decades later, I would have an office in that renovated, lovely sandstone structure when I was at Stanford's Asia-Pacific Research Center (APARC) in 2019–2020.

In China I had similar protracted anxiety, with its origins in the very nature of the PRC's political surveillance and social control system. After nearly six months of field research all over Hubei Province and in Beijing, my entire project boiled down to notes, on paper, and a set of paper computer punch cards configured in a way that I could systematically retrieve various categories of data. My whole project was in two vulnerable cardboard boxes. There was no way to get a complete copy out of China, except by taking the original notes through Customs and Immigration at the PRC's border or via international air mail which was subject to inspection. I had no materials about which authorities would rightfully have concerns, but I also wanted to protect sources.

Prior to my final departure from China, I had taken the precaution of sending a friend in England one copy of key materials and another copy home—hedging my risk on two continents.

But I still worried about my notes and about being able to take them with me upon leaving China. I could not be absolutely sure that some zealous border officer would not find something that they would declare to be "illegal." I had seen *neibu faxing* (internal use) information in my research in various locations. If I learned nothing else in the U.S. Army, it was that a white-gloved inspecting lieutenant can always find a problem with your foot or upright locker if they want to. For weeks I worried, and the closer I came to departure from China the more worried I became. In the end, I left behind all but my notes, rough draft articles, and data cards. This was my early personal introduction to the paranoia-inducing properties of the Chinese political system.

At the end of my field research, Susan joined me in China, and we took a boat journey on a vessel in the *Dongfanghong* [East Is Red] fleet from Chongqing down to Shanghai—five days and nights, the riverine version of the Trans-Siberian Railway. We went through the Three

Gorges in a severe wind and rain storm, with nearly ocean-scale waves creating geysers in the toilets, pitching glasses off shelves, and sending the rats in the bulkheads scurrying. We could only imagine what it was like in steerage, several decks below where passengers were packed in with chickens and other creatures.

Years later, in spring 1999, Susan and I accompanied an Aspen Institute Congressional Program trip from Chongqing to Yichang, passing the under-construction Three Gorges Dam, which became fully functional in 2012. Professor Lyman Van Slyke, one of my former Stanford professors who had written a book on the Yangtze River, was a seminar participant and lecturer for the Members of Congress. The trip was a lot less rugged in 1999 than seventeen years earlier.

One incident during the 1999 trip impressed me as our congressional delegation neared Yichang. As we approached the last bend in the river before the dam project would jut into sight, some of the congressional participants had an animated discussion about whether or not global environmental and multilateral financial institution pressure on Beijing might yet halt the project. As we rounded the bend and the concrete behemoth shot skyward, that discussion abruptly ended.

Overarching Themes

Nothing in the course of my research in Hubei struck me more deeply than the realization that localities, ministries, and organizations each have political cultures, values, and narratives. It is remarkable, for example, how similar the narratives of Hubei citizens and residents of Ohio were, in part by both being heartland areas of two approximately geographically equal-size continental countries. Residents of both localities were given to see themselves as the "flyover people," often ignored by distant and favored political and economic groups. They both are resentful of coastal elites. Predictably, many of China's earliest communist insurgents were from interior regions.

Organizations and politics in China can be understood in many respects by reference to processes we see in all political systems. It is not enough for Western analysts and critics to say, "China is a Leninist system"—end of story. Above all, China is an organizational system, manifesting regularities observed in many organizations around the world.

The Ministry of Water Conservancy, for instance, saw its primary mission as protecting the Chinese peasants along the river bank from floods. The Ministry of Electric Power, on the other hand, saw its mission as energizing urban industry and the cities. The Electric Power Ministry had enormous revenues and the Ministry of Water Conservancy relatively few. These two ministries repeatedly struggled over how to manage rivers and water impoundment areas, in part, because dams often have both flood control and hydropower purposes. Dams should be designed, built, and operated with both ministries' interests in mind. The two ministries constantly fight. When the two were pushed together into a single Ministry of Water Conservancy and Electric Power to create a unified hierarchy, they fought each other inside the combined organization. When split apart in the hope of reducing internal conflict, they then fought each other as separate entities. It was like a bad marriage. They couldn't live with each other, and they couldn't live without each other.

This observation contributed to the development of the "bargaining model" of Chinese politics,[3] which Ken Lieberthal, Michel Oksenberg, and I later individually and together in various combinations fashioned into the "fragmented authoritarian" framework of political analysis.[4] My Wuhan experience exerted such a powerful force on my thinking that in June 1983, shortly after my return from Hubei, I convened a field-wide conference on policy implementation in post-Mao China in Columbus, Ohio. The gathering was funded by Ohio State's Mershon Center and by the Joint Committee on Chinese Studies of ACLS and the SSRC. Part of my contribution to the resulting 1987 volume was a chapter titled "Water: Challenge to a Fragmented Political System."[5]

Another thought I continue to have in the wake of the Wuhan experience is that so much in life hinges on small things and happenstance. Documents held in the Wuhan University Library were key to my research success because many ministries and functional units in China's bureaucracy publish their own documentary series. Most of these had routinely stamped on the inside cover *neibu faxing* (internal use), not for circulation to outsiders. But these publications were the spaces in the

Chinese bureaucracy where insiders discussed real issues and provided data. These were the materials I needed. Documents provide the essential foundation for productive interviews. It is critical to interview people using the vocabulary they employ when speaking among themselves and to anchor questions in specifics and knowledge.

At this time in the early 1980s, the Wuhan University Library was housed in a dimly lit old building with a leaking roof, and generally not an inviting place to sit for hours on end. I sometimes had to position my materials on the table to dodge the raindrops in a downpour and carefully arrange tea cups to capture the water streaming through the ceiling. The library was unbearably hot in the summer and was an icebox in the winter—by fiat, coal was not to be used for heat south of the Yangtze River, and we were considered south of the Yangtze, even though Wuhan's metropolitan area straddles it.

After the first couple of trips to the library, the librarian got tired of going to the stacks looking for things I had requested. It was, in effect, the same set of library rules I had encountered four years earlier in Taiwan and had been so unhappy about. But in one important respect, the Wuhan librarian differed from his Taiwan counterpart. Finally, he told me to go into the stacks to retrieve things myself. Now I could go into the stacks and see what they had on the shelves, thumb through documents, find what they contained, and generally be much more productive. The librarian did not even want to acknowledge the *neibu* problem. He adopted the "hear no evil, see no evil, speak no evil" approach.

At the end of my research stay at *Wuda*, I asked a knowledgeable person why the librarian had been so cooperative. Paraphrasing his reply, he said: "The library is a low-ranking work unit where we put people who have no use anywhere else or are problematic in some way. He was lazy, and he would rather you do the work." It was with this comparison in mind that I earlier said that I had a better research experience in China in 1982 than I had in Taiwan in 1978. Taiwan and the mainland had the same system, the only difference being that in Taiwan the rule was enforced, and when I was in the PRC, it was not.

As I was preparing to leave Wuhan to return home in December 1982, The Yangtze River Valley Planning Authority (*Chang Ban*), in the person of my point of contact, Engineer Liu, asked me to deliver remarks to his colleagues (engineers and others) and to offer any "advice" I might have. *Chang Ban*, incidentally, was led by Lin Yishan, Chairman Mao's kindred spirit on dam building, particularly the Three Gorges Dam. I saw Lin a couple of times in the halls of *Chang Ban*, and once we sat at nearby tables in the otherwise deserted restaurant of an old French treaty port-era hotel, the Jiang Han. I wish I had the effrontery to just go and speak with him.

In my farewell remarks to *Chang Ban*, I did not really know what to say to the assembled professionals arrayed before me. They were technical experts, and I was a political scientist from America. After genuinely thanking them for their many courtesies and describing what I had done and where I had done it, I said that as a social scientist and a person who believed in economic incentives as a way to shape behavior, it had occurred to me that China needed an insurance industry. Audience eyes sharpened and ears perked, seemingly not understanding where I was headed. I went on to say that I noted throughout my travels in the river basin that people and industries kept rebuilding on vulnerable floodplains after successive disasters. It seemed to me that people did this because no cost was attached to the risk they assumed each time they rebuilt in a precarious place. SOEs didn't have to pay for the losses, and the government would rebuild. The risk-takers did not have to pay for the risks they assumed. There was no penalty for dangerous behavior. That is why we have insurance companies. "You need an insurance industry!"

It certainly was not cause and effect, but in subsequent years, China did build a huge insurance industry, and foreign companies such as AIG (founded in China and then relocated abroad post-1949) did very well.

LUCK OF THE DRAW

The title of my father's autobiography, *The Luck of the Draw!*, reflects my experience too. One symposium presentation at Yale, a marital relationship linking two key ministries in the PRC, converging national interests in deepening exchange, an overlap of state and province goals, and a university-to-university relationship involving my institution, all came together to advance my research agenda and those of my graduate students and colleagues at Ohio State. With this opportunity, a new vision of Chinese politics formed in my mind, the bargaining model.

My life would have unwound differently without Dr. Gao, to whom I owe an eternal debt of gratitude. I am sure I only vaguely comprehend his exertions on OSU's and my behalf. Vice President Gao was a great facilitator, even though he also was busy with his own work on virology, being one of China's most notable academics in that field. Over time Wuhan became a leading center for virus research as the world later came to know in the COVID-19 pandemic.

Looking at my experience more broadly, the system's decision to provide me with considerable access and transparency worked to China's benefit. This was true for access to documents and interviewees. When Chinese speak honestly to each other through internal publications, or enlighten the foreigner in straightforward interviews, problems can come to be seen as inherent in the human condition and circumstances. Their responses to problems begin to make sense. Often there is no mystery, and we would do much the same if we were in their shoes. When you understand the other guy's problems, you often become more understanding. Receiving empathy from others requires providing transparency. Openness breeds trust; closure promotes distrust.

APROPOS OF DISTRUST

Unfortunately, the positive developments chronicled here in the Ohio-China relationship came under assault about forty years later, an assault that is part of the much larger process of deterioration in U.S.-China relations described and explained in chapters 14–16. In 2023, a Senator in The Ohio Senate, Jerry Cirino from Kirtland, located twenty-five miles east of Cleveland, population 6,937, introduced Senate Bill 83, 1,094 lines of scattershot provisions affecting higher education. "Among the proposals, SB 83 would ban all academic and financial relationships between Ohio's public institutions and those located in China."[6] The senator's rationale? "Communist China's activities around the world and to their people are far more egregious than what Russia is doing in Ukraine." As of this writing, the fate of this and similar legislation in the Ohio General Assembly is unclear. Activist state legislatures around the nation are introducing bills to limit U.S. interactions and transactions with PRC citizens.

Serendipity kicked in two days after the developments noted above appeared in the *Columbus Dispatch*. I was in Gates Mills, a small community outside of Cleveland, Ohio, delivering a public lecture, in part addressing the state's history with China and the current and past gains it had made under those ties. I encountered only thoughtful, balanced audience responses. How issues are framed has everything to do with public reactions.

NOTES

1. Janet H. Cho, *The Plain Dealer*, "Former Ohio Gov. Jim Rhodes Left Lasting Impact on China's Great Wall," https://www.cleveland.com/business/2013/01/former_ohio_gov _jim_rhodes_left_lasting_impact_on_chinas_great_wall.html.

2. Paul Schroeder, "Why Jim Rhodes Talks the Way He Does?" *Columbus Monthly*, September 1979, 15, cited in David M. Lampton, *Paths to Power* (University of Michigan Center for Chinese Studies, 1989), 188.

3. David M. Lampton, "Chinese Politics: The Bargaining Treadmill," prepared for the 15th Sino-American Conference on Mainland China, June 8–14, 1986, Taipei, Taiwan. Published in conference proceedings. Also in *Issues and Studies* 23, no. 3 (1987): 11–42.

4. Kenneth G. Lieberthal and David M. Lampton, eds., *Bureaucracy, Politics, and Decision Making in Post-Mao China* (University of California Press, 1992).

5. David M. Lampton, ed., *Policy Implementation in Post-Mao China* (University of California Press, 1987).

6. Sheridan Hendrix and Peter Gill, "Some Ohio Faculty Members Worry about SB 83 Ban, Say Cutting Chinese Ties Would Affect Economy," *Columbus Dispatch*, April 17, 2023.

CHAPTER SEVEN

Science, Technology, and Leadership
(The Mid-1980s)

THE CIVIL WAR WAS STILL RAGING WHEN ABRAHAM LINCOLN CHAR-
tered the NAS in Washington, D.C., in March 1863. The first spike in the
Transcontinental Railroad was driven that year. America was opening its
West, industrializing, and building infrastructure. The academy's purpose
was to "investigate, examine, experiment, and report upon any subject of
science or art" when requested to do so by a U.S. government agency and
to serve as an objective, science-based think tank bringing together America's premier scientists to tackle issues with public policy implications.

One way the NAS discharges its duties is through the formation
of carefully composed study groups, each institutionally and otherwise
diverse and of appropriate disciplinary composition. The academy also
houses standing programs created to pursue recurring interests—the
Committee on International Security and Arms Control, for example.

For two years, between 1983 and 1985, I took leave from Ohio
State to go to Washington, D.C., to serve as Principal Staff Officer at
the CSCPRC; its permanent director, Dr. Mary Brown Bullock, was
on sabbatical. The committee already had enabled me to go to China
in 1976 and in 1982 had sponsored, negotiated, and partially funded
my research in Hubei. While at the CSCPRC, I worked closely and
well with Robert ("Bob") Geyer, who handled day-to-day management.
Susan, Kate, Adam, and I trundled off to North Arlington near Washington, D.C., where we lived for two years.

The NAS implemented most of its China-related activity through CSCPRC, and its offices at 2100 Pennsylvania Avenue, NW, were not far from the National Academy's neoclassical home constructed of white Dover marble with bronze doors.

CSCPRC was also sponsored by the American Council of Learned Societies (ACLS) and the SSRC, both in New York City. Its academic advisory structure was a *Who's Who* of scholars with deep China knowledge.

Adding further complexity to the CSCPRC's organizational ecosystem was (and is) an umbrella body, the National Research Council (NRC), composed of the NAS, the National Academy of Engineering (NAE), and the Institute of Medicine (IOM).

For a China scholar, this was an exciting time to be at the intersection of these organizations, particularly because NAS was led by the former science advisor to President Jimmy Carter, Frank Press, mentioned previously. At the same time, the NAE was led by Robert White, the brother of Theodore H. White who, with Annalee Jacoby, had written the classic *Thunder out of China* (1947). The chairman of CSCPRC was Herbert Simon, who had won the A.M. Turing Award in Computer Science in 1975 and the Nobel Prize in Economics in 1978. Simon, who had worked on decision-making ("bounded rationality" and "satisficing"), was at the cutting edge of work on artificial intelligence at Carnegie Mellon University. He was very interested in China.

I aspired to be in a setting where meaningful things were happening and to be led by superiors who cared deeply about the collective endeavor. During 1983–1985, NAS, NAE, NRC, and CSCPRC were just such organizations. I have always been grateful to Mary Bullock for giving me the opportunity to come to Washington. My colleagues at CSCPRC were splendid to work with. Also, there was a World Bank Education Project dealing with the PRC, headed by Halsey Beemer, located adjacent to CSCPRC.

There was a close fit between my past experiences and interests and what I was being asked to do in Washington. I managed several specific projects of priority to the sponsoring organizations.

My job description at CSCPRC-NAS included four projects. I go into some detail about them to demonstrate the role of S&T in the overall U.S.-China relationship. Some of the stresses in U.S.-China ties that later broke into the open were apparent in these early interactions. Nonetheless, by far the dominant impulse was to cooperate. This was a remarkably productive moment in the U.S.-China relationship.

RELATIONSHIP RESTORED

My first job was to work with George Beckmann, provost at the University of Washington, to form a Steering Committee to oversee a book-length study addressing the following questions:

1. What were the dimensions of the Sino-American academic relationship that already had been constructed, and how many students and researchers already were in each of the two countries, in what institutions, and in what fields of study? What were the trends moving forward?

2. What was the nature of these academic exchanges—were they two-way or one-way intellectual streets? Who was paying for these exchanges?

3. What impact were these activities having in various hard science, social science, and humanities fields in both countries, not least China Studies in America?

4. What issues had arisen in these undertakings?

5. What recommendations could we make to improve outcomes?

The resulting study (David M. Lampton with Joyce A. Madancy and Kristen M. Williams) was published by the National Academy Press in 1986 under the title *A Relationship Restored: Trends in U.S.-China Educational Exchanges, 1978–1984*.

Those questions are evidence of the decentralized, spontaneous combustion–like character of the U.S.-China educational relationship then. Simple questions such as "How many PRC students are in U.S.

institutions of higher education, in what fields of study, and who pays for them?" had not been answered because there was no central data bank with germane or comprehensive information.

In part, we lacked data because the U.S. and Chinese systems differed. The United States has a highly decentralized federal system. For instance, Governor "Big Jim" Rhodes in Ohio, so far as I am aware, never asked Washington for permission to initiate an educational relationship with the PRC. I would guess that no one in Ohio ever even thought to inform Washington, much less ask permission. China, too, has its decentralized character, with the additional reality that innocuous data of all sorts are treated as classified.

Nonetheless, I was genuinely shocked to find that the U.S. Department of State and immigration authorities did not even have a centralized database tracking how many PRC students had received visas to come to the United States, much less what kind of visa, the individual attributes of each student, and whether after completion of their studies, they returned home. Beyond anecdotes and hunches, we had no centralized, aggregated idea of what PRC scholars were studying in the United States. The technology employed by the U.S. government was practically using shoeboxes as storage devices, with the boxes scattered hither and yon, full of entry and exit slips that never were remarried.

The reason for this was simple but disconcerting. Chinese students received their visas from individual diplomatic posts in China, the transactions were conducted on paper, and the information on all these slips was never consolidated into a single electronic data set. When a Chinese student entered the United States, the immigration officer put one copy of the student's entry form into a box and stapled a companion departure slip into the student's passport/travel document, which was to be removed upon departure from the United States. The problem was that the departure authority that took the exit slip from the travel document when the student departed was the *airline* or other transportation company, not an immigration official. So, immigration had the arrival slip, the airline or other conveyance had the departure slip (if they remembered to remove it), and they had no capacity to reunite forms and determine who came in, who left, and whether the person returned home upon visa expiration.

Consequently, to obtain meaningful statistics, our study team had to send someone to China to go to each U.S. diplomatic post and examine their visa issuance files just to see who had been given visas and ascertain attribute data (age, gender, field of study, etc.) for every person who had been granted a visa. Yet even after we had done this, we could not be sure that all the students who had been granted visas in China actually departed for the United States. And thereafter, when in the United States, colleges and universities initially had varied capacities to keep track of what students did after their visas or terms of study expired and whether they graduated, transferred to other institutions, or went home. My impression is that several decades later, many of these record management problems have been addressed, particularly post-9/11.

Our difficulty collecting data reflects the fact that America is not built to control people. Our political culture and our legal system (appropriately, in my view) make it hard to do so. As a people, Americans are suspicious of government surveillance. Consequently, we hesitate to invest in what might be called bureaucratic control infrastructure. This is ironic—America did so much to start the information revolution but our government (except the military) is the slowest of adopters. So slow were parts of the government to join the information revolution, that the last "Wang Computer" I ever saw was in the U.S. government. No congressman ever got voted out of office denying the bureaucracy money for equipment and maintenance. As my superior in the U.S. Army, Colonel Pete Mcwane, once said, "There is no glory in maintenance." These built-in reflexes produce an inability to know our current situation—until we have a big problem; then we play catch-up.

In my view, the rapid growth in student numbers that resulted from President Carter's initial strategic decision to place no limits on the inflow was almost an unalloyed good. The fact that both Jimmy Carter and his successor Ronald Reagan were fine with admitting essentially unlimited numbers of Chinese students and scholars suggests that there was a broad bipartisan consensus on this. PRC student numbers grew unchecked. The process was not carefully monitored, much less government-regulated. American universities resist outside intrusion by the federal government, and they were happy to see numbers grow for reasons of talent, research capacity, and, before long, money. Moreover, most of those involved believed the entire process contributed to peace.

With some variations, this is what happened during the entire engagement era across many domains. Engagement was a happening, not the weakness or naiveté of American China scholars or any single group of citizens or bureaucrats. From my perspective, the gains of this untamed process far exceeded the costs, but that is a debatable proposition in our society today. Security systems began to be strengthened in the wake of 9/11, and then, when security worries concerning China went from low in the late 1970s to high in the 2010s and beyond, the prior laissez-faire approach was viewed at home in a progressively more skeptical light.

Among key findings of the CSCPRC study were these:

- "In the decade following the 1979 normalization . . . more students and scholars will have studied in the United States than did so between 1860 and 1950, when approximately 30,000 came here" (p. 2). Fifty percent of Chinese going abroad to study were coming to the United States.

- The number of PRC students and scholars coming to the United States initially was a small fraction of all foreign students in the United States. Nonetheless, that percentage was growing rapidly. "This trend is likely to continue" (p. 2). It did, reaching 370,000 in 2019.

- Initially, most PRC students coming to the United States were sponsored by the PRC government (J-1 visa) and consequently were obligated to return to China after study, at least for a time. They were overwhelmingly studying in STEM fields, not social sciences, the humanities, business, or even agriculture. Over time the percentage of privately funded students (F-1 visa) rose, and enrollments in business, social sciences, and humanities grew.

- Soon after normalization, American institutions of higher education picked up an increasing share of the costs of officially sponsored PRC students. In 1979 the PRC paid about half the costs of its official students; that percentage had dropped to about one-third by 1983. Of course, later, when self-paying students from China became a much bigger part of the story, tuition from them became a major source of revenue for U.S. tertiary institutions. As time wore on, full-paying Chinese students increasingly subsidized financial aid for American students. As for Chinese graduate students, before long many were paid for by American institutions because of their roles as research assistants, teaching assistants, lab section leaders, and valued members of research teams.

- The number of American students going to China to study was very much smaller (and always has been) than the flow of Chinese to the United States. Those who did were concentrated in humanities, social sciences, and Chinese language study.

- Our report cautioned that such intensive educational exchange could eventually produce a "backlash" in the PRC. "The issue of maintaining China's cultural identity will be ever present," the report noted (p. 7).

The uneasy conjunction of PRC official values and Western ideas took a decisive turn toward conflict in April 2013, with the rise of Xi Jinping and the issuance of Central Document 9 by the Party General Office, which warned against constitutionalism, civil society, universal norms, and the Western vision of media in an open society. Since 2013, limitations on Western content in PRC syllabi have grown. Writings I could get published in China until well into the new millennium can no longer be openly published there. Unfortunately, Hong Kong has become progressively harder as a backup site for free publication and research. By 2023, access to online data sets was being diminished.

THE SCIENCE, TECHNOLOGY, AND ECONOMIC DEVELOPMENT PROGRAM

In the decade-plus before the Cultural Revolution, science and technology (S&T), aside from the strategic military domain (missiles, submarines, and nuclear warheads), were not a priority on the mainland due to continual anti-intellectual campaigns and resource scarcities. In the Cultural Revolution, S&T was grievously harmed, though Mao was always interested in high-energy physics.

Deng Xiaoping would change this. Even before Mao Zedong died in September 1976, Deng had made a limited comeback in 1973 (before he was again purged in early 1976 in the wake of Premier Zhou Enlai's death). In that brief interlude, Deng's priority had been energizing S&T. Upon Mao's demise, his immediate transitional successor, Hua Guofeng, touted the "Four Modernizations," the modernization of agriculture, industry, defense, and science and technology. Modernizing S&T had wide support in the wake of the Chairman's death.

China's basic research structure was in shambles. Taking pure research and introducing it into practical application was also problematic. Equipment, materials, and data were in short supply. Trained personnel were even scarcer. The World Bank and the NAS, NAE, and CSCPRC addressed these challenges in their respective activities with the PRC in the early postnormalization period. Part of the reason for the huge flow of government-sponsored S&T students from China to the United States was precisely to make up for "the lost generation(s)" educationally.

My second task at CSCPRC, therefore, was to formulate, with the help of an advisory committee, a Science, Technology, and Economic Development Program (STED) in which NAS, the NAE, and CSCPRC would cooperate with American industry, universities, and other research institutions to identify China's major development challenges, the solution of which would have benefits beyond simply China; identify appropriate technologies to address them; and share experiences with the PRC when consistent with U.S. national interests.

This effort was fully consistent with the overall thrust of American foreign policy, as President Reagan made clear in an April 27, 1984, speech at the Great Hall of the People in Beijing: "We think progress in four areas is particularly promising: trade, technology, investment, and exchanges of scientific and managerial expertise."

The three STED programs that we developed and implemented during my tenure in Washington were revealing about where China was at that time, the scale of the challenges facing it, and how good-willed people can cooperate to mutual advantage. This program was about addressing development problems with global impact and providing economic opportunities to both Chinese and Americans.

The three-part STED program had been agreed to during a delegation visit to the PRC headed by Walter A. Rosenblith, foreign secretary of the NAS (former provost at MIT and one of the few persons ever to be a member of the NAS, NAE, and the IOM). The counterpart on the Chinese side was the State Science and Technology Commission headed by Director Song Jian. Song had played a role in China's submarine ballistic missile development, was an expert on cybernetics, and was key in the development of the one-child policy. An important part of each of the three STED programs was a joint conference where the field research could be discussed and recommendations considered.

The first STED program with the Chinese was aimed at reducing postharvest food losses of fruits and vegetables. The in-China meeting occurred in November 1984.

FOOD

What was China's problem with food?[1] Simply put, the PRC was losing about 50 percent of its fruits and vegetables between harvest and the dinner table. Though figures are scarce, and there are comparability problems, the range of figures for fruit and vegetable postharvest loss in the United States at the time was 2–15 percent, depending on the commodity. Though the Chinese did not provide comprehensive loss figures (I doubt they had them), one of the Chinese papers at our conference noted in passing that "simple storage facilities (caves, ditches, etc.) have a capacity of 15 percent of the total fruit output" (p. 153). One can only imagine how the other 85 percent of fruit and vegetables was stored. While China might have had a popular image abroad for frugality, in food production at that time, it was extremely wasteful. Reducing postharvest food loss was a better, quicker way to improve the nutritional status of the Chinese people than simply relying on expanded production acreage or the "green revolution," though those were important too.

Our program brought together scientists and food industry experts to jointly address this problem. Indeed, it was not just a Chinese problem—if the PRC reduced its postharvest food loss, this would be a humanitarian plus and help reduce pressures on the global food system.

The American delegation, headed by Malcolm Bourne, Professor of Food Science & Technology at Cornell University, included Pacific Fruit Express, Sunkist Growers, FMC Corporation, the Florida Tomato Committee, Campbell Soup Company, and Ocean Spray.

The firms had tangible interests in China addressing the problem. For example, subsequently I went to Camden, New Jersey, to the Campbell Soup Company headquarters to give a talk. At that time, the firm was contemplating growing and processing tomatoes in China as a substitute for hauling soup or ingredients across the Pacific because, after all, it was mostly water, which is heavy and expensive to haul. Moreover, various new tomato products made in the PRC could be sold directly in China and exported from there to other Asian locations. This in-China production would have positive back-linkages into China's entire agricultural and food production system.

Beyond all this, the problem of food variety in China was of concern. Diet was regionally specific and monotonous at this time—little citrus in the north in winter, for instance. In wintertime in North China, there was a surfeit of cabbage, stacked like cordwood on the sidewalks, in family courtyards, and in the corridors of apartment buildings, its pungent odor pervading entire buildings. Everyone ate cabbage, lots of it, until the next season's crop of something else became available. This pattern existed because there was so little capacity for long-term storage or long-distance transport of commodities. Later, better storage, transport, cold chains, warehousing, and packaging would reduce loss and increase diet variety.

While it took time, postharvest food loss in the PRC has been dramatically reduced over the intervening decades. I should note that most of the progress reflects the hard work of the Chinese. Of our three programs, I consider this to have been the most successful, embodying the kind of collaboration toward which both countries should strive.

Clean Coal

In the years since this field research and academic conference occurred in May 1985, many specialists have come to view "clean coal" as an oxymoron. That is true in terms of the global CO_2 emission problem. However, it also is true that part of China's coal problem is that coal combustion in the 1980s, and even today, was inefficient, sending enormous amounts of energy, sulfur, and coal particulate into the atmosphere. The emitted particulate and sulfur were ruinous to public health, causing and exacerbating respiratory problems. The sulfur produced acid rain, affecting agriculture in China, and it came down on the Korean Peninsula and Japan among other locations. This generated foreign policy friction. Interestingly, Ohio faced similar external complaints from Canada and internally from U.S. states downwind suffering from Ohio's power plant coal combustion emissions.

While the long-term solution to coal as an energy source was to ween China off it entirely, in the interim, significant health, environment, and efficiency gains could be achieved by simply washing and desulfurizing coal before combustion, increasing the efficiency of combustion and then scrubbing flu emissions to the degree possible. Coal is the PRC's largest conventional energy source. Considering alternatives, such as tapping its large hydro-power potential, creates other problems. Trying to "clean up coal" is a transitional improvement, not a solution.

An irony is that the more S&T reduces the downsides of coal combustion, the more one makes coal inadvertently more attractive to users. In 1998 China consumed twenty-nine exajoules of coal, and by 2020 that number had reached eighty-two, more than the rest of the world combined.

For our project, we had site visits and a seminar in Taiyuan, the heart of coal country (China's West Virginia). There we examined the pretreatment of coal, desulfurization, and methanol fuel blends.[2]

For me, one of the central conclusions of the project was that one problem cannot be considered in isolation from others. The delegation found that converting coal into methanol could theoretically provide a relatively clean burning auto fuel and that constructing conversion plants close to mine pitheads would be efficient. However, this strategy required huge water sources that were absent in the arid northwest. Similarly, developing coal slurry technology also required water that was unavailable. Even simply washing coal (which accomplishes a lot) required water. China's coal problem was linked to its water problem.

Addressing the water problem in the north leads one to contemplate gigantic water transfer projects from China's water-surplus south. This had long been a gleam in water planners' eyes and has subsequently come to pass. Yet, moving water from the Yangtze Basin to north of the Yellow River would have unknown ecological effects and could spread water-borne diseases from one basin to another. China has no small problems. Big problems often require big projects. Big projects have large uncertainties and undesirable impacts.

Another consideration is that, from the Chinese perspective, the outside world, not least the United States, is quick to criticize China's energy plans. Many energy sources have significant downsides, and the scale of any Chinese mass adoption of a particular technology seems threatening along some dimension. Think nuclear. Wind and solar energy are more acceptable ecologically but cannot resolve the entire problem, though the economics of these technologies is changing rapidly. The outside world finds big negatives for hydropower plants, coal-fired power generation, and nuclear energy, leaving the Chinese to wonder whether the West simply is indifferent to their energy needs and dilemmas. Even when China becomes the world's largest solar panel producer, Washington finds Beijing's subsidies to that industry to constitute unfair competition.

MOVING BASIC RESEARCH TO APPLICATION AND INTERNATIONAL TECHNOLOGY TRANSFER

The third seminar dealt with the factors inhibiting or promoting the transfer of basic S&T research into economic production. The challenge was to get useful basic research into the economy's bloodstream fast. We also were interested in the obstacles to the transfer of technology between America and China. This problem brought a PRC team to the Wingspread Conference Center in Racine, Wisconsin, in October 1985, to meet American counterparts.[3]

In this current era in which those who promoted engagement with China are often portrayed as enthusiasts unmindful of keeping America's competitive edge, in the mid-1980s, the NAS and NAE were in step with President Reagan's articulated policy of knocking down Cold War embargo–era restrictions on technology transfer to the PRC. Reagan put it crisply in his April 27, 1984, speech in Beijing.

> Last June, I instructed our government to liberalize controls over the export to China of high technology products, such as computers and laboratory instruments. Our policies on technology transfer will continue to evolve along with our overall relationship and the development of broader cooperation between us. May I emphasize to the members of the scientific community here today: The relaxing of export controls reflects my determination that China be treated as a friendly, non-allied nation *and that the United States be fully prepared to cooperate in your modernization.* [Emphasis added]

With respect to our NAS-NAE-CSCPRC program, the findings of this technology transfer project were several, one being that *both* nations faced challenges moving basic research into production, though some of the specific barriers differed between the two nations. One important problem area concerned the transfer of technology between the United States and China. Establishing copyright, patent, and licensing mechanisms was essential. Even at this early date, the Chinese were particularly focused on tech transfer in the micro-electronics and pharmaceutical industries. Chinese-made pharmaceuticals, as noted previously, have been a huge problem, as we can still see today in China's less-than-stellar development of COVID-19 vaccines and treatments. For technology to be effectively transferred to China required the development of a legal system there.

Another NAS study (*The Corson Report*, 1982, with which I was not associated) pertained to how to think about export controls with respect to the Soviet Union. The key formulation, which remains relevant as we think about China today, is the report's injunction that U.S. export control policy should seek to fence off fewer items of technology and, instead, build higher fences around only the most critical technologies for which the United States is practically the sole source. Washington's core strategy should be to out-innovate the competition, not construct a technological Great Wall. Such a strategy conforms to America's comparative advantage, its creative dynamism, and its capacities.

OUTWARD-FACING EXPERIENCES AT CSCPRC

My third duty while in Washington was to be outward facing for the CSCPRC concerning visiting Chinese delegations, meetings involving the U.S. government, the academies, private sector actors, and cultivating project funders. One occasion is worth recounting because it relates to the openness of the Reagan administration and the degree to which the work of the academies was pulling in the same direction as national policy. This vignette provides a glimpse of leadership in a profound, human way.

MEETING PRESIDENT REAGAN

By the spring of 1984, after a very rocky start for U.S.-China relations in the early days of the Reagan administration (largely over Taiwan arms sales), things had improved considerably. President Reagan's team was looking for a foreign policy success that would position the president well for his upcoming reelection campaign, and relations with Moscow were especially raw in the wake of the September 1983 Soviet shootdown of a civilian Boeing 747 South Korean Airlines (KAL 007) aircraft on its way from New York to Seoul, via Anchorage. Two hundred and sixty-eight souls perished, including a U.S. Congressman from Georgia, Larry McDonald. For the Reagan administration, the time seemed ripe to turn to China. U.S.-China educational relations were igniting interest.

One day in April 1984, a White House staff member called the CSCPRC office asking that we organize a group of Chinese students studying in the United States to meet with President Reagan and Vice President George H. W. Bush as part of the buildup to the president's China trip later that month. We agreed and identified twelve Chinese students in the D.C. area to meet the president in the Roosevelt Room of the White House.

In the days immediately before the White House meeting, President Reagan more than once said to those around him how much he looked forward to it, recalling that America had always been particularly helpful to Chinese students and supportive of Sino-American educational exchange. He mentioned the United States dedicating Chinese reparations from the Boxer Rebellion at the turn of the century for use to support the education of Chinese students in the United States (Boxer Indemnity Students) and the founding of Tsinghua College as a preparatory school for students going to the United States. Many of China's accomplished intellectuals benefited from this effort.

White House staff cautioned President Reagan that the combination of U.S. forces as part of the Eight-Power Expeditionary Force sent to quell the Boxer Rebellion violence, and the subsequent reparations themselves, were a sensitive topic in China. Reagan seemed not to be overly concerned. I understand that the president was "cautioned" more than once on this point.

On the day of the meeting on the afternoon of April 16, 1984, the door leading from the nearby Oval Office opened, and in walked President Reagan; Vice President George Herbert Walker Bush already was in the room. Both Reagan and Bush were all smiles, and, of course, the vice president had been Chief of the Liaison Office in Beijing some years earlier (1974–1976). The president got right to the point, with a National Archives record of the meeting preserving the interaction that I also heard:

> I just have a few minutes, and I know you've been in good hands here with the Vice President.

> You represent 11,000 students from China who are here in our country now. And I don't know how much history you've studied, but you know, this all began many years ago in the history of your country when there was a situation—similar to something we'd had in our own country—called the Boxer Rebellion. And countries from Europe and the United States and others, we went in with armed forces to rescue our people who were there from this strife and trouble.

> And as I have read history, all the other countries then imposed reparation payments on China except the United States. And the United

States said, "No, use our share as a scholarship fund to send your students here and ours to your country so we can get to know each other, and never again should there be any bitterness between our two peoples."

So, you are coming along here as a very definite part of what I think is a nice note in history that hasn't too often happened between great nations. *And you're certainly welcome, but we'd like to see the 11,000 become a hundred thousand. And we're going to work toward that goal.* [Emphasis added]

I'll probably be getting back to your country before you are. Why do I say, "getting back to it"? [Laughter] George has been there. I've never been there. It'll be my first trip, and I'm looking forward to it very much.

But I understand that the only way we can possibly have a chance to meet is that—it's so crowded in here—is if I step outside that door in the hall, and then if each of you come out one at a time, and we'll all have our pictures taken out there, and I get a chance to meet you individually.

But again, welcome. And I'll send them back in here.

I recount this at some length because it seems to me that at that moment, we saw genuine leadership at work. Reagan had a deep sense of what it takes to connect with people. Academics often think that getting all the facts straight is the secret of effectiveness. Leaders understand the deeper needs and motivations of people. The students weren't listening to whether Reagan had all the facts straight. They were amazed that he had ever heard of the Boxer Rebellion and that he had a constructive view of how the past could serve to make a better future.

On their way out, the PRC students couldn't stop talking about it. "*Taidu*" (attitude) or "*jingshen*" (spirit) get you a long way in China. With a positive attitude and spirit, errors can be forgiven; without them, nothing works. One Chinese remark has stuck with me over the years: "You

Americans think that if we solve problems, we can be friends. We Chinese say, if we are friends, we can solve problems."

ESTABLISHING AN OFFICE IN BEIJING

My fourth task at CSCPRC was to work to establish a NAS-CSCPRC Office in Beijing to help manage the explosive growth in student exchanges, facilitate American faculty and graduate student access for field and archival research, promote collaborative research, manage CSCPRC programs and in-China conferences, and "promote and maintain non-governmental programs between the scientific communities of the United States and the PRC."

While we achieved the objective of establishing a Beijing office, it subsequently ran into problems.

Our PRC counterpart was the Chinese Academy of Sciences (CAS). This was a natural, symmetrical partnership, though CAS is under governmental sway in a way NAS is not. The authoritative Chinese person with whom I dealt as the negotiating and planning process proceeded was Yan Dongsheng, the renowned ceramic engineer (nose cones and warheads) who had received his PhD from the University of Illinois in 1949 and did postdoctoral work in 1950 in the United States before returning to China that year. Persecuted during the Cultural Revolution, he was elected a vice president of CAS in 1981.

The motivating idea behind the push to open an office in China was that we needed a representative on the ground who had his/her fingers on the pulse of the relationship. We wanted to be as familiar with the Chinese academic and scientific community as possible. This might seem to have been obvious, but there was significant resistance to the idea from several quarters both in the United States and in China. With the establishment of an in-China office, we would need to recruit office management with deft hands.

While the office was established (on July 19, 1985), that deft on-the-ground management was not present at critical moments. In retrospect, it probably was unrealistic to think that any person could have been adroit under the circumstances that emerged in the very late 1980s. The office became an item of controversy by mid-1989.

The first obstacle to setting up the office was simply the fact that no Western academic or similar organization had done so before. The National Council for U.S.-China Trade opened an office in 1979, but it focused on business and trade. There was no template for an untethered foreign academic presence in Beijing. Thus, all aspects of setting up and running an academic office had to be invented. Never underestimate the power of people in any endeavor who say, "We never did this before," somehow thinking this is dispositive.

Beyond generic conservatism, institutions that play a gateway role in any society usually want to limit the opening of additional doors by others in their carefully constructed wall. Both the Chinese and the U.S. governments had their anxious elements when it came to having an independent Western academic presence in China. Up to this point, the U.S. government had taken the lead on driving ahead with all the national interagency agreements in the educational realm, a process in which I was deeply involved with Secretary Califano, though states and educational/research institutions also were making their own arrangements, as we saw in Ohio.

Consequently, the U.S. government, particularly the Press and Culture Section of the U.S. Embassy in Beijing, had concerns about whether a NAS-CSCPRC Office would supplant, or intrude into, its primacy and zone of responsibility. The embassy, for instance, had a key role in the Fulbright Program. Some in the U.S. Embassy seemed to worry that having an independent American academic "representative" would mean that there would be no hierarchical accountability within a very delicate corner of the U.S.-China relationship. The staffing plan announced upon the office's opening was that "visiting professors from the United States will serve as rotating advisors to the Office." As it worked out in the late 1980s, U.S. government anxieties proved warranted.

For their part, Chinese counterparts had their mirror-image concerns. China has always operated under the presumption that the presence of outsiders needs to be government managed. The bureaucratic vocabulary (*waiban*, managing outsiders) makes that clear. The concept of a nonbusiness organization operating in the realms of ideas and education having unmediated contact with Chinese citizens and other foreigners on PRC soil was heterodox, anxiety-inducing.

What might be called the "maximum fear" on the Chinese side was that this foreign presence could become entangled in PRC domestic politics, that U.S. academics might become involved with domestic dissidents, and that the Western commitment to academic freedom would create relationships that could prove volatile in Chinese politics.

There was, of course, also the large and more mundane issue of cost. We could not fund a "private" academic office with government money. The presence would be expensive. Private sector funding would have to carry the burden. Eventually, the Luce, Ford, Mellon, Starr, and Carnegie philanthropies played critical roles. Among America's institutional and diplomatic strengths is that it has a philanthropic sector to fund public goods, avoiding problems that taking government or business funds can create.

Despite all the misgivings and resistance, the office idea moved forward. It fell to Mary Bullock and her staff at CSCPRC to carry the ball over the finish line. They did a superb job. In my last conversation with Yan Dongsheng before returning to Ohio State, he said to me: "Mike, promise me that the office will never become involved in domestic politics in China." In good faith, I reflexively (without authority), and in retrospect naively, said, "Of course not." I was wrong.

By saying I was "wrong," I do not cast aspersions on those who were forced to make decisions in a future I did not foresee.

Nineteen eighty-nine was a tumultuous time in Beijing and in U.S.-China relations, even before the June 4 bloodshed in Tiananmen Square. President George H. W. Bush had come to Beijing in February, shortly after his inauguration, to solidify relations with Deng Xiaoping, hoping to dampen the possibility that Moscow and Beijing would once again move into closer alignment to Washington's disadvantage. This, as we would come to see, occurred about three decades later.

In the course of President Bush's visit, China's well-known dissident astrophysicist Fang Lizhi had been invited by the U.S. Embassy to the farewell banquet hosted by the U.S. president in honor of Deng Xiaoping at the Sheraton Great Wall Hotel. Deng Xiaoping had expressed great antipathy toward Fang, and the astrophysicist was intercepted by Public Security on the way to the banquet and prevented from attending. Professor Perry Link, head of the NAS-CSCPRC office in Beijing, was accompanying Professor Fang during the incident.

American interest in Fang, and his frustrated attempt to attend the event at which the American president and Deng Xiaoping would be present, put the professor even more squarely in the Chinese regime's crosshairs and elevated the astrophysicist's prominence in the ongoing American debate about China's human rights and the appropriate U.S. response.

Subsequently, in the context of the June 4 bloodshed of 1989, Professor Link actively helped Fang Lizhi and his wife reach the American Embassy to seek refuge amidst the domestic dragnet. Professor Fang and his spouse remained U.S. Ambassador and Mrs. Lilley's unexpected houseguests for almost exactly a year until they were permitted to leave the country, eventually settling in the United States.[4]

Fully understandable, and morally commendable, one thing was for certain. The NAS-CSCPRC Office in Beijing, which Professor Link led, found itself in the middle of Chinese politics and at the center of U.S.-China controversy. What Yan Dongsheng had most feared came to pass, and my blithe assurance about no political involvement seemed hollow to him, I would suppose.

After the news about Fang Lizhi being in the American Embassy broke, along with a full description of the role Professor Link had played, I called NAS President Frank Press, whom I so respect, to tell him about my earlier conversation with Yan Dongsheng and how different things now looked. I expressed concern for all the Chinese who had stuck their necks out by supporting the office's opening. I also urged Press not to halt scientific exchanges with China. Frank stood firmly with Link's decision, saying that as the leader of the NAS that had stood by the dissident Soviet physicist Andrei Sakharov in 1973, he and NAS could reach no other decision.[5]

I have often thought about what I would have done had I been in Link's shoes, particularly given my own prior assurances to Professor Yan. My bottom line is that there is no question that morally one must try to help the people on your doorstep, even at the expense of a prior assurance given under far different circumstances, an assurance that was never within my capacity to fulfill.

However, regarding the prior management of the NAS-CSCPRC Office's interaction with individuals and communities about whom the PRC regime had clearly expressed concern, my instinct would have been to be more circumspect. My impulse would have been to keep a greater distance from domestic politics in China for fear of jeopardizing the gradual progress that was being made domestically and in the U.S.-China relationship. I feel this way not simply because of organizational interests but also because association with Westerners in areas of controversy is not always doing the involved Chinese persons a favor, to put it delicately. I say this knowing that the then U.S. Ambassador to China, Winston Lord, and his spouse, the renowned writer Bette Bao Lord, had a lively interaction with intellectuals in salons and on campuses. Link was not out of line with where elements of the U.S. government and American society were pushing, bringing us closer to the regime's "red lines."

The stark reality is that managing U.S.-China academic relations is never free of the danger that political and academic affairs will become intertwined. This is inevitable. Chinese governing impulses are to control as much as possible, running into American ideas and values.

There is a sequel to the story about the NAS-CSCPRC Office in China. In the next chapter, I deal with the period of my presidency of NCUSCR. Because other U.S. organizations by then had offices in Beijing, I thought it was time for the National Committee to have one too.

NOTES

1. National Academy of Sciences/National Academy of Engineering, US-China Science, Technology, and Economic Development Program, *Postharvest Food Losses in Fruits and Vegetables* (National Academy Press, 1986).

2. National Academy of Sciences/National Academy of Engineering, US-China Science, Technology, and Economic Development Program, *Clean Coal: Pretreatment and Methanol Conversion* (National Academy of Sciences, National Academy of Engineering, 1988).

3. National Academy of Sciences/National Academy of Engineering, US-China Science, Technology, and Economic Development Program, *Transfer of Science and*

Technology Research into Production (National Academy of Sciences and National Academy of Engineering, 1987).

4. Even more than twenty years later, National Public Radio described what happened as: "Perry Link, an eminent China scholar, was living in China at the time as the Beijing director for the National Academy of Sciences. Months before Tiananmen Square, he met Fang Lizhi at a party and the two men hit it off and became friends." NPR Staff, "For Dissidents, Escape Means Fighting from Afar," May 5, 2012, https://www.npr.org/2012/05/05/152098555/for-dissidents-escape-means-fighting-from-afar.

5. Frank Press at NRC/EXOF, June 7, 1989, 3:19 p.m. (from the files of NAS).

CHAPTER EIGHT

Life Has No Tenure

(Into a New Decade)

WASHINGTON WAS A TRANSFORMATIVE EXPERIENCE FOR ME. AS WE returned to Ohio in 1985, I began to think of making a change. I was drawn to the boundaries between academia and public affairs, not only by my Washington experiences but also by my Ohio opportunities.

Ohio State had been good to me; I loved teaching and was determined to meet my duty to students, particularly those in the PhD program. I had excellent PhD students at Ohio State who went on to have varied, successful careers in colleges and universities, federal agencies, state government, and business, as well as individuals who went on to work in the PRC and Taiwan playing important roles in their respective governments and societies. One student from the PRC, after receiving his PhD from OSU, founded a pro-democracy NGO in China, an organization still in existence today. Another OSU Taiwan student became a minister in Taipei, as did a later Hopkins PhD student.

As I returned to Columbus for what proved to be two more academic years, I was receptive to new professional possibilities. One senior colleague asked, "You would give up tenure?" "Life has no tenure," I responded.

NEW YORK: THE NATIONAL COMMITTEE

In 1987 the NCUSCR's long-serving and successful president, Arthur Rosen ("Art"), announced he would retire once a successor was named.

Former Governor of Pennsylvania Raymond ("Ray") Shafer, the National Committee's chairman, promptly formed a search committee, and in the fullness of time, I was offered the job. I enthusiastically accepted.

One thing I had to decide concerning the committee's offer was whether to request a leave of absence from OSU, keeping a life preserver nearby if things did not work out in New York. Alternatively, I could make a clean break and put my full energy into this new endeavor. Should I burn my bridge? If I gave up tenure, the odds were strong that at a later date, I would be unable to return to academe—it can be unforgiving to those who leave the monastery.

Susan and I decided to make a clean break, one reason being that it is difficult to lead individuals, or an organization, if one has not fully thrown in your lot with them—your own fate must be linked to that of the organization and colleagues you presume to lead. Keeping a life preserver betrays a lack of confidence and undermines the legitimacy that accompanies sharing a destiny with colleagues.

Our family moved to the New York City area, Maplewood, New Jersey, to be precise, after the spring academic quarter at OSU had concluded in 1987. New Jersey is so much more than a punchline in a Saturday Night Live skit. In Maplewood everybody knew the long-serving Mayor Robert H. Grasmere, elected and reelected eleven times—he sometimes wore white buck shoes. Annually, there was a Fourth of July circus on the village lawn with a large fraction of the town turning out. The ambiance of Maplewood was much more in harmony with our Ohio experience than common lore might lead one to expect. It was a lot more than the *Sopranos* and petrol dumps along the Hudson River and its estuary. Its towns have great names, like Hoboken, Bayonne, West Orange, Hackensack, Holiday Heights, Saddle River, and my personal favorite, Ho-Ho-Kus. After joining the National Committee Board, former New Jersey Governor Tom Kean and I had great conversations about New Jersey, including Mayor Grasmere's effective leadership.

This move from the Midwest was not without its anxieties. For our children, it meant moving from an ordered, stable community and small private schools to big New Jersey public schools. We all shed a tear when we crossed the border of Ohio going east where one passes beneath a sign straddling the freeway announcing that we were leaving "The Heart of It All."

The succession at NCUSCR was carefully planned so that I could benefit from Art Rosen's mentoring, meet people in the New York philanthropic and corporate worlds, generally learn the ropes, and assume my new position on January 1, 1988. In due course, Professor Kevin O'Brien was recruited to take the slot I had occupied at Ohio State, where he stayed until he moved to the University of California-Berkeley in 2000.

Art Rosen possessed a wealth of experience, had advice a neophyte from the heartland and West Coast like me found invaluable (including how to do a fast walk in New York City), and he was empathetic—I admired him greatly. In 1946, after he mustered out of military service in World War II, Art was posted to Shanghai and subsequently served in the U.S. Foreign Service in Hong Kong, North Vietnam, Thailand, Singapore, and Australia. He was appointed "executive director" of the National Committee in January 1975, becoming president on May 1 of that year, succeeding Charles Yost, who became chairman of the board. Art passed away in December 2021 at the age of ninety-nine.

Between a new job, a new home in a different culture, and a rapidly changing China to deal with, my learning curve was steep.

At the very outset of my short apprenticeship in the second half of 1987, Deng Xiaoping's disabled son, Deng Pufang, was scheduled to visit the United States in October under Committee auspices, a trip during which he would meet the president. The younger Deng would be making a tour of the United States to publicize the challenges of disabled persons in China and be exposed to relevant practices then standard in America. Deng Pufang's health was tenuous due to paralysis sustained as a consequence of being pushed or otherwise falling from a building on the Peking University campus during the Cultural Revolution in 1968. His health was a constant worry for us. Among the special needs was an airplane that was configured for his safe, comfortable movement.

Having just arrived at the committee, I had not been involved in the trip's planning, but the younger Deng's imminent arrival was a major office preoccupation. With respect to securing a private aircraft suitable for Deng Pufang and his large entourage, Malcolm Forbes, chairman, publisher, and editor-in-chief of Forbes magazine, *The Capitalist Tool*, offered his corporate aircraft gratis. This plane had a nonrectangular large bed in its stateroom, a lavish bathroom with golden fixtures, and racks in the back for his lavender-colored Harley Davidson. It was the plane he flew around on with Elizabeth Taylor.

Living in New Jersey, I sometimes drove past the north end of the landing field at Newark Liberty International Airport. One day I noticed Malcolm Forbes's plane, with the "Capitalist Tool" logo emblazoned on its tail, parked on the tarmac, its gold and forest green paint job shimmering—it was a 727 with a range of four thousand miles. Before seeing this aircraft, I had not realized just what a statement the plane made, and I became concerned that an enterprising journalist/photographer would generate a story, with pictures, the gist of which would be, "China has gone capitalist and Deng Xiaoping's family leads the charge." As Americans, we always are attuned to signs that the long-awaited political transformation is at hand in communist systems. I didn't want to have my debut at the National Committee characterized by a public relations fiasco.

When I got into the office the day I saw the plane, I approached Art and asked if he realized the plane was named "The Capitalist Tool" and asked whether we should be concerned about how this might play out in the mass media, particularly if there were a picture of Deng Pufang getting on or off the aircraft. Art did not think that this was a big deal. I told him that I thought we ought to at least inform the PRC Foreign Ministry and get its concurrence so that if things went haywire, they would have been forewarned. I anticipated that the Foreign Ministry would at least take time to deliberate, and chances were that the Ministry would be gun-shy. In reality, the ministry got right back to us and essentially said, "No problem." We then proceeded, but we did take the precaution of having the plane pull into isolated spots at airfields to avoid photographs. There was no problem, as Art had predicted.

I learned two things from this: one was that China was changing, and, two, we Americans need to avoid trying to be more "Chinese" than the Chinese.

Figure 8.1.   Deng Pufang and Author during Deng's 1987 trip to America to assess best practices concerning the disabled. Photo by David M. Lampton.

New York fascinated me, not least because it is a strategically minded city. The National Committee was then located on the corner of 1st Avenue and East 44th Street (777 United Nations Plaza, 9th Floor), overlooking the United Nations, the East River, and the iconic Pepsi-Cola sign on the Queens side of the river. At each fall's gathering of the UN General Assembly, world leaders entered the semicircular drive in front of the Secretariat Building below my window, with sharpshooters ringing the area from their strategic high-elevations atop surrounding buildings (including ours); police boats patrolled the East River on the far side of the UN from my perch. Seeing Yasser Arafat from my window was memorable, exceeded only when I found Arafat and his thuggish-looking bodyguards a few feet behind me as we emerged from a Peking duck restaurant some years later in Beijing. Being from California and more recently Ohio, all this was exciting.

For me, joining the National Committee meant taking up a job where you actually had to meet a payroll, develop a vibrant program, and deal with a situation of U.S.-China relations that I already had concluded was headed for tumult. To cap it off, Henry Kissinger established a new and potentially competitive organization called the America-China Society. The two organizations with sizeable membership overlap eventually worked out a friendly absorption of the Society by the National Committee, due to the considerable efforts of board member, Herbert J. Hansell, a partner and later counsel at the Jones Day law firm chairing its international practice. In the 1977–1979 period, Herb had been Legal Advisor to the Department of State and developed the legal structure under which U.S.-China relations were conducted after normalization. Steve Orlins, later president of the National Committee, worked with Herb at the Department of State at this critical juncture.

THE NATIONAL COMMITTEE: HISTORY AND INVOLVEMENT
In 1981, while at Ohio State, I was asked to join the NCUSCR Board of Directors, my first such board membership opportunity. The committee, founded in 1966 by American academic, religious, civic, and business leaders, had been at the forefront of arguing, as A. Doak Barnett did in testimony before the Senate Committee on Foreign Relations that same

year, for "containment without isolation" as the desirable future touchstone for U.S. policy toward the PRC. The committee's founding was an act of spontaneous citizen organizing, not U.S. government initiative. It had its origins, in part, in trying to end a war for which China was a major component of the rationale.

In 1966, some members of the National Committee Board met with President Johnson who, on one hand, wanted to improve relations with China but, on the other, found that waging the Vietnam War made that politically infeasible. Using Chinese "aggression" as the rationale for the war, and simultaneously moving in a less confrontational direction with Beijing, seemed impossible. As to Beijing's receptivity to policy change, the surging Cultural Revolution meant it was difficult for Mao to simultaneously attack his domestic enemies for taking the capitalist road while he would be cozying up to American imperialism. The threat from the Soviet Union was not yet sufficiently alarming to force Mao to change strategic course to deter Moscow.

Three years after the committee's founding, it convened a National Convocation with 2,500 participants. Beyond armed clashes along the Sino-Soviet border, the convocation's timing was critical and auspicious, occurring as the transition to the Nixon administration was underway. The new president had indicated receptivity to changing directions with China two years earlier. John D. Rockefeller III took a forward-leaning position at the convocation, saying (as Mary Bullock reports): "Our thinking about that great country has been dominated by fear, so much so that in the recent past many regarded it as virtually treasonable to even raise the question of rethinking China policy."[1]

The extended Rockefeller family, through the Rockefeller Foundation, the Rockefeller Brothers Fund, and other vehicles, was a supporter of most key Asia-oriented NGOs, with members of the family in effect covering the fields of artistic and cultural endeavor (the Asia Society, Japan Society, and Asian Cultural Council), business (Chase Manhattan Bank), and foreign policy (the Council on Foreign Relations and NCUSCR).

There was considerable overlap among those active in the leadership of the National Committee and the Council on Foreign Relations. Many years later, David Rockefeller (youngest son of John D. Rockefeller Jr., and grandson of John D. Rockefeller), who was greatly interested in China, invited me to lunch at the Rainbow Room level of Rockefeller Center. On the way up in the elevator, with a start, he said, "Oh, I forgot to make a reservation!" I replied, "Mr. Rockefeller, I think they will have a table for you. This is the Rockefeller Center!" He laughed.

Preeminent China scholars were sequentially committee chairman in the organization's early years: Robert Scalapino, A. Doak Barnett, Alexander Eckstein, and Lucian Pye. Charles Yost, previously U.S. ambassador to the United Nations, was committee president from 1973– 1975 and thereafter served as chairman until 1981.[2] All continued their participation in the committee until their respective deaths, and the organization prospered by its ability to continually utilize their experience while providing enlarging opportunities for younger colleagues coming into the field. When the definitive history of the National Committee is told, one of its biggest contributions will be seen to have been the staff, interns, and others who got their first professional China opportunity at the organization and built a network in the field without parallel.

For me, joining the committee board opened up the world of NGOs and the challenges of being representative, bringing knowledge to bear on complex issues so that the broader public could understand, and dealing with the worlds of Congress and the executive branch, as well as, importantly, the Chinese. It changed my life.

My work with the National Committee Board was my first opportunity to see what running an organization entails: hiring and retaining excellent staff, meeting a payroll, dealing with a board of directors, addressing the human problems of personnel, and building bases of support in broader, diverse communities. Just learning what financial audits entail and how to read a balance sheet were additions to my knowledge. I made a lifetime of good friends and colleagues—Art Rosen, Doug Murray, Jan Berris, Ros Daly, and Elizabeth Knup were key players in the committee for decades. They are integral to the National Committee story and to its longevity and contributions. Doug Murray, variously president, board member, and program designer and participant, has a special place in the committee's history and heart.

Ros Daly, our vice president for administration, was key. She had administrative principles which I adopted: "Manage the organization like a business"; "Do as little as possible bureaucratically"; "Never trust instinct in hiring"; "Staff are first priority on budget"; and, "Always be prepared for Murphy's Law—if something can go wrong, it will." On only one issue in these regards did my instinct differ a bit from hers—I could never fully divorce instinct from hiring. Also, while staff is the priority, without an interesting and important program, one would be unable to attract financial and other support and retain skilled staff.

The time I came onto the board of directors (1981–1982) was an eventful moment in the committee's life. The organization's long-serving chairman, Ambassador Charles Yost, passed away in 1981, and MIT political scientist and China scholar Lucian Pye, himself having grown up in China's northwest coal country in a missionary family, served as interim chair until a permanent chair was found in the person of Raymond P. Shafer, the former Republican governor of Pennsylvania (1967–1971). Ray served as committee chair from 1982 to 1991.

Shafer was that now nearly extinct brand of big-tent Republican who was moderate on both foreign and domestic issues. Throughout his political career, Ray had a close association with Nelson Rockefeller, serving as his counselor when Rockefeller became vice president under President Gerald Ford (December 1974) after Richard Nixon's Watergate-precipitated resignation. The Rockefeller family not only had been associated with early calls to reassess China policy but, in the more distant past dating to the first decades of the twentieth century, had heavily invested in China's medical and educational development through the Rockefeller Foundation, as Mary Brown Bullock's lifetime body of writing amply demonstrates. When I was with Secretary Califano in China to sign the health agreement in 1979, an important stop for us was the Chinese Academy of Medical Sciences housed on the grounds of the old Peking Union Medical College, in its first decades supported by the Rockefeller Foundation and professionally guided by Johns Hopkins medical and public health talent.

Thus, Ray Shafer was a link to the moderate, centrist Republican coalition that represented not only the heartland of the country but also the cosmopolitan elites of the East. He was trusted by key players in the party of Ronald Reagan, who became president in 1981. Up until this moment, the committee had not been well connected to this part of the Republican Party. The issue was: Who can reach Reagan? Who can talk to Ed Meese (on the presidential transition team, counselor to the president, and later Attorney General) and Caspar Weinberger (Defense Secretary)? Ray could do these things and articulate the commonsense middle in politics.

Ray had relatively little prior knowledge of China but instinctively believed that it was central to America's future; thus, he wanted to contribute to the effort to make the relationship productive. Reflecting on Ray and organizational management more broadly, many different people, with different skills and interests, are necessary to make an organization work. One reason Ray and I got along so well is that we both grew up outside the East Coast corridor of power and social standing.

Tiananmen: A Gigantic Challenge
The Start

I had program inclinations when I assumed day-to-day responsibility for the committee on January 1, 1988. Although possible political instability in China remained in the back of my mind, as I had signaled in earlier writing, that was not the future for which the National Committee Board or I were planning.

The board's and my first concern was that ties between China and the United States were multiplying so fast, at so many levels, that the question would become, "Why do we need a special purpose National Committee to interact with a country with which so many throughout our society already are dealing?" What was our value added beyond the yawn-inducing mantra that China requires special handling? The biggest threat to an NGO is not opposition but apathy, indifference.

Following that concern was a second. I felt we were in a unique position to expand our activities in an area where we had a comparative advantage—bringing together decision-makers and opinion leaders in the two countries to address policy issues of common concern. The committee had convening power that no other U.S. organization possessed.

We needed to be proactive in addressing issues. We had to move beyond exchanging ping-pong and basketball teams, gymnasts, and martial arts troupes, although they all had been the perfect door openers to the PRC and played an indispensable role in getting the ball of normalization rolling. This story is wonderfully told in Pete Millwood's *Improbable Diplomats: How Ping-Pong Players, Musicians, and Scientists Remade US-China Relations.*

One of the early programs reflecting this direction was a diverse American group going to Tibet in 1991 and issuing a report upon its return. The report was delivered in person to the Dalai Lama among others. For me, this program interest built on my 1981 trip to Tibet, described in chapter 11. Dealing with such sensitive policy issues as Tibet meant that some National Committee programs ran the risk of running afoul of domestic politics in China, America, or both. At the board meeting considering this issue, the discussion was animated, but the board agreed to proceed.

A third issue was how to put U.S.-China relations in the appropriate global and multilateral contexts. The very name "National Committee on U.S.-China Relations" suggested an exclusively bilateral perspective was built into our self-conception. But the reality was that, for instance, Europe had major interests in China too. Having Europe and America coordinate policy would give the U.S. leverage with the PRC and rein in some of Washington's worst unilateralist impulses. In practice, Americans and Europeans rarely coordinated, or even talked, about China. I hoped the committee could help fill this gap. In this transatlantic thrust over the years, we cooperated with Professor David Shambaugh, who throughout his career had fostered transatlantic conversation on China policy and, starting in 1991, from his base at the School of Oriental and African Studies, was the editor of *The China Quarterly* in London.

Similarly, I felt that seeing Washington-Beijing ties in the context of Greater China (Taiwan, Hong Kong, and the Chinese diaspora) and in a multilateral context was important. The concept was that economic and security interdependencies among Hong Kong, Taiwan, and scattered Chinese ethnic populations meant that the United States and others did not have the luxury of making policy with respect to Beijing without considering the effects on Taiwan, Hong Kong, and the diaspora.[3] Environmental challenges and several other issues were intrinsically multilateral and global in character.

In short, we thought that encouraging Americans and Chinese to see U.S.-China relations in the context of the interests of others and in the context of addressing globally significant issues through multilateral cooperation would be a corrective to Washington's knee-jerk unilateralism, also nudging Beijing toward shared norms.

A fourth worry I had as I came to the committee was what I judged to be the organization's excessive dependence on U.S. government funding. My goal was gradually to push that percentage lower. I wanted to accomplish that by raising revenue from other nongovernmental sources, not by a cut in federal dollars. One problem with federal grants is that they rarely covered a project's full costs, leaving the "winner" of the competitive grant process to raise additional private sector money to conduct what was a government priority. Of course, close ties with federal agencies and carrying out projects important to Washington added credibility to our programs and NCUSCR's standing with Beijing. It also is true that the federal government collaborated with us on priorities central to the committee. Nonetheless, there were challenges, not least sticking with the organization's core values when government priorities were headed in other directions. The Chinese never saw us as independent of Washington as we were, and still are.

A core concern regarding excessive financial dependence on Washington was the independence of the committee: the only guarantee an NGO has of program independence is to have a diversity of funders with different interests and objectives. Foundations have agendas, corporations have agendas, wealthy individuals have agendas, and certainly governments do. If an NGO is to have a balanced, objective, independent program, it needs diversified financial support. Excessive dependence meant being held hostage to ever-changing political weather patterns on Capitol Hill and across administrations, particularly after the Tiananmen tragedy. As Pete Millwood recounts in his book, on some issues the National Committee took a tougher stance in negotiations with China than the U.S. executive branch did.

Consequently, we boosted corporate and foundation support. While the National Committee board of directors was of critical importance to policy, personnel, and programmatic decisions, and was an indispensable source of knowledge for the staff, during my time as president, the board overall was not a major revenue source for the organization, with the exception of Hank Greenberg and the Starr Foundation/AIG. The National Committee's always small general membership provided support and help in many intellectual and logistical areas, but, it was never a significant factor in committee revenues. That remains true today.

As the share of revenue from the government declined over time, members of the board (long after I left) constituted an ever-larger share of total revenues, particularly discretionary monies. Discretionary funds gave us needed resources to survive revenue shocks and are essential if an organization is to respond rapidly to crises and opportunities and not be overly dependent on single-issue donors.

To help meet revenue needs, we developed a corporate program that gradually became a more significant fraction of revenues. My successors, particularly Steve Orlins and Chairperson Carla Hills, really grew corporate and board revenues.

One funding vehicle that the board, Ros Daly, and I pushed forward was to promote what became the committee's Annual Gala in New York City, aimed particularly at enlarging corporate support, as well as being a public education program with its own substantive value. Under Steve Orlins's subsequent presidential leadership, the gala has become a major component of the organization's income.

A fifth agenda item arose from the fact that China was pluralizing vertically, horizontally, and in terms of state-society relations. The board and I felt that we needed to diversify our program to reach increasingly diverse levels, organizations, and segments of Chinese society. We predictably ran into the Leninist heritage of the CCP, as well as traditional ideas of managing foreigners, all of which led to being suspicious of unmediated contact between Chinese society and foreigners.

The committee's impulse to reach beyond Beijing held dangers, one of which was that our "counterpart organization" (*duikou danwei*), the Chinese People's Institute of Foreign Affairs (CPIFA, a nominally nongovernmental arm of the Foreign Ministry), would resist such efforts. One of CPIFA's core functions was regulating foreign access to PRC society and government and linking China to elites around the world. Our impulse was to reach broader swaths of Chinese society and government, this being one reason we wanted to secure permission to establish a National Committee Office in Beijing. Such a presence, we thought, would allow us to implement programs that would be more innovative and cost-effective, not reliant simply on moving people back and forth across the Pacific in expensive groups of twelve to fifteen.

A final item on our agenda going into 1988–1989 was making sure that we had open lines of communication with whichever U.S. presidential candidate won the 1988 general election. That election saw George H. W. Bush, President Reagan's vice president, running against Massachusetts Governor Michael Dukakis. The committee always avoided any form of electoral involvement, not only because it would have run afoul of our charter and tax law, but also because nonpartisanship was deeply embedded in the committee's DNA and was a core value. Becoming identified with any organized partisan political movement, organization, or endeavor could be a death sentence for the committee: the committee was about American interests, *broadly conceived*. The board of directors always had a bipartisan composition. In my observation, many of the individuals on the board and on the staff did not know one another's political affiliation. Even in cases where it was apparent, it just didn't matter. On the other hand, the Chinese frequently seemed interested in ascertaining my political identification.

When George H. W. Bush was sworn in on January 20, 1989, we had many avenues into the new administration—the new U.S. president had been head of the U.S. Liaison Office in Beijing; both the president and Mrs. Bush had been on our board of directors at various points; and Ray Shafer, our chair, was well-known to them and their closest aides. So, as we moved into 1989, we knew Washington's cast of characters in the China policy world, and they knew us.

Punched in the Mouth

As military leaders often observe, "The plan rarely survives the first shot of battle." Or, as the heavyweight boxing champion of the 1980s Mike Tyson put it, "Everybody has a plan until they get punched in the mouth."

With President Bush's previous personal familiarity with Beijing's elite, his interest in the PRC, and with individuals such as Brent Scowcroft, Richard Solomon, and James Lilley (who grew up in China and had a career in the CIA) on his national security and diplomatic teams, one could have anticipated that relations would enter a halcyon period. It was not to be.

Nineteen eighty-nine had started with the earlier-mentioned friction of President Bush's February 25–27 trip to Beijing (the Fang Lizhi fiasco) and Winston Lord leaving his ambassadorial post amidst mutual recriminations with the White House. Lord was replaced by James Lilley (who had a long-standing personal and family friendship with Barbara and George Bush). In the spring, student and popular unrest grew in the PRC capital and spread to numerous cities throughout the country. Instability gained momentum with former Party leader Hu Yaobang's April 15 death. Inflation was running high and resentment of corruption boiling over. People from all over the world and from all over China were converging on the capital. Mikhail Gorbachev was to be in Beijing May 15–18. The Bush administration feared a Beijing-Moscow rapprochement could reconfigure the geopolitical chessboard to America's disadvantage. The world's media were in Beijing to cover the Gorbachev visit as students and ordinary citizens converged on central Beijing, utilizing the assembled mass media to disseminate their messages of aspiration and exasperation to a tuned-in world.

Despite the ongoing demonstrations and the international attention they were attracting, very few persons initially expected the PLA would drive tanks and armored vehicles through central Beijing, indiscriminately using lethal force, producing an unknown number of dead and wounded, and indiscriminately firing at foreign-occupied buildings, much less to permit all this to be broadcast live on CNN. I will never forget sitting holding the hand of my daughter, Kate, watching the television screen as the carnage unfolded.

In the period between February 1989 and August of that year, *favorable* views of China in the United States fell by more than half, and *unfavorable* views of the PRC tripled. I always wondered how any favorable views remained. An architect friend of the committee called me in the aftermath of the violence to say that his lifetime architectural achievement building complex in Beijing was shot up by the PLA. U.S. Embassy personnel lived in quarters now pockmarked by bullets.

Beyond the death and destruction of the event itself, these developments created an organizational challenge for NCUSCR. Should/could engagement with China continue? Why or why not? Had engagement ended? What should be the balance between continuously dealing directly with China through exchanges and returning to the committee's roots in public education at home, our primary work prior to having brought the Chinese Ping-Pong Team to the United States in 1972? If engagement continued, what should be its terms, its foci, and with whom should we deal? Should we write a letter to Deng Xiaoping? What should it say? What would we say to the still-new U.S. administration and Congress? Who should say it? If we were invited to meet with Premier Li Peng, should we?

We had to think both strategically about the future and simultaneously deal with the total disruption of the committee's already-scheduled programs in what normally was its busiest period. As of June 3, groups were scheduled to soon arrive from China, we had delegations scheduled to travel there, and a major conference soon would be in the offing.

Unwinding and adapting to this new situation created organizational and financial mayhem. We had already spent much of our budgets on some activities that now had to be canceled or postponed. We had to spend money we didn't have to undo what we had just arranged. And finally, we had promised our funders actual programs, not a treadmill of assembling and disassembling activities at their expense. In the event, the U.S. government; the Ford, Starr, and Luce Foundations; and indeed all our funders were generous and flexible. Peter Geithner, T. C. Hsu, and Terry Lautz played especially significant roles in keeping engagement with China going from their posts at those three critical foundations.

The most pressing need was to address an almost spiritual set of questions for the National Committee's staff. It was idealism that had brought all of them to work at the committee, twelve hours a day, for modest compensation. They quite simply asked themselves, "How does one continue to deal with people who do bad things?" "How do you assess what price you are willing to pay to achieve uncertain long-term gains?" "Is progress illusory?" or, as James Mann put it, is progress in governance in China under the CCP at best a snare and a delusion, a "fantasy," or at worst a con job?

I did not have the answers, but I did say one thing I believed was meaningful and true then, and remains so today. "The question is less who we talk with than what we say when we speak with them." We would talk, but we would tell the truth. Something like that became our shared commitment moving forward.

Leadership in all organizations, particularly non-profit, mission-driven organizations, has an arguably spiritual core—you must help those you work with to answer for themselves a very basic question. Is what we are doing good, worthwhile, and meaningful? Before you can help colleagues answer that question for themselves, you had to answer it for yourself and believe it. If you cannot do so, almost everything else doesn't matter. Your colleagues and you, your funders, and your membership must together develop an answer to that basic question.

In early July, the board adopted a statement of policy and rationale sent to all relevant Chinese counterparts and our varied American constituencies, saying: "The National Committee acts upon this notion: China's policy of opening to the world has unleashed many of the forces of change with which that society is now coping. To help close that door is to help close the door on change. This we will not do."[4]

The essence of our response to the Chinese was that we were *postponing* events, *not canceling* them, and that the U.S.-China relationship was no less important now than before the tragic events of June 4 and its frightening and sobering aftermath. Both sides needed time to consider how to best proceed, but proceed we would. Our counterparts in China delivered us a compatible message.

There are crisis management lessons here. To start, the first signals one sends at times of crisis are the most credible because they most foretell the impulses that will guide your future behavior. So, as we sent messages to China, we also were sending messages to our fellow citizens. We had an obligation not only to reflect the values and interests of our citizens in the moment but also to think ahead.

PICKING UP THE PIECES

The afternoon of June 5, the National Committee's Executive Committee convened telephonically. At the outset of the call, there were expressions of outrage and shock at what had transpired in the PRC. However, as so often is the case in small groups facing crisis, one person compellingly frames the issues. In this case, it was former Committee Chairman Lucian Pye of MIT who asked: "But what are we going to do?"

The Executive Committee agreed to immediately move in the following directions, inform the full board of these responses, and solicit further advice from the board as expeditiously as possible:

- Continue with exchanges; focus on issues germane to expressing how much damage the violence had done to the relationship and the need for ongoing reform in China, all the while adhering to our past core principles.

- Write a public statement reiterating the damage done, the outrage felt, and the need for continued reform in the PRC. Not only distribute that document widely at home, but also send it directly to the Chinese leadership and Committee counterpart organizations in the PRC. We were to ask the PRC's Ambassador to the United States, Han Xu, to convey a copy to Deng Xiaoping, Foreign Minister Qian Qichen, and our most senior PRC counterparts.

- Increase the committee's domestic public education function, outreach focused on how and why such a tragedy occurred and what possible paths lie ahead for the United States in its ties with the PRC.

- At the earliest date feasible, dispatch a small group to the PRC, to be followed by a board trip, to express American outrage, see what constructive pathway forward might be found, and make recommendations to the full board.

- Convene a conference of U.S. organizations, government officials, and academics and thought leaders to discuss ways forward and forge consensus beyond the committee.

A guiding thought throughout was that many of those we had dealt with in China over the years were themselves victims of the violence, the subsequent repression, and the isolating response of many Western countries, international corporations, and other entities outside the PRC. We sought to avoid victimizing the victims with knee-jerk reactions.

In short, I came to the committee concerned that our work was losing relevance as so many other organizations were coming to deal with China directly. As history worked out, the bloodshed at Tiananmen and subsequent crackdown generated a quantum leap of interest in the committee's work. As other organizations severed ties with the Chinese for varied periods and diverse reasons, there was more demand than ever for the committee's capabilities to preserve and expand communication.

After that Executive Committee conference call, the committee staff immediately drafted a letter, the first of its kind ever issued by the NCUSCR, and conveyed it to Ambassador Han Xu for wide delivery in Beijing. The letter's purposes were to publicly express moral outrage and establish productive guidelines for the committee's policies going forth and to help shape the broader U.S. response. We also wanted the Chinese to know where we were headed. We conveyed the letter to human rights icon in the U.S. House of Representatives, Tom Lantos (D-CA), and asked him to have it placed in the *Congressional Record*, where it appeared on June 7, fewer than seventy-two hours after the tragedy in Beijing.[5]

In moving rapidly, the Executive Committee and staff had less immediate consultation with the full board than we would have liked, but when the board had a chance to weigh in over the next days, support for steps taken was unanimous, with only one board member asking whether or not we really needed to send a letter to Deng Xiaoping too.

CHAPTER EIGHT

June 5, 1989, was a new world compared to two days earlier. And yet, once the shock of June 4 lessened, and Deng Xiaoping by 1992 had reenergized the reform agenda, the committee was able to pursue the initial policy directions I had come to New York to advance. The principal exception was that the committee never was able to establish an office in Beijing. Though I had episodically talked to our Chinese counterparts about such a presence, the combined weight of the earlier Fang Lizhi incident and June 4 rendered such an idea fanciful.

In a very Chinese way, we never received a definitive, formal "no" on the office proposal; it just became clear that it was not going to happen. In retrospect, perhaps the absence of an office is a small mercy, ensuring that the committee would be less likely to become a participant in Chinese domestic politics in a way that could only spell trouble.

Committee Chairman Ray Shafer and his leadership at this moment deserve comment. Unknown to most in the committee's orbit at the time, Ray had decided to relinquish the board of directors chairmanship prior to June 4, as he had held the post for several years. We were quietly and methodically looking for a successor before Tiananmen. Immediately after the tragedy, the board asked Ray to remain on because he was a bridge to China and was credible in American political circles. He agreed.[6]

A person's mettle becomes obvious when they are pushed to the wall. Shortly before Tiananmen, Ray and I had scheduled a luncheon at the Metropolitan Club in Washington, D.C., with China's ambassador to the United States, Han Xu. The meeting was scheduled for what proved to be a few days after the Beijing bloodshed. Ambassador Han was a sinewy, gray-haired diplomat able to display great patience, while also having a short fuse to match his short haircut. Han preferred good relations with the United States but was a fierce defender of China's dignity, and his own. He was tough and sharp, like flint.

After the violence on June 4, I felt I should talk with Ray about whether or not to proceed with the scheduled luncheon and, if so, how to arrange it at the Club—should we reserve a secluded private room or sit in the main dining room with Ambassador Han surrounded by Washington's politically connected? Ray was adamant and decisive. The lunch would go forward if Ambassador Han wished. We would sit in the Main Dining Room. Either meet with a person or don't, but do not skulk around in the shadows, Ray declared. Ambassador Han was himself shaken by what had happened in his country. We would be frank in conveying to him the damage that had been done to bilateral relations and the PRC's global standing. Surely Ambassador Han did not need us to tell him that.

The day came and, out of character, Ambassador Han was half an hour late, leaving us to wonder whether he would come at all. He finally arrived, apologized profusely, and felt the need to explain that demonstrations in front of the PRC Embassy, then on Connecticut Avenue, NW, in the Kalorama neighborhood, forced him to exit from an inconspicuous garage. He was chagrined.

I had always been struck by the fact that whenever Ambassador Han had been in public previously, everyone wanted to burnish their Washington insider credentials by being seen shaking his hand and posturing as an old friend. That day in the Metropolitan Club was quite different: not a single person came up to say anything, either by way of condemnation, sympathy, or inquiry. Ray handled that day just right. You don't throw your friends overboard without knowing all the facts. Communication in periods of stress is essential.

Now What?

As we concluded the National Committee's Executive Committee meeting on June 5, our task was to tell fellow citizens, and the Chinese system, where we stood. The U.S. government was interested in what our policy was going to be, as were other NGOs and foundations. In addition, the committee is a membership organization that required that we either be in synch with members or explain why we were not, if we were to maintain legitimacy. This required that we listen and promptly develop guidance that would endure. Taking a step in one direction and then reversing the field would erode everyone's confidence. No do-overs.

On June 5, the Executive Committee adopted a statement sent out that day to our membership and interested organizations, asking for comment.[7] There was no substantive dissent from its principal points, and it was sent out globally in early July.

Its major points were as follows:

- "We view with shock and dismay the application of indiscriminate force by some Chinese government forces against its citizenry."
- "Only through progressively greater political openness and dialogue between the government of China and its people can the stability, reform, and economic improvement everyone so much desires be achieved."
- "It is inevitable that recent and ongoing events will have repercussions throughout the world and that China's cooperative international relations will be disrupted in many ways."
- "The National Committee regrets that events have necessitated the postponement of several of our programs."
- "Our policy will be to work with Chinese individuals and organizations which share our commitment to these goals and we look forward to a time when the atmosphere for productive programs will again exist."

On August 1, 1989, the full board of directors met in person and made further decisions aligning with the Executive Committee's June 5 principles. The board met in the Dean Acheson Room of Covington & Burling in Washington, D.C., with pictures on the walls of the former Secretary of State who was "present at the creation" of the postwar order and the Cold War. Henry Sailor, raised in China, and a partner at Covington & Burling, made arrangements for the meeting and undoubtedly spoke the most authentic Beijing dialect of anyone on the National Committee Board.

The board affirmed that the committee would proceed with exchanges "on a case-by-case basis, using as our criteria their professional excellence, forthright character, and non-propagandistic quality."[8] The next day, we informed the Chinese Embassy that the long-planned Ford Foundation–sponsored "Financial Instruments Delegation" from China scheduled for September–October 1989 would be welcome, as long as it was consistent with the above principles.

One might reasonably ask why, after such an enormous moral disaster in the PRC, the committee would make its first post–June 4 delegation exchange seemingly about money—stocks and bonds? The reasons were both practical and, we believed, ethical.

Practically, preparations for that delegation had been made prior to June 4, and this program was most feasibly implemented quickly. A second practical consideration was that it was feasible for the Chinese to implement because it did not raise disabling questions at home. Deng Xiaoping was saying he was still committed to economic reform and the open policy. We wanted to test that proposition.

Most importantly for us, however, was that this delegation was concerned with building financial markets. The absolute requirements for efficient and noncorrupt financial markets are open information, transparency, legal predictability, decentralized market-based decisions, and a level playing field. We wanted to support these impulses and directions. Furthermore, there was a need for empowering local governments in China. To achieve that in a financially sound manner, localities had to be able to responsibly borrow long-term money—hence bonds.

Also at the August 1 board meeting in Washington, the "Board asked Professor Doak Barnett and David M. Lampton to seek to arrange a visit to China in order to speak with counterpart organizations and key persons about the current state of relations and how to move forward." Barnett had grown up in Shanghai, the son of parents working with the YMCA, he had written the classic book *China on the Eve of the Communist Takeover* (1961), and he had been NCUSCR's second chairman. Barnett and I would report back to the National Committee Board *and* to all national conferees we had just convened in July. We were to "assess the general climate for exchanges and the feasibility of previously planned programs."

The conference referred to earlier was the "China in Flux" conclave held July 7–9, 1989, in Racine, Wisconsin, at the Johnson Foundation's Wingspread Conference Center, sponsored by the National Committee, the Johnson and Luce Foundations, and the Rockefeller Brothers Fund.

Its mission: "To examine the impact of the dramatic recent events in the People's Republic of China; how these affect American interests; and what appropriate American responses should be forthcoming from the public and private sectors."

Forty-five American representatives of educational and philanthropic organizations, think tanks, NGOs, corporations, and the executive and legislative branches attended. The conference as a whole made no recommendations and took no votes, so there was no group position. Speaking personally, however, I summarized what I saw as the conference outcomes in a memo to the business and professional associates of the National Committee,[9] and I wrote a piece for the *Christian Science Monitor*, July 10, 1989. The committee did publish a conference summary in its *China Policy Series*, No. 2 (August 1989).

What I saw as the conference conclusions included the following:

- We are looking at a transitional government in Beijing, one that is divided and will initially be dominated by the older generation, itself divided; persons with no formal position would for now play a decisive role.

- With respect to U.S.-China relations, there was general recognition that important strategic interests were at stake and that good relations with the PRC helped produce stability around China's periphery. There was heated debate, however, over whether or not there should be additional sanctions levied against China, particularly if arrests and executions continued.

- Given all the uncertainties, there was a general sense that a U.S. policy of "testing, probing, and waiting to see" was appropriate. Moving too quickly to renormalize would be to legitimate reprehensible behavior and be used for regime propaganda, and waiting too long would risk driving China into self-defeating isolation.

- The United States should act "in parallel with as many of our allies and international organizations as possible."

- The United States "should resist the efforts of various Chinese groups (students, emigres, and officials from both the PRC and

Taiwan) to turn the United States into an active partisan in Chinese politics."

With this guidance, on August 3, Board Chair Ray Shafer wrote our counterpart organization, CPIFA (headed by former Vice Foreign Minister Han Nianlong and former Ambassador to the United States Chai Zemin), asking whether they would receive Barnett and me. Our proposed trip was the next step in the process of "testing, probing, and waiting to see." In asking Beijing to receive us, we made clear that we would directly contact counterparts to request meetings, we would pay our expenses, and we did not desire formal, ceremonial meetings with senior leaders unless we had had prior working relationships with them. We desired no media coverage (our fear being that our purposes and statements might be distorted, in both countries). We proposed to land in Beijing on September 9, 1989, and depart Shanghai for Hong Kong on September 20.

We included Hong Kong (from which we departed to return home on the 23rd) because it had been affected by events, the committee had a growing Greater China program there, and we wanted to signal the city's importance to the United States as we moved toward Hong Kong's reversion to PRC sovereignty on July 1, 1997. Beijing promptly authorized our trip with no concerns expressed—our parameters were faithfully respected.

In the course of the September 10–23 trip, Doak and I had twenty-eight meetings in Beijing, twelve in Shanghai, and twelve in Hong Kong. A twenty-one-page report was submitted to the National Committee Board shortly after our return and subsequently sent to a range of outside organizations.

In that report, one of the important issues addressed concerned whether or not the committee could continue to play a policy role as it simultaneously fostered exchanges—was there mission conflict?

The committee's domestic policy analysis role (e.g., as reflected in its policy reports and conferences) requires the committee to give expression to views and analyses that the Chinese leadership, in many instances, will not like. This may complicate the task of fostering exchanges. On balance, however, we thought the Chinese would have more respect for the committee if it performed an analytic function and was not simply an organization with a logistical function. Nonetheless, there was, and is, tension between articulating honest policy analysis and conducting exchanges.[10] Among the Barnett-Lampton report's key findings were these:

- In the Chinese leadership, "there is a lack of policy agreement, and a struggle for power in the post-Deng era is underway." (In retrospect, this struggle was not basically resolved until Deng Xiaoping took his "Southern Journey" (*Nanxun*) in early 1992.)

- "U.S.-China relations probably have not yet quite 'hit bottom,' particularly if pending sanctions and immigration legislation are passed by the U.S. Congress. . . . There are worrisome anti-foreign themes in some Chinese pronouncements."

- "It is important to recognize that: there is a broad range of views [in China] about recent events; the severity of the current 'cleanup' campaign varies in intensity both by region and individual units within localities; and, some Chinese recognize the importance and implications of interdependence more than others."

- Given that the Beijing line was that Washington took the lead in sanctions and that "he who tied the knot should untie it," we said: "We do not believe a full [U.S.-China] dialogue would be productive at the moment." Small group discussions would be more useful.

- Both Chinese people and organizations we met, and U.S. government officials, "are most supportive of our maintaining contact where possible." "Exchanges will need to focus on topics that can be discussed in a professional non-ideological way." "Topics that relate to pressing economic and development needs are most feasible—those with a strong American studies component are less so."

- "The National Committee should more vigorously pursue its past policy of seeking to develop some exchanges with organizations outside Beijing, while not diminishing ties to the capital."

- "Expanding programs relevant to Hong Kong is one thing the Committee should seriously consider."

Concerning expanding Hong Kong programming, one of the first meetings Barnett and I had in the colony was with director (1983 to early 1990) of the *Xinhua News Agency*, Xu Jiatun, at his Wan Chai office, the PRC's de facto shadow government headquarters.[11] Barnett and I also met with the then-British Governor David Wilson (a former editor of *The China Quarterly*), who held the post from 1987 to 1992. We had an informative dinner with him at Government House on September 22.

The meeting with Xu (and its aftermath) gave us insight into the deep rifts within the Chinese Foreign Ministry concerning the management of Hong Kong internally and externally. For a Chinese official, Xu was open. He had been sent to Jiangsu Province immediately after Mao's death to bring order to the Gang of Four's stronghold and had been Party Secretary there from 1977 to 1983.

In Hong Kong, when we saw him, he was dealing with the Colony's reversion negotiations with London and the global blowback from June 4. My notes of our September 20 meeting record that both Doak and I were struck that while he (Xu) certainly did not refute Beijing's line (defending "the necessity" of the crackdown), he rather devoted all his attention to pleading for mutual understanding and damage limitation—looking to the future. He argued that Hong Kong people were not anti-China and that three things were key for stability there: stability in China, the open door and reform, and cooperation with the United Kingdom.[12] This formulation allowed Xu to talk to us two foreigners without defending something with which he was in deep disagreement, as the world would soon come to see.

As we later learned, Xu disagreed with his nemesis in the Foreign Ministry, Vice Minister Zhou Nan, on how to handle the people of Hong Kong. Xu wanted to get out among Hong Kong citizens and reassure them and the international community, but Zhou Nan had no such populist inclinations. Xu and Zhou also differed over what message they should be sending to Beijing. Xu wanted to tell Beijing things were going badly in the city and the center needed to change direction. This decidedly was not the message Zhou Nan wanted to deliver to his bosses in the capital. It was Zhou's policy that Xu was proposing the Center reject. As Xu himself put it to us, "I mentioned to Governor Wilson that I want the type of cooperation to be of the style of pre-June 4."

The contrast in personalities between Zhou and Xu was striking. Zhou Nan emoted false bravado, having to let you know in the first five minutes that he came from culturally illustrious stock, generations removed from Confucius. Xu, born in Nantong, Jiangsu, was much more cosmopolitan, self-assured, and at ease, not having to prove anything to you, except that he understood your point of view. Zhou wanted to make sure you knew his point of view.

Within two months of our meeting, Zhou Nan had set up a committee to investigate Xu and his financial affairs. Xu also carried the added political burden of having been close to party leader Zhao Ziyang, who had been sacked in the May–June 1989 turmoil. In January 1990, Zhou Nan took over as director of the Hong Kong Branch of *Xinhua News Agency*, replacing Xu. Sensing that he would soon be arrested, in early May 1990, Xu fled to the United States where he spent the rest of his life, unable to return home.

In short, Barnett and I were in Hong Kong as the hard line was in the process of prevailing over the soft line for the colony. Our perspective was to try to get as much positive interaction as possible going with Hong Kong soon, hoping to emphasize that the world, not least America, cared about Hong Kong.

THE PATH CHOSEN

From my point of view, our stop in Shanghai was critical to how things played out in a *relatively* positive way for the next twenty years. In Shanghai, Barnett and I met with Zhu Rongji, then Mayor and Party Secretary, getting together with him and an aide (Pan Chenglie) in the venerable Hengshan Hotel, in a dimly lit, musty-smelling upper-story room with wooden floors. The Hengshan was one of Jiang Qing's (Madam Mao) haunts during the Cultural Revolution and originally was the Art Deco Picardie Apartments dating back to the mid-1930s. I thought this was a nice, ironic touch that Zhu chose this site to meet us. The hotel was in the same part of Shanghai in which Doak had grown up; in a trip down memory lane, we walked over to his boyhood home which was still standing.

Zhu and former Shanghai Party Secretary Jiang Zemin, now General Secretary in Beijing, had quelled protests and unrest in Shanghai relatively peacefully. Zhu had in part calmed things down by saying in a brave June 8, 1989, speech that the people of Shanghai should avoid causing another tragedy in their own city and that history eventually would render its verdict on what had happened in Beijing.[13] At that moment, this was the furthest anyone had gone in suggesting that what had happened in Beijing was an error. The people of Shanghai did not need to exact vengeance because history would.

In our report's conclusions and recommendations, we argued that there were opportunities for contacts and exchanges with PRC localities. Generally, local government, both in China and in the United States, is problem-driven and results-oriented. China's local leaders were less tainted in American minds than Beijing officials were. While our two capitals couldn't talk to each other, we felt localities could.

On the spot in our meeting with Zhu, we probed as to whether the mayor might consider coming to the United States to lead what became "The Mayors Delegation" composed of six current Chinese mayors (Shanghai, Wuhan, Chongqing, Hefei, Ningbo, and Taiyuan, plus former Shanghai Mayor Wang Daohan). They arrived in the United States at JFK International Airport on Long Island on the evening of July 7, 1990.[14]

It would be fair to say that this was the first major public move in the United States to nudge things forward in the wake of June 4. Beyond Mayor Zhu, Jiang Zemin, Foreign Minister Qian Qichen, and former Shanghai Mayor Wang Daohan (Jiang Zemin's alter ego and a person Jiang referred to as "my boss") were decisive on the PRC side to making the trip happen. All were from Shanghai and its surrounding area. The Bush administration was supportive of our move but noninterventionist.

As the *Annus horribilis* 1989 slithered to an end, on December 17, 1989, I sent my friend, colleague, former University of Michigan professor, and former National Committee Board Member Richard (Dick)

Solomon, then Assistant Secretary for East Asia and Pacific Affairs at the Department of State, a long letter. This was a promised follow-up to the preceding day's meeting with him in Washington. I summarized what I had concluded from the preceding six months in terms of what U.S. policy choices were and recommended directions in which the Administration should move.

I suggested three options: (1) Tread water, "let the dust settle," let them stew in their own juices, and "wait them out." (2) High politics, symbolic moves, and the decisive initiative approach that could change the character of the relationship, an example of which might be a high-level meeting with a joint statement. (3) "Substantive engagement in pursuit of tangible American interests and letting 'the free market' determine the scale and form of interaction. . . . Now is the time to focus on linkages that can be defended in terms of American values *and* interests, not consuming ourselves in high profile, divisive ventures." I ended my letter calling for President Bush to deliver a nationwide address to make the moral case for the modest third option, immodestly suggesting words the president might use:

> The policy of the United States will be to engage in substantive relations with the Chinese leaders and people that enlarge the sources of information, increase interdependence, break down isolation, and create a climate in which global problems can be solved. This is our policy and it is the *right* thing to do.

This is the course the National Committee followed, and it captures the common thread of U.S. national policy during seven administrations from Richard Nixon to Barack Obama, until we got to the Donald Trump–Xi Jinping era a little more than twenty-five years after Tiananmen. The June 1990 visit of the mayor's delegation led by Zhu Rongji was the first flight test for this policy after Tiananmen. Though the Bush administration did not conceive of the delegation visit, it fully supported it behind the scenes, as evidenced by the access the mayor's delegation had in Washington.

Notes

1. Mary Brown Bullock, "Strategic Adaptation: American Foundations, Religious Organizations, and NGOs in China," in Anne F. Thurston, ed., *Engaging China: Fifty Years of Sino-American Relations* (Columbia University Press, 2021), 199.

2. Charles W. Yost, *History and Memory: A Statesman's Perceptions of the Twentieth Century* (W.W. Norton, 1980), 233–34, 244.

3. David M. Lampton, Ying-mao Kau, Terrill E. Lautz, Peter T. Mangione, James S. Martinsen, June Mei, W. S. Pau, and Mark Schlansky, "The Emergence of 'Greater China': Implications for the United States," National Committee China Policy Series (no. 5), October 1992.

4. David M. Lampton, "Chron Files," May–June, 1989 Volume. (RAC). "National Committee Program Purposes: Continuity in a New Era."

5. Hon. Tom Lantos, *Congressional Record*, Proceedings and Debates of the 101st Congress, First Session, 135, no. 74 (June 7, 1989).

6. David M. Lampton, "Chron Files," May–June 1989 Volume. (RAC). Letter dated June 18, 1989. Lampton letter to Shafer.

7. David M. Lampton, "Chron Files," Board of Directors Statement, June 5, 1989 (May–June 1989, Volume). (RAC).

8. David M. Lampton, "Chron Files," July 1989–September 1989, Volume, August 2, 1982, Lampton letters to Peter Geithner, Ford Foundation, and Bian Qingzu, Chinese Embassy. (RAC).

9. David M. Lampton, "Chron Files," "Memorandum: To Business and Professional Associates," July 12, 1989, July-September, 1989, Volume. (RAC).

10. David M. Lampton, "Chron Files," David M. Lampton and A. Doak Barnett, "Report to the National Committee Board of Directors: Trip to China," September 10–23, 1989. (RAC).

11. David M. Lampton, "Meeting with Xu Jiatun," A. Doak Barnett and David M. Lampton, September 20, 1989, in Interviews. (RAC).

12. David M. Lampton, *Following the Leader: Ruling China, from Deng Xiaoping to Xi Jinping*, 2nd ed.(University of California Press, 2019), 116–17.

13. David M. Lampton, Interview Notes, "Meeting with Shanghai Mayor Zhu Rongji," A. Doak Barnett and David M. Lampton, September 18, 1989, 4:40–5:45 p.m., Hengshan Hotel, Shanghai. (RAC).

14. Zhu Rongji, *Zhu Rongji: On the Record, The Shanghai Years, 1987–1991*, Translated by June Y. Mei (Brookings Institution Press, 2018), 524–30.

CHAPTER NINE

Shanghai

(Post-Tiananmen, 1989–1990)

SETTING THE STAGE

By late 1989 and early 1990, President George H. W. Bush was looking for ways to restore communication with the PRC without appearing indifferent to Beijing's repression; for his part, Deng Xiaoping was seeking a face-saving way out of China's isolation.

The two leaders were trying to navigate around the Scylla of recalcitrant elders in Beijing and the Charybdis of a U.S. Congress bent on retaliation for Tiananmen. Boosting the quotient of subnational ties was one way to navigate these waters. The NCUSCR began exploring ways to re-open ties without violating the Bush administration's ban on "high-level" exchanges. By inviting Mayor Zhu Rongji to the United States as Professor Barnett and I had done in September 1989, the committee helped the administration find a way out of the corner into which it had painted itself.

"High-level" exchange had been operationalized by Washington to mean minister/secretary and above-level officials. The ban was self-defeating. In an authoritarian system, senior officials make key decisions. If they are being isolated and shamed by outsiders (as was the ban's purpose), they will not empower subordinates to do what they are denied. Subordinates will not act if it appears that they are being treated better by foreigners than their bosses. Communication halts.

The beauty of the mayoral post in Shanghai is that it is of ministerial rank and confers senior rank in China's political hierarchy. In America, by way of contrast, a mayor is simply a local leader, though admittedly some are more consequential than others. The National Committee's invitation to Zhu offered a way for both sides to save face and restore high-level exchange.

At that time, the PRC was nominally led by Jiang Zemin, former Party Secretary and mayor of Shanghai. Jiang sought to avoid getting crosswise with China's conservatives, on the one hand, and Deng Xiaoping, on the other hand; Deng was committed to further economic and social reform, though not to the political change Zhao Ziyang had sought.

Jiang Zemin's patron and mentor was the former mayor of Shanghai, Wang Daohan, who had brought the McDonnell Douglas aircraft assembly venture to Shanghai in the first half of the 1980s. The foreign minister was Qian Qichen, a cosmopolitan in the mold of Zhou Enlai, who had assumed office in April 1988. Born the same year as Premier Zhou Enlai, Qian's roots were in Shanghai. In October 1989, not long after the dust had settled over Tiananmen Square, Qian made a low-profile effort at outreach when he attended the annual UN General Assembly session in New York, reassuring his listeners that China was proceeding with reform. Those of us present had the impression that he did not have much sympathy with how things had unfolded in his country while being careful not to step into a forbidden zone.

At that time, many of the key policy positions in Beijing and Shanghai were filled by persons inclined to use Shanghai as the launching pad for the PRC to break out of its post-Tiananmen isolation. Shanghai leaders were chomping at the bit to play this role. The city fathers were resentful that Shanghai had been brought to the table of "opening to the outside world" later than China's four southern special economic zones (SEZs). They also were aggravated that Shanghai was a revenue milk cow for the central government. During his meeting with Doak and me, Zhu complained that "eighty percent of [Shanghai state] enterprise profits go to the [central] state." He also complained that profiteers and the railroads were gouging Shanghai for the coal it needed. To address these problems, Zhu concluded his remarks to us by saying, "We must rely further on foreign cooperation."[1]

Finally, Zhu Rongji wanted to launch the Pudong (East Shanghai) development effort; this amounted to building an entirely new city across the Huangpu River from the older urban center of Puxi, West Shanghai. A trip to the United States would be an ideal platform from which to showcase the plans. The years 1989 and 1990 represented a favorable conjunction among local and national leaders, central needs to break out of isolation, and Shanghai's ambitions to achieve status as a global city. This kind of conjunction was the motive force behind much of engagement, not some master plan. Seize the day.

MEETING ZHU RONGJI

The delegation visit that developed was of a scope, scale, and duration we had not initially contemplated. In the end, the National Committee hosted a Chinese delegation composed of six sitting Chinese big-city mayors and one former mayor. They went to eleven cities and their suburbs over nearly three weeks. When we floated the idea in Shanghai, we had not anticipated that Beijing could quickly make a positive decision. The Chinese system can move with remarkable speed when it has a consensus.

At that moment, China's key local and national leaders were the most forward-looking, Western savvy, risk-taking combination of people the country had seen in modern times, Premier Li Peng and the old guard being glaring exceptions. Capable and forward-thinking people could also be found among second- and third-tier senior staff. A wonderful book is waiting to be written about this era's succession of leaders in and from Shanghai. On the top of my list would be Wang Daohan, Jiang Zemin, Zhu Rongji, and Xu Kuangdi; Huang Ju, in my experience, was less impressive. Vice Mayor Zhao Qizheng was exceptional.

We should appreciate the risks the Mayors' Delegation took at this moment. Those risks were implied when Zhu Rongji said to me early in his journey, "I wish they [the Western media] would quit calling me China's Gorbachev." The Soviet Bloc's and the USSR's precipitous collapse in 1989–1991, and the role America had played in that implosion, made it risky for a Chinese official to be so labeled. To be the darling of the West was the kiss of death in conservative corners of Beijing. During the trip, on the MacNeil-Lehrer *Newshour*, Robin MacNeil asked Zhu if he was China's Gorbachev. The mayor replied: "No, I am China's Zhu Rongji." Zhu made every effort to avoid being the West's pet at the expense of his superiors in Beijing. One problem for Zhu, before, during, and after his trip, was that people kept praising him for handling June 4 and its aftermath better than Beijing.

When Barnett and I met with Zhu in September 1989, the mayor went into excruciating detail about why it was easier for him to handle the Shanghai tumult than it had been for his hapless colleagues in the national capital.

> The situations in Shanghai and Beijing were different because Beijing is the capital, so it was the central stage of the struggle. . . . Shanghai has fewer students than Beijing and [Shanghai] is the largest industrial city. All the demonstrations and riots were directed by people in Beijing, so until Beijing solved the problem Shanghai could not. The solution in Beijing made it possible to solve the Shanghai situation peacefully. Jiang Zemin was in Beijing, so there was only one solution because there was student control. Shanghai had different conditions. The special condition [of Shanghai] is the large number of workers. The total of staff and workers is 5 million, of which 2.3 million are industrial workers. There are 7.3 million in the urban areas and 5 million in the suburbs and there were no problems [in the suburbs?]—very peaceful. The university students were 130,000 in number. Therefore, the picket line [of workers to control students] is overwhelming. The situation in Beijing was completely different. They had people coming from all over the country. Some people went from Shanghai to Beijing. Therefore, [they had] no other choice in Beijing and the situation [now] is "basically normal."[2]

Mayor Zhu did not want to be perceived to be inviting invidious comparisons with his bosses in the capital. The *Los Angeles Times* had this to say on July 23, 1990: "He [Zhu] has been compared to Soviet President Mikhail S. Gorbachev because of his extensive exposure to

Western economic thinking, and is credited with handling thousands of democracy demonstrators in Shanghai without the use of martial law." This praise elevated him in the West but could prove damaging at home.

LI PENG, THE CONTRAST

The very human considerations that animate a leader's behavior frequently are overlooked. Consider the contrast between Zhu and Premier Li Peng. Li had declared martial law and was its face.

Throughout almost all of his premiership (1988–1998), Li Peng was politically toxic in terms of being able to travel to Western capitals as Chinese premiers generally do. Even when foreign dignitaries and delegations visited the PRC in this period, they often debated among themselves whether they would permit themselves to be seen in Li's company—justifiably so. And yet, everyone knew that while the premier had played an important role in motivating conservative elders to use the iron fist, and he was a shrill advocate for repression, it was others, including Deng Xiaoping, who made the authoritative decisions. He was a willing, brutal instrument but not the cause.

Nonetheless, every bit of foreign praise Li Peng's subordinates such as Qian Qichen or Zhu Rongji garnered from interactions abroad was a humiliation for Li Peng, who was in diplomatic purgatory in much of the world. You could feel Li's resentment when he met Americans, holding them to be agents of his humiliation.

On August 31, 2002, when by then he was Chairman of the Standing Committee of the National People's Congress (NPC), Li Peng was in New York for a UN meeting. A complex maneuver resulted in him being served by a licensed private investigator with legal papers (a summons) for human rights violations in connection with Tiananmen—torture and murder. The papers were served at the Waldorf-Astoria Hotel where he was staying. A *New York Times* reporter and photographer accompanied the process server to document the event. The former premier was very upset to be publicly shamed in this way.[3] He viewed it as a premeditated act in which the U.S. government was complicit because the documents had been given to his U.S. security detail, which then conveyed them to the Chinese side.

The night before this incident, a small National Committee group of which I was a member had already heard from Li Peng directly about his low regard for the *New York Times*. While Americans might explain Li as having been served with papers as a concatenation of independent NGOs, independent federal courts, and independent media combining to make their case, to Chairman Li this looked like a conspiracy involving the U.S. government. Li knew how his government worked and projected that modus operandi onto Washington. Li departed New York irate but without further incident.

In short, Zhu Rongji was admired by much of the American public while Li was reviled.

Several American groups I accompanied to China during this period had heated internal debates, and then uncomfortable interactions with Chinese hosts, about whether to meet the premier and later NPC Standing Committee Chair Li Peng, how handshakes would be handled, and whether or not photos would be allowed. National Committee delegations and the committee's leadership met with Li Peng on numerous occasions, in low-profile ways, believing it was important to communicate forcefully and truthfully with those who made decisions. While we had no interest in humiliating Li, we also did not want to be used for propaganda purposes.

Li's political toxicity had practical consequences. For about nine years, China lost a key foreign policy actor in the West—its premier. This instrument found its way back into the PRC diplomatic toolbox only when Zhu Rongji became premier in 1998.

THE MAYORS' DELEGATION AND ZHU RONGJI
The Setting and Contexts
The Mayors' Delegation arrived at JFK Airport aboard a commercial Chinese flight late the evening of July 7, 1990; the formal program ended on July 26.

From the Chinese point of view, and that of the Bush administration, a central purpose of the journey was to improve the overall climate for Congress not overriding the president's already announced intention to renew most-favored-nation (MFN, later known as Normal

Trade Relations, or NTR) tariff treatment for the PRC. As Mayor Zhu explained in his 2018 book, *Zhu Rongji on the Record: The Shanghai Years, 1987–1991*, "The goal of our trip was to solidify our MFN status so that it would ultimately be approved by Congress. Another goal was to state our position on lifting economic 'sanctions' imposed on China." In pursuit of these goals, in one day alone, Zhu and his colleagues met with twenty-four representatives and senators on Capitol Hill, saying later in his book, "This was the most uncomfortable day of all."

For me, this day was exhausting in its intensity and nerve-racking given the variable atmosphere of successive meetings. As an American citizen, I was sometimes impressed and proud of the knowledge and sincerity of many members of Congress. Occasionally, I was appalled by the ignorance and narrow-mindedness, and in one case aghast that one senior member was in such an apparent state of mental decline that the member's senior staff aide treated the member like a Charlie McCarthy ventriloquial dummy. Zhu noted on the way out of that meeting that the member did "not appear well."

In bringing this group to Capitol Hill for such an intense day of meetings, one National Committee purpose was to let the Chinese see for themselves that Congress was an independent branch, with strong feelings and power. We also wanted members of Congress to see that China was a complex place, with a variety of political leaders, varied interests, and diverse possibilities. Pinning the label "authoritarian" on the Chinese system as a catch-all to describe all its leaders did not make good sense. We thought this delegation made that point powerfully.

Another context for the delegation's arrival was that Jiang Zemin was grooming Zhu for a big jump to the national capital, becoming vice premier in 1991 (along with assuming other major posts in the economic and finance arena), and then eventually elevating Zhu to become Premier from 1998 to 2003. As vice premier and later premier, he would lead China through its most severe unemployment and financial system challenges of the reform era and the Asian Financial Crisis (1997–1998). He also worked out China's World Trade Organization (WTO) entry in December 2001, which garnered him pointed domestic criticism but supercharged China's international trade performance.

In short, the Mayors' Delegation was about more than U.S.-China relations—it was about the future leadership of China and domestic reform. Some delegation members were concerned that untoward developments on the trip would weaken them back home. For Zhu and others on the delegation, a successful visit was paramount.

The group's itinerary suggests that its aspirations were much broader than often was the case for Chinese groups. Most Chinese leaders assumed that if they had been to Washington, New York, Los Angeles, and San Francisco, they had been to the United States. This group realized, as did the National Committee, that China had a problem with the American people as a whole, not just four big, cosmopolitan cities on two coasts of a very big, diverse continent.

Hence, the delegation spent time and energy in places and with groups not generally a priority for the PRC—altogether eleven cities and their metropolitan areas. Several of the visited localities had political leaders who would prove challenging. Zhu and his colleagues interacted with people in more effective ways than usual: less reading of speeches, more humor, more town hall meetings, and more talk about concrete plans.

Continually noting throughout the trip that the major American media (as opposed to regional or local press) were not paying much attention to the trip, Mayor Zhu decided to go over the national print media's head and speak directly to a nationwide audience. He exposed himself to an open-ended interview with Robert (Robin) MacNeil of the MacNeil/Lehrer *NewsHour*. The interview was broadcast live from a cramped San Francisco hotel room overlooking Union Square—his American interpreter, June Mei, America's most accomplished interpreter of Chinese, was in the *en suite* bathroom doing the simultaneous translation remotely from the bathtub!

The group visited New York and New Jersey, Washington, D.C., San Francisco, and Los Angeles, to be sure, but also Racine-Milwaukee, Wisconsin; Cleveland, Ohio; Boston suburbs; Lancaster, Pennsylvania; Chicago; and San Jose, California.

The composition of Zhu's delegation suggests the domestic coalition behind renormalization externally and reform internally. The

Figure 9.1.   Mayor Wang Daohan and Author, Hyde Park, New York, FDR Residence, June 1990. Photo by David M. Lampton.

Figure 9.2. Zhu Rongji delegation visits New York Harbor, June 1990. (Left to right) Chinese Consul General's spouse, former Shanghai Mayor Wang Daohan, Mayor Zhu Rongji, PRC Consul General Weng Fupei, and Author. Photo by David M. Lampton.

mayors came from Ningbo (in the Yangtze Delta); Chongqing (the major metropolis on the middle and upper reaches of the Yangtze); Taiyuan (in northwest coal country); Hefei, Anhui (in the lower Yangtze Delta and one of China's poorer provinces, also the home of Wang Daohan); and heartland Wuhan, where I had lived for six months in 1982. Several of the mayors were Tsinghua University graduates, giving substance to the university's claim to be the birthplace of China's political elite.

As an outsider, I could see in the delegation's interpersonal dynamics how important school ties were, kidding them about this being a Tsinghua Alumni Group. These were predominantly younger leaders who could envision a far different future for their country.

ZHU RONGJI UNREHEARSED

Leadership effectiveness is anchored in character. In our air and bus trips throughout the nearly three-week trip, bit by bit, pieces of Zhu's early life popped out. Subsequent opportunities to meet with him singly and in groups over the years, and conversations with other world leaders about their interactions with Zhu, have left me with indelible impressions about his character and qualities.

Zhu grew up in China's heartland province of Hunan, and he lost both parents at an early age. He was largely alone, raised by an uncle, receiving his early education in China's interior. He was educated in the school of hard knocks long before he graduated in engineering from Tsinghua University. This experience seems to have had the effect of making him empathetic to a degree not apparent in most Chinese leaders with whom I have dealt. He had an understanding of the Chinese heartland and was impatient with vacuous political rhetoric and dogmatism—he had a steel trap for a mind. He was a problem solver.

Zhu's credibility rested upon his cant-free pragmatism and cosmopolitan vision, inquisitiveness, humor, capacity to communicate across cultural divides, and candor. He also could deal harshly with those who lied and those who were corrupt in big or small ways. He was exacting.

On the evening of July 7, 1990, Zhu and his large delegation landed at Long Island's JFK Airport. As we rode into New York City, the Manhattan skyline and the illuminated bridges spanning the East River shot into view. Zhu turned to me and said, "Tell me. You have something here called the Port Authority of New York and New Jersey. What is it? What does it do? Why was it established?"

I did my best to explain that it was a multistate and municipality special-purpose jurisdiction to plan, develop, and operate infrastructure and promote region-wide economic and social development. It reflected the reality that although there were many political and administrative jurisdictions in the Greater New York City Region, the mutually beneficial functioning of the entire area required coordination for infrastructure development and finance, management, and compatible economic and regulatory policies. Showing his cosmopolitanism and practical nature, he said: "That is important. Though you are capitalist, you need planning. And we, though socialist, need a lot more market. In the end, we are all mixed systems."

Zhu not only was inquisitive in his interactions with others—this quality extended to his solitary behavior. I was interviewing a very senior Asia-Pacific Defense official who recounted that while visiting foreign dignitaries often were preoccupied with eating and drinking, "the Chinese are always on to something. One of our state officials was with Zhu Rongji, and he was interested in the dual-flush toilets we have. One half of the mechanism for a piss and the whole thing for a shit. Zhu was very interested; took it apart all over his [hotel] room."

Zhu's inquisitiveness extended way beyond plumbing. Having grown up within China's planned economy, and then having been a senior policy maker within it, Zhu was particularly interested in the U.S. Federal Reserve System. During his 1990 trip, he focused on how the Fed adjusted macro-economic performance through indirect market mechanisms, particularly the interest rate, reserve ratios, and open-market operations.

With his elevation to the post of vice premier in 1991, joining the Politburo, and appointment as Governor of the People's Bank of China, he pushed for much greater use of indirect economic instruments as opposed to blunt-force central directives (e.g., at the Dalian Conference of June 1993), though never tossing central administrative edicts from his toolbox. In the wake of Deng Xiaoping's early 1992 Southern Journey that rekindled economic reform, "Zhu Rongji set in motion a series of measures aimed at slowing investment and controlling money supply."[4] In this period, Zhu also increased the central government's share of revenues, abolished Foreign Exchange Certificates (a parallel currency system for foreigners), and reduced inflation. I have always thought that our visit to the Chicago Mercantile Exchange, along with Wall Street, left a deep imprint on his thinking. As we walked through the trading pits, he said, "You can feel the power of capitalism."

Equally impactful on this trip was the exposure of all the big city mayors to digital cell phone technology, permitting faster, clearer, and less cumbersome cell phone calls internationally and domestically. ATT brought its brand new cell phone technology to hedge fund manager D. Bruce McMahan's rural estate outside of New York City and let each mayor call home from the woods by a pond. The possibilities and meaning of globalization instantly became apparent. One mayor, with a tone of disbelief in his voice, told his family back home that he was calling from the woods, pond-side—with *no wires!*

Turning to leadership, if a speaker can get a person or audience laughing, or seeing things from their angle of view, in the first two minutes of talking with them, they are down the road to mutual understanding. Zhu was a master at that. He never spoke with a group before first asking who was in the audience. What did they care about? He very infrequently would read a speech verbatim. Also, unlike most Chinese leaders, he did not live in fear that someone in the audience would ask an embarrassing question. Congress was a particular challenge.

On the day that we headed for Capitol Hill during his 1990 trip to meet with what turned out to be over twenty members of Congress, he was undaunted by the prospect of meeting with a junior House member from California, Nancy Pelosi (also chapter 10). Congresswoman Pelosi was leading efforts to protect the visa status of Chinese students then studying in America and to tie MFN for China to its human rights behavior, if not take it away entirely as retribution for June 4. I cautioned Mayor Zhu that he would get what he might see as hostile, unfriendly questions. I also explained that he should not take personal offense at the way Congress operated in terms of protocol and ambiance. It wasn't personal. He would find members of Congress delivering criticism and then abruptly excusing themselves to go cast votes in the distant chambers of the Congress, thereafter returning to resume the meeting. It would all be very un-Chinese. Members would convey more moderate views privately to him, then go out and lambaste Beijing. This was not so much hypocrisy as politics in Washington.

As we departed the last meeting of that day, he said: "Well, that wasn't as bad as you warned. Reminds me of my barbershop. People come in, people go out, and everyone talks over everyone else. Yeah, like my barber shop."

Sometimes in a meeting, revealing your common humanity to your interlocutor makes things more manageable. When somewhat aggressively asked by one member of Congress what he was doing about

China's truly foul air quality, he said: "I only have one final wish before I go see God the Lord—that I will see clean scenery."

On another occasion back in China, when asked by a senior U.S. Senator to comment on his reported statement that he would need one hundred coffins to fight corruption—ninety-nine for the criminals and one for himself—Zhu replied: "I have never said one hundred coffins, one for myself. But I know this is a widespread rumor. But one hundred coffins are not enough for all the corrupt officials!"

My experience seeing many members of Congress interact with Chinese leaders over the years (particularly in my roles as a consultant for the Aspen Congressional Program and involvement with the congressional China Working Group) is that they identify a generally legitimate concern, come up with a proposed remedy or laundry list of to-dos, and are full of confidence that wisdom and virtue lie entirely with them.

Such was the case in April 2002 (about a year before the U.S. invasion of Iraq) when one senior member of Congress urged Zhu and the PRC leadership to support the U.S. invasion of Iraq to forestall what the George W. Bush administration argued was Baghdad's drive to acquire nuclear and other weapons of mass destruction. Zhu replied: "I cannot agree with you on the Iraq issue—you can't produce solid evidence that Iraq has nuclear weapons. To destroy a country at will is very dangerous. The whole Arab world will fall out with you—we don't hope to see this." Two decades later, America still lives with the consequences of not listening to this advice.

Often when a member of Congress goes to China or meets a visiting Chinese dignitary in Washington, he or she wants to report back to their constituents that they really "let the Chinese have it." They were looking for an interaction that would be to their political advantage with voters back home inclined to see every trip abroad as a boondoggle or cave-in. If each person in a congressional group has a pointed (political insurance) question in front of their mind, by the time the group gets done asking the Chinese principal questions, the overall interaction has been a sequence of mostly hostile queries, even if each member holds more sophisticated, differentiated views.

POTHOLES ALONG THE WAY OF ZHU'S TRIP

A couple of incidents on the 1990 mayors' trip capture the temper of the times. A third incident, the visit of another Shanghai Mayor, Xu Kuangdi, to New York City in November 1996, holds similar lessons.

Zhu Rongji's 1990 visit was born of the idea that exchanges involving subnational leaders offered a way around national-level gridlock. Local leaders, after all, are not generally responsible for national-level foreign policy, and in localities economic and development problems are central. Even so, localities have varied interests and political colorations. Local leaders also often aspire to higher-level offices. Sometimes big-city mayors and state governors think that the White House is their fitting residence. Hence, they seize opportunities to look like "statespersons" or project what they think will be an attractive national persona to voters and to show toughness and that they are "presidential timber."

Thus visits to localities can take unexpected twists. Localities have politics which make local leaders acting on an international stage tricky. While Zhu overall had a very successful trip and set of interactions across the United States, two incidents caused heartburn.

San Jose, California

We were nearing the conclusion of the Mayors' Delegation visit, with California as the final state on the formal itinerary. In Los Angeles, we had a very cordial meeting with Mayor Thomas Bradley, the first Black mayor of LA, the longest-serving mayor in that city's history, and a member of the National Committee's 1978 Mayors' Delegation to China. The visit was devoid of surprises. We visited Disneyland, where Mayor Wang Daohan, seventy-five years old, rode the biggest of the park's roller coasters. Summarizing the whole visit, an iconic picture came out showing Zhu Rongji meeting Mickey and Minnie Mouse under the title, "Zhu Rongji leads the Middle Kingdom towards the Magic Kingdom."

Early seeds of a Disney theme park near Shanghai were sown during this trip. The reader will recall in our earlier discussion of Ohio, Governor Jim Rhodes met Vice Premier Yu Qiuli in 1979 and had similarly suggested a theme park near Beijing.

After the LA stop, we flew an hour up to Northern California to visit San Jose and San Francisco, the two cities geographically bracketing Silicon Valley north and south. The visit seemed to be gliding to a positive and uneventful conclusion. San Francisco's Chinese American community was on balance supportive of the visit, and San Jose had fought hard to get on the itinerary.

In San Jose, we were scheduled to attend a large luncheon. Zhu was to deliver remarks. San Jose was an interesting and appropriate place to take the mayors. The city's mayor, Tom McEnery, was America's youngest big-city mayor. Being involved in start-up ventures in Silicon Valley, McEnery had built an entirely new city skyline in San Jose which not long before had been a rather sleepy town twenty minutes south of my boyhood home in Palo Alto. My wife, Susan, went to San Jose State College (as it was known until 1972). McEnery was a proponent of fiscal reform. In short, he had a lot in common with Zhu Rongji. As we drove up to the entrance of the hotel luncheon venue, there were no apparent security challenges. The scene was normal.

The ballroom was packed. I was not sure that the fire code was being observed; there was standing room only, with people lined up and standing cheek-by-jowl along the side and back walls. There was a buzz, all of which one associates with positive energy.

Zhu and I were seated near the podium, and after he was introduced, he rose to speak. Almost immediately, many of the people standing on the side and back walls unfurled banners with characters and began chanting, "*Sha Zhu.*" This was a play on words—the same sounds (though different tones) can stand for different characters. The written characters used on the banners and posters were "Kill the pig." Zhu Rongji's family name has the same sound as "pig" but is a different character. So, the protestors were chanting "Kill Zhu," "Kill the pig." I was stunned, as I believe was Zhu. We had no inkling that any protest was likely, much less one this threatening. There had been some police presence outside the hotel, as was appropriate, but we had not been informed of any anticipated problems. It was a bolt out of the blue.

I looked around to see if local police were converging on the room or podium. (This was long past the era, 1972–1978, when State Department security officers accompanied NCUSCR and CSCPRC-hosted delegations.) I looked toward the exits located at the rear of the room from our position. To extricate ourselves, we would have to walk the gauntlet of the entire crowd out the exit located at the rear. Even that narrow pathway was filling in with the alarmed crowd. I concluded that we had to get out of there promptly, or the opportunity to do so would be lost entirely. I stood up, walked toward the podium, signaled to Mayor Zhu that we had to get out, grabbed his forearm, and briskly walked through the crowd. There were the other mayors and the elderly Wang Daohan to be concerned about as well. All my National Committee colleagues extracted everyone safely, with what dignity was possible and prudent under the circumstances. They performed superbly.

By now, down on the street level, horse-mounted police were pushing back a growing crowd. We finally all got into our van with a police escort and departed, going north on US 101 to San Francisco, the freeway along which I had commuted for summer employment with United Air Lines more than twenty-five years earlier. This is the same stretch of highway upon which I had suggested to my father's somnolent carpool that United Air Lines should fly to China.

I sat next to Mayor Zhu, telling him that I felt some responsibility that we had not known about even the possibility of such a turn of events. Beyond that, I did not offer excuses. He reassured me. That was the last we ever talked about the incident, though during the rest of our trip, we were attuned to any possible security problems. I guess someone who had been on his own from a very early age, been called a "rightist" in the era of Mao Zedong, weathered the Cultural Revolution, and made it through June 4 would perhaps take this more in stride than I did.

Over the intervening years, I have thought about this incident. It seems to me that there is a strand in American political life in which some proclaim their commitment to "the masses," "the people," but exhibit little compassion or empathy toward individual humans as they find them.

San Francisco, California
The politics of China-Taiwan in the San Francisco Bay Area are complicated. Looking down from an upper floor of a building in the Montgomery and Grant Street area of San Francisco, one can see Taiwan and PRC flags fluttering above their "own" buildings, rather like gold-rush era miners of 1849 in the High Sierras staking out their mining claims with flags. Each building seems to be a proxy in the competition across the Taiwan Strait. Visible from above, and invisible from street level, the scene was like so much having to do with China and Greater China.

The other tense experience involving Zhu and the mayors occurred at one of our last meetings, this an early morning breakfast atop the Bank of America Center in the "Carnelian Room" on the 52nd floor, in San Francisco's Financial District. The stunning vista out the windows revealed the San Francisco Bay, with Alcatraz Island seemingly floating in the middle of the Bay in stark relief, as the rising sun provided a dappled, sparkling backdrop. The city's mayor, Art Agnos, was our host.

Earlier in his career, in December 1973, Agnos had been shot twice in an attack; he was a surviving victim of what had been called the "Zebra Murders." Before and after the assassination attempt, he was a northern California Democratic Party liberal, working himself up from a chief-of-staff slot in the California State Assembly to get elected to the assembly in his own right in 1976, representing the 16th District in San Francisco. He was extremely active on social, health, and civil rights issues. In 1987, he ran for mayor of the city, to replace Dianne Feinstein, who by law could not run for an additional term. Agnos took office in January 1988 and lasted one term. In 1990, Feinstein ran a losing race for governor of California but prevailed in a special election for U.S. senator in November 1992, thereafter becoming a national force in U.S.-China relations.

While she had been mayor of San Francisco, in January 1980, Feinstein had signed a sister-city agreement with Shanghai while visiting China, beating out LA in the process. Subsequently, when Jiang Zemin became mayor of Shanghai in 1985, Feinstein and Jiang interacted often, and their relationship continued after she became an increasingly influential U.S. senator in the 1990s.

Agnos and Feinstein disagreed on many issues, such as labor and policies concerning the police and fire departments. So, in the wake of Tiananmen, and later when Senator Feinstein emerged as a national voice for a productive China policy, Agnos for a multitude of reasons was otherwise inclined.

After pleasantries with Mayor Agnos with his back to the windows and Zhu admiring the Bay and mentioning Shanghai and San Francisco's decade-long association as sister cities, Mayor Agnos rather abruptly brought up Tiananmen, its admittedly horrific aftermath, and hardly afforded Mayor Zhu a chance to respond. This meal was heading very rapidly toward minor disaster as the eggs and toast arrived. I don't think anyone finished their meal.

I felt that San Francisco's mayor was rude, well beyond what one could characterize as hardball politics and bracing honesty. Having been shot, being heavily committed to civil rights, and having fought against police surveillance in San Francisco probably all go some distance in explaining Mayor Agnos's approach. However, when Zhu had met Congresswoman (from San Francisco) Nancy Pelosi earlier in the trip, she had managed to make the same points without being so strident as to be ineffective and rude. Agnos was in "send," not "receive," mode.

Sitting as I was to Zhu's right hand, I leaned over and said: "Mr. Mayor, you should know that I consider this rude, I don't think you need to endure this, and if you wish, I would suggest we leave." I may have been overly sensitive given what we had been through in San Jose. He turned to me and whispered: "Can we do this?" I said, "Yes, and I will excuse us now." Whereupon I turned to Mayor Agnos and said something to the effect of, "I don't think Americans treat guests this way. We need to be on our way." There was a stunned silence as we left.

In retrospect, I don't know that this was the best way to handle things, but civilized, respectful discourse gets you farther than offensive behavior. I think that was an important message I could send to our Chinese guests and our American hosts. The United States needs friends. It seems that in our righteous indignation, we often beat up on those with whom we may largely agree because we can never get our hands on those responsible for travesties.

NEW YORK CITY, XU KUANGDI, AND RUDOLF GIULIANI

Though later chronologically than the two San Francisco Bay Area incidents described above, this case fits neatly into the theme of the opportunities and dangers of using localities as workarounds to grid-locked national-level channels. New York City, like San Francisco, was a "sister city" of Shanghai. As such, when Shanghai city fathers came to either New York or San Francisco (or vice versa), it was expected that the city being visited would act as the gracious symbolic host with its mayor greeting his/her counterpart, at a minimum.

In New York City in the aftermath of June 4, in September 1989, Mayor Ed Koch renamed the Twelfth Avenue and 42nd Street inter-section (adjacent to the Chinese Consulate) "Tiananmen Square," much to Beijing's displeasure. Adding to this ambiance in this section of New York City called "Hell's Kitchen," the World War II Aircraft Carrier *Intrepid* was permanently moored at Pier 86, clearly visible from the PRC Consulate with a revolving carousel room atop the building. The entire scene carried with it a whiff of gunboat diplomacy. Mayor Koch had also suspended all twelve cooperative programs with Shanghai under the sister-city agreement.

Fast forwarding to November 1996, the National Committee hosted Shanghai Mayor Xu Kuangdi during a trip to the United States, a major stop being New York City to meet then-mayor Rudolf Giuliani. At that time, Giuliani was seen as an effective mayor, bringing more discipline to the city. Somewhat later he would become "America's Mayor" in the wake of his rallying the people of New York City on and after 9/11. This visit was about twenty-five years before Giuliani became a punchline about toupees, bleeding hair rinse, his corruption, accusations of attempts to improperly influence elections, servitude to Donald Trump, and insur-rectionist activities. It is hard to imagine a more glaring case of political self-immolation. In 1996, however, he was riding high.

On our draft itinerary with Mayor Xu's staff, we had penciled in a meeting between mayors Giuliani and Xu, but the specific time had not been confirmed. Though we had spoken to the mayor's office early in the planning process, we could not get a confirmed time for the Xu-Gi-uliani meeting. We assumed we were experiencing normal scheduling difficulties. As time marched on, and Xu Kuangdi arrived, the itinerary was still unconfirmed on the one meeting that Xu most wanted and expected. As time wore on, and as the mayor and I rode around in our limo from meeting to meeting, Xu regularly would ask, "And what is happening on the meeting with Mayor Giuliani?" I was getting alarmed but honestly replied that I thought we were just having predictable scheduling problems, dampening my concern with the soothing thought that when in China, meetings with senior PRC leaders rarely are confirmed much before they occur.

At this point, National Committee staff and I began to contact everyone in the committee's orbit with a connection to Mayor Giuliani to get a time and commitment to meet. We even called a Giuliani campaign contributor. Some of the people we contacted had long and deep connections with Giuliani and the Chinese. Finally, the message came back in effect saying, Mayor Giuliani is known as the anticorruption crime fighter; communist governments are corrupt, none more so than China; and he will not meet with Mayor Xu.

Immediately after learning this unwelcome news, I again was in the back seat of the limo with Mayor Xu headed to Wall Street. Mayor Xu asked the question I dreaded—"And how is the scheduling for the meeting coming?" At that point, I said something to the effect of, "Mr. Mayor, I have been informed by Mayor Giuliani's office that he will not meet with you." "Why?" Xu asked. I said that I owed him the unvarnished truth as I had just come to understand it. I explained that the residual of June 4 still lingered; that U.S. politicians have "brands," images of themselves that they sell; and Mayor Giuliani's political identity was that of crime buster and corruption fighter. He considered communists to be by definition corrupt, and he would not meet Mayor Xu. The fact that Giuliani was running for reelection in 1997 may have had something to do with it, I speculated. Mayor Xu looked out the car window for a long time, taking it all in.

From my point of view, we (the U.S. system) did it again. Here was a progressive mayor: he had modernized Shanghai, was an intellectual who loved classical music, later became the president of China's National Academy of Engineering, and, when Zhu Rongji had asked him to head Shanghai's Planning Commission, replied, "But I don't believe in planning."[5] We just keep beating up on the most cosmopolitan elements in the Chinese system simply because they are the ones to whom we are most often exposed, and therefore the people against whom we can lash out.

In an ironic exclamation point to this incident, in 1997 "Rudy" sent me a holiday card featuring a picture of the "City of Bridges" (New York). To me the mayor was burning bridges, not building them.

In stark contrast, on another occasion in this period, a different progressive senior leader of a major Chinese city met with a small group for dinner in New York at the Harvard Club. After the meal, several guests made remarks. When this official's moment to speak came, he stood at the lectern, subdued, speaking in a low, wavering voice, and told us that before embarking on his trip, he had attended a ceremony for the repatriation of remains of an American air crew on a supply mission to southwestern China that went down in the Himalayas during World War II. He reported that the crew in its last seconds before death had etched into the aluminum fuselage what had gone wrong with the plane before it crashed so the malfunction could be remedied to save future crews. The Chinese official then asked, how is it that our two countries could cooperate then, under such difficult circumstances, but now, with conditions objectively better, we were at such loggerheads? He broke down sobbing.

CAPITOL HILL BECOMES THE FOCUS

The Tiananmen tragedy had postponed Governor Shafer's plan to retire as Board Chair. Things were changing rapidly, however, and the committee resumed a low-key search for a new chair before long. Washington was coping with the aftermath of June 4; America soon had a new president, Democrat Bill Clinton; and the committee needed a chair able to work across party lines with China credentials. Having experience dealing with Congress would be a big plus.

As so often happens, serendipity drives developments.

From 1986 until August 31, 1991, Barber B. Conable Jr. was president of the World Bank. His work there was well known to the National

Committee. Before his time at the World Bank, he had been Ranking Minority Member (Republican) on the powerful House Ways and Means Committee. He had been named by his peers the most respected member of Congress.

Conable's spouse, Charlotte, had participated in NCUSCR activities and was familiar with Committee Vice President Jan Berris. Jan approached Charlotte to ask if she would ask Barber if he might be interested in becoming National Committee chair. An encouraging reply came back, and I scheduled a meeting with Barber after duly conferring with Governor Shafer and members of the board. After a short discussion, Barber agreed to undertake the challenge, if formally asked. On December 26, 1991, President George H. W. Bush wrote Barber congratulations upon taking up the chairmanship.

In the wake of Tiananmen, Conable had resisted the most punitive impulses of some in the Bush administration and Congress in his role as World Bank president. As he saw it, some in the Bush administration and those looking toward the 1992 general election wanted to use the World Bank to impose excessive punishment on China for Tiananmen. Barber felt this was ill-advised when Deng Xiaoping was in a domestic fight with opponents over whether or not to rekindle economic reform in China—don't pull the rug from under the reformers.

Barber also believed that the World Bank was not simply an instrument of U.S. policy. The UN, the World Bank, the International Monetary Fund, and other international multilateral agencies were positives for America, but they were not Washington's exclusive tools. He worked hard to get the World Bank Board of Governors to take an expansive view of humanitarian loans to China and augmented the bank's environmental portfolio because of the intrinsic merit of such investments. Humanitarian and environmental loans were relatively acceptable in Tiananmen's wake.

I am always interested in how people define their greatest achievements. When I asked Barber what he was most proud of in his World Bank interaction with China, he said: "We planted a billion trees in China."

When Barber became chairman of the National Committee, much policy action concerning China had shifted from the White House to Capitol Hill. He was a huge asset in credibly dealing with Congress.

NOTES

1. David M. Lampton, "Meeting with Shanghai Mayor Zhu Rongji," Hengshan Hotel, Shanghai, A. Doak Barnett and David M. Lampton, September 18, 1989, 6.

2. Notes by David M. Lampton, "Meeting with Shanghai Mayor Zhu Rongji," A. Doak Barnett and David M. Lampton, Hengshan Hotel, Shanghai, September 18, 1989, 2–3. (RAC).

3. Zhou v. Peng, "Memorandum of Order," https://casetext.com/case/zhou-v-peng.

4. Pieter Bottelier, "Working in the World Bank's Mission in the Mid-1990s," in World Bank Group, *At the Front Line: 1980–2020* (World Bank Group, 2021), 47.

5. David M. Lampton, *Same Bed, Different Dreams: Managing U.S.-China Relations, 1989–2000* (University of California Press, 2001), 277.

CHAPTER TEN

From the White House to Capitol Hill
(The 1990s Politically)

THE JUNE 4, 1989, BLOODSHED IN BEIJING LED TO PROFOUND CHANGES in Washington's management of U.S.-China relations.

Richard Nixon's trip to China, Jimmy Carter's establishment of formal diplomatic ties with Beijing, and Ronald Reagan's signing of the August 1982 Communique on arms sales to Taiwan were the result of behind-the-scenes negotiations between the U.S. Executive Branch and PRC officials—potent demonstrations of executive power. Legislators might have groused about policy after the fact, and, in the case of President Carter's formal diplomatic recognition of the PRC, pass the Taiwan Relations Act (TRA) of 1979 to fence in Carter's presidential action. However, at that time, Congress generally was more bystander than participant.

The presidential actions taken by Nixon, Carter, and Reagan were profound, but they did not require large congressional appropriations. Similarly, commerce—an area where Congress has substantial regulatory and taxing powers—was not a major consideration in the China opening. Moreover, anti-Soviet feeling was running so high in America that anything undertaken in the name of opposing Moscow did not face heavy scrutiny from Congress until the Soviet collapse. Consequently, the U.S.-China relationship in the first decade-plus after normalization was dominated by the Executive Branch, the TRA being an important exception.

Beijing's experiences with the Nixon-Ford-Carter-Reagan presidencies led it to think that U.S. presidents used the specter of Congress to serve as the "bad cop" to the executive's "good cop." For Beijing, Congress was a manufactured negotiating boogeyman, not a genuine force to reckon with. One implication of this perception was that Beijing took a long time to build up its congressional liaison capacities. This contrasted sharply with Taiwan's prowess with Congress.

One of many reasons I subsequently worked with former Iowa Senator Dick Clark and the Aspen Congressional Program (1998–2012) to get members of Congress to the PRC was not only so they could learn about China directly, but also so that Beijing would see more accurately the full role of Congress.

The Tiananmen bloodshed jolted Congress, energizing it to play a larger role in China policy. Once the genies of legislative interest and concern were out of the bottle, the Executive Branch faced constant challenges from Congress over how to manage Sino-American relations. One later example of congressional involvement was Speaker Nancy Pelosi's visit to Taipei (August 2022) despite President Biden's wish that she not go. The issue of human rights served as the entering wedge, but as U.S.-China trade became an expanding part of the bilateral relationship in the 1990s, Congress (particularly the House of Representatives) had another powerful, natural point of entry to influence policy. And later still, as China became a growing security challenge for Washington from 1995–1996, the congressional security and intelligence infrastructure of committees and subcommittees became more active, eventually culminating in House Republicans establishing a Select Committee on China in the wake of the 2022 mid-term elections, announcing that "even in divided government, we have an opportunity to build a united front against CCP aggression." Congress now talks less about "China" and more about the CCP.

The American political system also was changing, subjecting China policy to ever more fractious, diverse, and undisciplined forces. With the relative weakening of political parties as funding sources for congressional campaigns, and the arrival of the twenty-four-hour cable news cycle, members of Congress over the 1970s, 1980s, and 1990s increasingly saw their futures depending on directly cultivating personal support bases. Members of Congress became solo political entrepreneurs. Money bought air time, air time bought name recognition, and name recognition won elections. Hedrick Smith's insightful 1987 book, *The Power Game*, describes this transformation.

By the mid-1990s, the rise of the Tea Party had pushed congressional Republicans to the right, led by Speaker of the House Newt Gingrich. Also, particularly in the Senate, leaders with considerable Asia expertise began to fade away and, with a few exceptions such as Senators Max Baucus and Dianne Feinstein and Congressman Doug Bereuter in the House, new expertise did not ascend to replace them. Leaders such as Barber Conable, Bob Dole, Ted Kennedy, Mike Mansfield, Howard Baker, Nancy Kassebaum, John McCain, Sam Nunn, Richard Lugar, and Hugh Scott were a vanishing breed of centrist practitioners of the legislative craft and foreign policy, and they were knowledgeable about China. In Senator Mansfield's case, his association with China policy went back to the FDR administration.

With the accumulation of changes, America's China policy became just another club with which to beat domestic political opponents and mobilize diverse base voters.

ENTER NANCY PELOSI

In 1989–1990, junior Democratic congresswoman from San Francisco, Nancy Pelosi, became a major face of this transformation.

Elected to Congress in a 1987 special election, Nancy Pelosi came from a deeply committed, activist, and politically successful Democratic family in which her father and brother both had been mayors of Baltimore and her father had served in Congress. Moving to San Francisco in 1969, Pelosi became increasingly active in Democratic Party politics in California. Her 1987 victory came in a deep-blue district that a Republican had not won since 1949. The district's residents were 27 percent Asian American. That she left her family's secure Baltimore political base, moved to San Francisco (raised five children), and worked herself up in a very different political culture than the East Coast is testimony to her political skills and tenacity.

Having dealt with Nancy Pelosi on several occasions, I can attest that she is a deeply committed person of integrity, anchored in her Catholic faith. Skilled political calculation also played a large role in her ascent, with two of her mantras being "know you have the votes" before the final push and "own the ground"—mobilize your voters to get every last one to the polls. This combination of commitment, calculation, and mobilization skills accounts for her success. A junior congressperson such as Pelosi normally would have only gradually acquired foreign policy influence within Congress. And in those days, women in Congress faced considerable obstacles beyond lack of seniority.

Tiananmen provided Nancy Pelosi a context in which she could display her political values and skills on a very resonant issue, win support from key party leaders such as Senate Majority Leader George Mitchell (from Maine) who agreed with her on China, and take the lead attacking the Republican President George H. W. Bush, who in his desire to preserve ties with Beijing, was out of step with many in his political party and broader public opinion, not to mention the Democrats. Pelosi thus acquired a national constituency and name recognition very early in her career. In the aftermath of June 4, one former senior member of the House told me with a touch of exasperation that Nancy Pelosi was a very junior "backbencher" who would just have to wait her turn. This is not what happened.

Pelosi's secure political base and her values catapulted her to prominence well beyond what her modest seniority would otherwise have afforded her. She had a cause that resonated widely in her district, her party, and throughout the nation.

Three issues gave Congress a powerful role in China policy in the wake of Tiananmen. Pelosi seized all three, becoming the most prominent, most articulate voice for each:

1. President George H. W. Bush had imposed sanctions on China, but he did not want inflexible sanctions embedded in law which could tie his hands when he thought the time had come for them to be lifted or altered. Once policies become law, undoing them becomes challenging. Many in Congress also wanted more sanctions.

2. In 1989–1990, America faced the question of what could be done to protect the over thirty-three thousand Chinese students and scholars in the United States who, when their visas expired, could be forced back to China into the middle of the post-Tiananmen dragnet. Like Congress, the president wanted to afford them protection, but he did not wish to institutionalize that preference into law, fearing that Beijing would retaliate by not letting more Chinese students come to America. Beijing viewed affording a blanket extension to Chinese students in the United States as leading to strategic brain drain, a theft of the best Chinese minds. For President Bush, the way around the dilemma was to let them stay but be low-key about it, using executive action rather than legislation.

3. Finally, there was the issue of whether or not China should continue receiving an annual presidential waiver for MFN under the provisions of the Jackson-Vanik Amendment to the Trade Act of 1974, originally aimed principally at the USSR. The Amendment stipulated that Congress must be informed by the president of his intention to issue a waiver for a "nonmarket" (communist) economy to receive MFN for the next year. Before Tiananmen the China waiver had been a formality. The bloodshed changed this. While Representative Pelosi was at a conference in Cambridge, Massachusetts, in January 1990, with George Stephanopoulos (an ally of the Chinese students and later advisor to President Bill Clinton), she suggested that annually trying to stop the extension of MFN to Beijing would provide Congress leverage in the quest to advance human rights in the PRC.

In seizing a leadership role on all these issues, Pelosi dealt herself centrally into sanctions, trade, and immigration policy debates and had a moral position with broad appeal. She also had the outspoken support of Senate Majority Leader George Mitchell. In the 101st Congress of 1989–1991, the Democratic Party held a majority in both houses, while the presidency was in Republican hands. At this moment, political circumstances, her message, and available legislative tools converged. At NCUSCR I felt myself constantly crosswise with her policies.

In her righteousness, Congresswoman Pelosi is willing to stage events that look unimpeachable in the U.S. political context but can come at the expense of the people in China or Taiwan she wants to help. We saw this in 1991 when she and two other members of Congress ditched their Chinese handlers in Beijing and unfurled a banner in Tiananmen Square, making her point as she caused further tightening in China. Three decades later, she led a delegation to Taiwan (August 2022), and despite Biden administration preferences, she went, and extensive PRC military pressure on the island followed.

Tiananmen did not make Nancy Pelosi, but it did provide her visibility and a platform permitting her to demonstrate the full range of her skills, leading to her eventually becoming House Speaker in 2007.

First at NCUSCR, and later as a SAIS professor (1997–2018), dealing with Congress became a significant preoccupation of mine. I often testified before Congress and also had individual meetings with many members of Congress, from Ted Kennedy (D-MA) on the left to John Ashcroft (R-MO) on the right. In addition, I worked with the China Working Group led by Representatives Rick Larsen (D-WA) and Mark Kirk (R-IL, later senator from Illinois); participated in a study group convened by Senator Max Baucus (D-MT); worked with the U.S.-China Policy Foundation and others to get congressional staff to China; and served as a consultant to former Iowa Senator Dick Clark of the Aspen Institute's Congressional Program.

Over the years, this exposure to members of Congress shaped what I wrote and which issues I tackled, gradually giving me insight into the nature of Congress—its sometimes majestic character and its often disappointing, dysfunctional, and grimy flip-side. Many individuals in Congress are impressive, thoughtful, and want to do the right thing. But the sum is still less than the parts. Turnover, logrolling, and a constant stream of elections mean that the merits of an issue often take a back seat to a thousand other, sometimes petty, considerations.

The House of Representatives often is the "hotter" of the two chambers of Congress, which means that senators who do not so frequently face voters take a longer view. Senators represent broader, statewide constituencies and so, generally speaking, need to accommodate a broader range of opinions before taking a stand. Members of the House represent more variable, smaller constituencies. Districts can elect some truly bizarre characters. I once visited one House member's office that conjured up the image in my mind of a cult headquarters rather than a place in which to do the public's business.

Sometimes Congress acquiesces when presidents are determined to engage in ill-advised and pugilistic initiatives; at other times, Congress actively stampedes the Executive into disaster. But Congress has the virtue of also sometimes being the branch that can reverse course after taking full measure of an administration's missteps (e.g., Vietnam and Iraq). Executive branches seem more inclined to pour in resources hoping to salvage a failed policy. President Joe Biden's withdrawal from Afghanistan in 2021 was an untidy, wrenching exception to this pattern.

In the wake of June 4, Beijing tried to increase the size and effectiveness of its congressional liaison operation in Washington, but ultimately the ethos and practice of politics on Capitol Hill is something Beijing (unlike Taipei) seems unable to grasp. The PRC intrinsically knows how to deal with executive power but is a babe in the woods when it comes to dealing with Congress. One reason that Taipei is more adept at dealing with Congress is that it sees Congress as its ultimate life preserver—for Beijing, Congress has been a nuisance.

DEALING WITH CONGRESS

Between May 1990 and March 2016, I testified a total of nine times before Senate committees and subcommittees, four times before House committees and subcommittees, and four times in front of the U.S.-China Economic and Security Review Commission.

After the 1990s, the pace of my participation in formal congressional hearings on China slowed for a variety of reasons, including China's WTO entry with permanent NTR in 2001, thus eliminating the rationale for multiple hearings annually on MFN. Almost simultaneously, the 9/11 attacks on the United States diverted foreign policy attention to Central Asia, the Middle East, and counterterrorism. And finally, when the Republicans had a majority in Congress and a president of their party in the White House, congressional oversight declined with respect to the PRC.

As part of the WTO entry agreement of 2001, China was granted Permanent NTR. A component of the underlying deal in Washington was that two congressionally sanctioned "Commissions" (each structured differently) were created to help provide China policy oversight. The Congressional-Executive Commission on China focused on human rights, and the U.S.-China Economic and Security Review Commission focused on issues its name suggests. Both bodies became perches for people holding skeptical to hostile views of the PRC. Of the two commissions, the Economic and Security Review Commission has been the most sharply, consistently, and broadly critical of Beijing. Economic and Security Review commissioners were *not* members of Congress but rather political appointees, some electrically charged. The forces most skeptical of China effectively bargained to get these platforms as their price for going along with permanent NTR for China.

After 1989, Congress developed an ever-expanding agenda of concerns about China. Many of them were well-founded, beginning with the Tiananmen violence of 1989. Later, economic and trade issues grew in importance, and from the mid-1990s, security issues grew in number and severity, not least because of growing PLA modernization, activity in the waters off China, and episodic spikes in concerns about Taiwan.

My testimonies before Congress and the commissions addressed an expanding conflictual and shrill agenda, which I saw from several vantage points, first at the NCUSCR, then at SAIS in Washington. After Defense Secretary William Perry left office in 1997, at various points, I participated in his "Preventive Defense Project" from 1997 to 2017. The project afforded me opportunities for contact with the PRC and Taiwan militaries, including several generations of senior political leaders in both the PRC and Taiwan. NCUSCR cooperated with Perry and Ash Carter (later secretary of defense) on this. All this informed my Capitol Hill testimonies.

Other National Committee exchanges also shaped my testimonies. Committee programs involved U.S. military and national security leaders such as James Schlesinger, Robert McNamara, and many retired four-star officers, along with their counterparts in the PRC and Taiwan defense establishments. These exchanges left little doubt that nimbus clouds were churning on the horizon, thus shaping the content of my congressional testimony and my overall view that peace in Asia was growing tenuous.

Over time, I was invited to testify by both political parties. The Executive Branch (almost irrespective of which political party held the White House) was often in the position of defending attempts to manage the relationship with Beijing in the face of congressional calls for more muscular measures. I generally defended an expert-grounded, stable policy process that took into account the constraints facing Chinese leaders. My proclivities thus meant that I was more closely aligned with Executive Branch inclinations, irrespective of party, than the more diverse and unrestrained voices heard on the Hill—until the Trump era.

I made a major commitment of time and energy to the Aspen Institute's Congressional Program. This effort convened member-only, multiday seminars on China (including both legislative chambers and both political parties) outside the continental United States, sometimes in the PRC. The seminars addressed Chinese domestic and foreign policy and U.S.-China relations. In addition to American scholars as briefers, we generally included one or two scholars from the PRC. When the seminars were convened in places other than China, we sometimes invited influential persons from Taiwan to participate. One year we had Taipei Mayor (later president) Ma Ying-jeou and another year Madam Hsiao Bi-khim, then a member of Taiwan's Legislative Yuan and later head of the Taipei Economic and Cultural Representative Office (TECRO) in Washington, D.C. The Aspen Congressional Program supplemented these multiday seminars outside the continental United States with periodic Capitol Hill breakfast briefings for members only.

During the 1998–2012 period when I was the China Consultant for the Aspen Institute Congressional Program, the effort was under the leadership of former Iowa Senator Dick Clark and his long-time colleague Bill Nell. We held a total of ten large, multiday member seminars, four in China and six outside the PRC. Together these gatherings included twenty-eight senators and 112 members of the House. Some members attended several events over time, and House members out-numbered Senators by about four to one over the entire period. More Democrats participated than Republicans, but we made every effort to recruit from both sides of the aisle.

At the outset, we had protracted negotiations with our counterpart connected to China's Foreign Ministry to assure that Aspen would have complete control of delegation composition, itinerary, and contacts with various segments of PRC society. This meant declining nearly all Chinese government hospitality. A major feature of PRC thinking about foreign access is that it be monitored, if not controlled. The Aspen-Congress side could not accommodate this. If we had acquiesced, many members of Congress would not have participated, and such conditions would have been seen as indefensible by members' constituents and domestic oppo-nents, exposing them to criticism and attack.

Likewise, because Congress is a co-equal and independent branch in the U.S. constitutional system, the Aspen Program generally declined to meet with U.S. government officials in China. The U.S. Executive Branch chafed at this lack of interaction almost as much as the Chinese government. Everyone wants to see U.S. congresspersons so they can pro-mote their concerns. For their part, I imagine that the Chinese thought to themselves: "We will never understand these Americans. They are arms-length from not only our officials but their own as well."

The Chinese largely operated within the agreed parameters, with a little fraying around the edges on issues concerning providing security for groups. Quite reasonably, Beijing felt that if something untoward befell a congressional group while in the PRC, it would be a fiasco for bilateral relations and they would be blamed. To the Americans, a PRC security presence could be mistaken for control.

One example of the dilemma occurred when one of our delegations was on a boat steaming down the Yangtze River for several days. Ministry of Public Security vessels cleared our way along the choked waterway, and plainclothesmen provided on-the-ground security in remote areas, one memorable incident being security officers with ear pieces incon-spicuously posted in caves along the group's route. The Chinese never acknowledged the security, nor did we. From the Chinese perspective, it was simply unimaginable for central, much less ever-vigilant and nervous local, officials to have a large delegation of high-ranking foreigners wandering around with no provision for their security or monitoring. I recall that when NCUSCR was entrusted with the welfare of senior visiting Chinese in the United States, we were relieved to have federal security protection for our guests.

Aspen's work with Congress was important, particularly with the increasingly freelance behavior of members of Congress. In the more distant past, both chambers of Congress had legislators and staff who were knowledgeable and took the lead in guiding less-interested, less-knowledgeable members on issues of foreign policy. Because members of Congress must address such a broad range of domestic and foreign issues, not everyone can be equally knowledgeable across all topics, hence the need for specialization and leadership by issue.

During his lifetime, Representative and later Senator Mike Mansfield of Montana played such a leadership role on China policy since the administration of FDR. With Mansfield's retirement from the Senate in 1977 (whereupon he was named Ambassador to Japan), Senator Max Baucus (D-MT) assumed a similar role in terms of China policy, eventually becoming Ambassador to China (2014–2017), at which point he had become his state's longest-serving senator. Senator Baucus invested considerable energy in learning about China, periodically assembling a small group of experts in his upper-floor hideaway office in the Capitol where we ate carrots and discussed the PRC and Asia.

Nurturing cumulative knowledge in Congress is a frustrating, albeit essential, undertaking. Congress has 535 members, of whom 435 (the House) must run for reelection every two years; the other 100 (the Senate) face voters every six. Getting sustained focus on foreign policy in election years is difficult unless there is a calamity. Moreover, members of Congress lose elections, retire, or die, thereby generating high turnover, which means those seeking to elevate the overall knowledge level in Congress are on a treadmill. Staff turnover is constant, and the average age of congressional staff is thirty-one.

When members were together without staff and the media, as they were during Aspen seminars, they were collegial, thoughtful, flexible, and undogmatic. Once out of the seminar bubble, however, politics and the aphrodisiac of media attention took over. Some members worried that their constituents would view foreign travel as a "boondoggle" and thus avoided it altogether. Ignorance about the world can make for political bliss. Some in Congress just prefer their own beds at night.

It is in these contexts that the work of former Senator Dick Clark (D-IA), founder of the Aspen Institute Congressional Program, assumes importance. Dick became the standard against which I measure others in public life. In his precongressional career Dick was a professor of history and political science at Upper Iowa University. He was moderate, viscerally committed to human rights, and nonpartisan in political style. He believed in the power of education and knowledge to improve public life. During his term as Senator (1973–1979), he was influential on Africa policy as chair of the Senate Foreign Relations Committee's Africa Subcommittee. He opposed apartheid and the racist regime in South Africa, being sufficiently nettlesome to the South African government that it channeled $250,000 to defeat him in the 1978 election in Iowa.

After losing reelection, Dick joined the Aspen Institute (an international nonprofit organization established in 1949) and in 1983 founded its Congressional Program, an effort dedicated to educating members of Congress on foreign affairs. Its programs are bicameral and bipartisan, funded by genuine philanthropies, rather than self-interested groups looking to have influence. In 1998, when Dick's program expanded to include seminars and briefings on China, I was fortunate that he asked me to assist. I first met Dick and Bill Nell, his long-time and highly skilled staff colleague, at a program on Vietnam held in New York City when I was president of NCUSCR.

Dick and Barber Conable Jr. shared important qualities and assets, one of which was the respect they both received from congressional colleagues irrespective of party. I remember the way the Trade Subcommittee Chair of the Ways and Means Committee Sam Gibbons (D-FL) received Conable's testimony on February 24, 1994. The spirit of respect for knowledge and bipartisanship expressed by the Democratic Chair (Gibbons) to a former ranking Republican member (Conable) was remarkable in this otherwise rancorous period. Conable bluntly told the committee what his judgment was as to the prospects for democracy in China. "I am not going to tell you that China is moving rapidly toward democracy. I think such movement is inevitable, but I think it is also very slow. They do not have in their 4,000 year history a great democratic tradition and I think it would be unusual if they were to become a clone of the United States quickly."[1]

IN THE ARENA OF HEARINGS

The most useful way to convey the reality of, and directions in, U.S.-China relations is to examine two congressional hearings before which I testified, separated by about a decade. The first hearing took place in May 1990, before three jointly convened subcommittees of the House Committee on Foreign Affairs, during the earliest phase in which human rights in the PRC became a powerful issue in America and on Capitol Hill. Though there was powerful anger directed at Beijing following Tiananmen, that anger was offset to some extent by the hope that reform could be rekindled in China. At that moment, there was little sense in the region or America that China was a direct security challenge. A balance of forces in Congress and American society made management of the relationship challenging but possible. Many constituencies in the United States remained inclined toward moderation, patience, taking the long view, and reaping economic gains from trade and finance.

Moving to the second hearing in August 1999, with the PRC perceived as a mounting security problem, the relationship was entering more treacherous territory. Cracks had begun to widen perceptibly in 1995 and were on full display by the August 4, 1999, hearing of the Senate Committee on Foreign Relations before which I testified. A new era was dawning, though another decade-plus would pass before the transformation became fully apparent and deeply embedded.

MFN BATTLE AND THE MAY 1990 HEARINGS

The May 16, 1990, Joint Hearing by three subcommittees of the House Committee on Foreign Affairs on whether and/or how to continue extending MFN to China in Tiananmen's wake was a watershed.[2] The hearing framed the alternatives that would be debated for a decade. It signaled the important role that Congresswoman Pelosi would play.

Carried live in its entirety on C-SPAN, the hearing was chaired by Congressman Steve Solarz (D-NY), a notable policy voice on foreign affairs and Asia. His staff included respected China specialist Dr. Richard Bush and, before him, Dr. Edward Friedman, a long-time University of Wisconsin professor. The first panel consisted of former Ambassador to China under President George H. W. Bush, Winston Lord; me; Director of Human Rights Watch, Holly Burkhalter; and a Chinese student at Harvard University representing the Independent Federation of Chinese Students and Scholars—Zhao Haiqing.

George H. W. Bush's administration had spent the better part of the preceding year trying to coax better human and civil rights behavior out of Beijing, taking several initiatives. The president sent two special envoys (National Security Advisor Brent Scowcroft and Deputy Secretary of State Lawrence Eagleburger) to Beijing to urge restraint, a trip that when revealed publically became politically incendiary in Washington and the media. The administration also opposed popular *legislation* allowing Chinese students to stay in the United States, hoping Beijing would show restraint by continuing the flow of students abroad. The White House rejected further congressionally imposed sanctions.

Nonetheless, Beijing had done little in response, beyond releasing a few dissidents, taking every opportunity to assert that no government would allow another nation to tell it how to govern itself. Congresswoman Pelosi tapped into congressional and popular frustration with both Beijing and the Bush administration, calling for using MFN renewal to gain leverage. She spoke at this hearing.

When Congresswoman Pelosi's turn came to speak, her remarks homed in on my written testimony. "I am concerned about Mr. Lampton's testimony the most," she said. Later in the hearing, "Mr. Lampton, you cause me the most concern, most disagreement." I understood her to mean that I did not have a sufficiently punitive approach, my own view being that making public threats you cannot back up is unwise.

The hearing's most important outcome was that it specified *three policy approaches* to China and human rights policy, identifying the costs and gains of each: all three had downsides, some worse than others. The debate for the next decade revolved around this trio of alternatives.

Option 1 was to continue with the George H. W. Bush administration's approach of minimizing threats of muscular human rights pressure; continuing to protect Chinese students in the United States through *administrative measures*, rather than *law*; maintaining maximum flexibility for the president; and, most importantly, reinforcing the still powerful, but currently subdued, domestic pro-market forces in China to nudge Beijing back onto the reform path. All this was premised on the view that economic reform and social pluralization would come faster than change in the political system and that we should use what little influence we had to make progress where possible. I supported this approach.

There were several downsides, however, one of which was that we essentially were telling Congress that there was little it could do that wouldn't make things worse for the Chinese people, reform, and Hong Kong and Taiwan. I also was saying, don't victimize the victims.

Option 2 was to immediately curtail further MFN extensions until Beijing made important and measurable gains in civil and human rights. This had the downsides that it would rapidly and dramatically affect U.S. trade and economic groups, many Chinese who already had been victimized by Tiananmen would now be economically punished by the righteous indignation of America, and Taiwan and Hong Kong would become collateral damage because they were closely tied to the PRC economy. The Chinese student representative on the panel favored this option (calling for MFN "revocation at this time"), while conceding that there was not full agreement on this approach even among PRC students in America. Many in Taiwan and Hong Kong did not prefer this approach either. The political attraction of this path on Capitol Hill was that Congress could not be accused of inaction. I saw this as the "ready, fire, aim" approach.

Option 3 was to make *future* renewals of MFN (after the next 365 days) contingent upon Beijing making "overall, significant progress" in achieving U.S.-specified benchmarks for human rights gains. This approach had the advantage of delaying dropping the Sword of Damocles by one year, hoping Beijing would do enough to at least fashion a fig leaf of progress, thereby avoiding having to implement the threat. But Beijing could call Washington's bluff by doing nothing, and then what? Would Washington act? How would Congress define the "progress" it demanded, and how could compliance be measured? If Washington lost its nerve and failed to follow through, its credibility would be damaged, further emboldening Beijing. And, if the United States did implement the sanction, we then would have the downsides we would have had with Option 2 initially.

The Bush administration and I gravitated toward Option 1; Ambassador Lord was arguing for Option 3, with Congresswoman Pelosi saying at the hearing that she had not quite made up her mind between Options 2 and 3, while declaring that, "We can't face ourselves in the mirror if we just extend it [MFN]."

Given that President George H. W. Bush could count on thirty-four Senate votes to sustain a presidential veto of Options 2 and 3, realistically there was no chance that the two most punitive approaches would be put into effect during his term. Option 1 would win, barring another major PRC outrage. This fact, however, did not reduce the political attraction of relitigating the issue annually for a decade. Beijing might throw in a few token concessions along the way. Who knew? And all the interest groups could repeatedly get airtime to mobilize their supporters.

When Bill Clinton came into office in January 1993, having made opposing the "Butchers of Beijing" a theme of his victorious presidential campaign, and then appointing Winston Lord Assistant Secretary of State for East Asian and Pacific Affairs, Option 3 was effectively adopted as administration policy on May 28—the policy of "linkage" (Executive Order 128590), tying further extension of MFN beyond one year to Beijing making progress in meeting human rights markers defined in Washington. There was one important difference between the 1990 Option 3 and the Option 3 adopted by Bill Clinton in 1993—the terms of the linkage would be defined by the Executive Branch in policy, not enacted into law by Congress.

President Clinton's May 28, 1993, ultimatum essentially told Beijing to clean up its human rights situation within one year or lose MFN. But, having given Beijing the one-year deadline, the policy imploded when Beijing did virtually nothing in the next 363 days to meet Washington's conditions. When the policy abjectly failed to achieve its aims by mid-1994, President Clinton jumped ship, giving rise to howls of dissatisfaction in Congress. When presented with the choice between suffering all the predicted consequences of denying MFN to the PRC or backing down unceremoniously, Clinton retreated—for all the reasons predicted in the May 1990 hearing.

Standing back and objectively looking at how governments, authoritarian or democratic, actually behave, it is almost inconceivable that one nation's leaders would bow to a naked foreign demand to alter domestic governance to achieve trade gains. With President Clinton's retreat, Chinese leaders and citizens alike concluded that Washington was about symbolism, not substance. Americans, it seemed, choose their power and economic interests over humanitarian eyewash.

In the 1990 hearing, Congresswoman Pelosi revealed her core thinking. I thought then, and believe today, that she was profoundly mistaken: "If the economy [of China] suffers," she said, "democracy is served, because this will increase the displeasure of the Chinese people toward their government." Such pressure confirmed the thinking of those in China already believing that regime change and weakening the PRC was the U.S. agenda item written in invisible ink. I believe that economic deprivation and high degrees of turmoil throughout China's history generally have not fostered human rights. Attacking the PRC economy for human rights reasons activates the Chinese people to circle the wagons. The implementation of such a crude, but economically significant, threat would slow China's economic progress, impede its social pluralization, and inflict enormous costs on the regional and global economy, none of which serves democracy. Bill Clinton was correct to abandon the policy but wrong to have painted himself into the corner in the first place.

SECURITY AND TAIWAN

Standing at the threshold of the new millennium, the second hearing was convened by the Senate Committee on Foreign Relations on August 4, 1999, in the Dirksen Senate Office Building, coming to order at 10:30 a.m.[3] The hearing was convened to consider a bill proposed by North Carolina Senator Jesse Helms (R), the committee's chairman, and co-sponsored by Senator Robert Torricelli (D-NJ, appropriately known as "The Torch").[4] It was called "The Taiwan Security Enhancement Act (S-693)." From Beijing's perspective, this bill aligned Washington with Taipei in ways incompatible with the prior policies and practices of six U.S. administrations, particularly since President Reagan's August 1982 Joint Communique.

The period between the hearing of May 1990 recounted earlier and that of August 1999 discussed here saw U.S.-China ties shift onto a more ominous trajectory. This shift gradually became more pronounced during the subsequent George W. Bush, Barack Obama, Donald Trump, and Joe Biden eras in America, and the Hu Jintao and Xi Jinping periods in the PRC. The seeds for the more challenging times of the 2000s and beyond were sown in the mid-1990s, becoming apparent in the August 1999 hearing.

A signal event of the 1990s was the June 1995 visit of Taiwan's Lee Teng-hui, the island's first popularly elected president, to his alma mater Cornell University. Given that the Clinton administration had not prepared Beijing for President Lee being granted a visa, the PRC overreacted by lobbing missiles into the waters near Taiwan both in 1995 and again in 1996. The Clinton administration's 1996 response was to send two aircraft carrier groups to the island's vicinity to deter China from further using coercion. Beijing promptly de-escalated. This was the moment when both sides shifted from a policy of reassurance toward a policy of deterrence. Jiang Zemin unceremoniously backed off.

In meeting remarks made to a delegation I was with in March 1999 in China, former Defense Secretary William Perry recounted for President

Jiang Zemin what we had told cross-strait negotiator Wang Daohan in Hangzhou in previous days: "You have a two-pronged approach [to Taiwan]—deterrence and attraction. We understand both elements, but emphasize attraction and deemphasize deterrence."

In 1995–1996, President Jiang ordered the PLA to initiate a ten-year modernization program that would ensure China would not have to back down in the future like it just had done. What Washington considered an immediate victory had boomeranged, accelerating PLA modernization. This was no small matter because, from Washington's perspective, "normalization" had been predicated on "peaceful resolution" of cross-strait issues.

In the wake of the 1995–1996 imbroglio, other incidents reinforced the growing deterrence proclivities of both sides, not least a Chinese missile build-up. By the time of the 1999 hearing discussed here, Washington was contemplating selling theatre missile defense (TMD) systems to Taiwan, something Lee Teng-hui wanted. In a March 1999 meeting between Secretary Perry and President Lee at which I was present, President Lee said, "China acts like the Nazis before World War II and harbors ambitions."[5] He was asking for more U.S. defense help, and many on Capitol Hill and in the defense structure were supportive.

Other incidents reinforced the growing deterrence proclivities of both sides, not least the May 1999 mistaken U.S.-NATO bombing of the Chinese Embassy in Belgrade which killed three and wounded at least twenty PRC personnel. In the immediate wake of the bombing in Belgrade, the U.S. Embassy in Beijing came under popular, violent assault, demonstrations in which the regime channeled hostility at the U.S. Embassy while trying to ensure that it did not run out of control and result in dead Americans. I remember visiting the U.S. Ambassador's residence in Beijing shortly after this attack. The Marine guard gave departing U.S. Ambassador James Sasser and his wife, Mary, the flag flying over the mission on the day of the violent siege. At the ceremony, it was apparent that the ambassador and his spouse had bonded with their Marine guards in that ordeal.

May 1999 continued to be a bad month for U.S.-China ties when a congressional "Select Committee" report (*The Cox Report*) was released accusing Beijing of systematically pilfering U.S. defense (especially missile and warhead) technology and charging that U.S. companies had been negligent in protecting secrets. There also was the relentless Chinese occupation of land and tidal features in the South China Sea: notably Fiery Cross Reef in 1988 and Mischief Reef in 1994. And, adding to the growing feeling of Chinese assertiveness, Hong Kong reverted to PRC sovereignty on July 1, 1997, and Macau would "come back to the embrace of the motherland" in December 1999.

Beijing also had its worries. Taiwan's first popularly elected president, Lee Teng-hui, delivered internationally broadcast remarks on July 9, 1999, arguing that cross-strait interactions should be considered "state-to-state relations" [*liang guo*] which, for Beijing, came dangerously close to asserting that Taiwan was independent, Beijing's red line.

It was into this maelstrom that Senator Jesse Helms's legislation was thrust. Another decade would pass for the full erosion caused by this drip, drip process to become inescapably clear, but in retrospect, the August 4, 1999, Senate hearing made apparent where things were headed unless more restrained forces in Beijing, Taipei, and Washington asserted themselves.

The previously mentioned March 1999 delegation visit to China and Taipei led by former Defense Secretary Perry constituted part of the immediate background for my testimony. That delegation included former NSC advisor Brent Scowcroft; former Chairman of the Joint Chiefs of Staff, General Shalikashvili; future Defense Secretary Ashton Carter; and others. On that trip, we met with President Jiang Zemin, cross-strait negotiator and former mayor of Shanghai Wang Daohan, President Lee Teng-hui in Taipei, and cross-strait negotiator for Taipei Koo Chen-foo. The Perry Delegation, I think it fair to say, viewed cross-strait relations as the single most destabilizing issue in U.S.-China relations, and this was the view I tried to convey in my testimony, without invoking the views of others.

President Jiang Zemin was toying with the idea of establishing a *timetable* for the final resolution of cross-strait issues, something our delegation largely viewed as ill-advised and something toward which in more recent times Chinese President Xi Jinping has inched. In our conversation, President Jiang Zemin said: "I asked [President Bill] Clinton, can we do it [resolve the Taiwan issue, reunification] by 2005 or 2010?" In response, somewhere along this trip, I had remarked that Deng Xiaoping would not have painted himself into such a corner and that Mao had a one-hundred-year time horizon and Deng a fifty-year horizon. Years later, I was told that President Jiang was not amused.[6]

If the TSEA became law, it would enable or mandate changes in the levels and character of Washington's interactions with Taipei in ways conferring "officiality" on the island contrary to postnormalization practices, understandings, and agreements. It would facilitate a dramatic increase in the volume and sophistication of weapons sales to the island, including theater missile defense (TMD), proposing to sell a system we did not yet possess. This was unacceptable to Beijing and, in my view, could precipitate the use of force by Beijing.

This hearing was convened to examine the Helms-Torricelli Bill, its rationale, and its likely consequences. It is fair to say that all the senators at the hearing were uneasy with the ambiguity surrounding the clarity and credibility of the U.S. commitment to "peaceful resolution" of the Taiwan issue. Everyone was concerned about Washington's credibility in Beijing and how it could be enhanced. As Senator John Kerry put it, everyone wanted to "state that in a more clear way," but at the same time, Senator Kerry didn't want to be provocative to Beijing: "What are the implications of that? Do we trigger something that we then regret? Do we create greater instability, which is what Dr. Lampton has been suggesting we might create? And is there something short of that which might accomplish the goals without the downsides, if there are any?"

Senator Helms, in his wheelchair, presided. He was gracious, soft-spoken, and unfailingly polite as he dealt with witnesses and colleagues alike—Senator Joe Biden (ranking minority member) and Senator John Kerry key among them. Politeness aside, no one mistook his Southern courtesy for moderation on this set of issues.

Testifying in favor of S-693 were Richard V. Allen (former NSC advisor to Ronald Reagan), Caspar W. Weinberger (former defense secretary for Reagan), and James Woolsey Jr. (former CIA director for Bill Clinton). Then came my turn. To say it was intimidating to go up against these three other witnesses, and to testify against Chairman Helms's own bill to his face, is an understatement. I have always been grateful that as the hearing unfolded, Senators Joe Biden and John Kerry both articulated policy positions that I construed as compatible with my own. They also articulated concerns about PRC behavior that would only grow over time, concerns that I shared.

No one, myself included, was giving a defense of Beijing's actions. Rather Biden, Kerry, and I were trying in our separate, uncoordinated ways to avoid taking steps that would make the future more unmanageable and drag us into a potential armed conflict. A brief overview of the arguments made in the course of this hearing shows how far down the road of a more conflictual relationship the parties already had stumbled and how difficult it was going to be to manage bilateral relations and cross-strait interactions in future decades. Ironically, this bundle of issues again burst to the top of the Sino-American agenda in the Biden presidency, the core issue being whether or not to abandon Washington's policy of "strategic ambiguity."

Speaking in mid-2022, more than twenty years after this hearing, President Biden largely abandoned the "strategic ambiguity" policy for which he had argued at these hearings.

BATTLE LINES ARE DRAWN

Senator Helms began the Hearing by succinctly laying out his case. The three majority witnesses (Allen, Weinberger, and Woolsey) made supportive points. Helms: "We need to enhance our defense relationship with Taiwan. . . . The Reunification has become an increasingly high agitation issue for Beijing now that they have reabsorbed Hong Kong and, as of this coming December, Macau. . . . Beijing is also undergoing a multifaceted military buildup. . . . It was the Reagan Administration that signed the regrettable 1982 Communique [the Third] . . . and promised China that we would gradually reduce these [weapons] sales."

Senator Biden followed, his major points being: "We do not agree on everything. . . . I have reservations about TSEA. . . . This legislation would be the equivalent of waving a red cape in front of Beijing and inviting China to charge. . . . No amount of weaponry can guarantee

Taiwan's security. . . . A surefire way to spark such a conflict is for the U.S. to reinforce the growing perception in Beijing . . . that the United States is hostile to China or pursuing the fragmentation of China."

One central point that both Allen and Weinberger made in support of Helms was that the TRA was the law of the land and that the August 1982 Weapons Sales Communique with Beijing stated the intention to reduce (quantitatively and qualitatively) weapons sales to Taiwan over time and was simply a *nonbinding* executive agreement between the two governments. As Weinberger put it, "I do not feel that we should be hampered by, or felt [feel] that, we are in any way bound by what is said by the Communique." For Beijing, the "Three Communiques" were the Holy Grail representing an agreement between the two governments. The TRA was a unilateral act of the United States.

The points I made supported Senators Biden and Kerry, but I struck out in different veins as well. I rhetorically asked why Taipei itself did not seem to be doing much to reduce its own vulnerability. Taiwan's defense spending on its own behalf was paltry, and "if security were perceived to be so tenuous on Taiwan, and cross-strait ties so perilous, why is it that 40,000 Taiwan firms have contracted $40 billion of investment on the mainland?" "Why is it that one-third of Taiwan's total information industry output is produced in plants on the mainland?" . . . "The Proposed legislation would amount to a substantial restoration of the 1955 Mutual Defense Treaty with Taiwan, and therefore be inconsistent with the cornerstone of the normalization agreements of December 1978. . . . The United States also must discourage Taipei from so taking U.S. military support for granted that various political forces on the island feel they can change the status quo with impunity, and drag the United States into conflict." . . . "So, my principal recommendation is just very simple. Let us concentrate our efforts in directions for the moment that foster positive [cross-strait] interaction. There is plenty of time to consider other alternatives should they prove advisable."

Chairman Helms called our collective testimonies "very colorful."

At the hearing's conclusion, Senator Helms's eyes met mine, and he gestured for me to step forward to speak with him. "Son," he said, "I didn't agree with you, but you made a good argument."

Looking at the more than two decades that followed the defeat of Chairman Helms's legislation, three things stand out to me.

One is that during the next decade-plus, the U.S. and China avoided a major crisis in the Strait, and Bill Clinton's successor, George W. Bush, played a restraining role on Taiwan (making it clear to Taiwan President Chen Shui-bian [2003] that there were limits to Washington's support if he behaved recklessly). And, for its part, Taipei under the presidency of Ma Ying-jeou (2008–2016) accelerated cross-strait cooperation and lowered the temperature. Cross-strait ties flourished in many respects, but Beijing's underlying red lines were not jettisoned.

Two, China relentlessly built up its own military capabilities threatening Taiwan, but Taiwan domestic politics never put sufficient resources behind the island's own defense effort, one implication being that Taipei thought its own efforts always would be insufficient and that Washington would leap into the breach if necessary, so why bother?

And finally, in the Trump era, and thereafter in the Biden administration, both U.S. presidents failed to take most of the advice that Senator Biden had himself offered at the August 1999 hearing cited earlier, namely that the United States needed to keep some ambiguity concerning the conditions under which it might intervene and that Washington had to be careful not to reinforce Beijing's constant fear that Washington was pursuing the fragmentation of China. By late 2022, a tsunami of legislation in Congress inundated past policy, none more glaring than the National Defense Authorization Act of 2022 which ran to more than four thousand pages, offering grant aid to Taipei for an arms buildup in the face of growing PRC threats.

I believe that the three-pronged policy guidance I offered at the 1999 hearing's conclusion was the best approach: (1) "No [Chinese] force period." (2) "No unilateral independence [of Taiwan] with U.S. support." (3) "Start confidence-building measures [across the Strait]." Though this is what happened for the next almost two decades, as we entered the third decade of the new millennium, none of the three sides were any longer contributing to stability as I recommended. Xi Jinping has staked his legitimacy and legacy on some form of "reunification," sooner rather than later—dangerously close to the "timetable" President Jiang wisely did not adopt.

NOTES

1. Barber B. Conable Jr., "Testimony, Hearing, Subcommittee on Trade of the Committee on Ways and Means," House of Representatives, 103rd Congress, 2nd Session, February 24, 1994, 50–51.

2. David M. Lampton, "Testimony Prepared for the Subcommittee on Human Rights and International Organizations, The Subcommittee on Asian and Pacific Affairs, and the Subcommittee on International Economic Policy," May 16, 1990, 101st Congress, Second Session: https://www.c-span.org/video/?12338-1/chinas-favored-nation-status-part-1.

3. https://www.govinfo.gov/content/pkg/CHRG-106shrg60900/html/CHRG-106shrg60900.htm (transcript). https://www.c-span.org/video/?151366-1/taiwanese-security. Note there also were companion hearings held by the Committee on International Relations of the House of Representatives, Subcommittee on Asia and the Pacific, September 15, 1999. Doug Bereuter (R-NE) was committee chair, one of the truly constructive and knowledgeable forces in the U.S. Congress at the time.

4. Torricelli later was admonished by the Senate for campaign contribution violations and brought up on felony charges of bribery, tax evasion, and fraud in legal proceedings. In the period of his Senate and House career, Torricelli had close ties with Taiwan. In an October 31, 1999, opinion piece in the *Washington Post*, I wrote: "This river of money [from Taiwan] makes the alleged illegal campaign contributions of the People's Republic of China look like chump change." When I wrote that I did not have Torricelli front of mind.

5. David M. Lampton, "Notes of Meeting with ROC President Lee Teng-hui," Presidential Palace, Taipei, William Perry Delegation, March 8, 1999, 5. (RAC).

6. David M. Lampton, "Interview," January 17, 2013, China, 4–5. (RAC).

CHAPTER ELEVEN

Doing New Things with China

(*The 1990s, Opportunities*)

IN THE 1990S AND THEREAFTER, AS DEBATES IN WASHINGTON, AND between Washington and Beijing, ground on in apparent perpetual motion, parallel and productive possibilities for society-to-society collaboration and innovative exchanges expanded. Problems between the central governments multiplied, but society-to-society interactions deepened. There were entirely new ventures to be pursued.

These were the kinds of activities that the National Committee Board and I had hoped would come to constitute much of the organization's future activities after I arrived in New York in the late 1980s. That future had been delayed, but not canceled, by the June 4 tragedy.

How could growing strategic distrust and friction coexist with more collaborative, probing, and innovative programs? Simply put, Deng Xiaoping and his successor Jiang Zemin were committed to opening and sought to reassure the international system after June 4. In part, their commitment arose from having been exposed to Western thinking and education early in their formative years—Deng in France and Jiang through a Western-style teacher in China. Hu Jintao is an interesting case, but his connections with the progressive Youth League faction of the Communist Party kept him in the mainstream of Deng's policies. By way of contrast, Xi Jinping had minimal exposure to the West and he was not embedded in the network of progressives of which his two immediate predecessors were a part. The growing return flow to China of students and scholars educated abroad also played a catalytic role in creating innovative society-to-society collaborative efforts.

By the 1990s and the first decade of the new millennium, long before the rise of Xi Jinping, China was breaking out of poverty and on the road to development. Relative material prosperity brought with it the conjunction of a relatively stable social order, outward-looking leaders nationally and locally, and a more equal relationship between the United States and China, thus creating a more permissive environment for society-to-society cooperation. Those who have pronounced engagement a failure ignore the cooperative track at the society-to-society level from the 1990s to around 2010 and beyond. The NCUSCR wished to greatly strengthen this dimension of the relationship.

PEOPLE AND LEADERSHIP

To seize these opportunities required superb, skilled staff. In its programmatic endeavors, the National Committee has been blessed to have Ms. Jan Berris as vice president. Jan began her career at the United States Information Agency (USIA), taking leave from the agency to come to the committee in 1971 to work on the visit of the Chinese Ping-Pong Team to the United States in 1972. She has tilled the vineyards of U.S.-China relations with the committee ever since.

I never have seen anyone maintain Jan's energy level and innovative capacity for such an extended period. In overseeing and executing committee programs, Jan has trained dozens of young persons who, in turn, have gone into the world of organizations and academe to put to good use what she taught them. Jan is known personally to, and is respected by, more living Chinese societal and political leaders than any other living American—bar none.

For several years, Elizabeth Knup also played a key program role, demonstrating great intelligence and energy in developing and executing a variety of innovative programs. She went on to have a fascinating China-centered career, not least as the Ford Foundation's representative in China. She was also an exceedingly successful co-director of the Hopkins-Nanjing Center for Johns Hopkins. Much of the National Committee's success is thanks to the efforts of Jan and Elizabeth.

I also want to acknowledge the important role played by my successor on the committee, John Holden, who left an important legacy, expanding Committee programs into the Young Leaders area and broadening the committee's reach in Chinese society.

Many National Committee program participants have been leaders of national and sometimes international-level organizations, some of whom have large egos and low tolerance for direction—they are not wallflowers. Managing such people requires distinct capabilities and a level of self-confidence that usually develops only after decades of experience. National Committee staff have demonstrated capabilities well beyond their years.

This raises a general point about leadership. A team requires dedicated, excellent people. When you find such people, do all you can to retain them by making their endeavors gratifying. Moderate staff turnover is essential to keeping an organization vibrant, but losing good people is the most expensive practice in which an organization can engage.

Two programs that were undertaken in the early and mid-1990s indicate what is possible, the limitations we faced, and what will be lost if Washington and Beijing continue careening down their currently ruinous path.

PROGRAMS EXPLORING THE DEEPER REALITIES OF CHINA AND U.S.-CHINA RELATIONS

Tibet

Though my immediate purpose is to discuss one of NCUSCR's innovative programs implemented soon after I arrived in New York, our American Study Group to Tibet in the summer of 1991, I must first recount my 1981 experience taking a group there. That earlier trip energized us to put together the committee's Tibet project a decade later.

One sad truth of world history is that coastal, urban, and entrepreneurial peoples tend to expand across continents from their initial territorial footholds like gas expands to fill a sealed room. This expansion generally spells tragedy for the indigenous peoples in the path of these dynamic civilizations and their frontiersmen, as is so obvious in the case of America's westward expansion.

Geologically, the Himalayan Up-Thrust is the result of the collision of the Indian and the Eurasian tectonic plates. In historical and human terms, the "Tibet problem" is the result of the collision of two civilizations (cultural tectonic plates)—the Han and Tibetan peoples. One is larger, more entrepreneurial, and more capable of amassing bureaucratic power than the other.

And yet the Tibetans' Fourteenth Dalai Lama is a global charismatic figure who generates enormous popular and congressional support in the United States and throughout the world, even as in more recent years, His Holiness has tried to separate his spiritual role from the day-to-day governance of his people. For reasons complex and long-standing, Tibet has occupied a unique place in American thinking, a connection not grounded in much knowledge but powerful in its effect.

My First Trip to Tibet in 1981 as a Warm-Up

During my time at Ohio State, Robert Oxnam, then president of the Asia Society, invited me to accompany a small group of exceedingly wealthy people to visit Tibet Autonomous Region (TAR), the provincial-level administrative unit covering what Beijing calls Tibet (*Xizang*). Among the participants were Max and Marjorie Fisher and A. Alfred Taubman ("Al"). Al was an innovative shopping mall developer (later owner of Sotheby's who did jail time for price-fixing with Christie's).

Max Fisher, who went to Ohio State on a football scholarship, had been the owner of Aurora Gasoline Company, a large Midwest fuel chain that became a subsidiary of the Ohio Oil Company in 1959, and in 1962 assumed the name of its main brand, Marathon Oil Company. In 1982 United States Steel (USS) Corporation acquired Marathon Oil in the second-largest merger in U.S. history at that time. As it happened, the Marathon-USS acquisition was underway while we were on the trip to Tibet. Hence, one of my roles on the trip, assigned to me by Max, was to track Marathon's stock price every day the market in New York was open. This could be undertaken only through an international long-distance telephone network of creaky landlines and rusty sea cables. The Chinese long-distance telephone system was barely functional at the time and became successively less so the farther away one got from Beijing. Tibet is as far away from the capital as one can get in the PRC.

In the very early 1980s, only a handful of foreigners were granted entry into Tibet's vastness each year. Given its mystique derivative of popular culture (Shangri-La and the movies *Lost Horizon* and later *Seven Years in Tibet*) and its newsworthiness, people who had been everywhere else in the world saw Tibet as a new frontier to explore and, frankly, as an interesting item of cocktail conversation in rarified social circles.

The area designated as the TAR is twice as big as Texas and then had an ethnic Tibetan population of about 2.19 million. In addition, beyond the TAR was "Greater Tibet" composed of the TAR's population and territory plus contiguous areas inhabited by ethnic Tibetans in five nearby provincial-level units (Sichuan, Qinghai, Gansu, Yunnan, and Xinjiang), areas then with 2.9 million additional ethnic Tibetans and referred to as Amdo and Kham by Tibetans. This entire area with significant Tibetan population is what the Dalai Lama and many Tibetans consider Tibet, which means that the Dalai Lama's Tibet is much larger than Beijing's TAR. Consequently, when the Dalai Lama calls for a high degree of autonomy for Tibet—not independence—and its people, he is referring to much more real estate and population than Beijing. Quite frankly, talk of genuine autonomy for such a vast area is simply out of the question for the PRC.

Today, the TAR is run on a day-to-day basis by the central government's Minorities Affairs Commission (*Xiaoshu Minzu Weiyuanhui*, or *Minwei*), and the CCP is the force behind the screen. At the time of our trip in late 1981, Beijing had just cracked open the TAR's door for a very limited number of foreigners. There were no tourist hotels. The Holiday Inn-Lhasa, well-known to foreign visitors in later years, had yet to be built. The single guesthouse in Lhasa had no heat, and nighttime temperatures often dipped below freezing. The low-lying guesthouse was built of stone from the surrounding mountains that thrust upward from Lhasa's elevation of about twelve thousand feet and was divided into two wings of bunks—those with supplemental oxygen and those without. Visitors most sensitive to the high altitude were placed in bunks near oxygen, and those who acclimated well were in bunks without. Much of our group had a significantly adverse reaction to the altitude, though tolerance for the elevation was not strictly associated with age. The eighty-plus-year-old former ballerina in our group had no problem, and younger members of the party sometimes had episodes of vomiting and severe headaches. Some who became ill had ignored our hosts' admonitions to take it easy for a few hours and refrain from alcohol. I was fine, but at a low point early on in Lhasa, I wrote home: "The Lhasa experience is arduous and it is doubtful many will finish the trip." In the final analysis, they all did finish, though one had to be assisted onto the plane departing Lhasa. As for our low-land Han Chinese guide, he sucked on an oxygen pillow the whole time.

Most members of our group were not used to either discomfort or being told "no." When some in our group were not feeling well shortly after arrival, I heard requests to immediately return to the lower altitudes in China proper. "Charter a plane!" some in the group suggested. I informed them that there would be no plane for four to five days at the earliest, depending on weather and the absence of dust storms. The Lhasa Airport was on visual flight rules, and modern weather forecasting was in its infancy in China, as were telecommunications and automated landing systems. Our aircraft was propeller-driven. We saw it being "fixed" on the tarmac in Chengdu with a hammer delivering blows to one of the port engines after our first attempt to reach Lhasa had been aborted halfway there because of a dust storm that had come up *en route*. Pilots had to fly to the vicinity of Lhasa, assess the feasibility of landing by radioing the tower, then proceed if they could, returning to the departure airport if they must, where they would wait for another try as soon as conditions permitted.

The landing approach to arid Lhasa presented a landscape I can only compare to a moonscape or to flying over the Hindu Kush Mountains' Khyber Pass between Pakistan and Afghanistan in 2014. In my experiences seeing Tibet and Pakistan-Afghanistan from the air, I would say anyone contemplating ground intervention in these areas ought to see the terrain, the vastness, its bareness, and consider the implications. It is no wonder that almost every Western-dispatched insurgent parachuted into Tibet in the 1950s and 1960s was captured or killed. Parenthetically, one can visit what is left of Camp Hale in the Rocky Mountains' Pando Valley near Vail, Colorado, where U.S.-sponsored Tibetan insurgents were trained. A former SAIS student's father, John Kenneth Knaus, wrote a superb book on this endeavor, *Orphans of the Cold War*.

This experience taught me that there is nothing quite like being the facilitator for a group of strong-willed individuals, none of whom is used to hardship or to not getting their way. When told she must limit her baggage to twenty kilos, one lady said: "Honey, my makeup bag weighs twenty kilos!" However, in the end, the trip turned out to be a life-changing experience for the participants, once they acclimated and began to make sense of what they were witnessing.

Many people have a romantic, exotic image of Tibet, and then they confront a reality with which they are unprepared to cope. Of course, most people never have the chance to experience Tibet on the ground and hence are left with preexistent views having their origins in popular culture.

There are real and severe human rights, economic, and other problems in Tibet. Nonetheless, it is worth asking why Americans are so drawn to what could only be called a theocratic tradition when separation of church and state is such an article of faith in their own governing philosophy. It also is true that the Fourteenth Dalai Lama from his Dharamshala redoubt in Northern India has sought to distinguish between secular governance and religious life, but that separation is not strongly embedded in the hearts of his people. The unity and centrality of his theological and political leadership is something difficult to shed irrespective of his will.

In November 1981, when our group was in the TAR, the massive cultural destruction inflicted on Tibetan spiritual and material life, and the essential infrastructure for that way of life, was beyond description. We saw gaping wounds and scars on the otherwise pristine faces of the mountainsides. In the later 1991 NCUSCR trip to Tibet reported on shortly, our delegation observed that: "Except for eleven monasteries, and the Potala Palace (saved by personal order of Premier Zhou Enlai), every monastery in Tibet was destroyed and all monks were sent home or to labor reform camps where countless perished."[1] There had been at least 2,700 monasteries prior to the PRC's not so "peaceful liberation" of Tibet in 1959, at which point the Dalai Lama fled (with CIA help) to Northern India.[2] His Holiness and his followers have been ensconced there since, injecting further complications into New Delhi-Beijing ties.

In late 1981, when our group arrived in the TAR, the only remaining traces of most of these monasteries were foundation ruins clinging to the mountains. The three standing major monasteries (in and around Lhasa) had very few monks or novitiates, and monks and citizens alike kept old photos of the Dalai Lama tucked inside their vestments, discreetly revealing His Holiness's image by baring their chests when Han Chinese were absent. Virtually nothing was for sale; there were no traditional markets, and what little people had to sell (often jewelry) was hidden in their garments, revealed when safe; bargaining proceeded covertly.

Maoist excesses were so enormous in the Great Leap Forward and Cultural Revolution eras that in 1980, and again in 1982, the relatively reform-oriented General Secretary of the CCP, Hu Yaobang, personally visited Tibet and was shocked by what he saw. He initiated a brief period in which there was a large reduction of Han cadres in Tibet, social controls were relaxed, and markets returned. Our 1981 trip took place at the outset of this period of relative relaxation.

Second Trip to Tibet

My 1981 Tibet experience, combined with Tibet becoming a marquee human rights issue in the United States and globally, led me to be responsive when the Chinese government approached the National Committee in 1988, asking whether we would agree to receive a PRC delegation to exchange views on Tibet with a broad range of Americans. We were interested in the proposal but did not believe a single mission to the United States would be particularly enlightening or credible.

We proposed instead a multiphase project to "provide broad and thorough access to Tibet; forthrightly address the issues of human/civil rights and economic development; consist of more sustained and thoughtful interaction than a one-shot trip [to America]; and ensure that activities [with individuals] be off-the-record and have a substantially scholarly character."[3]

The key features of the project would be a visit to the TAR by a diverse group of Americans, a publicly disseminated policy report following the journey written by the American side, consultations with the Tibetan community in the United States and His Holiness the Dalai Lama, and a reciprocal trip by a PRC delegation to the United States. Each of the two delegations would participate in a two-day seminar while in the host country. On the U.S. side, funding for such an endeavor was too sensitive for the U.S. government, but the Ford Foundation and the United Board for Christian Higher Education in Asia were staunch supporters.

No sooner had we reached an agreement to cooperate after extensive discussions with the Chinese Embassy in Washington, and the Nationalities Affairs Commission in Beijing, than martial law was declared in Tibet in March 1989, following large protests in Lhasa demanding independence from China. The trip was postponed indefinitely. Subsequently, the June 4, 1989, violence occurred in Beijing, further deferring plans. Not until July 28 to August 7, 1991, was the American group finally able to go to Tibet. The Chinese group came to the United States shortly thereafter, from December 4–15, 1991.

We were pleased that Beijing reinstated the project in the post–June 4 environment. I saw this as a reflection of just how badly the PRC wanted to break out of its post-Tiananmen international isolation.

While the Beijing authorities presumably had to think long and hard about launching (and relaunching) the project, the National Committee Board also had its misgivings. The board meeting at which we decided to proceed with the undertaking was not rancorous, but it was intense. Those dubious about, or opposed to, resuming the effort feared that we could end up offending the Tibetan community in the United States, Congress, and human rights groups, thus bringing into question whether we were allowing ourselves to be used by the PRC propaganda machine.

I believe that we avoided these dangers in the end. One indication that Tibetans in the United States were not taking offense was His Holiness the Dalai Lama's meeting with our group in New York (October 11, 1991) after our trip. He wanted to hear our report and to share his thoughts with us. He praised the undertaking, and we worked closely with his long-time and trusted assistant and special envoy to the United States, Lodi Gyari, throughout.

One of the National Committee's preconditions for undertaking this effort was that we retain sole discretion over the composition of our delegation; it would include well-known members of the human rights community, someone with unquestioned Tibet expertise with language fluency, and credible people with diplomatic and negotiating experience.

In composing the delegation, we considered what combination of skills was required, interpersonal dynamics, and who would have credibility with the various key audiences when the group returned home and issued its findings. The delegation issued a report (*Tibet: Issues for Americans*) with analysis and recommendations.

Figure 11.1. A portion of American Tibet Study Team overlooking Potala Palace, Lhasa, Tibet, summer 1991. (Left to right) Richard Holbrooke; Chinese guide; Sidney Jones; Minwei representative; Tibetan aide; and Author. Photo by David M. Lampton.

We first had to choose a delegation leader. This was key because that choice would send signals to everyone—the group itself, Americans more broadly, Tibetans, and the Chinese. We chose Harold ("Hal") Saunders, former Assistant Secretary of State for Intelligence and Research (1975–1978) and former Assistant Secretary of State for Near Eastern and South Asian Affairs (1978–1981). He had helped negotiate the Camp David Accords and the Iran hostage crisis and also played a key role in the Kettering Foundation–sponsored Dartmouth Conference series of sustained dialogues with the Soviets (and later with Russia and Central Asian states) undertaken for many years. Hal and I knew each other well, having worked with the Kettering Foundation of Dayton, Ohio.

Our logic in choosing Saunders as the leader was that anyone who had worked on shuttle diplomacy with Henry Kissinger, negotiated with the Arabs and the Israelis, and dealt with the Iranians had to know something about dealing with controversy and minority-majority nationality conflicts. Hal turned out to be the perfect choice in terms of substance, interpersonal style, decency, and in interacting with the Chinese and Tibetans within and outside the TAR.

Our delegation also needed a person who had dealt with the Chinese on the full spectrum of issues, including Tibet, who had an unquestioned commitment to human rights, and who also understood that this issue existed within a matrix of other national and regional interests. We chose Richard Holbrooke ("Dick"), a person I knew through his involvement with the National Committee.

The choice of Holbrooke was not without its drawbacks, but the pluses heavily outweighed the minuses. Whenever I have been asked what it was like to spend two weeks with Richard Holbrooke, I have invariably responded: "Like a two-week root canal." When Dick was involved in something, he thought that meant he was in charge. Hal Saunders subtly managed to rein in his expectations.

Holbrooke had been at the State Department as Assistant Secretary for East Asian and Pacific Affairs (1977 to January 1981) under President Carter and Secretary of State Cyrus Vance. Dick was one of the few at the State Department who knew a little about what was going on concerning the secret normalization discussions with China in late

1978. But Dick was continually held at arms-length by Zbig Brzezinski (and his assistant Mike Oksenberg) at the NSC, who quite simply did not get along with Dick, not least because he had directly alienated President-elect Carter during the presidential transition by bad-mouthing the person who shortly thereafter became the president-elect's selection for National Security Advisor, Zbigniew Brzezinski.[4]

Beyond politically experienced Saunders and Holbrooke, we needed unquestioned substantive expertise on Tibetan society and history, language skills, and knowledge of human rights issues and economic development. We chose Case Western Reserve University's Tibet specialist Professor Melvyn C. Goldstein; Sidney Jones, who was executive director of Human Rights Watch-Asia; and Professor Dwight Perkins, Harvard China economist and development expert. Individually they were superb, and collectively we had the skills to make credible observations.

When the Chinese side saw this name list, I presume that they swallowed hard on seeing its human rights dimension, but given Beijing's desire to restore its reputation following June 4, and given the group's composition, Beijing agreed to move forward. Our designated Chinese counterpart agency was the State Nationalities Affairs Commission (*Min Wei*).

Overall, we had meaningful (even surprising) access to officials and citizens in Beijing and in the TAR. The biggest disagreement with our hosts was over our requested visit to the notorious Drapchi Prison (Prison No. 1) on the outskirts of Lhasa. We had asked to visit two prisons and were granted access to only one, being told it was the only prison under direct central control.

As we drove through the barren but majestic landscape toward the Drapchi complex, its growing silhouette on the horizon loomed as forbidding as the cells we would soon visit. The prison had been almost emptied of inmates before our arrival, except for the women's quarters, where we exchanged words with two of some thirty-seven women in custody, both of whom had been incarcerated for taking part in demonstrations.

We were not the first Americans to visit Drapchi. U.S. Ambassador to the PRC James Lilley had visited it about six months earlier, where he had unexpectedly been handed a letter by two prisoners. The missive was removed immediately from the ambassador's hands. Later, retribution reportedly was meted out to the offending inmates, though we did not know the form that retribution took. With this experience on our minds, we did not ask for prisoner interviews, though we did talk to the two nuns, with permission.

In the run-up to our prison visit, Holbrooke had defined the Drapchi visit as his litmus test determining the success or failure of the entire trip. Though we had initially requested that there be a visit to this facility, for the first several days of our stay in the TAR, it was not on the agenda. Every day, and at every opportunity, Dick demanded that Hal and I push harder for the prison visit, and he raised the issue with the Chinese side at every opportunity himself. Sidney Jones shared Dick's commitment.

While Hal Saunders raised the issue regularly with our hosts, I think he and I were both pretty sure that such a visit would be a Potemkin village–style exercise and might leave the prisoners worse off, especially if anything untoward happened during our visit, as had been the case with Ambassador Lilley. We also felt that the opening of Tibet to Americans was so tenuous that we had some responsibility not to make this the last opportunity for other foreigners to visit. Hal and I saw many other positive aspects to the trip, so a prison visit was not a litmus test for us. We weren't opposed to the prison visit, but we were ambivalent.

For reasons best known to the Chinese, we did visit Drapchi, but it was empty save for the few women prisoners. I couldn't help but think that the prison visit was as much about our delegation establishing credibility with the U.S. domestic audience as anything else. It was as if once Ambassador Lilley, or any other foreign visitor, was given access to a prison, that activity became the threshold event against which subsequent visits would be judged, whether or not such a visit advanced human rights or the welfare of particular detainees.

The TAR trip was full of notable, impactful events. One side trip in the TAR took us southeast of Lhasa to Lhokha (Shannan, or South of the Mountain) Special District toward the Indian border, and another north of Lhasa to a nomad district. In Lhasa we spoke with citizens, some monks, and local officials, having earlier met their superiors in Beijing. We also spoke with Han workers who had migrated for various durations to the TAR (referred to as "the floating population") to work, often in construction or commerce such as hauling watermelons from Gansu to Lhasa. The shorter- and longer-term Han migrants in the cities pretty well monopolized skilled jobs and commerce, leaving hard labor for Tibetans, often women.

Given his prior extended field research in Tibet and his facility with the language, the participation of Professor Mel Goldstein greatly increased the group's capacities to communicate and observe independently. He was our cultural interpreter. The one gaping hole in our observations and interactions concerned the large PLA presence in the TAR. We had no contact with the military system, beyond driving past garrisons. The Chinese military was a very large presence unto itself.

A Path Not Taken

In reading over our group's report and recommendations more than thirty years later, I am struck by the degree to which we identified the key issues, controversies still at the heart of the Tibet problem. A central challenge in Tibet then, as today, was how to protect Tibetan culture and identity and also achieve appropriate economic modernization. Our core observation was that time was not working in favor of a sustainable future for Tibetan culture and society, a life of dignity within a mutually agreeable framework of autonomy under PRC sovereignty. Other observations included:

- "As long as the Dalai Lama remains apart from his people, there will be continual unrest, resentment, discontent, and the potential for tragedy in Tibet. . . . It would be especially dangerous if he died in exile, thus creating conditions for a split over the selection of his successor."
- "Time is not on the side of protecting Tibetan culture and language and developing an economic environment for sustaining them. If present trends of Chinese in-migration are not addressed, the risk of another dangerous confrontation increases. . . . Creating an economic development strategy for enhancing Tibetan

capacities to assume increasing responsibility for their own future is thus essential."

- "One of the root causes of human rights violations in Tibet is the clash between the desire of some Tibetans for independence and the determination of the Chinese government to prevent it. Improvement of the human rights situation will depend to some extent on defusing that clash. In the meantime, the imprisonment of hundreds of political activists will continue to be a major obstacle in the U.S.-China relationship."

Unfortunately, the period in which this overall project on Tibet was possible proved fleeting. Beijing's subsequent policy has gone in different, less productive, more assimilative, and more coercive directions. Willingness to talk about meaningful autonomy has declined from its already low level in 1991. Foreign access to the TAR has declined. The policies encouraging Han inflow have continued. The "one country, two systems" framework used in post–July 1997 Hong Kong is not a credible conceptual starting point for discussion.

Moreover, Chinese concerns about big power interference and border security along the PRC's periphery have only increased, making Beijing even more defensive. If Americans were honest with themselves, they would admit that each time Washington becomes worried about Chinese internal or external behavior, it applies pressure along the PRC's periphery. This predictably enhances Beijing's determination to tighten periphery control.

There is what I would call an "iron law" of Chinese rule in Tibet. The more worried the Chinese are about their periphery and external actors, the worse the situation becomes for Tibetans. Chinese willingness to explore remotely feasible terms for the Dalai Lama's return has declined. Beijing thinks time is working in its favor, and thus no significant accommodation is required.

Adding one last measure of volatility to this situation since 1991, the Dalai Lama's following is under internal strain between young Tibetans who have given up hope for reconciliation with the PRC (and are attracted to a more assertive, sometimes violent, path) and others who remain committed to the Dalai Lama's more flexible, pacific inclinations. When His Holiness passes from the scene, the Chinese *will* assert the right to name his incarnation, while the Tibetan movement will choose a different incarnation in whom to invest its devotion.

In short, our Tibet report charted a path not taken.

During this period in the 1990s when program possibilities with China were growing, opportunities were far-ranging. The NCUSCR program on sustainable development and environmental issues is an example.

SUSTAINABLE DEVELOPMENT IN THE USSURI RIVER WATERSHED

Opportunities often result from converging developments in disconnected realms. In the early 1990s, Deng Xiaoping's efforts to break out of post-1989 isolation and rekindle domestic reform and opening created new possibilities for exchange and mutual learning, as did the rise of Jiang Zemin who, in retrospect, was more attuned to Western thinking than we could have anticipated.

Just as possibilities opened up on the PRC's southern periphery, in Tibet, so interesting possibilities also appeared along China's northern frontier. With the implosion of the Soviet Union in December 1991, Boris Yeltsin took over as Russia's first democratically elected President, moving Russia in an unsteady, messy, but arguably democratic direction. Yeltsin's new Russia was looking to develop economic ties to both its East and West. (Russia's national emblem is the "golden two-headed eagle.")

Yeltsin's quests for new patterns of domestic politics and foreign relations, along with the tyranny of distance in Russia, afforded local authorities in its vast Far East latitude to develop connections abroad, including with China and America. Moscow's fears about being seven time zones behind Vladivostok were well-founded, given that distance conferred opportunities for independent action. Chinese in-migration was also worrisome, as were often corrupt economic links being forged between Russians and Chinese (and Koreans) near the Far Eastern borders.

For its part, China's rust belt in its northeast (Heilongjiang Province in particular) had not done well economically in the opening and reform period compared to other regions, notably southern coastal provinces. The

PRC's northeast (*dongbei*) was looking to establish connections with the United States, international development organizations like the United Nations Development Programme (UNDP) and the World Bank, and energetically sought connections with the Russian Far East to help jump-start its lagging regional economy.

Both Moscow and Beijing had their own domestic problems and wanted to develop better bilateral relations, a task Mikhail Gorbachev launched when he visited Beijing in May 1989. By 1991, trends toward China-Russia cooperation provided opportunities for the National Committee.

NCUSCR wanted to promote cooperation around the need to solve transnational problems. Given growing interdependence, economically and environmentally, we saw an opportunity to pursue a three-way program on developing a "Sustainable Land Use and Allocation Program for the Ussuri/Wusuli River Watershed and Adjacent Territories" in Northeastern China and the Russian Far East. This topic harkened back to my earlier work on water management in the Yangtze Basin.

Encouraged by the State Planning Commission in Beijing, and Russia's Khabarovsk and Primorskii Krais, in 1993 the National Committee and Ecologically Sustainable Development (ESD), an NGO in Elizabethtown, New York, joined discussions in Harbin with the Heilongjiang Territory Society, whose leaders were officials of the Provincial Planning Commission. We held further talks in Khabarovsk and Vladivostok with two institutes of the Far East Branch of the Russian Academy of Sciences. On the Chinese and Russian sides, we worked closely with Du Youlin, Segei Ganzei, and Irina Klimova. A trilateral agreement was signed in May 1994, envisioned as a three-year program.[5]

National Committee staff member Elizabeth Knup (and later Marilyn Beach), and Anita Davis at ESD, played driving roles in project management for the American side, along with NCUSCR Board Member Douglas ("Doug") Murray. The committee partnered with George Davis, President of ESD. In this endeavor, we were generously supported by the MacArthur Foundation (its directors for Peace and Security Ruth Adams and Kennette Benedict being particularly helpful) and the Rockefeller Brothers Fund, the Trust for Mutual Understanding,

Weeden Foundation, the Asia Foundation, the Eurasia Foundation, and the United States Agency for International Development (USAID). George Davis was central throughout. This became the most multifaceted project NCUSCR had conducted.

In contemplating projects involving fieldwork, particularly in remote and vast areas, the challenges posed by logistics are easy to underestimate. The Russian Far East is unfathomably large, the boreal forest (*Taiga*) extends for thousands of miles, transportation is difficult and expensive, and weather is always a consideration. One of our flights out of Khabarovsk found our plane's landing gear mired in three feet of snow through which we passengers had to slog—the aircraft had to plow through the snow and ice to a runway sufficiently clear to take off.

For its part, Heilongjiang Province is very large and sparsely populated outside the cities. As an example, as the project began, an issue arose as to whether we needed to purchase a vehicle out of the American budget (it had to be a Toyota Land Cruiser, our Chinese partners argued) that would be left behind at the project's completion. We did not have funds for such an expenditure, and it would not have been permissible in any case, but the issue occasioned an extended discussion before being dropped. In the course of the project, aerial surveys had to be conducted, requiring the purchase of flight hours on a charter plane. The haggling over these issues was a lesson in negotiation.

In one flight from Anchorage, Alaska, to Khabarovsk in Russia along the Amur/Heilong River, headwinds were so severe that our plane had to make an unscheduled fuel stop in Magadan, the heart of the Soviet-era Gulag—"The Road of Bones." Our aircraft set down at an airfield consisting of a one-room building with a large fuel tank and one petrol truck next to it. The building and airstrip were surrounded by frozen mountains of Rocky Mountain grandeur. It was easy to understand how the Soviet Union could have a prison there without fences.

Also bearing on logistics, the USSR had fallen and the Russian Federation was born on December 26, 1991. With the movement toward a market economy ("big bang") that came in the wake of the Soviet collapse, adjustment problems for the Russian people were agonizing—life expectancy at birth *fell* from 68.47 years in 1991 to 64.46 in 1994, and GDP for the same years respectively *fell* 5.04 percent and 12.57 percent.

One indication of how bad things were was our experience with Russian restaurants. Our team would enter a restaurant in the Russian Far East, be handed an extensive menu, make a choice, inevitably be told it was unavailable, and be asked to make another selection. After several iterations of this, we learned to ask the service staff what was available. When our team went from China to the Russian Far East, before getting on the plane, our Chinese hosts made sure we took our own food; we purchased provisions in Harbin's free markets. Nonetheless, our considerate Russian hosts did all they could for us in this era of severe deprivation—our hosts were beyond generous.

As the Soviet Union fell apart and deprivation tightened its grip, regional authorities, particularly in the Russian Far East, sought maximal autonomy. This contributed to corruption throughout the vast region, not least where we were operating. Authorities on the Chinese side of the border developed their own, sometimes corrupt, arrangements with counterparts in Russia. Chinese merchants, peddlers, and laborers moved back and forth across the porous border in ways fueling illicit transactions as well as feeding xenophobia on both sides of the boundary. Predictably in Russia, citizens in the region and Moscow were worried about the growing Chinese economic and other influences.

All this translated into security problems for foreigners traveling on both sides of the border. Generally during this time, we moved around Heilongjiang with security. In one case, we were driven with a flashing red light and siren police escort (one car in front, one car behind) from Harbin to the Daqing Oil Field and back—102 miles each way. Elizabeth Knup and I received varied explanations for why this security was deemed necessary given our modest status. We were variously told that it was to protect us from Chinese citizens who might think we were Russians (an explanation with interesting implications) or bandits. Whatever the reasons, it had nothing to do with heavy traffic—there was none as we glided across the long, flat, frozen desolation and vastness.

In Harbin, the underground tunnel network (built to protect against Soviet attack) had been converted into commercial space, where we stumbled across a presumably illegal casino operating beneath the city.

In Vladivostok, criminal activity was so extensive that our hosts implored us not to venture beyond the gates of our guarded guesthouse on the outskirts of town. When passing through Immigration and Customs to catch a departing flight out of the Russian Far East, we came to expect a shakedown by border officials trying to separate the traveler from anything of value. The final agony of exit at the airport was wondering if the plane could even take off in the inclement weather. I was ambivalent about even attempting the takeoff, but my anxiety about that was exceeded by my reticence to put myself back into the clutches of Russian border authorities.

Here I must provide some background on the committee's connections to the Soviet Union/Russia leading up to this River Basin sustainable development initiative.

From the Soviet Union with Love

One of the early figures on the National Committee Board of Directors was Professor John Lewis of Stanford University, who was my PhD supervisor. John focused his research not only on China but also on North Korea and the Soviet Union, as well as on arms control issues. Very shortly after June 4, 1989, John phoned me and asked if NCUSCR would host in New York City Professor Mikhail Titarenko, Scientific Director of the Institute of Far Eastern Studies of the Russian Academy of Sciences, one of the Soviet Union's (and later Russia's) premier experts on China. John thought the National Committee could benefit from hearing about the Soviet Union's experiences dealing with China as we thought about our own reaction to the Tiananmen turmoil. There might be an opportunity for the committee to cooperate with Mikhail and his Institute.

I took John's advice, and on June 25, Mikhail Titarenko and his long-time loyal assistant Tamara Karganova, head of the Foreign Ties Department at the Institute, arrived in New York. We immediately liked each other.

Dr. Titarenko had a very clear message in his New York visit, during which we held a seminar in his honor; that message was that how the United States handled the post–June 4 crisis with Beijing would set the template for relations with China for a long time to come. The Soviet Union had made mistakes in its dealings with the PRC in the 1950s and 1960s (among which was too much intrusive involvement in China's internal affairs, thus arousing Chinese concerns about sovereignty). He advised us Americans not to repeat these missteps. China had a different political culture and moved at its own pace. One could coexist with it but could not shape it to one's own liking. He urged restraint and taking the long view. Upon his death, a Chinese obituary described him as an expert on "inter-civilizational relations in Northeast Asia."

After the National Committee's initial U.S.-China-Russia cooperation mentioned earlier (to be described in greater detail shortly), Mikhail invited me to Moscow to address the Russian Academy of Sciences Institute of Far Eastern Studies and be awarded an Honorary Doctorate, which occurred on October 25, 1995.

Before I arrived in Moscow, many Russian intellectuals and citizens already were becoming disillusioned by what they saw as meager and self-interested U.S. help for the struggling Russian democratic transition, dissatisfactions compounded by a 1995 NATO study of "enlargement" and the subsequent admission of the Czech Republic, Hungary, and Poland to NATO in 1999. This fed Moscow's consternation and contributed to Putin's rise on the back of Russian nationalism and security fears. For its part, Washington saw Putin's predecessor, President Boris Yeltsin, as erratic and mercurial, with a drinking problem. And, as we have subsequently come to know, while at one level Russia's political system seemed to be moving in a more liberal governance direction, the KGB and military intelligence systems remained intact and available to be mobilized by Putin as he gained power in the late 1990s.

During my 1995 trip to Moscow, people were personally friendly, though the shadow cast by disappointment with the United States already was getting longer. I felt the chill in the body language. Mikhail and I remained friends until his death in February 2016, but one could feel a powerful undertow in U.S.-Russia relations. The three-way

Sino-Russian-U.S. cooperation on environmental protection and sustainable development to which I now turn was the high-water mark of this kind of trilateral cooperation in this era.

The Project

The Ussuri/Wusuli River flows south to north, reaching the longer Amur/Heilong River, flowing west to east into the Pacific Ocean, with the two waterways forming the Sino-Russian boundary demarcating Northeast China from the Russian Far East. The Sino-Russian boundary also is the only international border in the world where European and Chinese cultures butt up against one another. The region spanning both sides of the rivers in the Far East is rich in biodiversity and has plentiful resources. Though the watershed embraces portions of two contiguous sovereign countries, the area is an integrated ecosystem that would benefit from holistic management.

The objective of our undertaking was to enhance "sustainable development" throughout the entire Ussuri watershed, which the three parties (China, Russia, and the United States) defined to mean "improving the quality of human life while living within the carrying capacity of supporting ecosystems."[6] The project was premised on the recognition that any environmental program was likely to be ineffective if it did not also hold out the prospect of economic betterment for the people living in the region. The project's mantra was "Listen to the Land and Listen to the People."

The project's core purpose was to delineate land use zones according to their various economic utilities and ecological strengths and vulnerabilities, with zones categorized by such specific uses as "preferred," "conditional," and "prohibited." The two governments would, based on these specific, and scientifically derived, land use categorizations, grant or deny land use permits. The project's task was for the parties to work together to define and refine the land use specification methodology, categorize specific pieces of territory by type, and then develop an implementation plan for allocating land by permitted use, with each country passing its own appropriate legislation and thereafter working together. NCUSCR's role was to provide expertise and was designed to end once an implementation outline had been developed, at which point we hoped the Russians and Chinese, international multilateral agencies, and others would drive progress forward with concrete legislation and other actions, such as establishing trans-border parks and animal reserves.[7]

This area of activity was interesting to the National Committee not only because we thought that Sino-American-Russian cooperation in such peaceful and globally significant endeavors was intrinsically desirable, but also because this region highlighted the importance and difficulty of reconciling popular demands for economic growth, preserving biodiversity, and restoring the carrying capacity of rapidly deteriorating land, particularly wetlands.

Among the endangered species in the watershed were the Red-Crowned Crane in China and on the Russian side were the Siberian Tiger, the Far Eastern Leopard, the Oriental White Stork, and the White-Tailed Eagle. As our final report explained, "A centerpiece of this program is the recommendation to designate four cross-border protected areas that will conserve the most ecologically important portions of the basin, while symbolizing the historical international cooperation of the project" (p. 10).

With these several goals in mind and the methodology agreed upon, the National Committee, ESD, and our Russian and Chinese partners then utilized new geographic information systems (GIS), and a planning concept developed by George Davis, to generate a sustainable macro-land use plan for the twenty-six million hectares in the watershed stretching along 1,100 kilometers of Sino-Russian border. To this end, field research was conducted on the ground, in the air, and in discussions with government entities, citizens, and others throughout the region in both countries. The report and accompanying land use map for the entire basin were published in November 1996, in three languages.[8]

So what resulted? Beyond the realm of developing methodologies to address the need for more intelligent, sustainable land use and preservation of biodiversity, beyond journal articles, beyond the report and map, and beyond bringing together more than 150 experts, officials, and civic society leaders across three countries in a cooperative endeavor, seven years later this project's results and follow-up were still under discussion by Russia and China. Frederic Lasserre looked carefully at follow-up, reporting in 2003 that: "[The] most important thing in the program was bringing the two countries [Russia and China] together around a common cause—a shared natural resource, with a view to reducing pollution and creating wildlife reservations. Bilateral talks have kept going, but few results have so far been achieved."[9]

This cold, but realistic, assessment, however, is not all that can be said. The project created a structure for ongoing conversation, trained a large number of people to think about promoting sustainable development in new ways, and helped keep the flickering flame of cooperation in international environmental issues alive. The modest on-the-ground results, however, show how difficult it is to forge development processes that preserve the world's ecological carrying capacity while satisfying expectations for economic betterment as state-to-state relations oscillate.

MANAGING WHAT IS: PUSHING FOR WHAT COULD BE

In the chapters up to this point, I have examined issues in U.S.-China relations to which the National Committee and I devoted ourselves, issues such as trade, human rights, Tibet, environmental cooperation, and security relations. Each of these recurrent issue areas has its associated universes of fact, precedent, and political combat, and each generates perpetual controversies preoccupying individuals and organizations in our respective countries. These issues are not going away, but they must be managed. Positive human interactions are essential if this is to occur.

Organizations and individuals need to look beyond the morass of recurrent issues that preoccupy national capitals to the realm of what could be, the positive, perhaps even visionary, goals toward which we as citizens of our respective nations can together strive. Realism must be leavened by idealism, and competition by cooperation.

NOTES

1. Harold H. Saunders, Melvyn C. Goldstein, Richard Holbrooke, Sidney R. Jones, David M. Lampton, and Dwight H. Perkins, "Tibet: Issues for Americans," National Committee on U.S.-China Relations, *China Policy Series* no. 4 (April 1992): 7.

2. John Kenneth Knaus, *Orphans of the Cold War: America and the Tibetan Struggle for Survival* (PublicAffairs, 1999), 166–69.

3. Harold H. Saunders, Melvyn C. Goldstein, Richard Holbrooke, Sidney R. Jones, David M. Lampton, and Dwight H. Perkins, "Tibet: Issues for Americans," National Committee on United States-China Relations, *China Policy Series* no. 4 (April 1992): i.

4. George Packer, *Our Man: Richard Holbrooke and the End of the American Century* (Alfred A. Knopf, 2019), 170–71. For additional information on the Holbrooke-Brzezinski interaction, see Charles Gati, ed., *ZBIG: The Strategy and Statecraft of Zbigniew Brzezinski* (Johns Hopkins University Press, 2013).

5. The results of the entire project were published as a book, written in three languages (Chinese, English, and Russian) under the title *A Sustainable Land Use and Allocation Program for the Ussuri/Wusuli River Watershed and Adjacent Territories* (November 1996). This was a cooperative project of: Ecologically Sustainable Development, Inc. (USA); FEB-RAS Institute of Aquatic and Ecological Problems (Russia); FEB-RAS Pacific Geographical Institute (Russia); Heilongjiang Province Territory Society (PRC); and the National Committee on United States-China Relations (USA). Agreement details can be found on p. 13, English-language section.

6. A Cooperative Project of Ecologically Sustainable Development, Inc. (USA); FEB-RAS Institute of Aquatic and Ecological Problems (Russia); FEB-RAS Pacific Geographical Institute (Russia); Heilongjiang Province Territory Society (PRC); National Committee on US-China Relations (USA), *A Sustainable Land Use and Allocation Program for the Ussuri/Wusuli River Watershed and Adjacent Territories (Northeastern China and the Russian Far East)*, November 1996, 12.

7. Bruce G. Marcot, Sergei S. Ganzei, Tiefu Zhang, and Boris Voronov, "A Sustainable Plan for Conserving Forest Biodiversity in Far Eastern Russia and Northeast China," *The Forestry Chronicle* 73, no. 5 (September–October 1997): 565–71. http://www.plexusowls.com/PDFs/sustainable_plan.pdf.

8. A Cooperative Project of Ecologically Sustainable Development, Inc. (USA); FEB-RAS Institute of Aquatic and Ecological Problems (Russia); FEB-RAS Pacific Geographical Institute (Russia); Heilongjiang Province Territory Society (PRC); National Committee on US-China Relations (USA), *A Sustainable Land Use and Allocation Program for the Ussuri/Wusuli River Watershed and Adjacent Territories (Northeastern China and the Russian Far East)*, November 1996.

9. Frederic Lasserre, "The Amur River Border: Once a Symbol of Conflict, Could It Turn into a Water Resource Stake?" *Cybergeo: European Journal of Geography* (2003): 242, footnote 48, https://journals.openedition.org/cybergeo/4141?lang=en#toctoln5.

CHAPTER TWELVE

Staffing the Leviathan: Human Resources

(Into the New Millennium)

After a decade at the National Committee, I knew that U.S.-China engagement had done much more than fashion government-to-government ties. These interactions had woven a deep and rich fabric of society-to-society linkages.

I had gone to the National Committee in 1987 feeling that much of academia was going down disciplinary rabbit holes. Now, I was ready to return to academia if I could find a setting and time in which the fusion of theory and practice was possible, comfortable, and valued. In New York, I had gained experience I wanted to share with students. I had something to say that had not been possible for me when I entered teaching fresh out of graduate school in 1974. We now needed to train the next generation of leaders and scholars in numbers sufficient to staff the great Leviathan of U.S.-China relations that had emerged.

It was time for me to get back to the teaching mission that had brought me into the field in the first place. I hoped to help empower students with the concepts and historical background that would enable them to adapt to ever-changing and unforeseen circumstances. I wanted to kindle in younger people a sense of possibilities. Teaching is not simply about facts and concepts; it is about inspiration, motivation, and vision of alternative futures, some to be sought, others avoided, and yet others to be managed as constructively as possible.

It was not simply the "pull" of academia that beckoned; there also was an internal "push"—the feeling that though I was excited by each day at the National Committee, loved working with my colleagues, the board, and the committee's diverse constituencies in China, America, Asia, and Europe, my job as committee president required constant innovation and fundraising.

NGOs are businesses. In the private sector, a firm must break even and achieve a rate of return acceptable to investors. There is a hard bottom line. NGOs have hard bottom lines too—namely they must break even, at least.

In the years I was on the committee, the organization grew modestly in terms of total personnel (ten staff and one intern in 1987 to twelve staff and three interns in 1997); our program became progressively more extensive and broad-ranging; revenue grew from $1,382,634 in 1987 to $2,304,507 in 1997 (up 66 percent); expenditures went from $1,246,156 in 1987 to $2,132,953 in 1997 (up 71 percent); and "net assets" were $255,372 at the end of 1987, rising to $1,562,357 at year-end 1997 (up more than six times).

Given the volatility of U.S.-China relations, however, lurking in the back of our minds was always the contingency of a big revenue shock. Lengthening the financial "runway" (for an emergency landing) was an important performance indicator for the board and me. By "runway" I mean the time between when an entire revenue shut-off occurs and when the organization's available assets and cash are exhausted.

Our Vice President for Administration and Development, Ros Daly, who I first met at the University of Michigan before coming to the committee, was essential to the committee's health and success before and during my entire tenure in New York. When I went to the committee, that runway length was about two-and-a-half months—when I left, it was nine months. This was a meaningful improvement, but we still needed to extend the runway.[1]

In leaving the committee, I felt I was following my mother's advice. "Mike," she often said, "everyone needs to be re-potted every decade or so; let your roots grow and find new nutrients." I dreaded leaving such wonderful colleagues, confiding to our Chairman, Barber Conable, after

I had accepted a new position at Johns Hopkins SAIS, that I wondered if I had made a mistake. He said: "There are no mistakes," by which I took him to mean that there are many roads to making contributions—make them where you can.

SAIS ENTERS THE PICTURE

While at NCUSCR, I continued with scholarly writing, doing so not because I thought writing would afford an off-ramp back to academia but rather because I have found that I do not really know what I think about a subject until I have put it to paper and have struggled with the underlying ideas. A theoretically grounded, systematic analysis of China's internal evolution, a conception of how and why economic and political development occur, and some sense of the powerful domestic and foreign currents affecting U.S-China relations was essential to keeping a brisk flow of innovative, relevant, and forward-looking programs going at the committee.

Having some intellectual North Stars is essential to avoid being constantly blown off course by every passing political or intellectual squall. Inconstancy does not inspire confidence among one's board of directors, colleagues, constituencies, Chinese interlocutors, or oneself.

Getting to Know SAIS

In about 1993, Professor Michael ("Mike") Mandelbaum at SAIS, and concurrently a project director at the Council on Foreign Relations, asked me to write a conference paper that would become a chapter in an edited volume on big power relations in East Asia. Published in 1995, the book was titled, *The Strategic Quadrangle*. The volume was written in the context of the Clinton administration coming to power in January 1993 and its new Advisor to the President for National Security Affairs, Anthony Lake, calling for the United States to organize its foreign policy around the idea of "enlargement," meaning that Washington should pursue the objective of expanding the space that democracies occupied in the global system.[2] Parenthetically, twenty-eight years later, the Biden administration tried to breathe air into this idea with its "Summit of Democracies" in the administration's first year. Lake's 1993 call, delivered at SAIS, reflected the post–Cold War flush of victory, the sense that America was "the indispensable nation," and that this was its unipolar moment. I was skeptical.

What did "enlargement" operationally imply? Was it feasible? Did the United States have the resources, the staying power? What means would be employed? How would other powers and our allies react? How would China respond? Wouldn't adding system change objectives to our mounting economic and human rights frictions with Beijing further destabilize already troubled ties? To me, this seemed like a policy destined to end badly, largely designed for a domestic audience.

In pursuit of such a concept, President Clinton had a few months earlier linked the continuation of MFN tariff treatment for Beijing to better PRC human rights behavior with a deadline of mid-1994, only to unceremoniously reverse course when the time to implement his threat arrived. Attempts to humiliate and publicly strong-arm Beijing do not generally work well.

In the 1995 Mandelbaum volume, I wrote:

> In China, economic progress, political reform, and social stability all must be achieved—a single-minded pursuit by the United States of political reform may well impede the possibility of achieving the other objectives and produce a resentful, destabilizing response from Beijing in the process. . . . A one-size-fits-all strategic policy of "enlargement" will not work; it will foster instability in the region, and ultimately it will set back the realization of both normative objectives and tangible interests.

In the course of my involvement in Mandelbaum's project, and against the background of my long association with Doak Barnett, who had been Hyman Professor and Director of China Studies at SAIS starting in 1982, it dawned on me that SAIS might be the perfect place for me. Susan and I had lived in Northern Virginia (1983–1985) when I was at CSCPRC, and we loved Washington and its surroundings.

SAIS was attractive to me in many respects, one being that over the years, Johns Hopkins had notable involvements with China. In the early twentieth century, Hopkins's third president, Professor Frank Goodnow, also the first president of the American Political Science Association (APSA) and an expert on administrative law, worked with Chinese President (later becoming emperor) Yuan Shikai to help draft a Western-style constitution emphasizing strong executive power (advocacy that drew critical fire in America). In a 1914 APSA paper, Goodnow wrote:

> It is of course not susceptible of doubt that a monarchy is better suited than a republic to China. China's history and traditions, her social and economic conditions, her relations with foreign powers all make it more probable that the country would develop constitutional government more easily as a monarchy than a republic.[3]

Later in his career, Goodnow wrote a book titled *China: An Analysis*. Also in the second decade of the twentieth century, Hopkins was leading in scientifically grounded medical, public health, and nursing research, education, and training and cooperated with the Rockefeller Foundation to establish and guide the Peking Union Medical College. Dr. Mary Brown Bullock has written authoritatively on this.

Subsequently, during World War II, Hopkins Professor Owen Lattimore was an advisor to Chiang Kai-shek, working closely with FDR, subsequently becoming a focus of attack in the McCarthy era of the early 1950s. Later still, A. Doak Barnett had called for the PRC's "containment without isolation" at March 1966 Hearings of the Senate Committee on Foreign Relations, subsequently moving to SAIS. In the mid-1980s, Hopkins President Steven Muller worked with Nanjing University President Kuang Yaming to establish the Hopkins-Nanjing Center (HNC), which opened in 1986, the first, and what has become the longest-enduring, post-1949 Sino-American educational joint venture. I believed HNC to be important, with Hopkins and Nanjing University agreeing to jointly confer a certificate and later a two-year MA degree.

I was asked to be on President Muller's advisory committee in the 1984–1986 period during which Johns Hopkins and Nanjing University moved from the rough concept to operational reality. From the very start, the program was bilingual, with Americans and other international students taking classes in Chinese from PRC professors, and Chinese students taking classes from international (predominantly American) professors in English. Over time the curriculum evolved, as did administrative practice. It was a joint venture in the best sense, most particularly when later a Sino-American/International faculty Joint Academic Committee was created to develop and approve curricular changes and academic procedures with best international practices as the standard.

All of this attracted me to Hopkins-SAIS because I believe that successful organizations build cultures, have history, and internally share objectives among units. The culture of constructive, joint action with China on issues of global importance was decisive in my decision. SAIS held further attraction for me because it occupied sparsely populated territory in American academia—being interdisciplinary, combining area and functional studies, emphasizing language proficiency, and demanding systematic study of economics.

When students came to SAIS, they generally already had significant real-world experience, more focus, and less angst about their life direction than do students who have gone straight from undergraduate to graduate school. SAIS students had enough experience to make them critical and practical, but not so much that they had become dogmatic or jaded. For the most part, the senior faculty members at SAIS had significant periods of public or private sector experience under their belts, along with recognized academic accomplishments. This was the broad skill set America needed to effectively deal with the future U.S.-China relationship. I kept bumping into SAIS and Hopkins while in New York.

Paul Wolfowitz and the Birth of Neoconservatism

Years earlier I had had a one-off meeting with Paul Wolfowitz when, in the Carter administration, at about the time of normalization, he, Mike Oksenberg, and I had lunch together near the Old Executive Office Building in Washington. At that time, Wolfowitz was Deputy Assistant Secretary of Defense for Regional Programs under Secretary of Defense Harold Brown. My post-lunch impression was that Paul was a lot more skeptical of China than Mike Oksenberg!

Subsequently, Wolfowitz held a series of posts: Assistant Secretary of State for East Asian and Pacific Affairs under President Reagan (December 1982–March 1986), ambassador to Indonesia (1986–1989), Under Secretary of Defense under George Herbert Walker Bush (1989–1993), and thereafter Dean of SAIS where he stayed until he joined the George W. Bush administration in its early days in 2001 as Deputy Secretary of Defense (2001–2005), becoming a motive force behind the war in Iraq. Thereafter, he became president of the World Bank (2005–2007), a tour that did not end well.

In 1980, Paul left the Carter administration and went to SAIS as a visiting professor (1980–1981). At about that time, he also joined the Republican Party (having been a Democrat), decrying what he viewed as the Democratic Party's having jettisoned the "hard-headed internationalism" of the World War II generation, embodied by figures such as Senator "Scoop" Jackson of the State of Washington, Harry Truman, and Ronald Reagan, who started political life as a Democrat. Paul believed in using American force, muscle, and raw power to produce maximum democratic political change—neoconservative for short. In his view, the Democratic Party had veered off track with the nomination of George McGovern as the Democratic Party's standard bearer in 1972.[4]

In these beliefs, he was joined by persons such as Richard Perle (who had worked for Scoop Jackson) and Ambassador Jeane Kirkpatrick, who once defined a neoconservative as a "liberal mugged by reality." Both became associated with the American Enterprise Institute (AEI) where I was founding head of the China Policy Studies Program in the 1985–1987 period, while I retained my principal post at OSU. Paul was associated with AEI over time.

By accident I was at the epicenter of the neoconservative revolution by being at AEI in the mid-1980s. I joined AEI when it was a traditional, business-oriented, Republican-leaning organization—fiscally conservative, internationalist, but not bellicose. "Compromise" was a perfectly good word then. When I came to AEI, no one even asked about my politics. But before long however, I woke up with traditional conservatives at AEI such as pipe-smoking former Federal Reserve Board Chair Arthur

F. Burns and University of Michigan economist Paul McCracken gone, to then be surrounded by Jeane Kirkpatrick and Richard Perle. Perle wore the moniker "The Prince of Darkness" as a badge of honor.

In 1987, I was offered the position of president of NCUSCR in New York City and left Ohio State with a sense of gratitude for the opportunities I had been afforded. I disconnected from AEI with a sigh of relief, alarmed at its lurch rightward.

I can only speculate why a decade later, by then Dean Paul Wolfowitz, recruited me to head China Studies at SAIS, beyond the fact that the school's Academic Board had voted to extend me the offer. In our few previous encounters, we had been cordial but were not kindred policy spirits. Perhaps Paul had concluded from my role at AEI a decade earlier that I shared his foreign policy inclinations, but that seems unlikely.

I had come to AEI under the leadership of its then president William J. Baroody Jr. and Robert J. ("Bob") Pranger, the latter being the institute's head of International Programs. Baroody Jr. and Pranger believed that AEI should be a "university without students," a broad intellectually ecumenical tent that had a small-government, realist, and national interest foreign policy center of gravity.

I left AEI in 1987 shortly after the institute made what I thought was a hard right turn by appointing a new president, Christopher Demuth (whom I took to Taiwan and South Korea as my last major act at AEI). I did not doubt that Demuth was committed to AEI's new starboard direction and responsive to the financial power of America's hard right, especially given that AEI confronted severe fiscal woes.

Baroody's attempts to keep a centrist institution financially afloat in the face of rising competitive pressures from hard-right organizations such as the Heritage Foundation were unsuccessful. Incidentally, Taiwan was very helpful to AEI in its moment of financial exigency. I believe that financial dependence threatens program independence.

Amidst this organizational turmoil at AEI, I invited the PRC Ambassador to the United States at the time, Han Xu, over to lunch with AEI's acting president, Paul McCracken, former Defense Secretary Melvin Laird, and me. Baroody Jr. had been dumped as president, and I wanted to do two things: get AEI's acting president conversant with the institute's China activities and send a message to Taiwan that the China Studies Program was not a wholly owned subsidiary.

On the appointed day, Ambassador Han arrived. I greeted him curbside on 17th Street, NW, and as we went up the elevator, the ambassador cheerily asked, "And how is President Baroody? Where is he?" To which I could only respond, "On the second floor" as the elevator zipped past that stop on the way to the upper executive suite where McCracken and Secretary Laird were awaiting our arrival. Ambassador Han had the look of someone finding out that a relative had been sent to a Qinghai reform through labor camp.

That lunch proved memorable in another way involving Fredrick Chien (Chien Foo), who then was Taiwan Coordination Council for North American Affairs (CCNAA) representative in Washington. Nearly screaming at me on the phone after that lunch with Ambassador Han, Chien indicated that inviting the PRC ambassador was deeply offensive to him and to Taipei. I had wanted to send the message that AEI's China Studies Program would be independent. I surely succeeded. I must also say that neither Paul McCracken nor Bob Pranger ever raised the issue with me. For them, fundraising and program content were realms to be insulated from one another to the degree possible.

While I was just getting my start in New York at the committee, Wolfowitz was compiling an admirable record at the Department of State, and, by all accounts, Paul was a very effective ambassador to Indonesia (1986–1989).

With George Herbert Walker Bush out and Bill Clinton in as president (1993–2001), the deanship of SAIS was an attractive place for Paul to spend an indeterminate amount of time (1994–2001, as it turned out), hoping that a Republican administration would roll along again and require his services. SAIS was a visible platform from which to articulate his policy views, particularly as they pertained to Iraq and Saddam Hussein. While I knew very little about Iraq, I always felt that SAIS deans should be circumspect in expressing polarizing, partisan political and policy views. There is a fine line between articulating policy choices (educationally framing issues) and advocating specific, polarizing policies, some of which could go disastrously wrong.

Paul was a man in a hurry, and he moved to bring new blood to SAIS, not least concerning Southeast Asia and China Studies. He also was worried about how to get the HNC onto a more sustainable financial trajectory, and he wanted someone to help lift that particular burden from his shoulders. Further, he knew the China Program was important to SAIS, but filling the post would prove difficult because of the multiple roles and varied internal constituencies at SAIS and within the broader university, not to mention Washington.

Paul and I were an odd couple. My army medical experience made me see war in human terms—I could put faces on decisions to go to war. My National Committee time made me value diplomacy and dialogue. My admiration of Hopkins and SAIS was rooted, in part, in their active and long engagement with China, about which Paul was skeptical. And while I certainly believed in democratic values, I did not believe democracy should generally be promoted out of the barrel of a gun.

Once Paul asked me why it was in U.S. national interests to train a more capable generation of Chinese communist leaders. That was a good question, and we had diverging answers. My answer was, and remains, I generally did not believe that mutual ignorance, whether in Beijing or elsewhere, improved policy or outcomes or served American interests.

While I thought that Paul was always skeptical of HNC, he never threw roadblocks in the way of China Studies, or in the way of the University President William R. ("Bill") Brody (1996–2009), who was very committed to the HNC. President Brody was so dedicated that he spent a year learning enough Chinese to deliver a speech in Nanjing in Chinese.

To secure a new head of China Studies at SAIS, Paul and the SAIS Academic Board launched a broad and protracted search for a chaired professor to succeed Doak Barnett. In the fullness of time, I was offered and accepted the Hyman Chair, agreeing to be in Washington in December 1997 and to start teaching the following January.

Paul's 2001 move into the George W. Bush administration, and the roles he subsequently played in the Iraq War and at the World Bank, were, and remain, very troubling to me. I am torn between gratitude for his having allowed me to come to SAIS and for his delegation of management of the China Program to me on the one hand, and my rejection of much of his foreign policy stance and subsequent World Bank controversies on the other.

Another interaction I had with Paul, however, rounds out the view of a complex person. Annually, the SAIS Student Government Association goes through a process of identifying a notable person to address each year's graduates. The school's administration plays little to no role in the selection but does invite the prospective guest speaker on behalf of the students. Their spring 2001 choice was His Holiness the Dalai Lama.

I was appreciative when Paul called me to check his instincts on this. He rightly suspected that we needed to anticipate some kind of PRC response, and obviously we had multiple connections to China that could be affected, not least the HNC. Paul and I had a short conversation since we were in full agreement. Our shared feeling was that Johns Hopkins is a private university, academic freedom is our core value, the Dalai Lama has a point of view about important ethical and global issues, and we would proceed with the invitation without consulting outside entities. The Dalai Lama delivered the graduation speech on the afternoon of May 24, 2001, in DAR Constitution Hall. We never heard a peep from the PRC.

I have listened to a lot of graduation speeches in my life, and the overwhelming majority have left no recoverable imprint on my mind. The first minute of the Dalai Lama's speech did. To paraphrase, he said: "I know that you graduating students will do well. The question is, will you do good?"

DIRECTIONS AND CHALLENGES AT SAIS, 1997–2018
Tasks and the Organizational Setting

My initial SAIS duties were to teach a total of four courses over two semesters each academic year, covering Chinese Domestic Politics, Chinese Foreign Policy, U.S.-China Relations, and an Advanced Research Seminar on either domestic or foreign policy issues germane to Greater China. I also was to fill the George and Sadie Hyman Chair of Chinese Studies; be director of the China Studies Program which involved advising MA and PhD students; hire adjunct faculty and staff for the

Figure 12.1.   His Holiness the Dalai Lama shakes hands with Author, SAIS grad-uation, May 24, 2001, DAR Constitution Hall, Washington, DC. Photo by David M. Lampton.

China Studies Program; assure that students had meaningful outside-of-the-classroom learning experiences, including field trips to the region; and watch over the HNC, both its Washington Office and operations in Nanjing for the American side of the joint venture, though the buck did not stop with me but rather with the Dean and our HNC directors. I had no line responsibility for Chinese language instruction, but we all were blessed with Qi Laoshi, who ran the program for all my years at SAIS. I only ever heard praise for her skill and kindness. During the Deanship of Vali Nasr (2012–2019), all my China duties were consoli-dated into what became "SAIS-China" which I headed from 2014 until my mid-2018 retirement.

Each of the two HNC offices (one in Washington and one in Nan-jing) had a director or co-director responsible for day-to-day manage-ment responsibility. I worked with a faculty committee and the dean to recruit the directors and co-directors.[5]

After Paul Wolfowitz had gone to the George W. Bush administration, former managing director at the World Bank, Jessica Einhorn, a graduate of SAIS herself, was named dean effective June 1, 2002. She created a new post, "Dean of Faculty," a position assumed initially by Frank Fukuyama for two years, after which I served in that post from July 2004 until June 2012, stepping down when Jessica retired. I kept my duties in China Studies throughout.

No single person could even remotely do all these jobs without being willing to delegate to skilled colleagues. With me at SAIS, from beginning to end, was Ji Zhaojin ("Zhaojin"), who kept our operation running, helped students with Chinese language, and maintained impeccable relations with the rest of the Hopkins bureaucracy. She also found time for Chinese brush painting; writing poetry; authoring a book, *A History of Modern Chinese Banking*; and was heavily involved in Chinese school and the education of her children bilingually and multiculturally. She is a truly admirable person.

Also, I was blessed with great academic colleagues who shared a common vision of what a rounded education involved while each had a distinct approach, skills, interests, values, and views. They were self-starters and innovators.

With respect to curriculum, I felt it was key to have one full-time faculty colleague specializing in the Chinese economy and a colleague studying grassroots China and humanitarian-related issues, given that my own interests were focused on elite and bureaucratic politics and foreign policy. Also, we always had a Modern History of China course and one or more persons dealing with the PRC's periphery, not least Taiwan. Later in the program's development, we generally had a course on Legal Development in China.[6]

SAIS emphasized language proficiency, but assuring proficiency in Chinese in a two-year master's program was always a problem since the language takes such a long time to learn. One way out of the dilemma was to make some prior Chinese language training a precondition for admission to the program—which we did. We also encouraged students to enroll in intensive summer programs. To supplement China Studies course offerings, other program units at SAIS, such as Southeast Asia,

South Asia, Japan, Korea, and Strategic Studies, covered many topics germane to China.

As the PRC became central to ever-more functional and geographic domains in international relations, other SAIS faculty with strong China credentials were added to the School's talent pool outside of China Studies. By the time I left SAIS, probably one-third of courses with heavy China content were taught by non–China Studies Program faculty.

Universities have distinct models of internal governance, with one point of differentiation being how much autonomy, discretion, and flexibility are given to department chairs and deans and how much authority is retained by university central (provost and president). While "accountability" and "best practices" are now buzzwords thought to promote sound management, when I first went to SAIS, discretion, delegation, and responsible entrepreneurship at the program level were the organizational trinity. I had the latitude to manage the China Program and correspondingly sought to delegate to my capable colleagues. Hire good people and trust them.

A high degree of autonomy for the major academic units within the university was the organizing principle, with the home campus in Baltimore and SAIS as a professional school located forty miles away in Washington. Hopkins and Harvard were at one end of the continuum of administrative designs—decentralized and entrepreneurial. That appealed to me. When, over time, the vocabulary within Hopkins evolved to emphasize "One Hopkins" and "best practices," the signal that gradual centralization and standardization were in the offing was clear. These alterations were associated with virtual and online learning, changing student expectations, standards-setting and quantitative performance measures, the Sarbanes-Oxley Act of 2002, and the tightening up in the wake of the 2008–2009 global financial crisis. Later, COVID-19 reinforced these trends.

Teaching

I remember my debut class session on Chinese Foreign Policy. The class had, as I recall, two persons from the Chinese Foreign Ministry, one person from Japan's Ministry of Foreign Affairs, several students with U.S.

government and military experience, a sprinkling of others from other nations in Asia, many American students who had lived and worked in China (including those who had attended the HNC), and other students attending class to complete requirements for academic concentrations other than China Studies.

From the start, I realized that with such a wealth of experience, political viewpoints, cultures, values, and interests represented in classes, I would have to be clear about my frameworks, be balanced in summoning data, and encourage students to bring their own experiences and interpretations to bear on the questions we were addressing. Invariably in each course, I would say to students, "It is interesting what you think, but if you want to be effective with others, particularly in negotiation, you should start by knowing what your interlocutor thinks, why they think that, and put yourself in their shoes. Only then might you stand a chance of being effective. There is a difference between empathy and sentimentality. Knowing your interlocutor's position, motivations, interests, values, and perceptions (empathy) need not mean losing sight of your own interests." Understanding and steadfastness are not opposed concepts.

In my years at SAIS, some students disagreed with me on substantive issues, but diverging views were managed (I hope and believe) by discussion and openness. SAIS students were serious, civil, and a joy to teach.

I have watched with interest the varied pursuits of former students, pleased that they have followed diverse paths, often adopting policy positions in public life that did not align with my own views but, nonetheless, represented a considered response to events. I think often of foreign student graduates of SAIS and OSU who have made contributions to enlightened public life on China's mainland, Taiwan, and around Asia.

Research

Johns Hopkins attracted me with its distinctive conceptual and organizational roots as America's first research university. Founded in 1876, Hopkins originally brought together senior researchers who took on mentees (graduate students) and developed close one-on-one intellectual relationships with them. At the institution's start, the focus was on graduate education. Mentors and mentees worked together on research;

systematic instruction supplemented the projects. The idea of learning through exploration and experimentation was, and remains, key for both graduate and undergraduate students throughout Hopkins.

Professors not only convey the knowledge and collective wisdom of the past, but also engage students by exposing them to, and involving them in, frontier areas of inquiry the professor is exploring. One reflection of this is that even a small academic unit within Hopkins such as SAIS has an active and highly selective PhD program. An important part of the PhD student admissions process was that an applicant had to identify a senior professor willing to assume responsibility for, and take an interest in, the student and his/her research and write a letter of recommendation for that applicant to the PhD Program Admissions Committee. Consequently, PhD students came knowing what they generally intended to do, and they had someone committed to their success.

During my SAIS years, I headed the dissertation committee of twenty-one PhD students, eighteen of whom have thus far completed their dissertations and been awarded their doctorate. Three continue their work. I had five completed PhD students at Ohio State.

CHALLENGES

Two challenges the China Studies Program faced during my years at SAIS are instructive, one in 2002–2003 because of a public health crisis and the other in 2017–2018 involving the mass media and academic freedom.

SARS

From November 2002 to February 2003, a mysterious, stealthy virus called SARS (Severe Acute Respiratory Syndrome) began to strike citizens in South China and by mid-March and April 2003 had spilled over elsewhere in China, also spreading to Hong Kong, Vietnam, Taiwan, Singapore, and Canada, eventually producing infections in twenty-nine countries, including the United States. Because we ran a school in Nanjing with our Nanjing University partners, this outbreak was of immediate and serious concern.

I must give full credit to Johns Hopkins President Bill Brody, and SAIS leadership under Dean Jessica Einhorn, for being the bedrock support for the U.S. side's creative response to this crisis. The guidance of the entire Johns Hopkins medical and public health establishment was irreplaceable. Great credit goes to Dan Wright, Executive Director of the Hopkins-Nanjing Center Office in Washington, for managing the overall effort within Hopkins and liaison with Nanjing University, and to Robert Daly, Co-Director in Nanjing and thereafter at the East-West Center in Hawaii during the fall semester relocation of 2003.

Only by June 27, 2003, did the World Health Organization (WHO) declare China "SARS free." In the meantime, the disease had infected 8,000 persons worldwide and killed 774.

Similar to COVID-19, local and other officials in China initially covered up infections in the early phase of the SARS outbreak, but, unlike COVID-19, the regime, by then under the new leadership of General Secretary Hu Jintao and the new Premier Wen Jiabao, sacked and punished one thousand officials, fairly quickly cooperated with WHO, and fired the minister of public health (Zhang Wenkang, Jiang Zemin's personal physician).

Local officials up the chain of command in China initially had tried to stanch news of the outbreak, in part for fear of taking bad news to superiors, in part wanting to avoid creating panic and slowing economic activity, and in part because major national government political meetings were imminent and underway and officials feared creating a "bad atmosphere." As with COVID-19, it took a courageous Chinese whistleblower's (retired PLA physician Jiang Yanyong) unauthorized warning of deaths in Beijing in early April to hit the world press before the PRC response got in gear. Unlike the later COVID-19 outbreak in 2020, however, Beijing soon reversed policy on SARS and became more transparent and followed a much more cooperative course internationally. The PRC leadership face of this effort was Vice Premier Madam Wu Yi, who had replaced Zhang Wenkang as Minister of Public Health and was soon internationally praised for her competence.

The lessons of SARS (and how Hopkins and Nanjing University handled it) were clear and could have provided the beginning of a template for handling COVID nearly two decades later—credibility and effectiveness in a pandemic go up with transparency, accountability, and cooperation. Among the many tragedies of COVID-19 was that the system under Xi Jinping had not learned the lessons of 2003. Also regrettable, the United States under President Trump made strategic missteps by dismantling much of its domestic epidemic crisis management system in the White House and slashing the level of CDC cooperation with China before the outbreak. The U.S. president and many of his political acolytes were oblivious to the lessons of SARS. In the early days of the COVID outbreak, the U.S. president was not forthright with the American people about the mounting danger, and he compounded problems by propagating misinformation and slinging degrading epithets.

In Nanjing, HNC had about a hundred students from the United States, China, and third countries enrolled at the time the SARS outbreak became public knowledge in early April 2003. For Hopkins, Nanjing University, and HNC, the nature of the disease, the initial epidemiological uncertainties surrounding it, and the academic calendar each presented problems requiring immediate attention. There would be no re-dos. And, since HNC was a joint venture, we needed Chinese buy-in for *school-wide* responses, though Hopkins retained control concerning American and other international students. Throughout this entire episode, we had the utmost cooperation from our Nanjing partners, and vice versa. The two university presidents were in close touch.

The first obvious fact was that more than half the students were Chinese and they did not have the option of leaving the PRC for a more secure location, if Johns Hopkins decided to do so concerning the international students. For the international (mostly American) students, and for Hopkins, a decision to evacuate was a real option, though exit procedures were initially unclear. The threshold question was, "Should we stay or leave for an indeterminate period of time?" Safety was the essential requirement, but what was "safe"? And, were we to decide to evacuate, the mere act of going to airports, rail stations, and being on airplanes was a risk of unknown magnitude. Moreover, there were lockdowns and spontaneous and planned interruptions of movement within China.

The first thing HNC's Dan Wright did was to set up the Crisis Response Team consisting of himself, a leading Johns Hopkins epidemiologist, the provost's office, Robert Daly in Nanjing, and me. Were the team to decide the health risk for international students, staff, and families was too great, we put in place the means to quickly exit.

Second, the school year normally would conclude in the spring (June 26), and if students could not complete their course of study, their diplomas could not be granted. Failing to graduate would affect students' plans for jobs, further graduate education, and so forth. Thus, if possible and safe, we wanted to finish requirements, even if it meant accelerating the teaching schedule. This we did, completing essential work by April 22, whereupon the university decided to grant degrees and get students out.

Third, the spring is when schools are involved with the admissions process for the following academic year's class. At that moment, we could not be sure how long the epidemic would last and whether or not there even would be an HNC class in Nanjing the following academic year. For their part, prospective new students did not want to apply or promise to enroll if HNC could not assure them that it would be open the following academic year. Without such assurances, students would seek and accept admission elsewhere. And, irrespective of what students or administrators thought, parents were highly anxious and needed accurate data on which to make sensible decisions. In short, we concurrently had to deal with the immediate issue of current students, their health and safety, graduation necessities, and, at the same time, plan for the following year to guarantee the school's continued operation. We were determined to keep faith with our partners and Chinese students.

The essence of our decision, announced by Hopkins President Bill Brody on May 19, 2003, was that we would guarantee to open HNC for the fall 2003 semester and that we would move Chinese and international students, faculty, and essential staff to the East-West Center in Honolulu for that semester. President Brody announced,

Fall semester classes will be taught beginning September 5 at the East-West Center in Honolulu, rather than in Nanjing. . . . The center's Chinese students and faculty will join their American and third-country colleagues and roommates in Hawaii for four months before returning to Nanjing for the spring 2004 semester, which opens in early March, after the Chinese New Year.

Like so much in life, luck and happenstance were critical. Prior to President Brody's announcement, Dan Wright and I had talked about setting up an alternative site in the United States where we could decamp all the students, faculty, and staff to continue our program until the epidemic had passed in China—we would not leave our Chinese students to the mercies of the virus if there were any choice.

During that period, I had happened to be at the East-West Center in Honolulu for a meeting with the center's President Charles E. Morrison, himself a SAIS graduate. I knew that over the years the East-West Center (EWC) had underutilized space and ruminated with Charles about finding a way to convene HNC classes at the EWC for an indeterminate period to get through the SARS epidemic. He soon got back to us saying he thought it could be done.

Armed with this, Dan Wright located President Brody in the Washington Metro system, quickly outlined the proposal, and Brody immediately expressed general support. With this and the critical buy-in of Nanjing University, HNC was able to work out arrangements with the EWC. Dean Jessica Einhorn was fully supportive and helpful every step of the way.

The next hurdle to be overcome was the great cost of such a move. It would be very expensive because from the start we were proposing to move all Chinese and international students and all Chinese and international teachers, plus relevant staff. From day one of the crisis, leaving behind our Chinese colleagues and students was unacceptable. Of all the moves we made that created an indelible legacy of trust between the two sides of the HNC, the decision to treat all students, faculty, and staff as of equal concern was key.

In terms of meeting the great added financial burdens without charging students more, this was the fastest, most effective fundraising experience I have ever been associated with. Almost immediately we raised the necessary funds. As President Brody put it on May 19, "We are grateful to the Asia Foundation and Mr. Daniel Koo, chairman of Shui Hing (HK) Limited, for assisting us during this extraordinary time. With their generous support, we are able to provide this opportunity at no additional tuition costs to our students."[7]

This case shows how important transparency and openness in China are in such emergencies, how important science-based decision-making is, and how expending effort to show concern and demonstrate trust is essential. Unfortunately, about seventeen years later when COVID-19 struck, the Xi and Trump administrations did exactly the opposite, with catastrophic results.

Another aspect of managing this situation was that at the same time we dealt with the immediate health crisis, both the Chinese and American sides made a major commitment to expand HNC's physical infrastructure and, shortly thereafter, create a new two-year master's degree program. As President Brody put it on May 19 as he announced the temporary move to Hawaii, "Nanjing remains the home of all center programs. Both universities have committed a combined $18 million to an infrastructure expansion project that will double the size of the center's campus and student body." Robert Daly, who subsequently became director of the Kissinger Institute on China and the United States at the Woodrow Wilson International Center for Scholars, not only oversaw the Hopkins side of the arduous process of constructing the enlarged and modernized physical plant, he also guided a major curricular reform along with Dan Wright.

The spirit animating this progress amidst crisis is the same spirit that Hank Greenberg of AIG mentioned to me in the context of the 1989 Tiananmen Crisis and AIG's corporate response. "When everyone else is heading for the revolving door exits, I enter."

Mass and Social Media and Reciprocal Suspicion

One morning in November 2017, I awoke to find that Foreignpolicy.com had carried a story by Bethany Allen-Ebrahimian, "This Beijing-Linked Billionaire Is Funding Policy Research at Washington's Most Influential Institutions." Hopkins and I felt obliged to respond to this piece and others, given the issues raised, not least concerning academic freedom and foreign influence. This and other pieces contributed to an environment in the United States in which PRC "covert influence operations" became the new slur by which normal academic relationships of integrity are transformed into nefarious activities.

Sometime before the article's publication, Allen-Ebrahimian (an HNC graduate) contacted me. She asked questions about a newly endowed professorship for China Studies and a sustained research/dialogue series called "The Pacific Community Initiative" (PCI) that aimed to bring together young academic and policy leaders in the Pacific Basin to talk about whether and how societies along the Pacific Rim might build a more cohesive and constructive community. This was a joint project undertaken by China Studies at SAIS and a Peking University Institute led by Professor Wang Jisi. On the Hopkins side, Professor David Bulman and I ran the program.

Allen-Ebrahimian's questions concerned the funder of PCI and the professorship—The China-U.S. Exchange Foundation (CUSEF), headed by C.H. Tung, the first chief executive of the Hong Kong SAR and a member of the Chinese People's Political Consultative Conference (CPPCC) in Beijing. Tung also was the scion of a Hong Kong shipping company fortune. The journalist asked about CUSEF with respect to the U.S. Foreign Agents Registration Act (FARA), projects CUSEF had funded with others, the implications of all this for academic freedom, and whether Hopkins would be subject to pressure by virtue of accepting CUSEF funds.

I answered the questions in written form, acknowledging CUSEF funding (as we had all along), explaining the purposes and uses of the funds, and categorically assuring her that CUSEF played no role in selecting personnel on the Hopkins side, and that "there are absolutely no conditions or limitations imposed upon the Pacific Community Initiative or our faculty members and program participants by reason of the gift or otherwise." I was concerned that by framing CUSEF as a registered "Foreign Agent," which is a perfectly law-abiding legal status for an institution or individual operating in the United States, it would be easy for the general reader to draw unwarranted conclusions.

So, when I read the published article's opening that November morning, I had a pretty good idea where it was heading. The author's opening announced that SAIS, a top school located in the heart of Washington, sends graduates to "a variety of government agencies," including the Department of State, the CIA, and the U.S. military. The second paragraph noted that in August SAIS had announced a new endowed professorship in the China Studies Program and a research project called the PCI, with subsequent paragraphs going on to say that CUSEF, the funder, is a registered "foreign agent" under U.S. law and that CUSEF's head, C. H. Tung, is "a high-ranking Chinese government official with close ties to a sprawling Chinese Communist Party apparatus that handles influence operations abroad, known as the 'united front.'" The article went on: "Even as Washington is embroiled in a debate over Russian influence in U.S. elections, it's China that has proved adept at inserting itself in American politics." After identifying other American research entities as cooperating in various ways with CUSEF (including Brookings Institution, the Center for Strategic and International Studies, the Atlantic Council, Center for American Progress, the Carnegie Endowment for Peace, the Carter Center, and others), the article concluded with the rhetorical question: "Who better to influence Americans than other Americans?"

Nowhere in this article was there any attempt to show actual influence. This was evidence-free analysis, substituting innuendo and assertion for examples. More basically, dialogue, exchange, and soft power were tools in the diplomatic toolbox of all powers.

As James Mann told us long ago in a piece in *Media Studies Journal* (Winter 1999), the mass media at any given moment has a "governing frame," a singular macro-story, a conceptual umbrella in a given substantive domain under which individual stories fit. When the macro-story shifts, for example, from "China as quasi U.S. ally against the Soviets" to "China as America's biggest competitor," the individual stories written in a given topical domain tend to follow the macro-story or frame. For example, when the media frame was "China as the largest reforming country," the years of cooperating with CUSEF had been an unremarkable or positive phenomenon. With the more recent rise of the "competitor" and "authoritarian threat" macro-story, cooperation and dialogue previously praised have become suspect undertakings, with little actual evidence required. It is an echo chamber.

This process snowballs, affecting the willingness of institutions to engage in dialogue with China. Some U.S. students and young faculty become reticent to study in China or participate in such dialogues for fear it will affect their ability to obtain a security clearance down the line. This process spills over into guilt by association, with, for example, the director of the FBI, Christopher Wray, calling for a "whole-of-society response" to stop Chinese spying and covert influence operations in his February 2018 testimony before the U.S. Senate Intelligence Committee and in other fora.

Unsurprisingly, it was not long before we began to see more displays of anti-Chinese, anti-Asian, and anti-Chinese American behavior and what later proved to be failed prosecutions directed at law-abiding Chinese American and Asian American citizens. In November 2018, the U.S. Department of Justice under Attorney General Jeff Sessions launched its "China Initiative" that ran through the remainder of the Trump administration and continued into the Biden administration, whereupon the program was nominally terminated in February 2022. Embarrassingly, the initiative has a record of court failures. Nonetheless, the Department of Justice continues the hunt for "non-traditional [intelligence] collectors."[8] And, of course, there are some.

Sadly, there is just enough unethical and untruthful behavior in academia and elsewhere that it is not possible to summarily dismiss all accusations. A particularly damaging case of such behavior involved Harvard Research Scientist Charles Lieber, chairman of Harvard's Chemistry and Chemical-Biology Department, a world-class nanoscientist. For whatever reasons, Lieber lied to federal authorities concerning his affiliation with China's Thousand Talents Program, a Chinese research and talent recruitment effort for which he received sizeable monetary payments from the PRC. This money was not declared to the U.S. tax authorities. He was convicted of (and sentenced for) making false statements to the FBI, federal authorities, and tax authorities.[9]

As we see in so many instances, a few unethical persons can disrupt the lives of many law-abiding citizens. In the case of China, ethnic Chinese in the United States, Chinese Americans, and Asian Americans are particularly vulnerable to accusations concerning PRC influence or espionage. When I was at Stanford University in 2019–2020 as a Research Fellow, the Asia Society and the Hoover Institution jointly published (in November 2018) a report, "Chinese Influence and American Interests: Promoting Constructive Vigilance." I felt, and said so publicly at the time, that the report would reinforce guilt-by-association thinking and would have negative consequences for law-abiding Chinese Americans, not to mention tarring hundreds of thousands of Chinese students in the United States with a broad brush. Without asserting cause and effect with any particular study, there was a notable uptick in abuse and violence directed at Chinese Americans and persons of Asian ethnicity after "influence operations" became new code words.

Unfortunately, China has fed every possible negative American impulse with its acts of omission and commission—no transparency with COVID-19, assertive foreign policy, Hong Kong clampdown, coercive pressure on Taiwan, internal governance toughening, theft of U.S. intellectual property and data, and Beijing's hedged, unhelpful response to the Russian invasion of Ukraine.

It also is true that security dragnets in China are growing in scope and intensity. In retrospect, the writing was on the Great Wall as early as the late 2013–2014 creation of the PRC's National Security Commission, aimed importantly at stopping "subversion" within the PRC. This had made Chinese of all stripes on the mainland circumspect in dealing with American NGOs, individual foreign researchers, and others. About two years later, Beijing's adoption of a restrictive NGO law further raised inhibitions on dealing with foreign NGOs, not least American entities. More recently, foreign researchers and others are concerned about what appears to be the increased use of "exits bans." Consequently, an unknown but sizeable fraction of the contemporary western China research community would think twice about going to the PRC and Hong Kong to attempt research on any sensitive topic. U.S. firms specializing in doing due diligence on Chinese firms are coming under pressure.

Conversely, it also is true that Chinese think tank researchers and university scholars sometimes have been stopped at the U.S. border and interrogated if thought to have links to the PRC's coercive, intelligence, military, and united front bureaucracies. On occasion they have been put on the next plane back to China. China has for years denied visas to foreign scholars deemed troublesome.

Access to archives, individuals, and institutions in China is drying up. Travel restrictions brought on by the global COVID-19 pandemic basically shut down face-to-face scholarly interaction, except what is possible in the Zoom and Skype worlds, until early 2023. Generally during video conferences, people are told they are being recorded and, in any event, assume that is the case. Because U.S. intelligence agencies monitor communications with PRC entities, Americans can incidentally be monitored if there is a PRC party on the other end, though there are supposed to be protections against the use of such inadvertent collection by U.S. authorities.

In December 2022, China ended its "Zero COVID" policy and attendant barriers to travel which offers the possibility of more scholarly interaction looking ahead. But the damage to exchanges and research access was caused by far more than COVID, and those barriers have not been perceptibly lessened and, in some ways, are becoming more stringent. The cost of air transportation to the PRC has skyrocketed with a reduced number of flights and longer routes of travel for U.S. carriers due to Russian prohibitions stemming from the war in Ukraine.

THE NIXON CENTER AND NATIONAL INTEREST

As I had founded the China Policy Studies Program at AEI in 1985, and then left it and Ohio State for the National Committee in 1987, once I decided to go to SAIS and depart the National Committee; I again wanted to put my foot back into think tank waters. At the National Committee, I had come to know and admire James ("Jim") Schlesinger, former Secretary of Defense, former Director of CIA, former head of the Atomic Energy Commission, and former (the first) Secretary of Energy. Having started his academic career at Harvard in economics, Jim was a Republican appointed by Democratic President Jimmy Carter to the

Energy Department post. He was associated with the Nixon Center, a Washington research organization founded in 1994.

I admired Jim for many reasons, not least that he could work for both Republican and Democratic presidents as different as Nixon and Carter. I also admired his decision as secretary of defense to protect against the erratic behavior of a distraught President Nixon with respect to the possible use of U.S. military forces at a time when pressure was building on the president to relinquish office due to Watergate (shades of General Mark Milley, chairman of the Joint Chiefs of Staff, in the waning days of the Trump presidency). An additional reason for my admiration was that I had traveled with Jim to China from August to September 1996 on one of NCUSCR's military exchanges. He effectively dealt with the Chinese military based on his experience in the Cold War. He was in the national interest school of realist foreign policy thinking to which I am attuned.

In early 1998, shortly after I arrived at SAIS, Secretary Schlesinger asked me to consider affiliating with the Nixon Center. After talking with the center's president, Dimitri Simes, I agreed to establish the Chinese Studies Program there, hire a staff person, oversee occasional policy-oriented publications, and convene lunches and dinners over which guests would discuss China-related issues of the day. I did so from May 1998 until May 2006.

During that period, the Nixon Center's Chinese Studies Program had excellent day-to-day staff, all of whom were SAIS students working with me, among whom were Daniel Ewing, Gregory May (later becoming Consul General in Hong Kong), and Travis Tanner. They went on to have diverse and successful careers, all dealing with China. Beyond providing this experience to students and generating policy-oriented publications, the Nixon Center's national interest orientation created the opportunity for me to get a hearing for my thinking on Capitol Hill and in the executive branch. The center's flagship publication, *The National Interest*, was first-rate, especially under its founding editor (1985–2001) Owen Harries. This was a venue I utilized to express my views, and I enjoyed working with Schlesinger, a member of the *National Interest*'s Advisory Board.

THE LIBERAL ARTS

Underlying my perspective are the liberal arts, the notion that education needs to be broad, multicultural, and multidisciplinary; prepare students to tackle unforeseen challenges inevitably arising during their lives; and to have human betterment through inquiry and application of knowledge as bedrock values. Liberal arts are anchored in the discussion of "final ends," the examined life. This approach led me to make a major personal commitment to Colorado College (CC) in Colorado Springs.

From 1999 to 2013, I was an active member of the Board of Trustees of Colorado College (head of the Academic Committee and then Secretary), a wonderful, innovative liberal arts institution. My initial association with the board arose when I met the college's president, Kathryn Mohrman, who had studied Asia in graduate school. Kathryn had gone to China under the auspices of NCUSCR and wanted to boost China/Asia offerings at CC. I joined the board to be helpful in that regard. The college already had a great foundation on China with Professor Timothy Cheek, who taught there until 2002. Later, Kathryn came to SAIS to be Washington Office Director of HNC. Succeeding Kathryn Mohrman at Colorado College was the former Governor of Ohio (1983–1991), Richard F. Celeste.

CONCLUSION

I reentered academia in late 1997 principally motivated to help train a generation of young scholars and future policy practitioners to understand China *from the inside out*. For almost all my career, this had been possible, productive, and enjoyable. However, with the onset of COVID-19 and as we moved into the 2020s, the forces of mutual suspicion leeched away much of the willingness in each society to provide one another's students and scholars the access each provided the other in an earlier, more trusting, and more hopeful era, even as considerable goodwill remains among individuals in the two societies.

One challenge facing scholars and practitioners in the United States henceforth is going to be developing increasingly effective means to learn about China with less capacity to learn from the inside. This will put a premium on the quality of the ideas and frameworks we employ to study

China and our ability to connect to the wider Asian context. We, however, will lose much of the human texture informing our views of China.

NOTES

1. These budget figures were provided by Committee Vice President Meredithe Mastrella in an email dated November 23, 2021. In David M. Lampton, "Chron Files" (RAC). Steve Orlins, who became president of the National Committee (in May 2005), dramatically improved the runway picture, as did Carla Hills, our long-standing and successful chairperson who had been Secretary of Housing and Urban Development and U.S. Trade Representative earlier in her career. She succeeded Barber Conable as Committee chair.

2. Anthony Lake, "From Containment to Enlargement," Address at Johns Hopkins University, School of Advanced International Studies, Washington, DC, September 21, 1993.

3. Jeremiah Jenne, "The Perils of Advising the Empire: Yuan Shikai and Frank Goodnow," https://www.chinafile.com/reporting-opinion/viewpoint/perils-advising-empire.

4. Paul Wolfowitz, YouTube, Oxford Union 2013, https://www.youtube.com/watch?v=Ujpn37ZUmB0.

5. Over the years when I was at SAIS, many persons contributed to direction of the Washington and Nanjing Offices and fundraising for HNC, all persons of enormous skill and dedication: Amy Celico, Robert Daly, David Davies, Carla Freeman (who played several key roles over the years), Anthony "Tony" Kane, Jan Kiely, Elizabeth Knup, Cornelius Kubler, Patricia Lloyd, Gene Martin, Kathryn Mohrman, Jason Patent, Madelyn Ross (who in my later years played a key role running our SAIS-China programs), and Daniel Wright. In addition, HNC has always had a very constructive and helpful Board of Advisors, none more so than Jill McGovern.

6. In economics, Pieter Bottelier, and subsequently David Bulman, were key. With respect to "Grassroots China" and civil society in the PRC, Anne Thurston was the leader. Ralph Clough, David Brown, and David Keegan, each with State Department experience, taught Taiwan courses and led field trips. With respect to China's periphery, Carla Freeman was a program stalwart colleague paying attention to the Korean Peninsula and South and Southeast Asia border areas, as well as global governance issues. Steven Phillips was a long and superb contributor on Modern Chinese History and was a member of the Office of the Historian at the Department of State for much of his association with SAIS. And finally, we were lucky to have Natalie Lichtenstein teach on the development of Chinese law bringing to bear her World Bank work and later experience as the Inaugural General Counsel of the Asian Infrastructure Investment Bank.

7. Just for the record, because I was later Chairman of the Asia Foundation Board of Trustees (2014–2019), and before that I was on the board of the Asia Foundation for a considerable period (2006–2019), I want to make clear that I had no institutional association or role with the Asia Foundation during the SARS crisis.

8. Department of Justice, "Information about the Department of Justice's China Initiative and a Compilation of China-Related Prosecutions since 2018," https://www.justice

.gov/nsd/information-about-department-justice-s-china-initiative-and-compilation-china-related.

9. Ellen Barry, "Top U.S. Chemist Guilty of Not Disclosing Chinese Ties," *New York Times* (National Edition), December 22, 2021, A22.

CHAPTER THIRTEEN

Ideas and Organizations

THE CHINA FIELD

Energized by ideas, propelled by vigorous minds, and sustained by organizations, academic fields grow, as do social and political movements. Academic fields and scholarly discourse can help alter popular understanding, frame debates, and thereby change reality. Reciprocally, fields adapt to their environment. Vibrant fields require entrepreneurial spirit and persons fusing abstract thought with organizational savvy. The China field of the 1960s and 1970s had these assets in abundance.

Those in the China field in the 1960s and 1970s did not all pursue the same goals or hold identical, or even consistent, views. Some, often younger, scholars believed that U.S. missteps in Asia reflected fundamentally flawed domestic governance requiring root and branch institutional and economic change in America. Others, among whom I counted myself, argued that reform was the antidote. America needed better information, better analytic frameworks, as well as better public education and outreach delivered by more effective civic organizations. The cure for what ailed U.S. Asia policy was mobilization based on knowledge, within our nation's traditional democratic institutions.

Some in the China field saw political and social conflict in the PRC as a never-ending factional power struggle devoid of purpose beyond group and individual aggrandizement and survival. Others thought that bureaucratic interests, inter-regional and class inequalities, and resentment of a privileged party elite not bound by the same rules as ordinary citizens were important sources of domestic fracture. And some saw the Cultural Revolution as Mao's noble effort to give the little guy a voice, while still others saw China as totalitarian which pretty much explained everything one needed to know.

In 1966, University of California-Berkeley sociology Professor Franz Schurmann published his field-shaping *magnum opus* titled *Ideology and Organization in Communist China*. Schurmann sought to explain the up-to-then seeming coherence of the CCP by reference to its tight ideology and disciplined organizational practices. Almost simultaneous with its publication, however, Mao Zedong upended Schurmann's thesis by turning against the very Communist Party the chairman had done so much to create, unleashing "the street" against the party. The vaunted cohesion and organization of the CCP had imploded.

Trying to bring order to the conceptual disarray, some scholars tried to use comparative generalizations drawn from other political systems and disciplines to shed light on PRC circumstances. Others thought that China had to be understood in its own terms—"China is China." Those of us in the middle of this debate welcomed comparative analysis while remaining convinced that the Middle Kingdom also had its particularities. It was an intellectually exhilarating time.

This also was an era of organization building, focused on human and material resource development, fashioning the infrastructure of a field, in part by providing seed funding for innovative research. This organizational infrastructure later facilitated access to China itself as the Mainland opened up and provided professionally relevant employment opportunities in the 1970s and 1980s.

Key organizations shaping the China field included: the Joint Committee on Contemporary China (JCCC), sponsored by the SSRC and the ACLS, which funded the research of individual social science scholars focused on contemporary China and convened conferences bringing scholars together to discuss their research. Two of my edited conference volumes were made possible by JCCC support. The ACLS also had a committee on Studies of Chinese Civilization and, like the JCCC, supported individual scholars of traditional China, funding their conferences.

As China began opening up to foreign researchers, the CSCPRC, later becoming the CSCC, sponsored by the NAS, ACLS, and SSRC, took the lead in helping place and fund American scholars doing research in China (the "National Program"), negotiating with the appropriate host organizations in the PRC.

For its part, NCUSCR, founded in 1966 and having a broad, diverse, and independent board of directors, expanded its activities greatly in the wake of its 1972 hosting of the Chinese Ping-Pong Team's U.S. visit. The committee progressively broadened the range of its cultural and public affairs endeavors, with a growing emphasis on elite interaction.

Other China-related organizations included the National Council for United States–China Trade (later becoming the U.S.-China Business Council) representing generally large U.S. firms. There also was the USC in Hong Kong providing a base for research for foreigners from around the world, not least Americans. USC was funded by the Ford Foundation and others over time. The infrastructure for Chinese language training in East Asia was mostly in Taiwan.

Thus, when I entered the field in the late 1960s and early 1970s, my role models were people who fused thought, action, and organization building. Most of them thought comparatively, notable among whom were: Robert Scalapino, Lucian Pye, Gabriel Almond, Doak Barnett, Jerry Cohen, John Lewis, and Alexander George. On my office wall for many years has hung a framed copy of the condolence letter I drafted on behalf of the NCUSCR board of directors in September 1991, written to Wilma Fairbank, the wife of the contemporary China field's energizing force Professor John King Fairbank at Harvard University. Each signatory of this letter was prominent in the China field in his or her own right. All had meaningful connections to Fairbank. Their signatures bore witness to what it takes to build a field.

Debates and disagreements aside, the China field generally was collegial, a field that was fun to be a part of, collectively trying to seize new opportunities to understand and interact with an emerging force that we all intuited would be of growing importance. We did not all agree on how China would be important, whether for good or ill, but important it would be. America had to deal with this emerging force with all the wisdom and knowledge it could muster. For me, the burn ward at Brooke Army Medical Center was a cautionary reminder of what failure meant.

The 1960s and 1970s were a period of intellectual blooming and contending, both as it related to China Studies and broader comparative studies. Scholars had big questions and big ideas. Political science as an academic discipline was flight-testing diverse methodological approaches. Money was available for large-scale, comparative projects. "Comparative communism" was a lively subfield. Area Studies was seen as a national security, Cold War priority.

Sufficiently little was known about on-the-ground reality in the PRC that many of us were open to comparative frameworks providing an intellectual skeleton on which to hang the few facts we gleaned from sources as diverse as refugee interviews, documents, the Hong Kong rumor mill, monitoring PRC domestic broadcasts and publications, harvesting the fruits of Taiwan intelligence raids on the Mainland, and intelligence collectors rummaging through the garbage of Hong Kong looking for data in discarded local PRC newspapers. In this era, one spent a lot of time in libraries and archives and, if one was lucky, considerable time in Hong Kong and Taiwan interviewing emigres from the mainland. In the process, we were building a global network of contacts and associates.

Broad comparative foreign policy and domestic politics questions animated us. We explored how deeply engrained political values and cultures shaped individual and organizational behavior around the world. Was there a logic of modernization? Indeed, what was modernization? How did urbanization change societies and politics? What were the effects of propaganda and mass communications on popular political behavior in diverse systems? How did varied political systems and individuals make decisions, to what effect? How do organizations and polities build and maintain coherence, and how do they assure compliance? What is political legitimacy, and why does it matter? What were the preconditions for democracy, and what was the soil that nurtured dangerous "isms": notably fascism, communism, and nationalism? How do nations deter one another from initiating war; how are wars terminated? What are the dangers and defining features of crisis behavior? Also, what is the role of national narratives?

As the PRC opened up in the mid- and late 1970s and throughout the 1980s and beyond, opportunities to test the evolving intellectual frameworks on the ground on the mainland became more numerous, more penetrating. We aimed to improve the alignment between what we now could more directly observe in the PRC and relevant theories and frameworks that we had previously developed.

QUESTIONS AND QUANDARIES

Several bundles of questions have persistently interested me; they have been my North Star. No matter the momentary distractions along the way, I always have headed back to the same handful of questions:

- *How do leaders, citizens, organizations, and localities in Greater China define and pursue their interests?* What political assets and strategies are effective in their pursuit?

- *What forces produce domestic fragmentation in the PRC, and how is conflict resolved and managed, and policy made?*

- In terms of political leadership, *who gets ahead and why?* How do leaders gain compliance, and what capacity do citizens, organiza-tions, and localities have to push back?

- *How are public goods delivered, and what considerations account for more or less effectiveness?* Health, education, water conservancy, rail-roads, and civil nuclear power generation all have interested me.

- Concerning foreign policy, how do key third parties affect the U.S.-China relationship, with Taiwan being a repetitive concern? *What lessons do past interactions hold for current decisions?*

- *How have Chinese and American foreign policy processes changed, and how do these alterations affect outcomes?*

The similarities China shares with other political systems have struck me with as much force as the differences. The PRC has much the same toolbox to deal with its challenges as other countries. Regularities of human behavior have not been suspended for the PRC, demographics being a notable example. The need to build coalitions is universal, with polities differentiated by the coalition building blocks specific to each society, the particular dispersal or concentration of political resources, and the forms of power various leaders and political cultures habitually employ. Values and ideology differentiate systems, but how one measures these differences, and the problem of discerning when they are just rationales for self-interested behavior, has always left me uncertain.

I have sought to reconcile two conflicting impulses—to use broad, comparative frameworks to make generalizations, on the one hand, and to advance narrower generalizations taking account of the particularities of China's circumstances on the other. I have agonized about whether I have been too Western-centric, or conversely, seduced by the "China is China" perspective. Was China best understood as a case of a communist (Leninist) state, Confucian civilization, or simply another, albeit enormous, developing country with an unusually large nationalistic chip on its shoulders?

Many analysts in the generation of which I am a part were committed to linking their academic work with public education, and some even hoped to have an impact on policy. These purposes did not always easily coexist. Young people, at the beginning of their careers, can feel the tension between being a good citizen and getting tenure.

In his written reflections on the Vietnam War and in several conversations with me over the years, Robert S. McNamara placed great importance on the lack of U.S. expertise in Asia as one explanation for Washington's march into the Vietnamese quagmire. There was an ocean of ignorance in Washington, to be sure. But there also was a willful disregard for the available expertise. I had many enlightening conversations with McNamara over the years, but when the subject got to the arrogance and intellectual laziness underlying our involvement in Vietnam, the conversations turned strained. I felt that we knew enough to avoid the quagmire if those making decisions had paid attention. It was the scholar's duty to accurately and effectively convey knowledge to those holding power and to the public. Unfortunately, sometimes you can feel as though telling the truth as you see it may not be a career-enhancing move, either in the public or academic spheres.

One incident I experienced during then-candidate Barack Obama's first presidential campaign is a personal example. I had been asked to represent the Obama campaign in a debate sponsored by the Chinese American organization, the Committee of 100, in October 2008. In the course of the debate with Republican presidential nominee John McCain's representative, Randall Schriver, a member of the audience asked whether the United States should sell submarines to Taiwan. I responded in academic mode, giving multiple reasons I thought this would be ill-advised. Having received no guidance (stupidly I did not ask for any), I did not know whether the Obama campaign would want to be identified with my views or not. *But I soon learned that it did not wish to be so identified.* The campaign dropped me like a hot potato.

In that moment of debate, I had framed my problem as being whether or not I should say what I thought. In retrospect, however, there was another approach that would have maintained my integrity. I simply could have said that I had received no guidance from the campaign on this issue and that this was the kind of question that would assume practical importance later. That was true. The underlying reality of my circumstance was that I had been asked to express what an *Obama administration* might think, not what I thought. The lesson I drew from this is tell the truth, but don't be too quick to turn each issue into a morality play and do not attribute one's own views to others, particularly when they are running for president and when they haven't had time to assess the issue.

Many of my generation endeavored to build new organizations, or strengthen preexisting ones, in the quest to bring useful and accurate information to bear on China policy. Naturally and appropriately, other scholars sought to speak almost exclusively to academic audiences, leaving possible policy implications and advocacy to others.

The research I have undertaken has had a strong fieldwork component—interviewing people to acquire information giving life to documents. Talking to PRC intellectuals and persons occupying varied positions in PRC society and government has provided me with valuable information and understanding, as has interviewing persons in other societies who interact with China. My impulse has been to pose what I felt was a meaningful question and then go in search of data permitting me to address it. I have been disinclined to seize on a newly available data set and to try to figure out a question that the data now permit me to address. Data in pursuit of a question can produce small-bore "answers." That China opened up on the ground just as I entered the field meant that my age cohort could ask questions across vast new real estate.

I had a principal concern: the two biggest hot wars of the Cold War (Korea and Vietnam) both involved China, the first more directly than the second. Misjudgments in Beijing and Washington played significant parts in both conflicts. From the beginning, this history animated me to adopt a core underlying mission—try to reduce the chances of future lethal conflict with China and to maximize cooperation. All this appears clearer in the rear-view mirror than it did through the windshield at the time.

THE INTELLECTUAL TOOLBOX
Several sets of ideas have shaped my thinking, the first having its roots in the work of Arthur F. Bentley, the late nineteenth and early twentieth-century political scientist. Bentley's classic was *The Process of Government: A Study of Social Pressures* (1908). He argued that the pursuit of interests was intrinsic to human interactions. The interplay among more or less formally organized groups pursuing their interests was politics. The question was how different individuals and groups (in different societies, over time) defined their interests, developed strategies, and pursued them. He argued that interests are pursued in authoritarian and democratic, traditional and modern, societies. Politics is about coalitions. Ideology is a way to systematically frame interests.

At the outset of my career, Bentley's insights seemed germane to Chinese politics, even though PRC leaders and citizens uniformly claimed they had banished the pursuit of parochial interests from their socialist People's Republic, except for a small number of class enemies to be liquidated. Work units, organizations, and individuals during the Cultural Revolution decried self-interest as they blatantly pursued self-interest. I knew things had changed in China when I first saw that a sign previously saying "Serve the People" (*wei renmin fuwu*) had been replaced by a sign saying "Serve Yourself" (*wei nin fuwu*).

Some colleagues in the China field were skeptical of an interest-centered view, believing that the dictator's power was the system's defining feature; its monopoly of the means of coercion and its monopoly of ideology were the unbending reality.

For me, the essential nature of the Cultural Revolution was that Mao built a massive coalition, comprised of himself and a few zealous central allies, some kindred ideological spirits in the wider Communist Party, and large chunks of the population disaffected by prior policies—populism. Chairman Mao unleashed these elements against the very party he had built over forty-five years. The military under Lin Biao ("the gun") was the chairman's backstop. In their populism and strategy of assault on their own parties, Mao and Donald Trump share similarities.

On my first trip to the PRC in 1976, in every unit we visited we met "the Revolutionary Three-in-One Committee," consisting of a "revolutionary Party member," a proletarian mass representative, and a military figure (often the head of the committee). Revolutionary Committees were the temporary institutional expression of Mao's interest-based coalition.

In the 1960s and first half of the 1970s, some foreign analysts saw the Cultural Revolution's unfolding mayhem as a clarion call for a more just and equitable future, not only for China but globally. I saw it as an unprincipled power grab by Chairman Mao, mobilizing the accumulated grievances of specific segments of society.

As China moved into Deng Xiaoping's reform era in the early stages of my career, PRC politicians and analysts themselves spoke with increasing candor about interest group activity and pluralism.

Another stream of work also influenced my research approach. The work of Alexander L. George, particularly his *Case Studies and Theory Development: The Method of Structured, Focused Comparison*. His writing inclined me toward finding comparable cases of a phenomenon (e.g., crisis decision-making or coercive diplomacy), studying several comparable instances in which outcomes differed, and identifying factors accounting for variation (or similarities) among cases.

A third body of work is epitomized by Philip Selznick's *TVA and the Grass Roots: A Study of Politics and Organization*, originally published in 1949. His research on Franklin D. Roosevelt's New Deal–era construction of the TVA makes a central point—while vast programs may be envisioned and adopted in faraway national capitals, local constituencies coopt national agents, bending them and their programs to local purposes.

An equally important contribution to my thinking has been Jeffrey Pressman and Aaron Wildavsky's *Implementation* (1973), a case study of how Lyndon Johnson's Great Society–era Economic Development Administration program for revitalizing Oakland, California, was dreamed up in Washington and deformed as it was implemented locally. Merilee S. Grindle, in her edited collection on *Politics and Policy Implementation in the Third World* (1980), brought these insights to bear on policy implementation in developing societies. The bottom line of this entire literature is that implementation is arduous everywhere. We should marvel more that things get done, rather than think it is delay that calls for explanation.

And finally, Aaron Wildavsky's *The Politics of the Budgetary Process* (1964) highlights how budgets drive decisions and budgetary incrementalism makes it challenging to change priorities. Making budgets is a central part of politics—everywhere, including China.

These streams of research speak to a universal problem—how to implement policy so that results align with the initial, central intention. Barry Naughton has called it the "implementation bias."[1] As directives cross multiple jurisdictions horizontally and vertically, the initial policy is deflected in the direction of implementers' interests. This is *not* unique to China. What *is* unique to China is the vastness of the PRC party-state-military bureaucracy, its massive territorial extent, and its ambitions to control.

China has more than four times the U.S. population, covering a territory slightly larger than the United States, and has not had a federal system (reserving extensive zones of governing autonomy for localities and the private sector) to lighten central burdens. Chinese leaders are overloaded by problems kicked up the hierarchy. This is but one of many reasons that PRC political reform is essential.

The ideas of Robert A. Dahl and Charles E. Lindblom, in their *Politics, Economics and Welfare* (1953), and Amitai Etzioni's *A Comparative Analysis of Complex Organizations* (1965) also greatly affected my understanding of politics, decision-making, and bureaucratic control.

Dahl and Lindblom argued that there are four basic mechanisms by which all regimes perform what they called "control" and "calculation" functions: market mechanisms, hierarchies, polyarchies (democracy, or preference counting systems), and bargaining (reciprocal deal-making among leaders and groups).

Etzioni's contribution was explaining that there are three types of power in a leader's toolbox: coercive, normative (belief or charismatic), and remunerative (economic). What differentiates one political system or leader from another is the power mix upon which different regimes, leaders, and cultures rely and how and why that power mix changes over time. Each form of power has its pluses and minuses.

One of the implications of all this is that political systems must "choose" among the kinds of control and calculation institutions they construct and the mix among them. The mix changes over time within and among systems. Recall, for example, my discussion with then Shanghai Mayor Zhu Rongji (chapter 8) in which he observed that "capitalist America" found it needed more economic planning and that China, which emphasized planning, required more market. Each system sought an optimal mix given its own ever-changing circumstances. Politicians are like orchestra conductors; they have a finite inventory of instruments, but distinguish themselves by the proportions in which various instruments are used, and how and when they are used.

To my foreign policy and U.S.-China relations interests, especially those concerning the origins of Sino-American conflict, I have found Alexander George's work on the difference between *deterrence* and *coercive diplomacy* to be particularly useful, as has been the broader literature on perceptions in international affairs. One core idea is that it is easier for one power, say the United States, to *deter* another state from possibly doing something in the future than it is to try to induce the adversary state to *undo* a step already taken. The costs of undoing an action include abandoning big sunk costs and losing face/credibility with both domestic and international audiences.

How one views the strength of an opponent and their intentions also is critical. The realms of perception concerning strength and intention are subject to catastrophic misjudgment. One may be stronger with respect to some goals than others. Moreover, while one state may see itself as trying to deter (having defensive intent), the adversary may perceive those actions as offensive. This occurred at the start of the U.S.-PRC relationship in 1950 when Washington could not imagine that the "Sick Man of Asia," China, would intervene on the Korean Peninsula against America and the UN. As General MacArthur moved toward China's borders, Beijing had no confidence that the U.S./UN forces would stop.

With the intellectual toolbox described earlier, I have examined domestic and foreign policies germane to improving the lives of both Chinese and Americans and reducing the odds of conflict between them.

INTERESTS AND FINDINGS

Several broad topics have been of enduring interest to me: the politics of medicine, public health, and education; water-related issues; leadership and elite mobility; the construction of infrastructure, particularly railway and civil nuclear power projects (in the PRC and elsewhere); and Chinese foreign policy and U.S.-China relations. What have I found?

Medicine and Public Health

Early on in my research (1972–1979), I focused on the politics of medicine, public health, and pharmaceutical regulatory policy in China. Several communities, aside from the China field narrowly defined, were interested in that work.

Resisting writing exclusively for one narrow audience has both risks and rewards. Writing for a broad audience runs the risk of losing credibility within your discipline. But if you focus excessively on the discipline, you can end up with a readership of about five people.[2] The key is balance, and to some extent, the tension is productive. The discipline helps assure that your analysis speaks to the work of others and is cumulative in theoretical terms. Speaking to functional and geographic audiences helps assure that the research has contemporary relevance.

Research grows organically with previous steps influencing later ones. Looking briefly back on the body of my health-related work, several conclusions emerged that shaped my future directions and had practical utility in U.S.-China relations.

- *China is not on the far side of the moon.* The PRC confronts the same problems faced by every political system. Decision makers there have a similar array of alternatives as others and must make choices within the context of resource scarcities and excess demand. There is the need to find a balance between spending resources on public health (preventive measures) and curative medicine, as there is the need to decide where and how health services are to be delivered—in large urban medical centers or dispersed among lower-tech, smaller facilities? Are expenses to be paid for by government or private payers, and how does this affect equity, equality, availability, and efficiency? Health professionals, and the associations representing them, often have preferences not aligning with the judgments or interests of politicians, or for that matter, patients. How much money should be spent on medical services compared to everything else? How does one address the growing burden of chronic disease as the population ages? How does the system control costs in the face of rapid technological advances? In short, it is often productive to ask: "In what ways is China the same as others?" rather than being preoccupied with differences.

- *Look at the organization chart.* Just as a military general needs to know the geographic terrain upon which the upcoming battle will be fought, the political coalition builder must know the structure of the bureaucracy, the formal decision-making system, and the informal pathways of power and influence. Each battle occurs on specific terrain. An effective bureaucratic player (or external analyst) must know the key actors and their assets and liabilities.

Informal relationships are important. Start with the "org chart." This is as true for foreign as domestic policy analysis.

- *The PRC can be going in several directions simultaneously.* Outside observers attribute to China more homogeneity of viewpoint and interest than often exists. The country's size and complexity create diverse realities even as our vocabulary implies uniformity. This has been evident in the health sphere. On the one hand, there have been many positive health outcomes, among which were the quick eradication of many infectious diseases after 1949 and the rapid increase in life expectancy from about forty-three years of age to sixty-three between 1950 and 1976, largely owing to basic public health measures. On the other hand, these positives were accompanied by new problems and gaping self-inflicted wounds such as assaults on the Western-style medical community and little or no oversight of pharmaceutical quality. Scant attention was paid to regulatory or safety issues, and lowered medical education standards all exacted heavy costs. Skilled medical professionals were sent to facilities that could not tap their skills. Quackery was rampant. The state tobacco monopoly promoted smoking to obtain revenue, despite its negative health consequences. Tens of millions starved to death in the late fifties and early sixties because of ill-advised agricultural policies and excessive crop requisitions. Exclusively focusing on either successes or shortcomings obscures the reality that China is going in diverse directions simultaneously. Simply defining China as "authoritarian" restricts our ability to understand why sometimes there is so much diversity and so little control in China.

- *While Marxism–Leninism came to China, interest tendencies of varied cohesion persisted.* In my early encounters with China, citizens and foreigners alike were bombarded by Leninist rhetoric asserting that interest group–like activity was a capitalist malady. The more I heard about shared values and common interests in China, the more I observed self-interested behavior. Doctors wanted more income, more equipment, and more infrastructure, and they generally did not want to be sent to treat rural citizens in remote areas forever. Patients sought pharmaceutical products that did not cause adverse reactions, and they wanted to see skilled doctors in a timely fashion. The tobacco industry and the Finance Ministry wanted more revenue. I remember a Minister of Public Health telling me that the most formidable obstacle to effective anti-smoking policy was the Finance Ministry which received enormous revenues from tobacco. The propaganda apparatus, the health minister complained, produced movies glorifying swaggering, unshaven, virile heroes puffing away on cigarettes.

- *Communists fight over money, personnel, and power—just like capitalists.* Where civic entities, governments, and individuals spend their money is a tangible expression of what they value. Following the 1949 revolution, China spent a very small fraction of the government budget and GDP on health care. Much bigger budgetary fractions went to industrial investment and defense.

Today we hear the PRC government calling for realignment of spending toward education, health, and retirement, but it is arduous to achieve budget realignment in reality. Traditional and current winners in the budget wars are reluctant to slink into the budgetary night to make room for new priorities. What calls for attention and admiration is that the health profile of Chinese people as a whole (excluding the late 1950s and early 1960s) has markedly improved over the decades, despite miserly health expenditures. This is in stark contrast to the U.S. experience where we spend about 19 percent of gross domestic product (GDP) on health care but have many highly deficient health outcomes (e.g., infant and maternal mortality rates).

- *Politics is about more than power struggles.* Every time China moves in more authoritarian or more chaotic internal directions and U.S.-China relations become more tension-filled, the analytic framework for analyzing Chinese politics turns to "power struggle" as an explanation. Xi Jinping's consolidation of power at the Twentieth Party Congress in fall 2022 certainly lends credence to that view. But my sense is that politics, everywhere, involves a clash over both power and policy, though the balance can shift over time. Genuine fights over policy issues are part of the fabric of Chinese politics.

- *Institutions and organizations have distinctive cultures and values.* In my work on medical care, and reinforced by my later research on water conservancy, civil nuclear power, railroads, and not least foreign policy, I observed that organizations are suffused with values and priorities that members internalize. For members of a cohesive organization, those values and priorities become central to their motivation, self-identity, and survival. When different organizations need to cooperate, distinct identities can be obstacles. When organizations are fighting for their survival, internal cohesion fostered by a shared mission is key.

Before and during the Cultural Revolution, Western-oriented doctors in the Ministry of Public Health were persecuted for their personal and professional commitment to the Ministry's traditional mission of providing quality, curative, modern medicine to China's people delivered principally in urban hospitals. Qian Xinzhong, the Minister of Public Health before the Cultural Revolution, was tongue-lashed by Mao for holding these values and promoting policies reflecting them. The chairman believed that hospitals had two big defects—they were in cities and ignored peasants, and hospitals were about cure, not prevention. Qian was purged and tortured, only resuming his ministerial role, and prior policies, once Mao was in his crystal sarcophagus. The price Qian was willing to pay for his commitment to these values, purposes, and priorities was evident when I saw him at a swimming pool, his back flayed and still scarred by his Cultural Revolution tormentors. When Joe Califano and the United States signed the health agreement with him in the wake of the Cultural Revolution, it was a vindication of sorts—the same applied to Jiang Nanxiang, the Minister of Education.

WATER CONSERVANCY AND RELATED ISSUES
Much can be learned by examining the functions that all systems perform.

In early 1982, with China opening up to foreign researchers and the broader world, I wanted to choose a research topic that would benefit from field research and that would not be viewed as politically treacherous by PRC gatekeepers whose approval and cooperation would be required to proceed. I also hoped a successful research experience by me would at least marginally bolster U.S.-China ties.

In chapter 6, I explained how colleagues in Washington, D.C., and Columbus, Ohio, managed to gain access for me to China for field research in the second half of 1982 when my topic was "Planning and Management in the Yangtze River Valley." I lived in Wuhan, midstream on the Yangtze, where the Han River joins it. The city is protected by enormous dikes that periodically had been overtopped or breached by onrushing deluges (measured in cubic miles of water) generating millions of refugees on the vast flood plain. Water stains on some of Wuhan's building walls remain like badges of honor, and high-water levels are memorialized on the surviving plaster or brickwork.

During my research there, I was housed at Wuhan University (*Wu Da*), directly under the Ministry of Education. However, my professional host organization was the Yangtze River Valley Planning Authority (*Chang Jiang Liuyu Guihua Bangongshi*, or *Chang Ban*) under the Ministry of Water Conservancy. The dual hosting arrangement was productive. Everyone was comfortable with the notion that I was researching a "technical" subject, not a "political" one.

During my six-month stay, I traveled south to near the border with Hunan Province, looking at relatively small-scale water projects; west to Yichang to see the Gezhouba reregulating dam being built in preparation for the Three Gorges Dam Project upstream; north on the Han River to Xiangfan and the not-too-distant Danjiangkou Dam and Reservoir on the provincial border with Henan; and I conducted numerous interviews in *Chang Ban* and other hydrological organizations in Wuhan, as well as in Beijing at the Ministry of Water Conservancy.

In terms of my evolving conception of Chinese politics, this was a very fruitful period.[3] As I was coming to an unfolding realization about Chinese politics, so too were Michel Oksenberg and Kenneth Lieberthal in their joint work on energy policy.[4] All three of us were trying to fully utilize interview opportunities, and we shared many academic interests and frameworks of analysis. Among my conclusions were the following:

- *Bargaining yes; democracy no.* Harking back to the work of Dahl and Lindblom, all political systems have limited options by which to perform the twin functions of "calculation" and "control" (decision-making and implementation): hierarchy, polyarchy (preference counting, e.g., voting and surveys), bargaining (among leaders and organizations at various levels), and market mechanisms. Generally speaking, China relied heavily on hierarchy and bargaining, rather than market and/or preference counting, though mixes have changed over time.

What I saw in Wuhan and Hubei was a Chinese system having many players in the most important issue areas. Each actor needed cooperation from others whom it could not directly command, and there was no legal framework or independent judicial system to resolve disputes. Therefore, any single player had one of two options to gain cooperation from others who resisted. The first was to find a higher-level organization/leader who could command all the subordinates to cooperate (hierarchy). Because higher-level leaders often were overloaded and/or had insufficient influence or knowledge, subordinate organizations worked out deals among themselves—bargaining. The result was that the default way of making decisions was through *bargaining* among lower-level entities.

It seemed to me that our earlier understanding of the Chinese political system had overemphasized hierarchical command, uniformity of decision, and consistent implementation. The reality was that political life in China was far more fluid, varied, and adaptable than the "Mao in command" (or leader-in-charge) model suggested. *China wasn't democratic, but it wasn't totalitarian in its actual capacities or its operation in many domains, particularly in technical and economic areas.* This insight came to be referred to as the "bargaining" or "fragmented authoritarian" school of Chinese political system analysis.[5] These insights also help explain foreign policy fiascos, with China's Foreign Ministry, and often its supreme leader, surprised by actions taken by a PRC military operating in its own bubble.

- *The masses can fight back; they often have agency.* My epiphany in this regard occurred when I visited the Danjiangkou Dam in northern Hubei in 1982. There I saw a dam that could not be completed (built to its designed height with water at the planned level) for many years because peasants refused to move and were living a foot or two (literally) above the current reservoir level. I asked why and how the peasants had stymied progress and was told that many had been paid more than once to move away, only to pocket the cash and return home on the water's edge, preventing authorities from further raising the lake's level and finishing the project. What kind of "totalitarian" system can't move poor peasants and, instead, permits them to stop a "key" state project for a protracted period, I asked myself? Chinese leaders are not always as powerful, ruthless, or unconstrained as we might think.

- *Implementation is problematic.* In all political systems, there is a gap between the initial intentions of central policy makers and the results of policy implementation. China's leaders may be divided among themselves over policy priorities, and they have limited attention spans and resources to make sure any given undertaking is implemented.

As policy trickles down a multilevel and stove-piped system, each implementer deflects policy in the direction of their interests. The cumulative distortion can be large. Local groups may simply not cooperate. Unexpected human resource and financing problems arise. Maybe there is corruption. China had not then, nor has it today, solved the implementation problem that is part of the human condition; its system only makes it worse.

- *Bureaucratic reorganization can get you only so far.* Given the earlier mentioned importance of the organization chart and given the intrinsic problems of fragmentation and implementation, Chinese leaders always are looking for a mystical bureaucratic silver bullet reorganization. There is a quest to get the organizational boxes in better alignment. There is a kind of perpetual organizational

Figure 13.1.   Danjiangkou Dam, Hubei Province, 1982. Authorities were unable to raise the water level to the designed height because of peasant resistance. Photo by David M. Lampton.

musical chairs. The reader may recall the earlier discussion in which Secretary Califano wanted to keep the federal educational function in his department (HEW) and President Carter wanted a freestanding Department of Education.

Such reorganization efforts often are only partially successful and sometimes entirely futile. The relationship between the Ministry of Electric Power and the Ministry of Water Conservancy in China is a case in point (chapter 6).

- *The West more often than not has critiques, not solutions.* I came out of my water conservancy field experience seeing U.S.-China relations from what I think is the perspective of many in the PRC. When Americans talk about issues in China, such as whether to construct a Three Gorges Dam (*San Xia*) or construct large numbers of nuclear power plants, or to just stick with coal-fired electrical generating plants because it has abundant coal, Americans find almost *every* alternative China actually has to be unacceptable.

We do not have a solution to China's energy problems, but we know what we don't like. We don't like coal, nuclear, or hydropower because of their heavy externalities, often regional or global. We just see problems, most of which are real. At some point, we can understand why many Chinese think that the United States simply opposes PRC economic development. Our individual project skepticism, often derivative of global interdependence and sound science, feeds a collective perception on the mainland that America has the strategic intention of "keeping China down." Also galling to the Chinese is the fact that the developed West used dirty development (coal, oil, and big dams) to get itself to the point that it can now afford stricter standards. Telling Beijing not to repeat our mistakes is not always compelling.

Leaders and Elite Mobility

The odds of becoming a principal leader of a major power are infinitesimal. What impels a few to try? What accounts for success? Once in office, what do leaders do to enhance the odds of their survival and goal achievement? What strategies and instruments of power do they employ, and which instruments are most effective under what circumstances?

For me, particularly impactful Western thinkers on leadership have included: James MacGregor Burns, James David Barber, Harold Lasswell, Lucian Pye, Alexander George, and Robert Caro. Central in the Chinese context were Mao Zedong's leadership writings ("Some Questions Concerning Methods of Leadership"). In my youth, history was told pretty much in terms of the titans, good or bad: FDR, Eisenhower, MacArthur, Stalin, Charles de Gaulle, Gandhi, Churchill, Chiang Kai-shek, Hitler, Martin Luther, Mao, and the Dalai Lama.

Part of what attracted me to John Lewis as a PhD advisor and mentor at Stanford was his book, *Leadership in Communist China* (1963). Later, I became particularly intrigued with mayor, subsequently premier, Zhu Rongji because he had risen under very adverse family circumstances; he didn't mouth the easy formulations of the CCP's propaganda apparatus;

he had become the focus of Mao Zedong's ire early in his career and lived to tell the story; and he was upright, standing tall in a polity the first rule of which is to keep your head down—"the tall tree catches the wind."

Aside from my baseline interest in Chinese leaders was the fact that Mao had played an enormous and schizophrenic role in China's modern history: Deng Xiaoping had risen under Mao, suffered under Mao, and been promoted and sacked by Mao multiple times, eventually succeeding Mao and thereafter jettisoning much of the chairman's legacy.

Leadership was a subject I pursued throughout my career, writing *Paths to Power: Elite Mobility in Contemporary China* (1986, 1989) and much later *Following the Leader: Ruling China from Deng Xiaoping to Xi Jinping*. With the ascension of Xi Jinping to power in 2012–2013, I agreed with the Canadian Security and Intelligence Service to research Xi Jinping and his recently created National Security Commission. The work resulted in an essay that won the Sabel Award given by the *Journal of Contemporary China* (2015). The article was titled "Xi Jinping and the National Security Commission."

This piece argued that Xi was leading China in a new and, from a Western perspective, problematic direction. Xi was tightening politically at home, becoming more assertive abroad and increasingly suspicious of the West, particularly America. He created the National Security Commission to tighten his grip on the PRC's domestic and international security institutions, in part motivated by his concerns over alleged U.S. and Western subversion (not least in Hong Kong) and his fear of internal disorder born of personal experience in the Cultural Revolution and being witness to the implosion of the Soviet Union.

I undertook an earlier piece on leadership at the invitation of Deng Xiaoping's youngest daughter, Deng Maomao (Deng Rong) in 1995. Having known her for some time, she invited me to write the foreword for the English-language edition of the first volume of her biography of her father, principally covering the period through the communist victory in 1949. It was challenging to write a balanced, enlightening introduction to a daughter's biography of her father—not least in the wake of Tiananmen, a tragedy in which Deng Rong's father had played such a decisive role. I could easily come off looking like an apologist for communist atrocity. Americans and Chinese alike would smell a white-wash a mile away. Maomao observed a hands-off policy on the foreword as we had agreed beforehand, save for a single word.

Looking at my leadership work as a whole, several themes ricochet throughout:

- *Leaders count.* There have been two epoch-changing leadership transitions in Beijing during my professional lifetime (in the second half of the 1970s with the death of Mao and the rise of Deng, and then the change from Jiang Zemin, through Hu Jintao, to the decisive departure represented by Xi Jinping). Over the years, Western intelligence agencies have reached out to understand how these successors had grasped power, what their formative experiences had been, and, looking to the future, what their policy proclivities might be. The underlying questions in both transitions were: "Where was the new leader headed, and what did it mean for us?"

Academics can appropriately debate all the factors limiting individual leader capacities to produce change. Nonetheless, the irreducible historical fact has been that some leadership shifts set in train entirely new dynamics having vast implications, as we now are experiencing with Xi Jinping and, in a far different setting, Donald Trump and his acolytes in America.

- *Chinese leaders vary greatly.* While acknowledging the emergence of somewhat more autonomous bases of economic power in the post-Mao era, the principal routes to leadership remain the party-state bureaucracy, provincial administrations, and the military. Strategies for upward mobility vary by one's political base. What it takes to rise in each setting varies. Different elite aspirants have diverse strategies for upward mobility depending on circumstances. Some aspiring leaders are adept in small group settings, others play more to the streets. Some seek power through slavish devotion to the supreme leader. Some do not care if they are liked, while others seek to please. Some have an affinity for foreigners and crave their praise, some can take them or leave them, and some are affirmatively hostile. Some have policy aspirations, and others primarily seek power.

- *Upward mobility requires a fit between circumstance and skills.* There are three broad strategies for getting ahead in China: *Patron-client*—harnessing one's career wagon to a patron, making whatever contortions are required to stick with him or her. *Bureaucratic*—anchoring one's fate to organizational success. And finally, cultivating influence in an important *Territory.* Leaders who have anchors in multiple bases are stronger than those with only one. Deng Xiaoping was notable for being so strongly anchored in all three bases that he did not even need a formal position to exercise power. Persons who rose by virtue of ascending by a helicopter piloted by Mao in the Cultural Revolution (patron-client) did not last long after the chairman's demise. Transitional leader Hua Guofeng is a good example.

- *Jiang Zemin is the most underestimated supreme leader of post-1949 China.* In personal interactions, President Jiang sometimes seemed scattered and unfocused, occasionally engaging in displays of song and English-language capacity, leading one to wonder about his seriousness. When meeting with foreigners, he cultivated the notion that he was letting you in on his inner thinking. His retinue of aides often seemed to be wondering what he might say, showing genuine interest as they sat in their back-row chairs scribbling away.

Nonetheless, Jiang had a remarkable record, starting with the mere fact of his survival for two terms after taking over in the wake of internal recrimination and foreign-imposed sanctions and isolation following Tiananmen in 1989. At the end of his party and state leadership, he managed to maintain the chairmanship of the Central Military Commission for two years longer, though I believe that to have been an unwise violation of the emerging term limit norm. In terms of infrastructure building for the twenty-first century, Jiang energized the space program and the high-speed rail system vision, as well as modernizing Shanghai. He did much of this working with Zhu Rongji, showing rarely seen confidence to share the limelight with a charismatic subordinate for the sake of the larger mission. Politically, Jiang acknowledged that the CCP needed to broaden its support base to include newly successful entrepreneurs and intellectuals as never before in the PRC's history. Regarding foreign policy, he got China through the 1989, 1995–1996, 1999, and 2001 crises with Washington and launched China on a military budget trajectory that fostered armed forces modernization, while cementing U.S.-China relations for a decade beyond 9/11 by aligning himself with America in the "global war on terror." President Jiang managed to preside over a China that was relentlessly growing economically and militarily while not setting off alarm bells in the region or globally. He launched the effort to develop China's west that had been left economically behind and launched the go global effort of investing abroad. President Jiang, of course, made mistakes, some big, among which I would number the repression of the Falun Gong and Tibet. But, on balance, it was an extraordinary record. Immediately after his death in November 2022, a wave of nostalgia for him swept across the country, an implicit rebuke of Xi Jinping.

THINK COMPARATIVELY

China's foreign policy, although not immune to outside developments and often reactive to the outside world, has its principal origins in the PRC's domestic system. Domestic politics in China can be volatile, and hence external policy can vary, sometimes dramatically. An intelligent U.S. foreign policy needs to take account of Chinese domestic realities. And as we consider China's differences and pathologies, we should devote more attention to how its problems may be similar to our own, not to mention those of other countries.

For U.S. foreign policy to be strong and realistic, it must be founded on knowledge, empathy, and accurately assessed capabilities and weaknesses.

NOTES

1. Barry Naughton, "The Decline of Central Control over Investment in Post-Mao China," in David M. Lampton, ed., *Policy Implementation in Post-Mao China* (University of California Press, 1987), 51–80.

2. David M. Lampton, "The Roots of Interprovincial Inequality in Education and Health Services in China since 1949," *American Political Science Review* 73, no. 2 (1979): 459–77.

3. David M. Lampton, "Chinese Politics: The Bargaining Treadmill," *Issues & Studies* 23, no. 3 (March 1987): 11–41.

4. Kenneth Lieberthal and Michel Oksenberg, *Policy Making in China: Leaders, Structures, and Processes* (Princeton University Press, 1988).

5. David M. Lampton, "Water: Challenge to a Fragmented Political System," in David M. Lampton, ed., *Policy Implementation in Post-Mao China* (University of California Press, 1987), 157–89. Kenneth Lieberthal and I further developed this approach in a 1992 conference volume titled *Bureaucracy, Politics, and Decision Making in Post-Mao China* (University of California Press, 1992).

CHAPTER FOURTEEN

Sino-American Relations and Chinese Foreign Policy

THREE CONSIDERATIONS SHAPE U.S.-CHINA TIES AND BEIJING'S ACTIONS globally: (1) *Perceptions and images* that elites and citizens in China and America hold of each other, particularly in crises; (2) *third parties* add complexity, and often danger, to the bilateral relationship; and (3) *foreign policy-making processes and domestic politics* in both countries.

My approach to learning about China has been using engagement (such as joint projects, exchanges, and site visits) as sources of information and insight, along with statistics and documents. My colleagues and I have worked with counterparts not only throughout Greater China (the PRC, Taiwan, Hong Kong, and Macau) but elsewhere in the world including Russia, Northeast and Southeast Asia, and Europe.

As of March 2020, when COVID-19 led to severe travel barriers, I had visited all Chinese provinces, save one (Qinghai); all four provincial-level municipalities (Beijing, Chongqing, Shanghai, and Tianjin); three of five autonomous regions (Xinjiang, Tibet, and Guangxi Zhuang); and both special administrative regions, Hong Kong and Macau. By early 2020, however, travel came to a screeching halt because of public health concerns, the CCP's anxieties about subversion, and foreign researchers' mounting concerns that their research might get them or their PRC associates into trouble. Video calls became a principal means by which some level of dialogue was maintained, with a couple of National Committee colleagues and me keeping in touch with a few well-connected foreign policy figures. Beyond that, my in-person contact with Chinese official-dom during the March 2020 to December 2022 period was confined to consular authorities in San Francisco, embassy officials in Washington, and a very few PRC visitors. With the January 2023 termination of the Zero-COVID policy and the elimination or easing of quarantine and visa obstacles, energized by the recognition that shutting itself off from travel and exchange was compounding Beijing's foreign policy isolation and hurting the economy, travel to the PRC by foreign scholars began to pick up. I went to the Boao Forum in March 2023 on Hainan Island. This trip was only partially satisfying: light on substantive contacts and heavy on controlled settings.

Though Chinese colleagues have endeavored to keep channels open, political shifts under Xi Jinping represent the partial return of an unwelcome way of life and modus operandi that many Chinese and outsiders had thought, or hoped, had perished with Mao Zedong. Authoritarianism runs deep.

Dialogues and Research Projects

Interaction with Chinese individuals and organizations has been a core feature of my approach to learning about China. This naturally raises questions. Am I talking to people who have knowledge about the subject at hand? Are they telling me the truth? Are they candid informants or purposeful vectors of disinformation? The answer to these questions is that "it depends." It depends on the degree to which there is documentary material to confirm, deny, or at least inferentially validate what I am being told. It also depends on whether or not I am prepared for the encounter. Do I have a command of the publicly available data concerning my topic? A prepared interviewer makes for better interviewees. It also depends on the length and character of my prior association with the interlocutor. And finally, it depends on the phase of the political cycle in China and in U.S.-China relations in which one is operating. Since the 1950s, field access to China has been highly variable. With Xi Jinping, the opening has narrowed considerably. Research strategies must adapt.

I made what turned out to be long-term commitments to three sustained dialogues throughout my career, in addition to many shorter-term dialogues conducted by the National Committee, other American organizations, and counterparts throughout Greater China and beyond. These have provided information useful in my research, outreach, and policy work.

The most enduring of these commitments has been the Kettering Foundation "Sustained Dialogue" with China's Academy of Social Sciences (CASS), in which I have been involved since 1984. For much of that long period, this conversation, which started with close associates of Deng Xiaoping (Huan Xiang, Zheng Bijian, and Li Shenzhi), also included the Chinese military. Among the most memorable interlocutors from the Chinese military was the irascible, indeed volcanic, Deputy Chief of Staff for Intelligence General Xu Xin. He was succeeded by General Xiong Guangkai, otherwise known as "Bear." Bear and his wife had lived for some time in West Germany, and he was a collector of books signed by foreign authors. He liked to demonstrate his proficiency in English and things foreign. He was also close to President, General Secretary, and Military Commission Chairman Jiang Zemin.

Figure 14.1.   (Left to right) Author; Xiong Guangkai ("Bear"); U.S. Ambassador Joseph Prueher. Photo by David M. Lampton.

One of my most memorable moments with Bear involved an "off-the-record" talk I had given at Columbia University to a small faculty and student group shortly before going to China. On meeting Bear after arriving in China, the General began the conversation with, "About your talk at Columbia University—." He had full command of what I had said at that closed meeting. This experience contributed to my adoption of what I call the "beach theory" of PRC intelligence collection—a grain of information here, a grain there, and soon you have a beach.

The American side of the Kettering Foundation's sustained dialogue was led by the Foundation's President David Mathews, who had been President Gerald Ford's Secretary of HEW. Harold ("Hal") Saunders, who had been an aide to both Henry Kissinger and President Jimmy Carter, played a leading role. Other frequent participants were Robert McNamara; Don Oberdorfer, *Washington Post* international affairs reporter and columnist; and William Howard Taft IV, great-grandson of President Taft. In his own right, Taft had been Acting Secretary of Defense, Deputy Secretary of Defense, and Ambassador to NATO in the Reagan and George H. W. Bush years. These individuals devoted significant time to this sustained dialogue that remained below the radar. Maxine Thomas, Kettering's vice president, secretary, and general counsel, has overseen the program, with me as consultant.

A second enduring commitment to dialogue was the earlier mentioned Aspen Congressional Program for which I was staff consultant from late 1998 to early 2012. I say this was a "dialogue," though it was so only because we often invited PRC and Taiwan scholars to join American experts and practitioners to participate in the congressional seminars. In January 2003, for example, we included Taipei Mayor, and later Taiwan's president, Ma Ying-jeou. As noted earlier, these Aspen Congressional Seminars were founded and led by former Iowa Senator Dick Clark.

And finally, from the late 1990s until well into the new millennium, I was involved in a protracted program led by former Defense Secretary William Perry and future Defense Secretary Ashton Carter—their "Preventive Defense Project." In the portion of the project involving China, Perry partnered with NCUSCR. Our principal Chinese interlocutors were President Jiang Zemin and Jiang's mentor and former boss, Wang Daohan. We also often met with "Bear."

MULTILATERAL DIALOGUES AND COOPERATIVE PROJECTS

In addition to the three sustained dialogues just mentioned, some large-scale cooperative projects, sometimes undertaken with PRC Chinese and sometimes others, have boosted my understanding of China's operation and outward connections.

Beyond the U.S.-China-Russia Ussuri Sustainable Development project discussed in chapter 11, another multilateral project involved NCUSCR and the Atlantic Council of the United States forming a Committee on U.S.-China Policy (with a *Who's Who* of seventy-two American leaders) in 1992. Thereafter we cooperated with *The China Quarterly*, the Ditchley Foundation, and the Japan Institute of International Affairs to convene a significant meeting in England, based on the committee's report.

The Committee on U.S.-China Policy, in which Al Wilhem Jr. at the Atlantic Council played a key role, aimed to rebuild a post–June 4, 1989, consensus among Americans about future China policy, a consensus allies and friends could accept. We sought to accomplish this by drafting and circulating for comment a policy paper released in February 1993. Thereafter, in 1995, we published a book composed of the revised policy paper and nineteen issue papers prepared in the course of our work.[1] On this basis, we joined with British and Japanese colleagues to convene an international conference to discuss ways to move forward together.

In the course of writing the policy paper, a small working group consisting of National Committee chairman, Barber Conable; former Deputy Secretary of State John C. Whitehead; Al Wilhelm Jr. of the Atlantic Council; and I went to Hong Kong, Taiwan, the PRC, and Japan in August to September 1992, where we solicited the views of leaders and citizens of these societies concerning the desirable direction of U.S. policy toward the PRC in the wake of Tiananmen.

Our meeting with former Japanese Prime Minister (1987–1989) Noboru Takeshita in Tokyo had a notable impact on me. Speaking to us in measured tones, Takeshita circled his main point like a bird of prey, gradually descending, then suddenly lunging at the jugular—Americans have to be more subtle in dealing with China, he advised.

In such projects over the years, I have tried to solicit views on U.S.-China relations from Japan, Europe, Australia, South Korea, and post-Soviet Russia to inject their concerns and rationales into U.S. policy discourse. Living relatively close to the PRC, they have had to balance their anxieties about China with the positive interests they have by virtue of their proximity and economic interconnectedness. The Europeans and China's neighbors must reconcile their own diverse values and interests with those of the Middle Kingdom, while America often drenches itself in its own exceptionalism and rectitude. I have hoped that Europeans and China's Asian neighbors could help invigorate America's more productive, thoughtful, moderate, and inclusive policy angels.

The China Policy Report's release provided the basis for a specially convened conference ("China after Deng") held at Ditchley Park, England, from October 19–21, 1995. Ditchley was Winston Churchill's secret Oxfordshire retreat early in World War II. The Palladian building constructed in the 1720s sits on three hundred acres and is the place where Churchill met FDR's envoy Harry Hopkins to secure U.S. support against Hitler when Americans were reluctant to get deeply involved. The 1995 conference was a collaboration of the Ditchley Foundation, NCUSCR, the Japan Institute of International Affairs, and *The China Quarterly*, of which David Shambaugh was editor. Barber Conable occupied Churchill's room with the bathtub from which the Prime Minister delivered dictation to aides.

Sir David Wilson, who had been the second-to-last governor of Hong Kong (from 1987–1992), and who had been succeeded by Chris Patten (who served from 1992–1997), was the conference convener. After the meeting's conclusion, Ditchley's Director released his "personal impressions of the conference," among which were: (1) Jiang Zemin was a different sort of leader from his predecessors; (2) The main lines of China's reform were unlikely to be revised because they had "massive popular support"; (3) A rising middle class would push for more liberalization, but there was "no inheritance of democratic expectation," and the current "philosophical vacuum" in China meant that the void in belief might be "filled by emphasis on national dignity and pride as the unifying force." The report concluded that Western nations needed to consult more frequently about China policy and that there was no one-size-fits-all approach to the PRC that would meet diverse needs. The general view of the conference, however, was steady as you go, avoid gratuitous cold war vocabulary, and work to help strengthen China's "sense of being an accountable stakeholder, not a free-riding outsider."

At Ditchley Park, I had the honor of briefing Her Royal Highness Queen Elizabeth II, as did a couple of other fellow participants. The Queen seemed engaged and remarked on the scale and complexity of problems facing China. Given all that she just had heard, I thought she succinctly articulated the key point, doing so with a warm and engaging personality. I had been forewarned not to violate the Queen's large personal space. When she extended her hand in greeting, after a moment of hesitancy, I shook it. Her hand had been in more history than any other I ever shook.

Twenty-eight policymakers, scholars, and civil society leaders coming from ten countries and groupings, including Russia, the European Union, and Japan, attended the Ditchley Conference. With respect to the attendance of a senior Russian official (Igor Rogachev, Russian Ambassador to China), this was a moment of democratic optimism concerning the Russian Federation under Boris Yeltsin.[2] The conveners hoped that this would become part of a larger effort to bring Russia into a more collaborative relationship with the West. That did not happen as Putin came to power.

At the moment of our meeting at Ditchley, Britain was in the rancorous throes of negotiating the reversion of Hong Kong to PRC sovereignty that would occur on July 1, 1997. Conferees were desirous that the city's upcoming transfer to Beijing's sovereignty preserved as much of the past social, political, and economic system there as possible.

Considering our hopes for long-term cooperation with Russia, and for a long-term, relatively liberal order in Hong Kong, fast forwarding twenty-five-plus years, these aspirations were not realized. Signs of the long-term problems in Hong Kong were readily apparent when I attended the reversion ceremonies in the city less than two years after Ditchley.

Figure 14.2. Her Majesty Queen Elizabeth II meets Ditchley China Conference participants, October 1995, Ditchley Park, England. Photo by David M. Lampton.

HONG KONG'S REVERSION, JUNE–JULY 1997

I will not repeat the enormous literature on the intricacies of the lead-up to and execution of the resumption of PRC sovereignty in Hong Kong.[3] I recount, instead, developments and events with which I was involved along the way. These events constituted warning signs, driven by long-standing resentments between Britain and China and a genuine fear among Western allies that even before its formal assumption of power, Beijing was cutting democratic corners in the metropolis. These events simultaneously deepened Beijing's thinking that the two English-speaking powers (the United States and Britain) were a band of Anglo-Saxon brothers devoted to keeping China weak and divided. This is but one example of how China's and America's interactions with third parties can affect the U.S.-China relationship, sometimes precipitating high levels of conflict.

On April 9, a couple of months before leaving for Hong Kong reversion ceremonies in June–July 1997 (to which I had been invited by all three participating governments: Hong Kong, the PRC, and Great Britain), I had been invited down to Washington, D.C., to join a few others in briefing Secretary of State Madeleine Albright about U.S.-China relations. One of the several issues on the Secretary's mind concerned her attending the reversion ceremonies to be held by Britain, the PRC, and Hong Kong culminating on July 1, 1997.

The core issue was whether or not she should attend the swearing-in for SAR government officials and most particularly the Provisional Legislature, in the course of attending other planned events. Jiang Zemin, with Li Peng, would lead those ceremonies. One concern was that Hong Kong's to be newly installed Provisional Legislature did not come close to meeting democratic standards. By going to other events, but skipping that swearing-in of new SAR officials and legislators, the United States could recognize the legitimacy of the reversion itself and pay homage to Britain's historical role, without sanctifying the nondemocratic features of the new legislative and executive arrangements going forward. While the United States had an interest in trying to get things off on a reasonably good foot in Hong Kong, and Washington had no wish to embarrass Jiang Zemin, simultaneously Secretary Albright had no desire to be in Li Peng's presence. There also were huge trade and economic interests to be protected, so boycotting the entire event was not in the cards.

How should Secretary Albright participate in the tangle of reversion ceremonies in a way that would respect her (and America's) democratic instincts, on the one hand, while not setting Washington against a Hong Kong that would have to live with the arrangements to which London and Beijing had agreed? The issue also was entangled in U.S. politics. Vocal elements of the human rights community wanted to use the occasion to underscore their concerns, while trade and economic groups sought to avoid rocking the boat looking ahead.

Secretary Albright went around the dinner table at the State Department asking what each of us thought. When she got to me, I said that I judged that on balance attending all events, other than the government's and the Provisional Legislature's swearing-in, was best. This, along with the Hong Kong Policy Act of 1992 that said the United States would grant the new Hong Kong SAR its traditional privileges under U.S. law as long as its autonomy was respected by Beijing, would signal U.S. concerns without being gratuitously provocative. Further, not attending the swearing-in portion of the program would signal to some on Capitol Hill that the administration took their concerns seriously. This was important given that MFN was coming up for another of its annual renewal votes in Congress. Doing nothing to demonstrate concern about Hong Kong would roil congressional waters.

In the end, Secretary Albright (and indeed Prime Minister Tony Blair) did not attend the swearing-in.

As for me, as a private citizen and head of NCUSCR, I attended all the ceremonies, receiving mild criticism from some in Washington concerning my swearing-in attendance. I wanted to put my hand on the scale of hope for a positive future. Also, it seemed to me that it was going to take the new Hong Kong SAR government and Beijing to make the arrangement work, so I saw no reason to offend both at the onset. Nonetheless, it may seem inconsistent for me to have advised the Secretary of State to take steps that I did not myself adopt. I guess this is the difference between what is prudent for an official and what may be right for a citizen, especially heading the NCUSCR. In the final analysis, I felt that our officials not attending the swearing-in set us against the new SAR administration which, after all, was all that the Hong Kong people had. On the other hand, domestic politics in Washington made limited nonattendance the least that could be done.

I was invited to attend the various functions convened by Britain, the PRC, and Hong Kong—the "Farewell" at 6:15 p.m., June 30; the

"Banquet" at 9:15 p.m., June 30; the "Handover" and "Swearing-in," beginning at 11:30 p.m., June 30, extending into the early hours of July 1; the "Celebration," 10:00 a.m., July 1; and, the "Reception" at 4:00 p.m., July 1. My detailed notes record several instructive events,[4] one of which was the five-thousand-person banquet starting at 9:15 p.m. the evening of June 30. From the very start of the sequence of activities, one could see that the decision of Albright and Blair not to attend the swearing-in led each side to engage in retaliations of not attending each other's events.

> The banquet [Britain was the host] had about 5,000 people . . . Jiang Zemin didn't come and C. H. Tung had skipped the [British] Farewell [that preceded the banquet]; both absences really upset the British. So, the British disinvited some of C.H.'s [C.H. Tung, the new SAR Chief Executive to be] guests to the Farewell . . . Foreign Secretary Cook hosted the dinner [banquet]. A diminutive, bearded man, Cook stiffly read a card toasting President Jiang, the Prime Minister, the Queen, and all others (all very staid and set piece). In contrast, Foreign Minister Qian [Qichen], as if to do Cook one better, delivered all his toasts without a robotic reading and he translated his own Chinese into his own English—quite a piece of one-upmanship! He ended saying, "To the Queen," and he flashed a smile.

The swearing-in ceremony of the new Chief Executive and others followed the banquet late into the night from which Secretary of State Albright, Prime Minister Tony Blair, and Foreign Secretary Cook absented themselves. This was just one visible indication of the friction underlying the handover:

> Jiang Zemin swore-in C. H. Tung and Li Peng swore-in the others. Li Peng is so awkward and he tries to stay no more than a half step behind Jiang, which is an awkward interval—too close and too far.

At the "Celebration" the next morning, my notes record:

> As I was moving toward my seat prior to the start of the program, I stepped in front of Margaret Thatcher, who smiled. . . . Throughout the

program she listened intently (sitting next to Rupert Murdock). She was sitting in a British section [where I also was seated nearby], where she seemed to be the only Brit around—I think the British didn't feel like celebrating this moment.

My notes also summarized what, at that moment, I thought/hoped Hong Kong's future would be like:

> Just as the British flags went limp the Chinese flags unfurled into the artificial breeze. It was sad to see this, but my guess is that Hong Kong will both do fine and be a different, more corrupt, less predictable place. More exciting, less rule abiding.

In the end, this was about half right—it was not "fine" from the vantage point of twenty-five years later—it was "less rule-abiding" and less secure for the individual. Governor Patten's stirring remarks at the Tamar Basin Farewell ceremony captured both the hope and angst of the moment: "It is Hong Kong's 'unshakable destiny' to be free and prosperous," he intoned. That certainly was our hope, but not how things worked out. In retrospect, the ability to even cordially pull off the reversion events spoke volumes. That was a cautionary note. That one dear British friend upbraided me for prematurely wearing a Hong Kong (Bauhinia) reversion pin was an indication of the scarcely concealed resentments. During the reversion ceremonies of rain and gloom, with me soaked to the bone after hearing Prince Charles read his rain-soaked and ink-bleeding speech at the Farewell, Terry and Ellen Lautz shared their room with me. I have always been grateful to them for providing me refuge from the meteorological and political deluge.

DRIVERS OF CHINESE FOREIGN POLICY BEHAVIOR

Documents, interviews, field trips, and cooperative programs with Chinese and others as described above have contributed to my belief that *perceptions* and *interactions with third parties* can be important drivers of bilateral U.S.-China relations.

Perceptions

Because the outside world provides an infinite volume of information, humans must reduce and organize the torrent. We make assumptions about what we most need to know about "the other" to predict their behavior. The lenses through which we view the *intentions* and *capabilities* of the other are particularly important. One's perceptions about the other's intentions and capabilities shape a policymaker's sense of urgency. This insight still leaves one to speculate about whose perceptions count, which ones are most decisive, and how all this can be measured.

My first political science journal article (in *The Western Political Quarterly*, March 1973) was entitled "The U.S. Image of Peking in Three International Crises" and addressed the issue of perceptions and images by looking at U.S.-China crises involving Korea, Laos, and Vietnam in the 1950s and 1960s. These conflicts were the largest hot conflicts of the Cold War.

The Nixon administration was widening the Indochina War by attacking insurgent redoubts in Cambodia in 1970. There were ongoing massive U.S. air attacks affecting Laos in the 1960s which lasted until 1975. Even today unexploded U.S. ordnance continues to blow Laotian peasants (often children) to pieces and makes building infrastructure dangerous, costly, and slow, as Selina Ho, Cheng-Chwee Kuik, and I discovered during our field research in northern Laos in mid-2017 looking at the construction of a high-speed rail line from China.

The U.S. purpose in raining this violence on the region was to arrest China's perceived proxy expansionism in Asia. By examining these three cases, I hoped to learn whether or not, and how, our images of Beijing shaped Washington's decisions concerning whether or not to become involved and to assess the accuracy, components, and implications of those perceptions.

In Vietnam in 1954, the United States backed off immediate large-scale intervention to "save the French" from the massacre at their ill-chosen valley base at Dien Bien Phu, only thereafter to become ever-more entangled ourselves in the growing conflict with Ho Chi Minh. Ho thereafter endeavored to topple a succession of unsavory and non-democratic U.S.-backed regimes in Saigon. Washington's ever-deeper involvement eventually sparked a growing antiwar movement in the United States leading to popular and policy turmoil in America and unleashing carnage in Southeast Asia lasting for a decade in the 1960s and 1970s. Beijing supported Ho Chi Minh's resistance, with advisors, supplies, and limited manpower, as did the Soviet Union.

In the early 1960s, we avoided ground-troop involvement in Laos for the most part but inflicted enormous damage on the small country and its people in a "secret" air war conducted from 1960–1975. One Lao official with whom our research team met in 2017 told us: "Today we still have to clear millions of unexploded ordnance. Because of [U.S. Secretary of Defense] McNamara's policy, three million bombs were dropped in Laos. They still affect the daily lives of ordinary people. . . . 'I forgive but I will not forget.'"[5]

In the end, both Laos and Vietnam fell to communist forces. Of course, the "secret" dimensions of these operations only remained hidden from U.S. citizens, not those under attack in Asia. The Johnson administration kept reports of Americans dying at the hands of PRC aircraft and anti-aircraft fire under wraps during the war in Indochina.[6] The White House feared that citizen reaction to the news of a wider war would drive the administration in one of two unacceptable directions. One possibility was that outraged U.S. public opinion might call for expanding the war to the PRC. The other possibility was that such news could be the last straw precipitating an unceremonious exit from the long Indochina conflict, consequences be damned. This eventually happened in April 1975 with the fall of Saigon.

No sooner had we withdrawn from Indochina than the long underlying animosity between Vietnam and China reasserted itself; they turned against each other. A short, costly war between Hanoi and Beijing erupted in early 1979. I was in Kunming in mid-1979 in the immediate aftermath of that conflict. The dusty town with mostly wooden buildings was full of Chinese troops who just fought the same Vietnamese regulars that Americans fought in the Vietnam War. The PLA troops did not acquit themselves well against Vietnam's forces, took enormous casualties, and provided Deng Xiaoping the rationale to emphasize economic and social modernization, deferring military modernization.

Several findings from my three case studies have shaped my thinking about perceptions ever since. Deeply etched in my mind is the decision authorizing U.S. and UN troops to cross the 38th parallel into North Korea from South Korea in early October 1950. The goal of the U.S./UN mission was to liquidate the North Korean regime of Kim Il-sung which had invaded the South headed by strongman Syngman Rhee the preceding June. The U.S./UN mission was to restore order on the entire peninsula and hold elections to reunify its two halves (then divided at the 38th parallel) under a freely elected government.

The October U.S./UN counterattack across the 38th parallel occurred despite warnings from Beijing not to do so. The consequences of ignoring PRC warnings immediately became apparent when Chinese troops poured into North Korea and then themselves crossed the 38th parallel heading south. Battle lines soon stabilized near the 38th parallel, thereafter becoming a war of attrition along largely static lines.

Prior to China's direct intervention, Beijing's warnings went unheeded in Washington for what seemed to be sound reasons at the time. The Truman administration perceived China to be weak and concluded that Beijing would have to be delusional to challenge America. To Washington it seemed obvious that China was in no position in the fall of 1950 to get into a ground war with a great power that had just defeated Germany and Japan. As one senior U.S. official said when asked if Beijing would intervene if U.S./UN troops crossed into North Korea: "I don't think China wants to be chopped up."

There was only one problem with this perception—Beijing did intervene, sending U.S./UN troops on their longest retreat in American military history, and bogging down both countries in a bitter, protracted war. In late November 1950, Harry Truman made nuclear threats, and his successor, Dwight Eisenhower, who came into office in 1953, also threatened to use nukes if the Chinese refused to negotiate.

One of my Stanford mentors, Professor Alexander George, who took advantage of three hundred interviews of Chinese communist prisoners of war captured in Korea, wrote a classic volume, *The Chinese Communist Army in Action*. His book described a Chinese army barely hanging together under excruciating American air and artillery bombardment.

But my personal takeaway from all this was that the PLA *did* hang together under very adverse conditions to defend the PRC border. Mao Zedong's son died in the effort. *Will* is central to capability. Perceptions of strength are subject to catastrophic error if one discounts *will*, as the Russians did in 2022 in their invasion of Ukraine.

Many years later, when I visited Dandong, on the Chinese side of the Yalu River, facing North Korea's Sinuiju City, in front of me was the Yalu River (Broken) Bridge, severed precisely at the river's midline. In the course of the Korean conflict, the span had been cut in half by precision U.S. Air Force aerial bombardment. Taking out half the bridge required flying along the river's midline, thereby subjecting the U.S. pilots to antiaircraft fire from both banks of the river. My colleague at Johns Hopkins-SAIS, Professor Andrew Mertha, recounted a conversation he had in 2004 with a Chinese citizen in Dandong concerning this bridge. The conversation captures both the nature of the war and the more peaceful subsequent era of Sino-American engagement that followed decades later.

The Chinese citizen asked Professor Mertha:

"Do you know why one of those bridges is only half standing?"

"You Americans blew up that bridge. You Americans. You Americans . . ."

"I respect you Americans!"

"You Americans flew in and blew up the Korean side of the bridge and left the Chinese side standing, all with 1950s technology. You Americans!"

Mertha ends by recounting that his interlocutor,

"Flashed the thumbs up sign" and they then had a good laugh toasting "Long live American imperialism."[7]

In Beijing's narrative, Broken Bridge symbolized the PRC's resistance to imperialism and an unwavering defense of sovereignty. But what Mertha's Chinese interlocutor marveled at were U.S. capabilities and the ironies of history. In cutting the bridge and leaving the portion on the Chinese side standing, America *respected* Chinese sovereignty.

The Korean War came to a halt pretty much where it had started. The conflict was suspended with an armistice, not a peace treaty. The Korean War marked the onset of "limited war" (objectives short of "total victory"), unlike World War I and World War II, and ignited growing American frustration with indecisive, much less losing, conflicts. This experience also convinced Beijing that it needed to acquire nuclear weapons on a crash basis, detonating its first atomic device in October 1964.

Over time, Beijing promoted protracted guerrilla war in scattered locations around the world to drain U.S. and allied strength and will, all the while building its nuclear deterrent. Wars have long-tailed consequences. Washington's error concerning Chinese intervention in Korea stemmed not only from deficient military intelligence. More fundamentally, it reflected an inability to perceive China as anything but the "sick man of Asia." Our perceptions were wildly out of whack.

Throughout my career, I have been skeptical of analyses built around unbalanced assessments of Chinese capacities. Americans tend to exaggerate the power of their own technology and underestimate the importance of an opponent's sheer force of numbers, popular will, and steadfastness in defending territory. But eventually, fatigue wins out. The last moments of the U.S. exit from Vietnam in 1975 and from Afghanistan more than forty-five years later (in August 2021) were shattering experiences generating eerily similar images—U.S. aircraft lifting off with those unable to obtain space inside the passenger cabin running alongside the plane, hanging on for dear life, dropping off or crushed one by one.

My second case study addressed the Truman and Eisenhower administrations' decisions of the early and mid-1950s to try to "save the French" who were then embroiled in a grinding conflict in Indochina against Ho Chi Minh (who Washington viewed as little more than a Mao Zedong marionette). Our error there was approximately the opposite of the one we made in Korea. So badly had we been burned in Korea by underestimating Chinese power that now Washington perceived Beijing's handiwork in every brushfire and nationalist insurgency in Southeast Asia. Washington traded in a flawed view of China as pathetically weak for an equally deficient image of a China on steroids.

As I summed it up in my *Western Political Quarterly* piece, "In the case of Indochina, Eisenhower and Dulles were both so preoccupied with the military dimensions of the Chinese thinking that they were preparing to fight just as Peking wanted to talk, in part because launching the Third Five-Year Plan for domestic economic development was such a high priority. In the very process of trying to prevent war with the Chinese, Dulles and Eisenhower were making it more likely." In their effort to stop the spread of communism step by step, they walked into a quagmire in Indochina, effectively substituting for the French.

Years later, having visited Vietnam several times, descending into the bomb shelter where Joan Baez sang antiwar songs (she, too, had attended Palo Alto High School, graduating in 1958, six years ahead of me), and drinking Graham Greene daiquiris in the French Colonial Metropole Hotel in Hanoi, I could not help but wonder what all the carnage I had seen at Brooke Army Medical Center in Texas had been for. The films *The Quiet American* and *Apocalypse Now* are two cinematic headstones of this era.

So what is the moral of this story? There is more than one way to go wrong with China, and we oscillate between overestimating PRC strength and underestimating it. It is imperative to assess the opponent's comprehensive capacities realistically and look our own weaknesses straight in the eyes. The costs of error are measured in wounded in hospitals, deaths on battlefields, and foregone opportunities.

PARADIGM SHIFT: CHINA GETS STRONGER

Another major challenge to maintaining equilibrium in our thinking about Chinese power came with the violence and bloodshed in and around Tiananmen Square on June 4, 1989. Until then, many Americans had thought China was going to be the next domino in the sequence of failing communist regimes. For example, when reacting to my 1990 Testimony in the House of Representatives (see chapter 10), Congresswoman Nancy Pelosi said: "If the economy [of China] suffers, democracy is served, because this will increase the displeasure of the Chinese people toward their government." She seemingly believed that U.S. sanctions and other pressures to punish Beijing for its oppression would weaken the regime.

By way of contrast, NCUSCR programs in the wake of the Tiananmen bloodshed urged Americans to keep their balance and recognize the underlying strengths of the Chinese regime. Whether we liked it or not, China was not going the way of the Soviet Union anytime soon. The leadership of the National Committee believed that America should play the long game, increasing its own national capabilities on the one hand, and staying engaged with China on the other. Trying to sanction China into submission is a fool's errand.

Globalization introduced new challenges (and opportunities) for the United States as China became the "workshop for the world" and in the process gained economic leverage over an ever-broader slice of the international community. The PRC's trade surplus with America relentlessly grew, as did Beijing's purchase of American financial and tangible assets. China weathered the Asian Financial Crisis of 1997–1998 comparatively well. As I said in my book *The Three Faces of Chinese Power: Might, Money, and Minds* (2008):

> Washington should seek to foster an environment in which the PRC's principal emphasis remains directed inward and will not be turned outward, coercively. If Washington treats Beijing as though it is placing primacy on its military, when it is not, it will push Beijing in undesirable directions and squander U.S. resources better employed to meet the actual economic and intellectual challenges that the PRC represents. . . . Realizing the competitive dynamic where it exists, and cooperating where necessary and possible, is the only sensible way forward under current and likely future conditions. (pp. 272–73)

While Chinese heft was increasing, several events suggested to Beijing that America was in decline. The September 11, 2001, terrorist attacks, the resulting U.S. intervention in Afghanistan, and the failure to hunt down Osama Bin Laden until about a decade later, drained American attention and resources. The 2003 invasion of Iraq and concomitant failure to find nuclear weapons or other weapons of mass destruction there further degraded PRC respect for America's power and realism. The 2008–2009 global financial crisis with origins in Wall Street shenanigans was yet another development confirming PRC doubts about Washington's trajectory.

One example of this was an April 5, 2002, meeting I attended in the Purple Pavilion in Beijing's Zhongnanhai with Premier Zhu Rongji more than a year before the George W. Bush administration attacked Iraq. At that meeting, there was the following exchange between the Premier and a member of the U.S. Congress, as silk-sheathed tea servers hovered pouring the soothing and fragrant fluid. Zhu warned the United States to be careful as it pushed for war with Iraq:

> *Member of the U.S. Congress*: The issue is, when, where, and how will we face weapons of mass destruction—medical [dirty bombs], nuclear material, etc.? Iraq has used this [on its own people]. I believe that in 2–5 years they [Iraq] will have these [weapons]. Many Americans believe that we have to end the reign of Saddam [Hussein].

> *Premier Zhu Rongji*: I cannot agree with you on the Iraq issue—you can't produce solid evidence that Iraq has nuclear weapons. To destroy a country at will is very dangerous.

The whole Arab world will fall out with you—"we don't hope to see this."

In fall 2005, I wrote an article for *The National Interest* titled "Paradigm Lost: The Demise of 'Weak China,'" building on the idea that how we viewed China's comprehensive national strength, and our own power in relationship to it, would play a large role in shaping Washington's policy and behavior. Reciprocally, Beijing's perception of U.S. strength, as well as its sense of its own power, would play a central role in shaping events.

We [the U.S.] have witnessed a marked paradigm shift in thinking about China in the last few years, one that threatens to substitute one flawed framework (a "weak China") with another (a "China on steroids"). An April public opinion poll conducted by the Canada Institute of the Woodrow Wilson International Center found that 31 percent of Americans polled agreed with the statement, "China will soon dominate the world." (p. 73)

By way of contrast, in the 1970s and 1980s, Americans seemingly had good reason to be relaxed about the PRC's power—many observers thought that its fundamental problems were so great that progress would be measured in decades, and America would not be standing still. In the 1980s and 1990s, it seemed self-evident to me that "[Beijing] changing all this [its problems] would take a long time, even without considering the disabilities of the one-party state (corruption) and the natural-resource, environmental and population constraints. All of this argued for reserved predictions about China's progress" (p. 74).

Many factors contributed to the paradigm shift to the image of a "strong China." A decisive point, however, was reached by 2005 when the Organization for Economic Cooperation and Development (OECD) and World Bank statistics on Chinese economic performance revealed that the PRC accounted for 68 percent of global growth in oil consumption in the 1995–2003 period. China was soon being referred to as an engine of the global economy. Its ongoing disabilities had slipped from sight. The PRC joining the WTO in 2001 energized PRC growth.

By 2010, Beijing's assertive dealings with Japan, aggressive moves in the South China Sea, and relentlessly growing military strength became progressively less reassuring. Anxiety grew regionally and in America. As the PRC's power grew and Beijing flexed its muscles, Washington's unipolar moment was on the wane, and the post–World War II world order seemed in jeopardy.

Since my earliest research on Sino-American mutual perceptions in the 1970s, the difficulties of building a stable domestic consensus around realistic assessments of Chinese power have become increasingly apparent. The Chinese have a similar problem calibrating U.S. strength, oscillating between putting America on a pedestal of power and capacity, to seeing it as in steep decline and malevolent. Both nations suffer from a persistent inability to fully appreciate the resilience of the other. U.S. policy lurches from relaxed to alarmed, at the same time China has wide swings in its views of America.

On May 6, 2015, in a speech at the Carter Center in Atlanta titled "A Tipping Point in U.S.-China Relations Is Upon Us," I said: "Things [in the U.S.-China relationship] unfortunately have changed dramatically since about 2010. The tipping point is near. Our respective fears are nearer to outweighing our hopes than at any time since normalization." Things are unlikely to improve until leaders in both countries can have more objective perceptions of each other's strengths and weaknesses, and until both sides use what power they have to reassure each other and provide reciprocal positive incentives. In the eras of Trump and Xi, and Biden and Xi, "deterrence," *not* "reassurance," has become the watchword. That signals that each country will continue to administer heavy doses of threat to the other and each will relentlessly build its capabilities to deal with its often exaggerated view of the other's intentions and capabilities.

There are several ways that the relationship could go terribly wrong: First, one side could see itself as strong, the other weak, and overplay its hand. Alternatively, each could see itself as weaker than its opponent and try to salvage the situation by any number of preemptive and high-risk moves. Also alarming would be the circumstance in which a self-righteous America pushes China too far, particularly regarding Taiwan, or Beijing misjudges White House determination to defend the island. The mere presence of increasing amounts of military hardware close to one another in Asia holds its own risks. We should be particularly alert when Washington says Beijing needs America more than America needs China, as is occurring in 2023.

This brings me to the role of third parties in Sino-American ties.

THIRD PARTIES

Third parties of various types (nations, nonstate actors, multilateral organizations, and internationally active civil society organizations) affect the U.S.-China relationship. Managing the complications, dangers, and opportunities third parties present has concerned American leaders since George Washington and Thomas Jefferson warned against "entangling alliances."

DIASPORA AND IMMIGRANTS

Former Secretary of Defense James Schlesinger, involved with the Nixon Center when I headed its Chinese Studies Program (1998–2006), attached great importance to the roles ethnic/immigrant groups play in U.S. foreign policy. He argued that politicians seeking the votes of naturalized Americans and their natural-born offspring shape their foreign policy stance to attract these often issue-specific and committed voters.[8] U.S. policy abroad often reflects the intense commitment of these groups, sometimes unmindful of the costs to broader U.S. national interests.

There are other problems as well, such as those facing Americans of Chinese descent (and others of Asian ethnicity). Chinese Americans sometimes are tarred with the brush of being insufficiently mindful of U.S. interests with respect to policy toward the PRC and Taiwan. Accusations of disloyalty, xenophobia, can become attractive. Anti-Chinese and anti-Asian violence spiked in the COVID-19 era, in part due to growing suspicion of the PRC and anti-immigrant feelings.

This charged atmosphere feeds back into the overall U.S.-China relationship. Every act of violence or disrespect aimed against Chinese Americans and persons of Asian ethnicity in the United States is amplified in its recounting by the PRC, reinforcing the PRC's long-standing narrative about U.S. racism. Further, Beijing's policy with respect to Overseas Chinese (*huaqiao*) often implies that all persons of Chinese ethnicity globally have an obligation to China. Beijing's public security, intelligence, and consular authorities keep close tabs on PRC nationals and others abroad, including students, accused fugitives, political dissidents, and others.

The recent uptick in anti-Chinese, and anti-Asian, violence in America is one reflection of these forces. As a consequence, for many years I have been an advisor to the Committee of 100, a U.S. NGO focusing on issues of concern to the Chinese American community and

Sino-American relations. I am proud that the committee presented me with its "2018 Lifetime Achievement Award."

Another set of third-party challenges revolves around disaffected PRC persons who have ended up in America. They often strive to realize their aspirations for their old home from their new shores. For instance, the Falun Gong leader, Li Hongzhi, lives in New York (Dragon Springs) where he established a branch of Falun Gong. Rebiya Kadeer heads the World Uyghur Congress while living in exile in America. Without prejudice to their causes and rights, some Chinese exiles strive to mobilize allies and gain support from various corners of the U.S. government, NGOs, overseas Chinese, and the broader American citizenry.

In China itself, politically vulnerable individuals have sought refuge from persecution in the U.S. Embassy in Beijing or consular posts. Two notable examples are the blind lawyer Cheng Guangcheng and astrophysicist and vice president of the Chinese University of Science and Technology Fang Lizhi. Both sought refuge in the U.S. Embassy in Beijing at different times. As each was holed up for substantial periods, protracted negotiations wore on until their departure could be arranged. Both Fang and Chen ended up in America. In August 2020, Chen Guangcheng spoke at the Republican National Convention where he endorsed President Trump for reelection, calling for America to "use its values of freedom, democracy and the rule of law to gather a coalition of other democracies to stop [the] CCP's aggression."

Taiwan and U.S.-PRC Relations

Since 1949, Taiwan consistently has been a highly neuralgic issue in U.S.-PRC relations. Less observed have been incidents when Taipei has actually brought Beijing and Washington closer together, though usually only for a brief time.

The Taiwan American community is well organized and in certain localities (California, New York, Texas, and New Jersey) wields considerable political clout. As one former senior member of Congress said to me when we visited Taiwan in the early 1990s: "These are our kind of Chinese," expressing his preference for the democratic and open ethos he found on the island. I have former students who are and have been very senior officials in Taipei. These bonds of friendship, shared values, and human sentiment are strong.

Testifying before Congress alongside someone who had fled PRC oppression or represented Taiwan in its struggle for autonomy, dignity, and democracy always left me aware of a trap into which one easily could fall. Such persons had an intrinsic credibility advantage. Every caveat or "but" in my testimony could sound like an apology for Beijing, rather than a rounded exposition of U.S. interests.

Both KMT and Democratic Progressive Party (DPP) administrations in Taipei have used, and are using, intermediary foundations, companies, and other vehicles to get funds into the hands of some American politicians, think tanks, and opinion leaders (influencers). Many, perhaps most, of these avenues are lawful. A recent notable example of this was former U.S. Secretary of State Mike Pompeo's March 4, 2022, speech in Taipei before the Taiwan government-affiliated Prospect Foundation. The foundation acknowledged publicly that it had contracted with Pompeo to give a paid speech in Taipei. In and of itself, this is unremarkable.

In Pompeo's case, however, there was uncertainty among outsiders over the precise amount of his compensation. The most commonly mentioned figure was $150,000. What *was* remarkable is that a very recent former secretary of state (then contemplating a presidential run) would go to one of the most consequential hot-button world areas to articulate a policy at odds with every U.S. president since Richard Nixon, including the president for whom Pompeo had just worked—Donald Trump. In his remarks, Pompeo called upon the U.S. government to "offer the Republic of China, Taiwan, America's diplomatic recognition as a free and sovereign country."

That he would do so in the middle of a war in Europe for which Washington was seeking PRC help in exerting pressure on Moscow was irresponsible, not to mention the incendiary nature of the proposal itself. I would assume that were the U.S. government to heed Pompeo's call, it would spark war of some magnitude.

For its part, the PRC wisely chose to give Pompeo's proposal the back of its diplomatic hand—to ignore it. But in Beijing's upper-most councils of power, this must have been deeply disturbing. How could a conspiratorial-minded government in China not ascribe significance to this? In back-channel National Committee conversations with senior PRC Chinese representatives in early March 2022, Beijing's concerns about Pompeo's trip and statement were made abundantly clear to us. In truth, Pompeo's remarks were a domestically driven gambit with virtually no regard for America's broader interests or circumstances, or, for that matter, the welfare and security of the people of Taiwan who would pay heavy costs if things spiraled out of control.

On the subject of Taiwan money greasing Washington wheels, in a *Washington Post* op-ed of October 31, 1999, I called attention to Taipei's deft use of money in Washington, contrasting it with the paltry sums Beijing was accused of ladling out at that time: "This river of money makes the alleged illegal campaign contributions from the People's Republic of China (PRC) look like chump change." Of course, as the PRC has become wealthier and its firms have assumed global scale, the resources Beijing devotes to influence surely have grown.

All this is not to take away from a more elemental and important fact—as Taiwan became more democratic over the last three-plus decades, it also has had a progressively better story to tell the American people. In contrast, during Xi Jinping's reign, Beijing's story has become less congenial to Americans, whether from the angle of internal governance or foreign policy. As U.S. strategic ties with Beijing deteriorate, American politicians and security thinkers attach more strategic importance to Taiwan, hence weakening the One-China Policy. This process reached a new, dangerous level in May 2022 when President Biden committed his administration to intervene militarily were Taiwan attacked, something the TRA does not require. He repeated his pledge several times, while his staff asserted that Washington's policy had not changed. Beijing believes Washington is headed toward "One China, One Taiwan"—a formula for kinetic conflict.

Two thousand and twenty-one Senate testimony by Assistant Secretary of Defense Ely Ratner shows how as Washington–Beijing relations deteriorate, Washington's impulses to attach growing strategic importance to the island 95 miles from PRC shores become greater. Ratner said: "Taiwan is located at a critical node within the first island chain, anchoring a network of U.S. allies and partners . . . that is critical to the region's security and critical to the defense of vital U.S. interests in the Indo-Pacific."

All these difficulties aside, on rare occasions Taipei drives Washington and Beijing into each other's arms.

THE CASE OF CHEN SHUI-BIAN

In 2000, Chen Shui-bian became the first Taiwan president who was a member of the DPP.[9] He had scarcely concealed proclivities toward Taiwan independence. Chen was a constant worry to those in and out of the U.S. government concerned about stability in the Taiwan Strait.

Former Secretary of Defense William Perry (and future Defense Secretary Ash Carter), with the support of the NCUSCR, conducted a sustained dialogue on cross-strait relations in the late 1990s and well into the new millennium, part of which involved going to Taipei and Beijing/ Shanghai over time. Perry and his colleagues believed that the Taiwan Strait was a volatile flashpoint, as was North Korea. PRC President Jiang Zemin had given his blessing to the Perry Dialogue Channel, and former Shanghai Mayor and President Jiang Zemin's mentor, Wang Daohan, was our interlocutor. We simultaneously kept in touch with the highest levels in Taipei, including the island's presidents, emerging leaders, foreign ministers, military leadership, and Wang Daohan's counterpart, Koo Chen-fu, the cement king of Taiwan. Wang Daohan had been on the Zhu Rongji trip to the United States in 1990. We knew each other well. He gave me his fax number in case I wanted to share ideas with him.

For several years, the Perry Group kept channels of communication open with then-Taipei mayor and presidential hopeful Chen Shui-bian, well before Chen became president in 2000. Our objective was to have Mayor Chen appreciate the interests and concerns Washington had about management of cross-strait affairs—by that we meant that we were concerned that those harboring Taiwan independence objectives could catalyze dangerous conflict that would harm the United States, the wider region, and the people of Taiwan. We wanted to lend support to the further liberalization of the island's political system, even while mindful that the objectives of reinforcing democratic trends and avoiding cross-strait provocation sometimes were in tension.

After Chen's initial election as president in 2000 (he was reelected in 2004), Beijing had shown no flexibility and had offered Taiwan zero carrots, leaving President Chen angered and making serial proposals concerning Taiwan autonomy and identity, including proposing referenda and constitutional revisions. Chen's moves ran the risk that Beijing would claim Taipei had crossed its "no independence" red line. Each of Chen's moves was more worrisome to Beijing (and Washington) than the preceding one. By 2003, Chen was mobilizing his voter base in anticipation of the 2004 presidential election on the island, holding out the aphrodisiac of more international recognition, respect, and global involvement for Taiwan.

President George W. Bush had come into office in 2001 more sympathetic to Taiwan than any U.S. president in decades. Nonetheless, Bush had his hands full fighting terrorists, North Korea had an active nuclear weapons-building program that the U.S. administration hoped Beijing would help stanch, and the U.S. president faced a reelection campaign in 2004. He didn't need another foreign policy migraine in the Taiwan Strait.

In a November 2002 trip during which the Perry-National Committee group stopped in Taipei, we met with President Chen Shui-bian. Dr. Perry wanted to make sure the Taiwan president understood how American foreign and defense attitudes had changed in the wake of the 9/11 terrorist attacks against New York, Washington, and Pennsylvania. My notes record that Chen was told the following:

> President Bush made a strong diplomatic statement ["Do whatever it takes" to defend Taiwan]; the United States Government was prepared to use or threaten force against the PRC [on behalf of Taiwan's defense]. But at the same time [the U.S. president] said he would not support Taiwan making moves toward independence. This [the Perry Group] is not an official delegation and no one speaks for the [U.S.] Government, but we all support the Bush Administration on this! This support is across branches and within the Executive Branch. . . . The new [U.S.] National Security Strategy [asserts] that the main threats

are not other powers, but the forces of disintegration [terrorists], and the powers should try to cooperate on these issues. There is strong bipartisan support for this too.

With detectable irritation, impatience, and relish, President Chen gave these concerns a wave of his hand. He seemed to be saying that his government and people would make their own decisions about how far to go in asserting their independent identity, and it was America's moral obligation to support them, no matter what. As Chen put it:

> The United States doesn't like to listen to [this], but all Taiwan people consider themselves independent and sovereign and not part of any country. Last August 3rd, [I said] *"Yi Bian, Yi Guo,"* [one country on each side of the Taiwan Strait] different countries—this is a fact! One side is the PRC and the other the ROC. [This is] not to the liking of the United States, but we must make this clear.[10]

Without speaking for others, I bristled at this assertion. I sensed throughout this period that President George W. Bush felt a certain ingratitude on Chen's part; Chen was proposing to write security checks that might have to be cashed in American blood. President Chen continued to roil the waters as he waged a tight presidential campaign.

In December 2003, Chinese Premier Wen Jiabao made a trip to the United States, with a meeting scheduled with President George W. Bush on the ninth in Washington. To prepare for that meeting, having just arrived at JFK Airport the evening of the seventh, Premier Wen met with five American NGO leaders and academic experts in a Waldorf Astoria Towers suite in Midtown Manhattan. I participated.

Wen's top agenda item was to express Beijing's hope that the U.S. president would exert influence over Chen Shui-bian to lower the temperature of his statements and actions concerning Taiwan's future and identity—to stop what Beijing viewed as provocations.

The premier was concerned that President Chen Shui-bian was a potential IED (improvised explosive device) buried just below the surface of the U.S.-China relationship and the One-China Policy. Chen could precipitate serious Sino-American friction by embedding the island's separate political identity in constitutional changes and referenda on selected hot-button issues.

At our meeting, some of us encouraged Premier Wen not to adopt a strident tone toward Taiwan, either publicly or in his meeting with President Bush. Doing so would make it harder for Bush to exert a restraining influence on Chen: Wen responded, "It is my hope that President Bush will do all the talking on Taiwan."

The Americans at that evening's meeting were unsure what President Bush would say in the get-together with Premier Wen two days hence. The U.S. president had earlier (April 2001) strongly indicated he would defend Taiwan—"Do whatever it took to help Taiwan defend herself." In the Waldorf meeting, I told Premier Wen, "I believe the Administration now sees that mistake and in a number of recent statements by the President, privately, and others publicly . . . the Administration has underscored its concerns about Taiwan provocations." I went on to suggest: "Let the U.S. try to restrain him [Chen] and you [the PRC] provide more carrots [to Taiwan]." I noted that the "One Country, Two Systems" formula "has no attraction I can discern on Taiwan."[11] One Country, Two Systems was not a "carrot."

Thereafter, in Premier Wen's meeting at the White House, President Bush made public remarks. He took President Chen to the rhetorical woodshed to a greater and more public degree than I believe any of us at the December 7 meeting in New York had expected. Before the Waldorf meeting, we could sense Bush's direction, but not the degree of his frustration with President Chen. In an ill-advised tactical move, shortly before Tuesday's White House visit by Premier Wen, on Monday, President Chen made the mistake of ignoring a private White House plea that President Chen refrain from doing things that might upset the status quo across the Taiwan Strait. The next day, at the White House, the U.S. president, in effect, gave Chen a dressing down.

After Bush's publicly expressed support for the One-China Policy and criticism of Chen, I believe Beijing's leaders had more confidence in George W. Bush, concluding that even though he was sympathetic to Taiwan, he would not allow Taipei to upend the strategically critical U.S.-China relationship, particularly with multiple conflicts and strategic problems in the Middle East, in Central Asia, and on the Korean Peninsula. Beijing's baseline confidence lasted through the rest of the Bush administration and into the Obama years.

That confidence almost entirely evaporated in the Trump and Biden years, with Beijing coming to perceive that Washington was peeling away elements of the One-China Policy layer by layer—a diplomatic version of death by a thousand slices.

In more than one meeting with Chen Shui-bian, I was struck with the low regard in which he held the U.S. Executive Branch (whether Republican or Democratic), finding them too accommodating to China's mainland, too prone to emphasize interests and depreciate values. His dissatisfaction was palatable—he preferred Congress. Capitol Hill was his 911 number.

Over the longer sweep of history, whether Chiang Kai-shek first on the mainland and later on Taiwan, or the succession of post-Chiang administrations in Taipei, in times of trouble the emergency number for Taiwan always has been the U.S. Congress. In February 1943, Madam Chiang Kai-shek addressed the House and the Senate pleading for more aid to Taiwan in its fight against Japan and thanking the United States for what already had been provided. "America is not only the cauldron of democracy, but the incubator of democratic principles," she memorably said.[12] And basically, so it has gone ever since, long after the Chiangs passed from the scene and as KMT and DPP governments have succeeded one another. James Schlesinger attributed to Alexis de Tocqueville an observation that captures one aspect of Taiwan's grip on the American psyche: "Nations, like men, love that which flatters their passions—even more than that which serves their interests." When Taiwan appeals to U.S. democratic angels, it is easy for Americans to sublimate other interests.

ECONOMICALLY ENTANGLED FRIENDS

For the entire decade-long debate over MFN extension for China in the 1990s, many members of Congress did not vote to pull the trigger on Beijing by terminating MFN because they knew that doing so would inflict great collateral damage on Hong Kong, Taiwan, Japan, and South

Korea, each of which was intertwined with the PRC economically. These societies were the very ones about which Washington professed to be concerned. This was a point I hammered home in almost all my Congressional Testimony on the subject throughout the 1990s—"Don't victimize the victims," "Don't victimize our friends." Very quietly many in Taiwan and Hong Kong (and throughout Asia) were imploring Washington to spare Beijing from MFN withdrawal, not for the PRC's sake but for their own.

THE 9/11 ATTACKS AS AN ADHESIVE IN U.S.-CHINA TIES

Another instance of a third-party interaction fostering U.S.-China cooperation was on display in the wake of the September 11, 2001, Al-Qaeda attacks on America. President George W. Bush had reacted to the attacks by telling a joint session of Congress that he would judge nations by a simple standard: "Either you are with us, or you are with the terrorists." PRC President Jiang Zemin immediately reassured the beleaguered Bush that China was with him. To a degree, Jiang made his rhetoric tangible by cooperating with Washington to assure the safety of the enormous numbers of freight containers coming to America from Chinese ports, the fear being that weapons of mass destruction could enter any U.S. harbor in any one of millions of standard cargo containers from the PRC. The two sides also shared intelligence.

Jiang's reassurance encouraged an overstretched White House not to adopt a harder-edged policy toward Beijing, which had been the new administration's initial inclination. At this time, I wrote an article for *The National Interest*, "Small Mercies," the "small mercy" being that the 9/11 attacks had forestalled the Bush administration from making a strategic mistake with respect to China. Jiang's deft and supportive response to 9/11 delayed a rift between Washington and Beijing by five to ten years. One can only speculate about the effects on U.S.-China relations had President Xi Jinping reacted in a similarly reassuring manner in February 2022 when Moscow invaded Ukraine.

The Russia-China-Georgia Triangle

Another instance of a third-party issue drawing America and China together occurred in 2008, this time with Beijing standing up against Moscow's territorial infringement on the sovereignty of Georgia, a Caucasus state where Asia meets Europe. As Putin was trying to dismember Georgia, Beijing opposed Russian encroachment, preventing the Shanghai Cooperation Organization (SCO) from supporting Moscow, citing the principle of ensuring sovereignty and territorial integrity as a global-order principle. Were Moscow to annex part or all of Georgia, what would be the argument against Western "splittist" efforts regarding Taiwan?

Beijing's Blunder on Ukraine in 2022

U.S.-China relations might now be very different had Beijing adopted a similar posture in reaction to Moscow's brutal aggression against first Crimea in 2014 and then against Ukraine as a whole on February 24, 2022. Beijing refused to condemn Moscow's brutal invasion of sovereign Ukraine, thus shredding its own nearly seven decades-long commitment to the sanctity of sovereign borders.

To make matters worse, with Putin in Beijing for the opening of the Winter Olympic Games, and Moscow's ominous buildup encircling Ukraine well underway, on February 4, 2022, President Xi Jinping and Putin issued a "Joint Statement," declaring their "no limits" partnership, emphasizing that "there are no forbidden areas of cooperation" and that a transformative era in "global governance architecture and world order" was their joint endeavor.[13] The Chinese side noted "the significance of the efforts taken by the Russian side to establish a just multipolar system of international relations." The day before that Joint Statement, a very senior U.S. diplomat told a small group of which I was a part, that, "China really has shifted closely to Russia." Even before Moscow's all-out invasion of Ukraine, the Biden administration believed that Beijing already had gone over to the dark side.

This Sino-Russian Joint Statement eliminated the opportunity, however slight, for a midcourse correction in U.S.-China relations and was a PRC blunder weakening its own position concerning Taiwan.

Subsequent fall meetings, between Putin and Xi in Uzbekistan and a Putin meeting with Politburo Standing Committee Member Li Zhanshu in Vladivostok, ratcheted up Chinese support for Russia. China was, in part, reacting to President Biden's increasingly clear support for Taipei. Both Beijing and Washington were pushing each other's hot buttons.

In this critical period, two colleagues at the National Committee and I kept a faint channel open to Beijing, convening virtually about once every month or two with senior persons. The exchange of February 17, 2022, was telling. We urged Beijing to separate from Russia, noting that the *New York Times* already had referred to China as "a critical ally" of Russia. We needed to see Beijing push back publicly against Moscow and not be its enabler in the UN Security Council.

Within forty-eight hours of our conversation, Foreign Minister Wang Yi issued a statement that sounded like hedged distancing from Moscow, saying: "The sovereignty, independence, and territorial integrity of any country [Ukraine] should be respected and safeguarded," a sentence considerably diluted by a simultaneous admonition to the United States and NATO that Russia's security concerns also should be respected. A few days later (February 22), as an all-out Russian attack seemed imminent, another statement from Wang Yi did not include respecting sovereignty, citing only the need to respect Moscow's security concerns. With the Russian invasion ("special military operation") fully in gear as of February 24, Beijing had aligned with Moscow.

After our conversation with the PRC representatives on February 17, I wondered how much the PRC Foreign Ministry and other bureaucratic officials (presumably beyond a tight circle around Xi) knew about Russian plans, the imminence of war, and its possible objectives. Was this a case of the Ministry of Foreign Affairs being uninformed? It is hard to imagine that when Putin and Xi met on February 4 in Beijing, the Russian did not share with China's president in some detail his plans for Ukraine once the Olympic Games had concluded. Xi was either very naïve or complicit. In a March 2023 conversation with persons in the foreign affairs system, we were told: "Putin didn't tell China it would invade." Whether this is in error, disinformation, misinformation, or true, I do not know. Maybe Xi did not ask because he knew the answer. In any case, from our conversation I concluded that Xi did not try to dissuade Putin.

In our various interactions with our Chinese interlocutors, we had discerned division among them, one revealing what I think was the dominant line of thinking in Beijing's security community and reflective of Xi Jinping's orientation. The official essentially said that the turmoil in Europe benefited China by deflecting American attention from the PRC to the heart of Europe. I replied by pointing out, "That is a very unfriendly thought to both Americans and Europeans."[14] Almost two decades before, as the United States was bogged down in Iraq, one Chinese strategist plainly described for me Beijing's strategic reflex: "As long as you [the United States] are preoccupied with the Greater Middle East, China is safe!"[15]

By mid-March 2022, with Russia bogging down in Ukraine, other audible PRC voices were arguing that China would benefit only if Putin won, and that was unlikely.[16] The official, Hu Wei, called Russia's military action "an irreversible mistake." China's interests lie in being with the winner, and, if Putin lost in Ukraine, China would be isolated and possibly left with a relatively dependent Russia to assist economically— China would be isolated and face a now stronger United States. The PRC itself could be subjected to secondary economic sanctions by the West. A China that only wants to go with the winner is not a very attractive partner in the long run. I sense that much of China's intelligentsia thinks that Xi Jinping led China into a diplomatic box canyon from which there may be no escape. Hu Wei says that Xi's tilt toward Russia divided the policy community in the PRC into "two implacably opposing sides."

Admittedly, Beijing's actions were not occurring in a vacuum. Washington had just released its Indo-Pacific Strategy (on February 11, 2022), amidst the beating of war drums in Europe. Moreover, Secretary Blinken went to Melbourne to meet with Indian, Japanese, and Australian counterparts (The Quad) on February 18 to coordinate China policy. Both actions were strong statements to Beijing that Washington saw the PRC as its central long-term strategic problem irrespective of immediate circumstances in Europe. If China was America's long-run enemy, so went CCP logic, "Why help America in the short run?"

In the fiftieth anniversary year of Nixon's visit to China, the logic of that journey was turned on its head.

CONCLUSIONS

There are many ways to explore the considerations shaping U.S.-China relations. I have used policy-oriented programs and cooperative inter-actions with China among my methods. Working with colleagues in China and elsewhere to address issues such as food policy, technology transfer, environmental sustainability, crisis management, railroads, and civil nuclear power have taught me much about domestic and foreign policy dynamics.

With respect to foreign policy, it is easier for America to get into quagmires than to extricate itself. One reason is a lack of clarity about what constitutes power in various circumstances. America oscillates between underestimating and overestimating China's capacities. In Korea, we underestimated Chinese staying power as we entered the fray on the Peninsula. In Indochina, we overestimated China's capacities as we underestimated Vietnam's will to stay free of both U.S. and Chinese domination.

Finally, America's policy over long periods has been to prevent any country, or hostile coalition, from dominating the expansive Eurasian landmass. This has been true with respect to imperial Britain, Tsarist Russia, Japan in World War II, and the Soviet Union later. Generally, I have felt that cooperation between Moscow and Beijing is not their default condition. When Moscow and Beijing cooperate to America's disadvantage, Washington should consider whether or not it has played its economic, diplomatic, or military cards skillfully. America should be more adept at avoiding pushing them together.

NOTES

1. David M. Lampton and Alfred D. Wilhelm Jr., *United States and China Relations at a Crossroads* (University Press of America, 1995).

2. It was during the Yeltsin democratic interlude in Russia, in 1995, that the Russian Academy of Sciences, Institute of Far Eastern Studies, awarded me an honorary doctorate.

3. A singular account of Hong Kong's return is Dalena Wright, *Diplomacy Ends at Midnight: The Long Return of Hong Kong to China* (Penguin Books, forthcoming 2024).

4. David M. Lampton, "Diary on Hong Kong Handover," unpublished. (RAC).

5. David M. Lampton, Selina Ho, and Cheng-Chwee Kuik, "Interview with Foreign Affairs System Official," June 7, 2017, Vientiane, Laos, 7. (RAC).

6. Robert Beckhusen, "The NSA Listened as Chinese MIGs Shot Down American Warplanes," https://medium.com/war-is-boring/the-nsa-listened-as-chinese-migs-shot-down-american-warplanes-521fb522369f.

7. Andrew Mertha, "A Half Century of Engagement: The Study of China and the Role of the China Scholar Community," in *Engaging China: Fifty Years of Sino-American Relations*, Anne F. Thurston, ed. (New York: Columbia University Press, 2021), 103.

8. James Schlesinger, "Fragmentation and Hubris: A Shaky Basis for American Leadership," *The National Interest* no. 49 (Fall 1997): 3–9.

9. In September 2009, Chen was jailed for corruption.

10. "Meeting with President Chen Shui-bian," Presidential Palace, Taipei, Taiwan, November 18, 2002, 4. Notes by David M. Lampton. (RAC).

11. David M. Lampton, "Notes of Meeting with Premier Wen Jiabao," Waldorf-Astoria Towers, New York City, December 7, 2003, (RAC).

12. On March 16, 2022, Ukrainian President Volodymyr Zelensky ripped a page out of Mme. Chiang's speech in virtual remarks to the U.S. Congress.

13. "Joint Statement of the Russian Federation and the People's Republic of China on the International Relations Entering a New Era and the Global Sustainable Development," February 4, 2022, http://en.kremlin.ru/supplement/5770, 1, 13.

14. David M. Lampton, "Notes of Meeting with Former Official," XXX, February 17, 2022, 11. (RAC).

15. David M. Lampton, "Notes of Remarks of Senior Chinese Strategist," Washington, DC, May 19, 2004, 1. (RAC).

16. Hu Wei, "Possible Outcomes of the Russo-Ukrainian War and China's Choice," https://uscnpm.org/2022/03/12/hu-wei-russia-ukraine-war-china-choice/.

CHAPTER FIFTEEN

Schizophrenia: Connectivity and Insularity

ONE CONCEPT MISS TURNER, MY HIGH SCHOOL TEACHER, IMPARTED TO her students was that in its attempt to define and attain a respected and secure role in the world, China has sought to reconcile two objectives, each in tension with the other—maintaining China's cultural essence (*ti*) while adopting the methods of the West that would produce technological and economic progress, wealth, and power (*yong*), thereby enabling China to fend off the predations of outsiders (*waiguoren*). The Middle Kingdom's problem has been its inability to introduce the science, technology, and organizations capable of competing with the West without changing its essence.

Consequently, Chinese history has oscillated between periods emphasizing reform and modernization involving heavy borrowing from others, and periods of rejection of Western modernity, closure, and charting a future more resonant with its past. Particularly difficult to digest have been Western concepts of political modernization.

Western-style modernization challenged China's legitimating self-identity and the power interests of its Confucian elite. If the Middle Kingdom's legitimating myth was that it was halfway between heaven and earth (*Zhongguo*), it was by definition unique, having to be understood in singular terms. While the United States had the First Amendment securing free speech, religion, and assembly, China had the *baojia* (the mutual supervision, collective responsibility, and civil control mechanism) in which family and social groupings were responsible for the behavior of their members and collectively accountable for infractions. State power

353

was constitutionally unconstrained. We see echoes of this in the PRC's surveillance state.

China has been unable to find a stable and productive equilibrium reconciling the assertion of its uniqueness with the homogenizing effects of foreign military power, science, open economic and information systems, rule of law, and democracy. Each term is imprecise and debatable, but the point Miss Turner was making was that China has had trouble reconciling the demands of the outside world with its self-conception, much less convincing China's elites to adopt a new vision in which they might have a diminished, or no, role.

When China's leaders have moved too abruptly toward more Western-resonant modernization and greater integration with the outside world, China's antibodies have kicked in and mass movements have ignited to expel the intrusive forces in periodic wrenching, violent spasms. The mid-nineteenth-century Taiping Rebellion that depopulated large swaths of China is one example. Another was China's limited reform era in the late 1800s to early 1900s and a counter-reaction to it—the Boxer Rebellion. This instability was, in turn, followed by the collapse of the Qing Dynasty in 1911. China's sequence of civil wars from 1911 on were attempts to define a new vision, to fashion supporting institutions that could work in the twentieth century. There was a period of forward movement during the Republican era, led by Chiang Kai-shek's Nationalist Party, but this was brutally disrupted by Japan's invasion of China. The communist era's Great Leap Forward and subsequent Cultural Revolution in the late 1950s, 1960s, and 1970s continued this pattern, with these movements, in part, reactions to the Soviet Union's model of modernization that was deemed by Mao Zedong to be incompatible with the PRC's needs, sovereignty, and identity. The underlying dilemma has always been how to make China strong and respected without losing its essence, whatever that essence was deemed to be according to the reigning dogma of the day.

Miss Turner's approach to understanding China's evolution was embodied in Ssu-yu Teng and John King Fairbank's *China's Response to the West*, published in 1954, and John King Fairbank's *The United States and China* published six years earlier. The idea was that the Western modernization paradigm was encountering China's very different history, understandings, values, and institutions. This clash of civilizations had a profound and energizing effect on relations between America and China. Each society had to be understood on its terms, but it was the tensions and attractions between them that animated history. This is what Tongqi Lin called the "Clash of Modernity Approach," or the "Impact-Response" model.[1] When China tried to reform, Americans were enthusiastic; when it reverted to antecedent patterns, Americans were disappointed. One may ask why it was America's right to be "disappointed."

This was the intellectual framework to which I first was exposed. I have never entirely jettisoned it. This approach remains germane to interpreting the comparatively successful forty-five-year-long reform era extending from the 1970s into the new millennium, followed by Xi Jinping's rejection of much of that agenda despite its enormous gains.

Xi's self-proclaimed "New Era" is defined by the backward-looking slogan of "The Great Rejuvenation of the Chinese Nation." The last rejuvenations of China before the communist period arguably were the glory days of the Ming and Qing dynasties. Xi Jinping's underlying charge is that the West (particularly the United States) seeks to keep China weak, subverting the PRC through "peaceful evolution"—to change its essence. Leaving nothing to the imagination, at the time of the National People's Congress meeting of early 2023, the supreme leader said that China was facing a "comprehensive containment and suppression by Western countries led by the U.S. over the past few years, which have brought unprecedented and severe challenges for China's development."

Whatever one thinks about this historical action-reaction model, as I moved out of Miss Turner's classroom into the wider intellectual world, I realized that my interests were somewhat different. I wanted to know how China works, on the ground, and how this shaped governance at home and behavior abroad. Scholars can look at broad historical frameworks, from thirty thousand feet, or they can focus closer to *terra firma* and seek to discern why things happen as they do, in real places, with real people, with real constraints and opportunities.

At Stanford, I was influenced by scholars focusing on developments in China itself, developments driven by the PRC's own demographic and resource constraints; distinctive political dynamics, institutions, and political culture; local economic systems, interconnected but insular; the peculiarities of individual leaders and their paths to power; and by universal processes such as bureaucratic politics, the need to make budgets, and much more. The PRC's internal and external behavior was understandable in terms applicable to most political systems—communist or not, Chinese or not, Confucian or not. China had distinctive qualities, but it was not immune to broader patterns.

Chinese history was being made in China, not principally because of the West. Professor John Lewis was looking at specific localities to find out how the PRC worked at the local level, in his case Hebei province's city of Tangshan. Professor Michel Oksenberg was investigating how water conservancy projects were being built in China's heartland. Professor Robert North admonished his students to remember that if you wanted to know what Chinese leaders think and value, do not read Mao's *Little Red Book*. Instead, look at China's local and national budgets. North understood that people value what they spend their money on. Alexander George was documenting how actual PRC Korean War prisoners and the Chinese military as a whole reacted to the application of massive U.S. firepower on PLA troops in Korea. The point was to look at people, real situations, and practical constraints, many of which are universal. China was best studied if one did not start with the *a priori* assertion that "China is China is China." This was what the "behavioral revolution" in social science meant to me.

For most of my career, China acted largely on its domestic, sometimes regional, stage. What China did sometimes affected others beyond its region, but generally what happened in China stayed in China or along its periphery to a considerable extent. As the 1990s rolled into the new millennium, and China entered the WTO in 2001, however, the PRC's global impact expanded rapidly, reflecting rising national capacities, prior investments in education, new infrastructure, more open policies, a less constrained domestic intellectual environment, and a massive influx of outside investment seeking to reduce costs in global supply chains and sell products to China's fast-growing middle class and the growing societies along its periphery.

Some of these foreign investments had negative externalities abroad, as well as inside the PRC itself. Foreign investments in China in the furniture industry, for example, almost extinguished that industry in the United States. Western investments in China likewise could make waves there, with Western disposal of electronic waste in the PRC being one illustration.

What China did internally and abroad increasingly mattered to the global citizenry and affected systems worldwide, running the gamut from the environment to food, human rights, trade and finance, and development practices abroad. Pet food and toothpaste laced with antifreeze in some Chinese exports (in the 2007–2008 period) was just one example, an occurrence that led one member of Congress I accompanied to Beijing to express his frustration with adulterated Chinese products by telling a Politburo Standing Committee Member with whom we were meeting in the Great Hall of the People that: "Poison food for pets or people is a very big issue in every U.S. town."[2]

In this period, the PRC embraced connectedness and interdependence as it never had before. This impulse was particularly apparent after China entered the WTO. President Jiang once said in my presence that he considered himself Western-educated, mentioning that his English language teacher used as teaching materials the great political documents and speeches of American and British history. Early on he was introduced to the Constitution of the United States and the Gettysburg Address. At one point, in paraphrase, he said that he wished that U.S. presidents knew as much about China as he knew about America.

Some in China embraced integration as the wave of the future, while others were ambivalent and wanted to slow, or even dial back, change. Some leaders wanted to reverse trends they saw as weakening their internal control and threatening China's essence, whether defined as socialism or traditional values. The impacts that Xi Jinping most feared were the dissolution of the CCP, the corrosive effect of Western ideology, and loss of power, with one informant telling me in paraphrase that: "He [Xi] believes holding on to power is the only way to enhance his security. He can't live if he gives up power."[3]

Although Xi Jinping embodies this hesitancy to embrace interdependence, he also has been schizophrenic. On the one hand, in 2013 he launched his One Belt, One Road (OBOR) policy, later rebranded the Belt and Road Initiative (BRI), a huge six-corridor Eurasian infrastructure construction endeavor. Even if only partly realized, BRI would make China the economic hub of its part of the world, with tentacles extending to Europe and beyond. Infrastructure would be the arteries through which Chinese power would flow. Xi's launch of this effort implied acceptance of great interdependence.

On the other hand, many of his other policies betrayed a fear of the subversive nature of connectivity. China's great firewall against polluting ideas is one manifestation of this concern. Along with BRI, Xi established a "National Security Commission" in 2013–2014,[4] aimed at blunting foreign subversion and strengthening party control in important areas that Deng Xiaoping and his two successors, Jiang Zemin and Hu Jintao, had loosened: the economy, civil society, and information.

In short, under Xi Jinping, China has been headed in two very different directions simultaneously. This is the PRC's core contradiction, and when instability grows, as I believe it will, this will be a major contributor, along with inequity, corruption, injustice, and environmental blowback. America has many ills as well. We ought not be too smug, but we also should not wish to trade circumstances with PRC leaders.

In 2014–2015, I was considering my intellectual agenda going forward. I was attracted to one of two basic frames for the next phase of my research. One was to focus on some aspect of how Xi was unwinding certain key dimensions of reform, how he engineered that politically, what implications this might have for domestic stability, and what this would mean for relations with the West, not least America.

But if I focused my work in this way, I would be destined to recapitulate the familiar storyline of the "impact-response model." China put its toes into the ocean of reform, only to fear taking the bracing plunge, and it drew back to a more authoritarian, bureaucratic, state-led path energized by a strong man. The conclusion already was obvious—a Leninist Party was reasserting itself, playing upon all the cultural tropes of a meddlesome West trying to keep China down or change it entirely.

I wanted to do something different, something that might shed light in other corners—be more forward-looking. I also wanted to do something that connected to my prior infrastructure work and would get me into the field. The alternative research frame I had in mind was to focus on that aspect of Xi Jinping's agenda and era that was headed in the direction of connectivity and globalization—the PRC effort to connect seven Southeast Asian neighbors to China through a system of high-speed rail lines. With BRI and this rail effort, Xi was placing a considerable bet on interconnectedness even as many of his other endeavors sought insulation.

The questions I wanted to ask were: Could China do it? How? What interests in China could sustain such an effort? What problems would the PRC and its partners encounter implementing it? Would China learn from its mistakes as it worked with a sequence of different political and social systems to complete an interconnectivity network of massive scale? What effects would this effort have on Chinese society? What impact would it have on the wider world?

RIVERS OF IRON

This line of thinking led me and Professors Selina Ho and Cheng-Chwee Kuik to undertake a five-year field examination of China's role in planning, designing, negotiating, and implementing an emerging regional connectivity network of high-speed rail (HSR) and medium-speed rail (MSR), envisioned as eventually running from Yunnan Province (Kunming City) in southwest China to Singapore via three north-south trunk lines.[5]

When (if) completed, it would traverse seven continental Southeast Asian countries. Each one of the lines would be longer than the Transcontinental Railroad built in America from 1863–1869, an undertaking that transformed the U.S. economy, knit the country together, and provided a springboard for power projection across the Pacific.

At the time, the Transcontinental also had its American doubters. Corruption was rampant. Native Americans and Chinese laborers were victims of human rights abuses. But within a decade of its construction, American citizens largely praised the undertaking. The railroad provided "robber baron" Leland Stanford such a vast fortune that he founded what would become a university that, nearly a hundred years later, took the lead in bringing Chinese scholars and students to the United States, even before normalization. He built his fortune on the backs of Chinese labor but later gave back opportunities to successor generations of Chinese youth. The university also became a driving force in the development of Silicon Valley, energizing the computing, information, and bioscience industries.

My two research colleagues and I believed that a multicountry Pan-Asia HSR system would not only be transformative, but studying its emergence would illuminate many significant questions, among which are: How and why was Xi Jinping's China initiating an effort to build infrastructure to connect China to the world, while simultaneously seeking to insulate the PRC from the corrosive effects of globalization and connectivity? Could these two purposes long coexist? What did such an effort tell us about Chinese domestic politics, how fast China was learning from the world, and what was the capacity of the PRC's smaller neighbors to shape their destinies?

The study took us to nine countries: China, Cambodia, Indonesia, Laos, Malaysia, Myanmar (Burma), Singapore, Thailand, and Vietnam, and involved site visits, interviews, and scouring local publications and government documents. The most ambitious phase was ground travel from Bangkok to the PRC-Laos border at Boten in the summer of 2017. Beyond the extensive travel in Thailand and Laos, at other times we moved by ground and interviewed in Malaysia, Cambodia, Vietnam, and Singapore. We generally had quite extensive access, largely because of my colleagues' interpersonal networks, the help of the Asia Foundation, and my own connections.

This was a massive, comparative research undertaking, involving interviews with hundreds of people and well over 150 organizations. Meetings included government representatives (among which were past and current prime ministers, cabinet-level officials, and a sultan), representatives of private and state-owned multinational corporations, international multilateral agencies, elements of civil society where accessible, universities, and think tanks.

To do all this, a team was essential, and ours was composed of a Singaporean, a Malaysian, an American, and, at a critical phase, one Thai professor. The mere act of conducting such a geographically far-flung comparative study on the ground, dealing with so many economically and politically diverse areas, often in forbidding terrain, one of which was lawless (Cambodia), was daunting. Our research team dealt with the kinds of challenges that those who would negotiate and construct the rail network itself would confront. Moving with efficiency, making sure we had people with local knowledge helping us, all the while speaking with the right people and winning confidence, across language and cultural barriers, were challenges. Logistics and funding were key. Our team is grateful to the Smith Richardson Foundation for its support.

In Myanmar (Burma), a group I was with met with Aung San Suu Kyi, who spouted a bone-chilling refutation of Western descriptions of the Burmese military's persecution of the Rohingya in Rakhine State. One of the intrinsic dangers of infrastructure projects is the unstable social milieu in which such projects often are built. The conversation with Aung San Suu Kyi gave me a sense of how deep and vicious ethnic antagonism still is in many parts of this region. If Beijing is going to build infrastructure in these kinds of areas, it has to be prepared to accept the risks of economic loss, political entanglement in human rights debacles, and sometimes attacks on its personnel.

In Malaysia, our conversation with former Prime Minister Mahathir gave us a sense of how colonial-era British rail development had early on convinced him of the importance of trains. His boyhood experience drove his later policy commitments. We also interviewed the Sultan of Perak, in whose domain the Chinese had a rolling stock facility.[6]

In Thailand we interviewed a high-level official who was self-assured in negotiating with outside powers because Thailand, in his words, was like a "beautiful lady" with many suitors—giving it options and leverage.

In Indonesia in January 2016, I met with the Governor of Jakarta, Ahok, a popular Christian leader of Chinese extraction in a predominately Muslim nation, who had misgivings about PRC HSR development in his country. He told me that the proposed high-speed train to be built between Jakarta and Bandung traveled so fast that it would have

Figure 15.1.   At Sultan of Perak's Palace, Jalan Changkat, Bukit Persekutuan, Kuala Lumpur, Malaysia, May 29, 2018. (Left to right) Malaysian aide; Author; His Royal Highness Sultan Nazrin Muizzuddin Shah; Cheng-Chwee Kuik; and Selina Ho. Photo by David M. Lampton.

to initiate braking before reaching the capital's sprawling city limits. He concluded that a slower-speed, easier-to-maintain train, such as GE manufactures, might be more suited to local circumstances.

In our team's travels in Laos, we saw hydro-dam projects under construction by Chinese firms that would generate and distribute electrical power to China, Vietnam, and perhaps elsewhere, holding the potential to transform Laos into the "battery" of Southeast Asia—Chinese-built dams would be powering Chinese-built high-speed trains in the region. These projects also, of course, imposed large environmental, displacement, and financial dependency costs.

Each of these places, projects, and leaders provided us insight into the complex and diverse geological, social, political, and economic circumstances with which China was dealing. Lessons learned in one country or region would not necessarily be transferable to other circumstances. China's state enterprises knew how to deal with conditions at home, but venturing abroad was a different and far more complex task. They would have to be fast learners.

IN THE FIELD

One of the many virtues of field research is that it forces researchers to reconcile preconceptions with objective circumstances. It helps the researcher define the problem through the eyes of actual participants, rather than being a voyeur eight thousand miles away imposing his/her biases on a distant reality. Trudging through the red clay of Laos or Thailand's mud-bathed railway right-of-way quickly got us attuned to reality.

Over my years of interviewing, many conversations have been memorable, but few more so than those our team conducted with bureaucrats, legislators, academics, and others in Laos in June 2017. One interviewee was a transportation and public works planner in Laos' capital Vientiane. We spoke with him on June 6, 2017, shortly after arriving in the dusty, sleepy town.[7] It was memorable because our interlocutor, the "Planner," was not only frank, but he thought historically and developmentally. He had confidence and spoke with precision. The Planner saw the broad picture and the fine detail. In all my various infrastructure research projects over the years, I came to appreciate engineers the most. For them, facts are the coin of the realm.

As we started our conversation with the Planner, I imagined that he was starting from the presumption that we Westerners were inclined to think that Laos was simply becoming a dependency of China, a principal manifestation of which was the massive debt to Beijing that Laos was assuming by building the rail line. The Planner, it seemed to me, thought it important that we understand the circumstances in which Laos found itself and the development theory they embraced as they proceeded. He made these points:

- Laos is the only landlocked country in Southeast Asia. Historically, rivers and oceans have provided decisive assets to the world's most vibrant societies during their development. Laos had to build its own manmade "iron river" to create the pathways of connectivity that nature had failed to provide.

- Laos had an asset, as well as liabilities, the asset being that it is centrally located and is the most direct route by which a relatively high-speed (160 km/hr) railroad could go to connect China with some of the most dynamic parts of Southeast Asia. Laos, he argued, had location, location, and location. Beijing would pay for transit rights and construction contracts. If somehow little Laos could manage to capture just 5 percent of the value flowing along its new rail corridor linking the two regions, the Planner said, it would be a huge boon for his country.

- China wanted to develop Yunnan Province on the border with Laos, which meant that Laos could benefit from all the investment going in next door.

- If Vientiane failed to join with Beijing, the PRC had alternative routes around Laos (to the east through Vietnam and Cambodia, and to the west through Myanmar). If either alternative route was selected, Laos would be cut out of the economic flows and resulting development along the rail right-of-way. His small mountainous country would be condemned to remain the landlocked backwater it had always been. "Laos has asked China to think about Laos and not turn away from Laos or divert from Laos to Myanmar and Vietnam—'we ask them not to forget Laos—we don't want to be left behind,'" the Planner said.

- Once China finished the line from Kunming to near Nong Khai on the Thai side of the Thai-Lao border along the Mekong River (which happened at the end of 2021), Thailand would then almost be compelled to link to the Laos line to gain access to China. Once Thailand did that, Malaysia and Singapore would be incentivized to hook up to the line. Thailand had its dream—becoming the Chicago of Southeast Asia, the East-West, North-South transportation hub linking India to Vietnam and China to Singapore. If Singapore and Kuala Lumpur failed to link up with Bangkok, the Chinese would use Myanmar to circumvent Singapore and Malaysia altogether, or perhaps terminate in Malaysia, leaving Singapore out. The Planner had in mind a very dynamic, sophisticated game. The fact that people are poor and their country small doesn't mean they aren't sophisticated.

Our book, *Rivers of Iron: Railroads and Chinese Power in Southeast Asia*, written with Professors Selina Ho and Cheng-Chwee Kuik, systematically reports our findings, but here I want to enumerate some of how my thinking was affected by our team's on-the-ground encounters in Southeast Asia and in China.

ON INITIATIVE

Americans often have a storyline about the PRC and then superimpose that template on quite distinct cases. The storyline on China's BRI is that a rapacious and strategically ambitious Beijing takes the initiative; lures poor, vulnerable, and often corrupt regimes into undertaking major infrastructure projects that have an insufficient economic return; and "traps" the regimes into unsustainable debt rendering them unable to resist PRC goals and influence, undermining their sovereignty, and sometimes seizing collateral. Though unsatisfactory outcomes do occur, a conscious strategy of this nature attributes more capacity to control outcomes and attributes motives to the PRC that often do not exist.[8]

Our team found that it often is the potential partner state that takes the initiative in approaching China, not Beijing imposing itself on others. When a Chinese BRI official came by my office in Washington one day, saying that the problem with BRI was that too many countries were coming to Beijing with investment requests, aid, and infrastructure projects, I initially was skeptical. Xi Jinping, this official said, was a problem because he was trotting around the globe making fifty-billion-dollar commitments hither and yon without regard to the PRC's financial or human resource capacities.

As our team visited various countries in Southeast Asia, we repeatedly asked how the HSR idea arose and who had taken the initiative. Often as not we were told that it was the Southeast Asian state that initially floated the idea of connectivity and partnership with China. This was the case in Malaysia when, in the late 1990s, Prime Minister Mahathir asked Zhu Rongji for assistance on rail construction and Zhu responded by saying that China had its problems for now. Later, when China's capabilities increased and the PRC had built out its infrastructure, subsequent entreaties by Prime Minister Mahathir's successor, Najib Razak, bore fruit in Beijing (and spawned considerable corruption for which he [Najib] was convicted of money laundering and other felonious behavior, eventually being sentenced to twelve years in jail in August 2022).

When we were in Laos and asked a senior foreign affairs official about where the idea for HSR development in Laos involving the PRC came from, he said: "We have experienced high-speed train[s] from Shanghai to Beijing. We think why not construct a high-speed railroad in Laos? We need connectivity, not only within Laos but also [to] connect with other countries in the region. 'We then began to negotiate with China.' . . . 'So we have to ask and talk to China.' 'Before Xi's announcement of OBOR [One Belt, One Road], Laos already have [had] talked with China. We want to export our goods, our products to China.' . . . 'Then when Xi announced [OBOR], we began to have more talks with China.' . . . 'China said no problem, we have experience and technology.'"[9]

My conclusion is that it is not always Beijing that assertively pushes bad ideas, but rather, sometimes China has good ideas and sometimes it responds to the proposals of others. With Beijing's diplomatic aims, combined with strategic lobbying by countries that want Chinese support, combined with justifiable PRC pride in its HSR technology, combined with large domestic state-owned enterprises (SOEs) pushing for government support and help in getting a foothold in foreign markets, combined with a security apparatus that can see strategic benefits, taken as a whole these forces constitute a powerful domestic PRC coalition in support of these efforts. Sometimes provinces push projects as well, with Beijing several steps behind.

Some people inside and outside of China worry that in the process of building railroads and other large projects, Beijing may accumulate a surplus of risky debtors. Indeed, many efforts may prove unsustainable. *But this is neither a plot nor a strategy.* The excesses of the PRC's domestic coalition pushing for railway and other development undertakings have produced many critics of these efforts within China. Many PRC citizens and groups do not see how investing in economically or politically risky projects abroad are in China's long-term interests, especially given competing domestic needs for capital and leadership attention, and particularly as blistering mainland growth slows.

The analytic problem for Americans when viewing all this is that we seem to think we are the only ones with domestic politics. To build a coalition in China, as elsewhere, one must provide benefits to more members, a process that easily snowballs—logrolling. In American politics, it is easier to conjure up a nefarious strategy (like "debt trap diplomacy") than accept that domestic politics often drives excesses in China as elsewhere.

Nonetheless, the PRC may be saddled with borrower repayment problems, some of large scale. This, in turn, fuels domestic unhappiness with Xi, with unpredictable consequences. The PRC may also be driven to try to impose onerous repayment regimens on borrowers, producing foreign policy friction.

On Choices

Countries, particularly poor countries, face tough choices. These choices reflect each country's circumstances, sometimes dire. I found convincing a Laotian Foreign Ministry official who forthrightly laid out his country's position regarding the HSR line, already under construction: "When you want something, you have to sacrifice something else. Yes, it will be a big burden for the next generations, but we will have no choice."[10]

Big infrastructure construction inflicts great human and other costs in the short run, the hope being that once completed, the project will provide even larger future gains. Compounding the difficulty of cost-benefit calculations is the fact that both predicted costs and gains are imprecise at the time decisions must be made, a challenge further aggravated by the fact that various groups weigh costs and gains differently. Whatever the initial cost-benefit analysis may suggest, unanticipated challenges boost costs, no matter how good-faith the initial estimate may have been. And good faith cannot be assumed in the initial cost-benefit assessment. Proponents exaggerate gains and minimize costs, while opponents exaggerate costs and minimize gains.

In judging China and its infrastructure projects, do not forget the prices that we and other earlier developing countries paid to achieve our gains and the stumbles we have had along the way, up to the present day. For instance, the initial cost estimate of Boston's "Big Dig" (Central Artery/Tunnel Project) under the central city was $2.8 billion when the project started. When finished (twenty-five years later), the cost had reached a staggering $14.78 billion.

The experiences of other transformative infrastructure projects around the world are instructive.[11]

- **Transcontinental Railroad** (United States): 1,200 estimated deaths. *The Sacramento Reporter* wrote that "about 20,000 pounds of bones" dug up from shallow graves were taken by train for return to China, calculating that this amounted to 1,200 Chinese. All this is vaguely documented, a fact that itself bears witness to how little importance was attached to the carnage.

- **Suez Canal** (Egypt): 120,000 deaths. Built by 1.5 million forced and hired laborers, mostly Egyptians, the canal took eleven years to construct and now handles over half of the world's intercontinental shipping.

- **The Panama Canal:** 30,609 deaths, many from malaria and yellow fever, is similar to the Suez story. The Panama Canal, combined with the Transcontinental Railroad, helped make America a Pacific power.

- **The Hawks' Nest Tunnel** (West Virginia, 1931): 764 deaths, "known as one of the worst industrial disasters in United States history because of the certainty of death." Many of the five thousand workforce died because of silicosis, "an incurable lung disease that can take a few years to become fatal. For example, it is estimated that at least 764 of the 1,213 men who worked underground for a mere two months died within five years of the tunnel's completion, but other estimates raise this figure to over 2,000."

- **Qatar World Cup** (6,750 deaths): By March 2021, about 6,750 migrants had died working on multiple projects for the 2022 World Cup. "Due to the combination of heat exhaustion, long hours, poor living conditions, and contracts that can trap workers for up to five years, as many as two million migrant workers face slavery-like conditions. . . . The Qatari government is turning a blind eye to the situation."

The point here is not to excuse PRC misdeeds or incompetence with the fiascos of others, but rather to point out that constructing big public infrastructure has been, and remains, a costly undertaking in human and other terms, and this generalization is not limited to specific political, economic, or social systems. It is expensive in human terms to move from being poor to being rich. The Chinese public is aware of these costs, with one young person traveling with me on a bus ride in Yunnan Province's mountainous border area mentioning offhandedly that tunnel boring for the HSR through the region's flaky karst mountains was dangerous work and that many workers died in the process. China should do more to increase worker safety.

SMALL AND MEDIUM POWERS HAVE LEVERAGE AND AGENCY

One of the most potent weapons smaller countries have to safeguard their interests is to "just say no." Vietnam sometimes employs this tool unapologetically when it comes to China. Thailand rarely says "no" but keeps finding reasons to defer final decisions on the project (citing considerations of right-of-way, its own constitutional strictures, financing arrangements, and development rights along the line). Moreover, changing regimes and administrations, and political flux, keep creating new contexts for ongoing negotiations in many countries. A foreign diplomat we interviewed in Vientiane noted that Laos might be small but had multiple ways of throwing "sand in the gears" of undertakings to which it was not committed.[12]

The level of commitment to projects can vary among potential PRC partners, and a once-committed regime or leader in any given country can suddenly vanish from the scene, confronting the PRC with more skeptical successors. The toolbox of resistance among potential partners includes unwillingness or inability to meet matching capital obligations, inability to acquire the land necessary for the project, and the ability to dangle future projects in front of the Chinese to extract more benefits in current negotiations. The Vietnamese, Indonesians, and others have employed the specter of awarding contracts to the Japanese to squeeze one last pound of flesh from Beijing. In more pluralized partner countries, civil society organizations can throw up roadblocks. This is diplomatic rope-a-dope of the kind that Muhammad Ali used so skillfully in his 1974 fight in Zaire with George Foreman, "The Rumble in the Jungle." Lie on the ropes and let the opponent slug away, eventually exhausting himself, so he is easy to finish off in the late rounds.

Conclusions

This chapter began with the observation that Xi Jinping and his allies in China are pursuing mutually contradictory paths. They are, on the one hand, tightening up on internal political controls and pursuing a nonreassuring foreign policy. On the one hand, Beijing seeks to promote connectivity with the international system to an ever-greater extent, even as it simultaneously talks internally about self-reliance or "dual circulation."

Such a schizophrenic strategy will be difficult to sustain because the non-reassuring aspects of PRC foreign and domestic policies drive PRC neighbors and others to balance economic linkages with Beijing by forging security and supply chain linkages with others, not least the United States. China's neighbors try to diversify their dependencies to the extent possible. For their part, other big and medium powers will band together to deny or slow the acquisition of critical technologies by Beijing and perhaps constrict the PRC's access to their domestic markets. They also may form commercial consortia to compete with Chinese state enterprises to win contracts. The Association of Southeast Asian Nations (ASEAN) as an organization can also be part of the repertoire of counterweights to Beijing. Many countries can use the competition between Beijing and Tokyo to gain leverage.

Within the PRC, the forty-plus years of growing global engagement built domestic constituencies favoring the openness that the Xi regime is trying to limit in order to keep the Communist Party in power. This will create a backlash and counter pressures—but of what magnitude, over what time frame, is hard to say. While acknowledging the basic contradictions in PRC policy, some elements of Chinese policy are indeed attractive to developing countries which tend to subscribe to the theory that, "If you want to get rich, build a road." America's approach should not be to seek to impede China's connectivity efforts at every turn, but rather to help construct a system of balanced connectivity with others (maybe sometimes even including China) that leads to other destinations besides Beijing.

NOTES

1. Tongqi Lin, Review essay, "The China-Centered Approach: Traits, Tendencies, and Tensions," *Bulletin of Concerned Asian Scholars* 18, no. 4 (1986): 49–59. https://doi.org/10.1080/14672715.1986.10409772.

2. "Meeting Notes, David M. Lampton, Senior Chinese Leader," August 28, 2007, Great Hall of the People, Beijing, 2. (RAC).

3. David M. Lampton, "Interview with XXX," October 10, 2022, 3–4. (RAC).

4. David M. Lampton, "Xi Jinping and the National Security Commission: Policy Coordination and Political Power," *Journal of Contemporary China* 24, no. 95 (September 2015): 769.

5. For the conceptual map for this set of projects, see David M. Lampton, Selina Ho, and Cheng-Chwee Kuik, *Rivers of Iron: Railroads and Chinese Power in Southeast Asia* (University of California Press, 2020), 5.

6. David Lampton, Selina Ho, and Cheng-Chwee Kuik, "Conversation with Sultan of Perak," May 29, 2018, 8. (RAC).

7. Selina Ho, "Notes of Meeting, Director-General of Planning and Cooperation, Ministry of Public Works and Transport," Vientiane, Laos, June 6, 2017. (RAC).

8. Deborah Brautigam and Meg Rithmire, "The Chinese 'Debt Trap' Is a Myth," https://www.theatlantic.com/international/archive/2021/02/china-debt-trap-diplomacy/617953/; see also, Deborah Brautigam, "Misdiagnosing the Chinese Infrastructure Push," https://www.the-american-interest.com/2019/04/04/misdiagnosing-the-chinese-infrastructure-push/.

9. David M. Lampton, Selina Ho, and Cheng-Chwee Kuik, "Meeting with Lao Foreign Ministry System Official," Vientiane, Laos, June 7, 2017. (RAC).

10. David M. Lampton, Selina Ho, and Cheng-Chwee Kuik, "Meeting with Lao Foreign Ministry System Official," Vientiane, Laos, June 7, 2017, 6. (RAC).

11. "The Human Costs of Construction: An Inside Look at the World's Most Notable and Deadliest Construction Projects," *Building Safety Journal*, May 1, 2021, https://www

.iccsafe.org/building-safety-journal/bsj-dives/the-human-cost-of-construction-an-inside
-look-at-the-worlds-most-notable-and-deadliest-construction-projects/.

12. David M. Lampton, "Lunch Conversation with XXX," diplomat, Yokohama Restaurant, Vientiane, Laos, PDR, June 5, 2017, 3. (RAC).

CHAPTER SIXTEEN

History: Not Over, Nor Just Begun
(Looking Ahead)

Strength and ambitions, once revealed, cannot be easily concealed again . . . Russian aggression and China's reluctance to criticize Russian aggression [against Ukraine] . . . has revitalized the idea of "The West" which after the Cold War was loosening and in some danger of entirely decomposing. Moreover, the idea of "The West" that is reconstituting itself, is a robust idea.

—BILAHARI KAUSIKAN[1]

THE BASELINE: COLD WAR REDUX?

How are today's circumstances similar to, and different from, those my generation faced? How are we to assess engagement?

On February 14, 1950, nearly four years after I was born, Joseph Stalin and Mao Zedong signed in Moscow a thirty-year Treaty of Friendship, Alliance, and Mutual Assistance; concluded two additional agreements; and exchanged three notes. This was Mao's first-ever trip abroad, and that was an unhappy experience for him, though we did not know this then. Stalin did his best to ignore Mao.

The treaty and associated documents constituted a military and economic development pact between Moscow and Beijing, dramatically tilting the debate in America over national strategy. The debate concerned whether or not to formally recognize the just-established PRC or adopt a policy to contain China and move toward tighter alignment with Chiang Kai-shek and the Republic of China (ROC). In the concluding stage of the civil war between the Nationalists and Communists, Chiang had been driven offshore to Taiwan and a few other specks of land sticking their heads out of the Pacific. With the combined shocks of Chiang's defeat, the pact between Moscow and Beijing, and Kim Il-sung's invasion of South Korea a few months later, the Truman administration soon was in full containment mode.

Washington saw Moscow as the overarching strategic threat, but Beijing was an important secondary concern, and its alliance with Moscow created the specter of a single, ideological, purposeful condominium dominating the Eurasian landmass from Central Europe through Indochina. An initial, long step in containment's development was a National Security Council policy paper (NSC 68) adopted in April 1950. The committee that drafted the document was chaired by Paul Nitze, co-founder of SAIS.

When North Korea invaded South Korea in June 1950, having been given the green light by Moscow and Beijing, China was further elevated as a strategic concern. In the fall of 1950, with Beijing's direct intervention in the Korean War against General Douglas MacArthur's advancing U.S.-UN troops, Beijing became the principal active belligerent in a war in which 33,652 Americans would die, along with countless Chinese and Koreans. All this reenergized the U.S. commitment to the ROC and Chiang Kai-shek and provided the basis for the Mutual Defense Treaty with Taipei signed in December 1954.

In the space of some two years (1949–1951), the Truman administration had gone from wavering about future diplomatic ties with Beijing to tight, steadfast alignment against it, enlisting allies and like-minded countries in a common cause. On the Chinese side, Mao used the American threat to launch the movement to "Resist U.S. Aggression and Aid Korea" as a pillar of efforts to consolidate domestic control and wring all the aid possible from Moscow.

Seventy years later, we still live with the consequences of all this. The echoes of the past reverberate today. In 2023, the parallels in the two eras, while imperfect, are notable. The similarities with 1950 are eerie, notwithstanding the important economic and global interdependencies we now share with the PRC. Moreover, Beijing now is the big brother in the relationship with Moscow.

On February 4, 2022, China and Russia signed a "Joint Statement" when Vladimir Putin was in Beijing for the Winter Olympic Games. One of the Russian leader's objectives presumably was to shore up support for his planned military invasion of Ukraine. As to Xi's aims, one was to make sure a prospective military move by Moscow did not ruin his Olympic Games by requesting that the Russian leader delay the initiation of conflict until after the sports competition. Western leaders generally declined to attend the Winter Games. Putin's visit was symbolic for Xi, who was sending the message that if Washington was going to bring allies to America's side in its mounting competition with the PRC, Beijing could play that game too—with Moscow. This was Nixon's strategic triangle turned upside down.

While the February 4 Joint Statement between Beijing and Moscow does not have either the force or the gravity of a treaty, unlike the Sino-Soviet Pact of 1950, it nonetheless is significant, not least because shortly after its release, Russia attacked Ukraine. One of the key elements of the Joint Statement was its declaration that the friendship of Moscow and Beijing "has no limits" and that "there are no 'forbidden' areas of cooperation."

This phraseology played a key role in hardening an already tough White House policy toward China. Secretary of State Antony Blinken said as much in his May 26, 2022, speech conveying the results of the Biden administration's post–2020 election review of China policy: "President Xi and President Putin declared that the friendship between their countries was—and I quote—'without limits.'" In the wake of Russia's invasion of Ukraine, Beijing refused to credibly affirm its long-standing principle of the inviolability of sovereignty, refused to distance itself from Moscow, and, instead, placed blame for the breakdown of peace on the shoulders of Washington and NATO—accusing them of threatening Russia's security through the process of NATO enlargement and military cooperation with Ukraine.

A comparison of Blinken's May 26, 2022, speech with the "Conclusions and Recommendations" section of NSC 68 ("United States Objectives and Programs for National Security," April 1950) is illuminating. NSC 68 was the initial Cold War strategic document shaping the U.S. response to the Soviet Union and China for the following two-plus decades. There are numerous similarities between NSC 68's analysis and the recommendations and key points of Secretary Blinken's speech, as well as the subsequently released *National Security Strategy* (October 2022) and the *Nuclear Posture Review* (October 2022). The *Nuclear Posture Review* said that: "[T]he PRC likely intends to possess at least 1,000 deliverable warheads by the end of the decade," up from the very low hundreds Beijing possessed over prior decades.

Though in his May 26 speech, Secretary Blinken emphasized that Washington was putting "diplomacy back at the center of American foreign policy," I fear a repetition of what George Kennan believed happened to his concept of containment as it was implemented in the 1950s and 1960s: what was meant to be a primarily diplomatic strategy in Kennan's view became a largely military one.

In 1950, NSC 68 said: "The gravest threat to the security of the United States within the foreseeable future stems from the hostile designs and formidable power of the USSR, and from the nature of the Soviet system." Blinken said: "China is the only country with both the intent to reshape the international order and, increasingly, the economic, diplomatic, military, and technological power to do it." He went on to proclaim, "We will remain focused on the most serious long-term challenge to the international order—and that's posed by the People's Republic of China." Near the conclusion of his remarks, the Secretary laid out the implications: "President Biden has instructed the Department of Defense to hold China as its pacing challenge, to ensure that our military stays ahead."

In terms of strategic objectives, NSC 68 said that: "Soviet domination of the potential power of Eurasia, whether achieved by armed aggression or by political and subversive means, would be strategically and politically unacceptable to the United States." Blinken said, "China has rapidly modernized its military and intends to become a top-tier fighting force with global reach. And it has announced its ambition to create a sphere of influence in the Indo-Pacific and to become the world's leading power. . . . Under President Xi Jinping, the ruling Chinese Communist Party has become more repressive at home and more aggressive abroad." NSC 68 said that the purposes of U.S. policy were: "to create situations which will compel the Soviet Government to recognize the practical undesirability of acting on the basis of its present concepts and the necessity of behaving in accordance with precepts of international conduct, as set forth in the purposes and principles of the UN Charter." Blinken said: "But we cannot rely on Beijing to change its trajectory. So we will shape the strategic environment around Beijing to advance our vision for an open, inclusive international system." NSC 68 said: "Strengthen the orientation toward the United States of the non-Soviet nations; and help such of those nations as are able and willing to make an important contribution to U.S. security, to increase their economic and political stability and their military capability." Blinken said: "The second piece of our strategy is aligning with our allies and partners to advance a shared vision for the future. From day one, the Biden administration has worked to reenergize America's unmatched network of alliances and partnerships and to reengage in international institutions."

While U.S. citizens have no access to Beijing's corresponding foundational policy documents, directives, and decisions, there can be little doubt that most Americans would be alarmed were they available.

The problem is that Beijing and Washington each view the policies being pursued by the other as highly adversarial. Beijing sees Washington's policy as "containment," and the U.S. government views the PRC as trying to surpass American dominance and change the character of the post–World War II order. *The ascribed goal of each country is unacceptable to the other.* Both are developing their respective military, economic, and diplomatic toolboxes of coercive means to deal with the other. Deterrence is the name of the game, not reassurance. Each side is transforming the other into its existential threat, which will accelerate a stair-step action-reaction cycle, a cycle accelerated by quickly evolving tools in the cyber and artificial intelligence realms.

As with the first Cold War, as the bilateral relationship deteriorates, each attaches increasing weight to Taiwan, the single most volatile flash point in bilateral ties. On May 23, 2022, President Biden again emphasized his commitment to defend Taiwan militarily if it is attacked. (There is no legal imperative to do so under the 1979 Taiwan Relations Act.) Beijing reacted by joining with Russia to send a joint flight of six bombers near Japan and South Korea, and southward into South China Sea airspace immediately after Biden's remarks, while the U.S. president still was in Asia.

And in turn, as Taiwan's security becomes more problematic, Tokyo becomes more alarmed. As Japan's anxieties grow, it aligns more closely with Washington and enhances its military capabilities. In December 2022, Tokyo announced a doubling of defense expenditures as a percentage of GDP over five years. Further, South Korea and Japan began to firm up their long-strained relationship out of common concern about Beijing. This process reached a new high with President Biden's summit meeting with the Japanese and South Korean leaders at Camp David in August 2023. The meeting's purpose was to "enhance strategic coordination."

Among the dangers is the fact that the norms and practices that Washington and Beijing observed concerning Taiwan over eight successive administrations from Richard Nixon through Barack Obama are on life support. While China was not a nuclear power until late 1964, today it bristles with a growing number of nuclear and conventional warheads and increasingly potent means of their delivery. To date, Washington has never launched a direct attack on a nuclear-armed power, but it is hard to see how a war across the Taiwan Strait could be fought without immediately cascading into attacks on the Chinese homeland and PRC attacks on U.S. bases and platforms in Asia and perhaps escalating beyond. This would amount to strategic attacks by two nuclear powers on each other.

The fiftieth anniversary of the Nixon China trip was in 2022. The strategic core of the Nixon-Mao rapprochement was to use the combined strategic weight of China and the United States to offset the Soviet Union. Today, Beijing and Moscow are jointly working to America's detriment, though beneath the surface the Sino-Russo relationship is brittle.

The question is, what will the generations coming to policy dominance in the United States and China do now? Their first responsibility is to avoid general war and their second to cooperate on existential global issues. Achieving these tasks requires rebuilding a shared strategic foundation resting on broadly shared interests, pursued in negotiations. The current state of truncated dialogue is the exactly wrong path.

Memory and Purpose

The last seventy years have seen a full cycle of Sino-American relations—strategic hostility, followed by rapprochement and considerable cooperation (1970–2010), in turn followed by mounting and now dangerous strategic friction, with Taiwan again near the center of the struggle. Dangerous strategic competitions have been the bookends of the engagement period which preoccupied most of my professional life. Hence, this book's subtitle, *From Cold War to Cold War*.

This brings me back to where I began this story—my early years at Stanford and my father. As I recounted earlier, about fifty-five years ago Dad asked me, "Who's going to pay you to do that?"—study China. Leapfrogging to shortly before his 2017 death, in his soft voice he matter-of-factly asked me, "Are you disappointed with how things have worked out with China?" Quickly adding, "You should not be," suggesting that I not take today's circumstances as a personal failing. I did not, and I do not, for many reasons, the most obvious being that the era of engagement ushered in four-plus decades of peace and gains through cooperation and because eras change for many reasons. Historical development is a series of probabilistic occurrences; the mere acts of observation and intervention set events in unanticipated directions.

Dad's question, however, raises the issue of how one assesses the meaning of one's career. History, like the Mann Gulch Fire described in the preface, assumes its form not through preordination, but rather from the confluence of developments, each often independent of the other, but nonetheless colliding, sometimes to catastrophic effect. In this kaleidoscopic jumble of causation individual decisions, nature, economic forces, national psychologies, and more assume importance.

Nonetheless, one cannot dodge important questions: Was engagement a big mistake, a naïve period in which the United States strengthened a prospective enemy? Was constructive engagement misguided, rationalized by assumptions about the inevitability of democracy through economic and social interaction and the presumed palliative effects of modernization and globalization? Is engagement to be understood simply as a period in which short-term thinking, profit-hungry American businesses, and in their own way American universities, pursued perishable economic gains by building up what almost inevitably would become a strategic, economic, and technological competitor—a threat? Did we pay insufficient heed to the CCP and its goals, the country's vast reservoir of intelligent and increasingly well-educated people with a collective nationalist chip on its shoulders, and the PRC's need for legitimacy achieved not through political reform but by reclaiming the expansive territorial extent of the Qing Dynasty at its height?

Changing Coalitions and Changing Mission

The era of constructive engagement between America and China lasted a long time by the standards of foreign policy eras. By my reckoning, it extended from 1970 to 2010, forty or so years. If, however, one considers the period from the founding of the PRC in late 1949 to the third decade of the new millennium, a span of about seventy-five years, approximately thirty-four of those years have been characterized by growing, often high levels of Sino-American tension. Neither good times nor bad are eternal. We should manage ties to prolong productive periods and to minimize the damage of downturns.

Politics and history are propelled by broad societal coalitions, constantly reconfiguring themselves in reaction to the ever-changing constellation of local, regional, and national leaders, fluid public perceptions, altered power balances, technological change, and the perceived and actual results of prior policies.

Periods of cooperative U.S.-China relations have been sustained by a dominant coalition in each country. Over time, however, perceived or actual "losers" in these halcyon periods accumulate in each system, and political entrepreneurs in each country gradually come forth to build a new, dominant coalition that seeks to overcome the perceived deficiencies and downsides of the prior period. This mutual hardening triggers an action-reaction process that spirals progressively toward higher levels of friction. As relations deteriorate during these downturns, the costs of conflict accumulate in each society. At some point (which could be decades), either one or both societies search for less costly, more mutually beneficial policies anchored in new coalitions that create a renewed basis for expanding cooperation.

This cycle creates a task to which we as scholars, public servants, or citizens can devote ourselves—trying to slow the downswings by reducing the accumulation of frustrations, trying to reinforce positives on the upswings, and thereby maximizing total welfare throughout the cyclical process. Conflict and tragedy can never be fully eliminated, but you can put your weight, whatever it may be, on the scales of history to maximize gains and minimize losses—faint echoes of John Stuart Mill and utilitarianism.

Thinking about the Gains of Cooperation

To play such a role, one needs to appreciate the high costs of downswings and the potentially enormous gains of upswings. At this moment in America and China, insufficient attention is being paid to prior gains, thereby making conflict seem less costly than it is.

When we talk about the costs of downturns and the gains achieved in upswings, we are talking about developments *directly* involving 25 percent of the global population. We are talking about two countries that together constitute 41.89 percent and 34.75 percent of global GDP in nominal and PPP terms, respectively, and alone account for 38 percent of global greenhouse emissions. In terms of defense expenditures, the two combined account for 52 percent of global military spending. A productive U.S.-China relationship is of consequence to the world. Both countries' public and private leaders must manage ties with the rest of the world in mind, to make room for each other.

As we focus on the problems of this downswing, we ought not to lose sight of what the last upswing produced and what future upswings could bring.

Constructive engagement built the human connections and human resources both societies will need once they rediscover their need for cooperation. When Nixon and Mao decided to talk, it was those who had lived, worked, and studied in each other's societies much earlier that provided the individuals capable of rapidly reestablishing a more productive relationship in the 1970s. That is why our 1986 book was titled *A Relationship Restored.* In this regard on the American side, the Rockefeller and Luce families, John King Fairbank, Michael Blumenthal, Arthur Hummel, James Lilley, and Stapleton Roy are among those who come immediately to mind. They each had long-standing connections to China well prior to the first Cold War. Among the Chinese equivalents were Yan Dongsheng, Zhou Peiyuan, Ji Chaozhu, and Xie Xide, who had studied and lived in America before the communist takeover. In other words, each preceding cyclical upswing creates the human infrastructure that will facilitate the future upswing when the time is propitious.[2]

Because I have written elsewhere about the broad dimensions of gain during the forty-plus-year upswing starting in 1970, I will not rehearse that argument here other than to say that whether one considers the nutritional status of the Chinese people, life expectancy there, or their life opportunities, the gains have been enormous.[3] Americans also benefited mightily from China's entry into the global economic system, and the PRC's economic gains fueled relatively high U.S. growth and helped keep inflation at bay for decades. While China benefited considerably in economic terms, the absolute gap in per capita GDP between the U.S. and PRC greatly widened in absolute terms in America's favor during the engagement period. There were, however, great inequities in the distribution of those gains in America. How America distributes its growth internally is its decision, not China's. That the United States squandered some gains in misguided wars and neglected human and physical infrastructure domestically for a long time is on Americans, not the Chinese.

After the rapprochement with China in the early 1970s and the fall of the Eastern Bloc (1989) and the Soviet Union (1991), America enjoyed a peace dividend. The share of GDP allocated to defense in the United States dropped from 6.52 percent of GDP in 1972, bottoming out at 3.12 percent in 2001. As for China, Deng Xiaoping, much to his own military's disquiet, initially imposed an absolute reduction in defense spending and then kept military expenditures fairly flat as a percentage of GDP until around 2000. This gave the PLA growing resources without increasing the relative domestic burden of defense. Now, with China's growth rate slowing, and friction with America and others mounting, PRC defense expenditures are becoming more onerous and domestically contentious. For its part, Washington increased national defense spending for fiscal year 2023 by about 8 percent.

MAKING THE PAST SERVE THE FUTURE

Given global volatility, there is no substitute for a north-star purpose and an ethical framework. Without these we become flotsam on a roiling sea of contending and ever-shifting interests. We need navigational instruments that include philosophical groundings and core values and concepts about how change occurs. Of course, different people have quite varied frameworks.[4] Some argue that preparing for war is the best way to prevent it while others, including me, argue that managing frictions and promoting cooperation are no less important. Avoiding war and maximizing cooperation have been my twin objectives. I have several conclusions drawn from my experiences:

- *Achieving security by indirection.* Human beings privilege safety goals over self-actualization goals—"be all that you can be." Consequently, when a threat is perceived as rising or high, expenditures and leadership attention bend toward security as a priority, which is true whether we are talking about traditional or modern, authoritarian or democratic societies. Often overlooked, however, is the fact that economic power and the capacity to innovate are the foundations on which security-related capabilities rest. Paradoxically, achieving security goals requires building human and physical infrastructure and requires restraint on resource allocation toward defense directly, maximizing soft power, and using low-cost diplomacy whenever possible. Sound domestic governance is essential.

Not emphasizing economic strength, domestic governance, and innovative capability weakens the capacity to achieve and sustain real, durable, hard security in the medium and long runs. Under-investment in human resources reduces social cohesion. An America with its citizens storming the Capitol as occurred on January 6, 2021, or that has inadequate financial regulation to avoid a global financial crisis such as occurred in 2008–2009, or that fails to provide adequate education and safety in the classroom to many of its children, is not an exemplar and undermines America's security and capacities.

- *Ideology and the frame of U.S.-China relations.* The Biden administration, unlike its nine predecessors (including the Trump administration), has cast U.S.-China relations in starkly ideological terms—democracy versus authoritarianism. Doing so leaves little room for flexibility or compromise, signaling to the other party that regime change is Washington's ultimate goal, that engagement is an attempt to weaken Beijing's legitimacy in the eyes of its people.

- *Technology has its own logic.* We are in an arms race with China now and have been for some time. The zones of competition and escalation are apparent in the cyber, artificial intelligence, space, land, air, and sea domains. Balloons in the high atmosphere became an area of concern in 2023. Because technological development involves lead times measured in decades, each side identifies future technological possibilities that could be turned into their own, or the opponent's, advantage, and each side adopts long lead-time programs to respond. Each side is stimulating the other to move toward countering threats that are more or less in the future, more or less hypothetical. Both sides react to technological possibilities, not current actualities. Both sides often are not reacting to what each side necessarily *intends to do*; they are reacting to what *the other side could do*. The only way through this miasma is to have strategic and arms control discussions that through dialogue, confidence-building, and verification seek to dampen this process.

- *High degrees of security competition are incompatible with full Chinese cooperation on global issues.* In his May 26, 2022, speech, Secretary Blinken reiterated what one might hope is true, but in reality is not. "We'll work together with Beijing where our interests come together [e.g., climate change]. We can't let the disagreements that divide us stop us from moving forward on the priorities that demand that we work together." This is a hopeful sentiment, and China will do what it finds in its core interests. But overall, it is unlikely to work for many reasons among which, as one senior PRC foreign policy official put it in a virtual May 9, 2022, conversation in which I participated: "Everything happened when the U.S. was bashing China. So nothing the U.S. does can gain support from China. China cannot capitulate to the atmosphere in Washington." In an earlier March 9 virtual conversation with colleagues, one Chinese participant exploded, "Look at what you are saying, how can China come back and kiss your . . . don't want to say?" Simply put, Beijing will not be inclined to cooperate as long as it is defined as Washington's central strategic challenge. The parallel reality is that Beijing defines U.S. strategic aims as its central threat.
- *Don't try to fight something with nothing.* This lesson applies to two realms in U.S.-China relations, one being in the zone of economic and social development policy abroad, and the other in the zone of Sino-American narratives.

For several decades, the United States has avoided supporting big infrastructure projects for fear of their adverse impacts, financial cost, and tendency to involve high levels of corruption in developing countries. In contrast, Beijing has advanced BRI by articulating a belief shared with most developing and middle-income countries that infrastructure is the road to wealth. Recently Washington has sought, largely rhetorically, to address this imbalance. But developing countries we seek to attract are not going to accept rhetoric. America needs to become a greater participant, perhaps cooperating with other strong market-based economies, to jointly build projects developing countries need.

In another way, one also can't fight something with nothing—that concerns the uniformly conflictual nature of the Sino-American narrative in both countries. The two sides need to cooperate in some significant zone providing something to offset the current exclusively negative narratives. Waiting to cooperate until the narrative becomes more accommodating will not get us out of the cul-de-sac. Loosening controls on media access, reopening closed consular facilities, augmenting global health cooperation, and boosting channels of scholarly exchange surely would improve the current imbalance.

- *The breakdown of norms concerning managing the Taiwan issue is dangerous.* Americans implicitly think that if China thought it would fail in an attempt to coercively take Taiwan, it would refrain from the attempt. I believe that a more accurate way to put it is that if Beijing was put in the corner of acquiescing to what would be seen at home as the "loss" of Taiwan, it would fight, even though victory in the conflict was uncertain, perhaps unlikely. China prefers not to fight, much less lose, but it would do both rather than acquiesce to what would be portrayed at home as permanent separation from the island. Somewhat analogously, in December 1941, Tokyo attacked Pearl Harbor realizing that in all probability it would lose a protracted war with America, but assessing that acquiescing to Washington's sanctions and dominance in the Pacific was a worse fate than possible defeat and that its own comparative strength was declining. Excessive deterrence can ignite a war.

Both the Trump and Biden administrations have continually pushed the boundaries of previously accepted norms for managing the Taiwan situation. Xi Jinping has greater ambitions, and less patience, than his predecessors, and he too has pushed unwisely. As to Taiwan itself, there is a greater desire to throw off previous isolating constraints. And, for his part, President Biden has tried to create more certainty about a forceful U.S. response to a possible PRC use of force, hoping thereby to bolster deterrence. All sides are pushing the limits to a dangerous extent. Miscalculation is a growing danger.

We already have seen the dangers of miscalculation across the Taiwan Strait in the June to August 1995 to spring 1996 period. On August 29, 1995, I had a conversation with a senior PRC Foreign Ministry official. The conversation was in the immediate wake of PLA missile firings near Taiwan from August 15–25, 1995. The White House's approval of extending a visa to Taiwan President Lee Teng-hui for a private visit to his alma mater, Cornell University, had elicited furious PRC diplomatic and military responses—including the missile firings. The notes of my meeting with the PRC official on August 29 recount the following exchange:

Lampton: "I expected once Congress got back [from recess] there would be pressure to sell theater missile defenses to Taiwan and probably other weapons [in response to the missile firings]. And, in the event force was used by Beijing, he [the Chinese official] ought not to rule out American intervention or some significant response."

PRC Official: "'It is bullshit that the US will intervene.' You did nothing in 1954 and 1958, Quemoy and Matsu, and you are doing nothing in Bosnia. This government and this president [Bill Clinton] will not react. 'You are bluffing.'"

Lampton: "It would be a grave mistake to assume intervention of some sort would not occur. . . . Had China considered what Lee Teng-hui apparently said about [Taiwan's] nuclear options? . . . As to 1954 and 1958 and the [official's] assertion that we did nothing, I said my reading of the U.S. response at that time was much different and at a minimum 1954 actions by China produced the alliance with Taiwan [ROC] of 1955."

Official: "'The U.S. will do nothing.'"

Lampton: "I said it is one thing to assume we are bluffing, which I do not predict is what we would do, and it is one thing to say that Taiwan is bluffing. But, it is quite different and risky to assume everyone is bluffing. This kind of thinking is subject to serious miscalculation."[5]

About a half-year later, on March 8–15, 1996, Beijing launched another wave of missile tests into the waters near Taiwan. On the same day, March 8, President Clinton ordered the carrier group *Independence* to head toward Taiwan's waters and on March 11 ordered another carrier group, *Nimitz*, to head in that direction. The Chinese were surprised and de-escalated, but at the same time, President Jiang Zemin stepped up long-term military modernization so he would never again find himself in a spot from which retreat was the principal option. In the long run, everyone was a loser in this interaction.

- *And finally, while I am not advocating spheres of influence, we do need to respect buffer zones around the major powers.* It is a fact of life that nations, particularly those with power projection capabilities, prefer insulation around their periphery, particularly in an age of high-speed and long-range strike weapons and surveillance devices. In a different age, the twelve nautical mile limit protected from cannon fire. Today, much longer distances afford less real protection. We need to develop shared norms regarding provocative behavior around the peripheries of the major powers. North Atlantic Treaty Organization (NATO) enlargement is a cautionary tale. Like it or not, Moscow has bristled and become more aggressive as it has seen nearby states align ever more closely with NATO. Of course, Russia's imperial compulsions push its neighbors to seek security in the West. And, when the shoe is on the other foot, as China boosts its military presence in Cuba, Washington becomes agitated.

This story ends in some sense where it began. My career started with joining collective efforts to end one war, in Vietnam and in Indochina. Today, as my career moves toward its conclusion, many like-minded persons are seeking to reduce the prospects of another war in Asia, possibly a direct conflict between Washington and Beijing. Virtually no person, country, or continent would remain insulated from such a catastrophe. Waging peace is a never-ending task—as fires are never-ending for the firefighter.

Notes

1. Bilahari Kausikan, "China's Strategic Dilemmas," *Asia Sentinel*, Speech Delivered March 22, 2022, in Canberra, Australia. https://www.asiasentinel.com/p/china-strategic-dilemmas.

2. Terry Lautz, *Americans in China: Encounters with the People's Republic* (Oxford University Press, 2022).

3. David M. Lampton, "Engagement with China: A Eulogy and Reflections on a Gathering Storm," in *Engaging China: Fifty Years of Sino-American Relations*, Anne F. Thurston, ed. (Columbia University Press, 2021), 391–422.

4. David M. Lampton, "Ethical Operational Codes and Dealing with China," *Asian Perspective* 45, no. 1 (Winter 2021): 241–54.

5. David M. Lampton, "Memorandum of Conversation," with XXX, August 29, 1995, 10:00–11:00 a.m. (RAC).

INDEX

CIA. *See* Central Intelligence
Agency
Cirino, Jerry, 127
Clark, Dick, 208, 212, 215–18,
318. *See also* Aspen Institute
Congressional Program
"Clash of Modernity Approach,"
in PRC, 355
clean coal industry, in People's
Republic of China, 139–40
Clinton, Bill, 204, 267, 388; Jiang
Zemin and, 227; MFN tariff
treatment under, 262; response
to human rights in PRC,
223–24; Taiwan and, 224–28;
Taiwan Security Enhancement
Act, 224; U.S.-China relations
under, 222–28
Clough, Ralph, 287n6
coercive diplomacy, deterrence
compared to, 299–300
Cohen, Jerry, 44, 291
colleges and
universities: liberal arts
programs, 286; "Memorandum
of Understanding on
Educational Exchange
Programs between the United
States and the People's
Republic of China," 103; social
sciences as study in PRC,
116. *See also* China Studies
programs; student exchanges;
specific colleges; specific universities
Colorado College, 286

Columbia University, 22, 25
Committee of 100, 295
Committee of Concerned Asian
Scholars (CCAS), 28
"Committee of One Million
against the Admission of Red
China to the United Nations,"
10–11
Committee on International
Security and Arms
Control, 129
Committee on Scholarly
Communication with the
People's Republic of China
(CSCPRC), 62–64, 66, 129,
131; American Council of
Learned Societies, 130; Beijing
office for, 145–49; Reagan and,
142–45; STED Program, 136;
student exchange programs,
134–35
communism. *See specific communist
parties*
Communist China. *See* People's
Republic of China
*A Comparative Analysis of Complex
Organizations* (Etzioni), 299
Conable, Barber B. Jr., 204–6,
209, 218–19, 260–61, 287n1,
319–20. *See also* National
Committee on United States-
China Relations
Conable, Charlotte, 205
Confucianism, 18
Confucius, 178

Paths to Power (Lampton, D.), 34, 83, 310
Patten, Chris, 320, 326
PCI. *See* Pacific Community Initiative
Peking Union Medical College, 159, 263
Peking University, 153
Pelosi, Nancy, 195, 201, 333; response to human rights policies in PRC, 223; role in U.S.-China relations, 209–13; visit to Taipei, 208
Peng Chong, 81
Pentagon Papers, 27
People's Bank of China, 194
People's Liberation Army (PLA), 51, 71–72, 83; in Tibet Autonomous Region, 246
People's Republic of China (PRC): during Asian Financial Crisis and, 333; Barnett on, 263; Belt and Road Initiative, 358, 365–67; Big Gang of Four in, 73, *74,* 177; Buchwald in, 101–2, *102,* 106; Bush, G. H. W., visit to, 165; Califano visit to, 100–101, 112; Chinese Academy of Sciences, 145; Chinese Communist Party, 6–7, 51; Chinese refugees from, 49–50; "Clash of Modernity Approach" in, 355; coal industry in, 139–40; Committee of Concerned Asian Scholars in, 28; compliance cycles in, 53; during COVID-19 pandemic, 76–77; COVID-19 vaccines in, 76; Democracy Wall, 100, *100*; development as global power, 1–2; domestic politics in, 313; as duty culture, 105–6; Fifth Modernization in, 99; First Five-Year Plan, 81; food issues in, 137–38; Four Modernizations policy in, 99; Fourteenth National People's Congress, 71; Great Leap Forward, 49–50, 354; green revolution in, 137; Health Agreement with, 101; Heilongjiang Province, 248–49; Hong Kong reunification/reversion to sovereignty under, 175, 228, 322–26; human rights policies in, 20–221; "Impact-Response" model in, 355; Indonesia and, 24; Indo-Pacific Strategy, 349; infrastructure projects in, 359–60, 367–69; intelligence services in, 77–78; kaleidoscopic quality of, 1–2; Lampton, S., in, 122–23; Laos dependency on, 363–64; Leninist Party in, 358–59; Little Gang of Four in, 73, *74*; medicine policies in, 300–304; mental health policies in, 107–8; MFN status for, 188–89, 195, 219–20, 345–46;